Socio-Economic Segregation in European Capital Cities

Growing inequalities in Europe are a major challenge threatening the sustainability of urban communities and the competitiveness of European cities. While the levels of socio-economic segregation in European cities are still modest compared to some parts of the world, the poor are increasingly concentrating spatially within capital cities across Europe. An overlooked area of research, this book offers a systematic and representative account of the spatial dimension of rising inequalities in Europe.

This book provides rigorous comparative evidence on socio-economic segregation from 13 European cities. Cities include Amsterdam, Athens, Budapest, London, Madrid, Milan, Oslo, Prague, Riga, Stockholm, Tallinn, Vienna and Vilnius. Comparing 2001 and 2011, this multi-factor approach links segregation to four underlying universal structural factors: social inequalities, global city status, welfare regimes and housing systems. Hypothetical segregation levels derived from those factors are compared to actual segregation levels in all cities. Each chapter provides an in-depth and context-sensitive discussion of the unique features shaping inequalities and segregation in the case study cities.

The main conclusion of the book is that the spatial gap between the poor and the rich is widening in capital cities across Europe, which threatens to harm the social stability of European cities. This book will be a key reference on increasing segregation and will provide valuable insights to students, researchers and policy makers who are interested in the spatial dimension of social inequality in European cities.

A PDF version of the introduction and conclusion are available from Open Access at www.tandfebooks.com. It has been made available under a Creative Commons Attribution-Non Commercial-No Derivatives 3.0 license.

Tiit Tammaru is Professor of Urban and Population Geography and Head of the Centre for Migration and Urban Studies at the University of Tartu, Estonia.

Szymon Marcińczak is Assistant Professor at the Institute of Urban Geography and Tourism, Lódź, Poland.

Maarten van Ham is Professor of Urban Renewal at Delft University of Technology, the Netherlands and Professor of Geography at the University of St Andrews, UK.

Sako Musterd is Professor of Urban Geography at the University of Amsterdam, the Netherlands.

Regions and Cities
Series Editor in Chief
Susan M. Christopherson, *Cornell University, USA*

Editors
Maryann Feldman, *University of Georgia, USA*
Gernot Grabher, *HafenCity University Hamburg, Germany*
Ron Martin, *University of Cambridge, UK*
Martin Perry, *Massey University, New Zealand*

In today's Globalised, knowledge-driven and networked world, regions and cities have assumed heightened significance as the interconnected nodes of economic, social and cultural production, and as sites of new modes of economic and territorial governance and policy experimentation. This book series brings together incisive and critically engaged international and interdisciplinary research on this resurgence of regions and cities, and should be of interest to geographers, economists, sociologists, political scientists and cultural scholars, as well as to policy-makers involved in regional and urban development.

For more information on the Regional Studies Association visit www. regionalstudies.org.

There is a **30% discount** available to RSA members on books in the *Regions and Cities* series, and other subject related Taylor and Francis books and e-books including Routledge titles. To order just e-mail alex.robinson@tandf.co.uk, or phone on +44 (0) 20 7017 6924 and declare your RSA membership. You can also visit www.routledge.com and use the discount code: **RSA0901**.

Socio-Economic Segregation in European Capital Cities

East meets West

Edited by Tiit Tammaru,
Szymon Marcińczak,
Maarten van Ham and Sako Musterd

Routledge
Taylor & Francis Group

LONDON AND NEW YORK

First published 2016
by Routledge

2 Park Square, Milton Park, Abingdon, Oxfordshire OX14 4RN
52 Vanderbilt Avenue, New York, NY 10017

Routledge is an imprint of the Taylor & Francis Group, an informa business

First issued in paperback 2019

British Library Cataloguing in Publication Data
A catalogue record for this book is available from the British Library

Library of Congress Cataloging in Publication Data
A catalog record for this book has been requested

ISBN: 978-1-138-79493-1 (hbk)
ISBN: 978-0-367-87020-1 (pbk)

Typeset in Times New Roman
By Swales and Willis Ltd, Exeter, Devon, UK

Contents

Figures

Tables

Contributors

Roger Andersson, Uppsala University, Sweden

Māris Bērziņš, University of Tartu, Estonia

Donatas Burneika, Lithuanian Social Research Centre

Gerhard Hatz, University of Vienna, Austria

Ron Johnston, University of Bristol, UK

Kelvyn Jones, University of Bristol, UK

Anneli Kährik, Uppsala University, Sweden and University of Tartu, Estonia

Josef Kohlbacher, Austrian Academy of Sciences

Zuzana Kopecká, Charles University in Prague, Czech Republic

Zoltán Kovács, Hungarian Academy of Sciences and University of Szeged

Kalju Kratovitš, University of Tartu, Estonia

Zaiga Krišjāne, University of Latvia

Jesús Leal, Complutense University, Madrid, Spain

Kadri Leetmaa, University of Tartu, Estonia

Kadi Mägi, University of Tartu, Estonia and Delft University of Technology, the Netherlands

Thomas Maloutas, Harokopio University, Greece

David Manley, University of Bristol, UK and Delft University of Technology, the Netherlands

Szymon Marcińczak, University of Łódź, Poland

Sako Musterd, University of Amsterdam, the Netherlands

Jakub Novák, Charles University in Prague, Czech Republic

Martin Ouředníček, Charles University in Prague, Czech Republic

Dewi Owen, University of Bristol, UK

Petros Petsimeris, Université Paris I Panthéon-Sorbonne, France

Lucie Pospíšilová, Charles University in Prague, Czech Republic

Ursula Reeger, Austrian Academy of Sciences

Stefania Rimoldi, University of Milano-Bicocca, Italy

Daniel Sorando, Complutense University Madrid, Spain

Petra Špačková, Charles University in Prague, Czech Republic

Balázs Szabó, Hungarian Academy of Sciences

Tiit Tammaru, University of Tartu, Estonia and Delft University of Technology, the Netherlands

Rūta Ubarevičienė, Lithuanian social research centre and Delft University of Technology, the Netherlands

Vytautas Valatka, Lithuanian social research centre and Vilnius University, Lthuania

Wouter van Gent, University of Amsterdam, the Netherlands

Maarten van Ham, Delft University of Technology, the Netherlands and University of St Andrews, Scotland

Terje Wessel, University of Oslo, Norway

Preface

The history of this edited volume goes back to February 2013 when the idea for this book first emerged during a coffee break at Umeå University in Sweden when we realised that little was known about recent changes in socio-economic segregation in European cities. Although many have claimed that segregation is increasing, there was no recent international comparative and systematic research available on segregation. In March 2013 many of the authors of the chapters in this book came to the University of Tartu in Estonia for the conference *Mobility, Segregation, and Neighbourhood Change* and agreed to contribute to this book project. The resulting volume contributes to the literature on residential segregation in Europe in three ways. First, the existing literature mainly focuses on ethnic segregation while this book is about recent changes in socio-economic segregation. Second, for the first time, residential segregation is compared between Eastern and Western European cities. And third, the book provides a rigorous multi-factor approach to understanding segregation in European cities, combining structural factors with a context-sensitive presentation of each case study city. This methodologically rigorous approach is important for a better understanding of the spatial representations of socio-economic inequalities in European cities. The book shows how levels of socio-economic segregation in Europe have increased in the context of globalisation and economic restructuring, combined with different welfare contexts as well as different historical development pathways.

This book would not have been possible without contributions from authors from thirteen European political and economic capitals: Amsterdam, Athens, Budapest, London, Madrid, Milan, Oslo, Prague, Riga, Stockholm, Tallinn, Vienna and Vilnius. We are also grateful for the help of Annika Väiko in preparing the final manuscript of this book. Much of the time invested in this book by Tiit Tammaru and Maarten van Ham was covered by funding from the Estonian Research Council (Institutional Research Grant IUT no. 2-17 on Spatial Population Mobility and Geographical Changes in Urban Regions); the European Research Council under the European Union's Seventh Framework Programme (FP/2007-2013)/ERC Grant Agreement no. 615159 (ERC Consolidator Grant DEPRIVEDHOODS, Socio-spatial Inequality, Deprived Neighbourhoods and Neighbourhood Effects); and from the Marie Curie programme under the European

Union's Seventh Framework Programme (FP/2007-2013)/Career Integration Grant no. PCIG10-GA-2011-303728 (CIG Grant NBHCHOICE, Neighbourhood Choice, Neighbourhood Sorting, and Neighbourhood Effects).

Tiit Tammaru, Szymon Marcińczak,
Maarten van Ham, Sako Musterd
February 2015

1 A multi-factor approach to understanding socio-economic segregation in European capital cities[1]

Tiit Tammaru, Sako Musterd, Maarten van Ham and Szymon Marcińczak

Abstract

Growing inequalities in Europe, even in the most egalitarian countries, are a major challenge threatening the sustainability of urban communities and the competiveness of European cities. Surprisingly, though, there is a lack of systematic and representative research on the spatial dimension of rising inequalities. This gap is filled by our book project *Socio-Economic Segregation in European Capital Cities: East Meets West*, with empirical evidence from Amsterdam, Athens, Budapest, London, Madrid, Milan, Oslo, Prague, Riga, Stockholm, Tallinn, Vienna and Vilnius. This introductory chapter outlines the background to this international comparative research and introduces a multi-factor approach to studying socio-economic segregation. The chapter focuses on four underlying universal structural factors: social inequalities, global city status, welfare regime and the housing system. Based on these factors, we propose a hypothetical ranking of segregation levels in the thirteen case study cities. As the conclusions of this book show, the hypothetical ranking and the actual ranking of cities by segregation levels only match partly; the explanation for this can be sought in context-specific factors which will be discussed in-depth in each of the case study chapters.

Introduction

Although it is often claimed that socio-economic segregation is increasing in European cities, there is no recent internationally comparative and systematic research into changing levels of this form of segregation. Most research on segregation focuses on ethnic rather than socio-economic segregation, and although the two are related, the latter deserves more attention in light of increasing levels of incquality in Europe, which is also likely to be expressed spatially. Governments all over Europe fear that in the future such socio-economic segregation may lead to social unrest, referring to recent riots in several European cities. Although often openly ethno-religious, the deeper underpinnings of such urban unrest stem from rising socio-economic inequalities that are also clustered into urban space (Malmberg *et al.* 2013). This book will be the first to rigorously compare levels of socio-economic segregation for a large number of European cities, and to use a multi-factor approach to understand segregation that combines structural factors with a context sensitive presentation of each case study city. We ask whether rising inequalities in Europe lead to what Kesteloot (2005) suggests is a shift from a city of social class divisions to a city of socio-spatial divisions, with top, middle and low socio-economic groups being increasingly separated from each other in urban space.

By socio-economic segregation we mean residential segregation of population groups based on occupation and income. In the last three decades we have seen some remarkable changes in advanced capitalist countries, characterised by a transformation from industrial to post-industrial societies, accompanied by growing levels of liberalisation and globalisation of capital and labour flows. These changes have impacted on occupational structures and have led to wage inequalities even in the most egalitarian European countries (Sachs 2012; European Commission 2010). The fall of the Iron Curtain in 1989 and the demise of the Soviet Union in 1991 integrated many former communist countries in Central and Eastern Europe (East Europe hereafter[2]) into ongoing globalisation and neoliberalisation processes. The combination of these processes with transformations from centrally planned to market economies brought about a rapid decline in real per capita income between 1988 and 1993: minus 41 per cent in the Baltic states and minus 25 per cent in the Visegrad countries (Deacon 2000: 148). Before 1989/1991, wage inequalities in East European countries were small but have grown dramatically since (Słomczyński and Shabad 1996; Tsenkova 2006). In addition, in most East European countries housing was supported by state patronage under socialism, but during the 1990s more than 90 per cent of the housing stock was privatised as states withdrew from the costly housing sector (Hegedüs 2013).

These fundamental changes were the inspiration for formulating the overarching goal of this book: to provide new insights into the spatial dimension of growing socio-economic inequalities in Europe, in the light of the processes of globalisation, neoliberalisation and welfare state retrenchment. The book delivers a set of theoretically informed, methodologically sound, and policy and planning relevant systematic comparative studies that provide new evidence of the changing levels and patterns of socio-economic segregation across a diverse set of European cities: Amsterdam, Athens, Budapest, London, Milan, Madrid, Oslo, Prague, Riga, Stockholm, Tallinn, Vienna and Vilnius. We focus on these economic and political capital cities because they have been the most influenced by globalisation (Beaverstock *et al.* 2015). Especially in East Europe, many important changes induced by globalisation occurred in the capital cities first (Marcińczak *et al.* 2015; Stanilov 2007; Smith and Timár 2010). Although the case study cities are diverse in size, they do share similar positions in their countries as important locations for government services, as centres for education and jobs, and for international investments.

The study is based on a multi-factor approach that focuses on key structural indicators shaping socio-economic segregation: globalisation, social inequalities, welfare regimes and housing systems, as well as the occupational structure of cities (Hamnett 1994; Kemeny 1995; Marcińczak *et al.* 2015; Musterd and Ostendorf 1998; Sassen 1991). This approach is combined with more nuanced institutional and contextual approaches that have found their way into studies of residential segregation (Burgers and Musterd 2002; Kazepov 2005; Maloutas 2012; Van Kempen and Murie 2009). The latter approaches emphasise the role of local institutional, morphological, historical and spatial contexts in mediating effects of more universal/generic structural factors on patterns of segregation. Since such city-specific factors are very important, along with the more generic ones for understanding segregation, each chapter of this book will deliver a detailed account of the unique features of a given case study city.

The next section of this introductory chapter contains a literature review on the key structural factors that shape socio-economic segregation. Because cities in East Europe are still understudied with respect to inequalities and segregation (cf. Van Kempen and Murie 2009), we will briefly elaborate on the urban experiences in the formerly state socialist countries in a separate section. The main focus here will be on the legacies of central planning and some distinct features of the socialist city that are important for understanding socio-economic segregation. The importance of context will be discussed in more detail in the next section. Then we will develop a multi-factor analytical framework that guides the analyses of the thirteen cities in the rest of the book. The operationalisation of this framework leads to a hypothetical ranking of our case study cities by their expected levels of socio-economic segregation. We will then present the data and methods behind our analysis in the next section. In a separate section we introduce the rest of the book chapters, which will each deliver a contextually sensitive and empirically detailed account of socio-economic segregation in one of the thirteen cities in 2001 and 2011 (corresponding with the years of the census in many countries). Finally, we will reflect on the expected levels of segregation in our case study cities. Taken together, this introductory chapter, the thirteen case studies and the concluding chapter of this book will provide new perspectives and insights on the evolution of socio-economic segregation and its contributory factors in major European cities.

Literature review: structural factors shaping socio-economic segregation

Cities are both the main drivers of innovation and economic growth, as well as places where the biggest diversity and largest social inequalities can be found. In this review, we focus on the key structural factors that link social and spatial inequalities. Research on patterns of socio-economic residential segregation has followed four important phases: the ecological approach; research on the relationship between social and spatial inequalities inspired by a global city thesis; studies that begin with the impact of welfare regimes on residential segregation; and, most recently, studies that emphasise the importance of the contextual embeddedness of residential segregation (Maloutas 2012; Marcińczak *et al.* 2015; Musterd and Ostendorf 1998; Van Kempen and Murie 2009).

Charles Booth's (1887) detailed social and spatial description of Tower Hamlets in London could be considered as the beginning of a more systematic research on segregation. Extending from description to explanation, scholars from the Chicago School provided a human ecology framework of invasion and succession to explain the evolving segregation patterns in cities (Park *et al.* 1925). The ecological approach explained the evolution of segregation by referring to natural forces that are the same in all cities. Consequently, cities develop towards similar spatial structures with different social and ethnic groups clustering into different parts of the city (Häusserman and Haila 2005). The Chicago School developed an important toolbox of segregation indices that are still used in segregation research today (Massey and Denton 1988; Marcińczak *et al.* 2015; Peach 2009). Applying these indices to real data typically reveals a U-shaped segregation pattern across occupational groups, with the biggest spatial distance being between the highest and lowest social categories or occupations (Duncan and Duncan 1955; Ladányi 1989; Morgan 1975; 1980). The ecological approach developed into a factorial ecology during the post-war positivist research tradition (Berry and Kasarda 1977), and later into GIS-based studies of segregation and advanced spatial modelling (Wong 2003).

Methodologically, these studies stressed that for a rigorous spatial analysis, the units used should be internally homogeneous so that the variation of interest, for example the distribution of socio-economic groups across the city, becomes visible between the units as an ecological variation (Janson 1980). This indicated the problem of how to define neighbourhoods (known as the modifiable area unit problem) and raised the question of how the conceptualisation of neighbourhoods affects segregation measures (Fotheringham and Wong 1991). Following the research by Kish (1954) on within-unit and inter-unit variation of a given phenomenon in and across neighbourhoods, Manley *et al.* (2016) make an important methodological contribution to this book by extending the ecological tradition into a multilevel research setting. It should also be noted that in parallel with the advancements of the ecological approach, behavioural (Wolpert 1965) and institutional (Rex and Moore 1967) approaches towards studying segregation started to emerge. These are beyond the scope of this book.

Income inequalities started to grow in advanced capitalist countries in the 1980s (Piketty 2013) and in Eastern Europe in the 1990s (Sztompka 1996), and this reinvigorated the interest in relations between social inequalities and socio-economic segregation. These relations play a major role in the social polarisation versus professionalisation debate (Manley and Johnston 2014; Hamnett 1994; Sassen 1991). The concentration of higher-order management and coordination and service functions of multinational corporations into large cities is a direct result of globalisation and economic restructuring. According to the global city thesis this leads to social polarisation; a class of well-paid workers in the financial and other higher-order services emerges on the one hand, and since they require consumer services this provides jobs for many low-skilled workers on the other hand (Sassen 1991). Others argue that professionalisation rather than polarisation takes place in the global cities (Hamnett 1994; Préteceille 2000).

The widespread pursuit of free market efficiency in the housing sector in Europe in tandem with globalisation and economic restructuring since the 1980s, and the retrenching of welfare states, implied significant cuts in universal housing subsidies, privatisation of part of the social housing stock and the promotion of home ownership (Arbaci 2007). Major changes in the housing sector started in the UK with the right-to-buy policy in the 1980s, which led to an increase in home ownership and a decline of the social housing sector, residualising this sector and increasing socio-housing divides (Kleinhans and van Ham 2013). This trend of decreasing importance of social (or public) housing subsequently spread across Western Europe (Jones and Murie 2006), while at the same time people with a lower social status became increasingly overrepresented in social housing (Van Kempen and Murie 2009; van Ham and Manley 2009; Manley *et al.* 2013). Since social housing is often concentrated in certain parts of cities, the developments in the housing market combined with a growing social polarisation, *ceteris paribus,* should lead to rising levels of residential segregation.[3] Globalisation and economic restructuring thus create socio-housing divisions that become the core drivers of residential segregation (Figure 1.1[4]). Further, since these changes in the housing sector spread across most Western European countries in the 1980s, it has been argued that this leads to increasing convergence of European housing systems (Arbaci 2007).

European countries are still characterised by high levels of social protection and income redistribution (although declining) that cushions the effects of globalisation and economic restructuring (Musterd and Ostendorf 1998). This is also the core argument why we find lower levels of residential segregation in

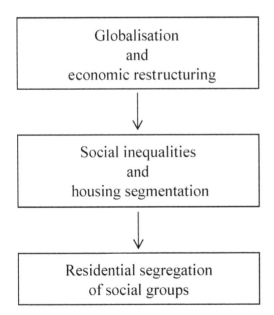

Figure 1.1 Globalisation and socio-economic segregation.

Western European cities compared to USA cities (Musterd 2005; Van Kempen and Murie 2009). Essentially, the welfare state helps to lower residential segregation through direct reductions of social inequality, or through housing policy, or through both (Figure 1.2). The cutbacks in welfare and housing benefits across Western Europe directly affect those who are dependent on such benefits, such as unemployed or lower-income groups, increasingly pushing them into lower-cost housing (Marcuse and Van Kempen 2000). Retrenchment of the welfare state, the promotion of home ownership together with social and economic change (professionalisation) and spatial change (gentrification, suburbanisation) thus potentially contribute to increasing levels of socio-economic segregation. The sorting of social groups across housing and neighbourhood types increasingly emerges from market transactions, favouring middle-income and high-income population groups over low-income groups (Van Kempen and Murie 2009; Dewilde and Lancee 2013).

Despite converging tendencies, European countries still represent different types of welfare regimes (social democratic, corporatist and liberal; see Esping-Andersen 1990) and housing systems (unitary, dual; see Kemeny 1995). The corporatist (and its distinct Mediterranean variant) and social-democratic welfare types are characterised by a relatively large social housing sector and unitary rental system in which social and private renting are integrated into a single rental market, with high levels of socio-tenure mix and low levels of residential segregation (Arbaci 2007). The liberal and Southern European welfare types are characterised by a dualist rental system, in which the state controls and residualises the social rental sector for vulnerable and low-income groups, leading to higher levels of socio-tenure segmentation and residential segregation but often at a very micro scale (ibid.).

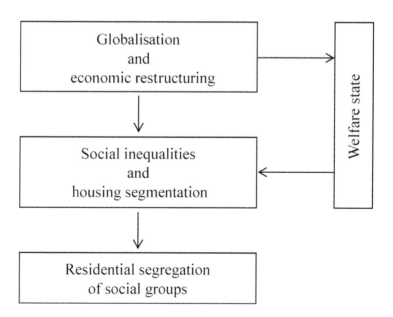

Figure 1.2 Social inequalities, welfare state and socio-economic segregation.

Fenger (2007) found that East European countries are both collectively distinct from the Western countries and different from each other. Namely, Visegrad countries (including the Czech Republic and Hungary represented in this book) could be characterised as post-socialist corporatist regimes, while Baltic countries Estonia, Latvia and Lithuania could be characterised as post-socialist liberal welfare regimes. The main differences between the two country groups relate to the social stratification dimension, with higher social inequalities being found in the Baltic countries compared to the Visegrad countries. Next, we will elaborate more on the specific features of Eastern European cities that stem from their socialist legacy.

Eastern Europe: central planning and the socialist city

Cities in Western Europe are generally less segregated than in the USA, and the literature provides some evidence that the communist rule and centrally planned production and consumption policies in East European countries resulted in less socio-economically segregated cities there in comparison to Western Europe (Dangschat 1987; Ladanyi 1989; Musil 1987; Węcławowicz 1979). The socialist states nationalised the means of production and had a central role in the production and redistribution of goods, with housing being one of the most valued (Kornai 1992; Verdery 1996). Urbanisation had a particular significance in the formerly centrally planned countries: on the one hand, it facilitated the fulfilment of ambitions for industrialisation and signified modernisation and progress, and on the other hand it encouraged collective rather than individual identity with the aim of creating a socially just society (Kährik and Tammaru 2010; Smith 1996). A more uniform city with little economising of space and little urban diversity emerged in countries under central planning (Gentile *et al.* 2012; Szelényi 1996). The high degree of urban homogeneity was a function of the share of the urban fabric constructed under socialism when the focus was on standardised mass construction of high-rise housing estates. In the context of the pool of cities included in this book, the imprint of the socialist legacy, for example in the form of socialist housing estates, is larger in the Baltic capitals in comparison to Visegrad capitals (Marcińczak *et al.* 2015).

When it comes to segregation, the administrative allocation of housing free of charge (apart from cooperative housing that formed a minor part of the new housing construction) became an important tool for building the desired uniform and egalitarian society. The production and administrative allocation of goods, which were either free of charge or heavily subsidised, was broader than housing and characterised many key aspects of society – ranging from subsidised food, transport, guaranteed employment, adequate health and education (Deacon 2000). This implies that state paternalistic welfare, sometimes called the totalitarian corporatist welfare state (Sennett 2003), characterised countries under central planning (Verdery 1996). With time, market elements were introduced in some domains of the economy, first in the Visegrad countries and later, from the mid-1980s, in the Soviet Union in the form of *perestroika* – the policy to restructure Soviet political and economic systems – introduced by the Soviet leader Gorbachev.

Budapest was the first to introduce market-relations in housing (Bodnár and Böröcz 1998) and, interestingly, at the end of socialism it was the most segregated East European capital city among the pool of cities included in this book (Kovács 2009; Marcińczak *et al.* 2015).

Although the mass construction of standardised housing was common in many non-communist Western European countries in the 1960s through the 1980s, the scale was much higher in East European cities (Gentile and Sjöberg 2013). In other words, the redistributive effect of the state in the form of public housing allocation (see Figure 1.2) in countries under central planning was stronger than in the West. As a result of the construction of vast high-rise housing estates, East European cities were characterised by less sprawl than Western cities (Bertaud and Renaud 1997; Tammaru 2001). Moreover, the Iron Curtain sealed off Eastern Europe from the effects of globalisation and economic restructuring, and manufacturing industry remained the main pillar of its economic base. The result was a less segregated and spatially compact city with socially mixed neighbourhoods (Marcińczak *et al.* 2015). In the literature, it has been labelled as a distinct city type: the socialist city (Sýkora 2009). In comparison to many West European large housing estates, which are often in deprived areas, similar estates in East European cities show a much greater share of higher socio-economic groups (Turkington *et al.* 2004). In the West such housing estates originally also included middle-class families, and in some areas this is still the case, but in many places downgrading or residualisation occurred. An important question then is whether this downgrading of large housing estates will also occur in high-rise estates in Eastern Europe, as some scholars already envisaged in the 1990s (Szelényi 1996).

Important changes to East European cities after the fall of the Iron Curtain twenty-five years ago are related to the economising of space, increased social inequality and increased urban diversity (Gentile *et al.* 2012; Hirt 2013; Szelényi 1996; Tsenkova and Nedović-Budić 2006). Large-scale privatisation and restitution of properties to pre-World War II owners were the two important specific factors shaping housing markets in East European cities in the 1990s. The concrete spatial manifestations of such changes are under debate. Segregation could be reduced further when those parts of the socialist city that were left in decay under socialism – mainly higher-density, pre-World War II inner-city areas and lower-density outer city areas – go through a process of socio-spatial upgrading, while large housing estates start to lose the relatively high status they used to enjoy under socialism. Eventually, this might cause these large housing estates to take similar positions on the housing market as in the case in many Western European cities. This in turn leads to the paradox of post-socialist transition: despite increasing social inequalities, levels of segregation either decreased from already low levels (Sýkora 2009; Marcińczak *et al.* 2013) or virtually did not change (Marcińczak *et al.* 2014) in the 1990s.

This paradox, however, could be a temporary phase of urban socio-spatial change; the evolutionary view predicts that, with time, new residential socio-economic segregation patterns will emerge as the residential choices of managers and professionals, as well as *in situ* demographic and social change (effects of changes on the labour market were more extensive compared to residential mobility in East Europe in the 1990s), start to redefine the residential geographies of cities (Sýkora and Bouzarovski 2012; Tammaru *et al.* 2016). The gentrification of inner cities and suburbanisation of the middle class are the most eye-catching manifestations of such spatial change that could ultimately lead to higher levels of segregation. Such paradox is not unique to East European cities, though. Gentrification often lowers levels of segregation in its initial phase as higher socio-economic groups start to move into low-income inner city areas, and evidence of it can be found in many parts of Europe (for example Leal and Sorando 2016; Musterd and Van Gent 2016). Likewise, *in situ* change in social and demographic structures can also contribute to lowering the levels of segregation in a neighbourhood (Hochstenbach *et al.* 2014), for example through professionalisation or increase of income of people not moving or as a result of *in situ* demographic change. The latter can occur as children achieve a higher occupational status than their parents but, later, leave the parental home, move into a different dwelling in the same neighbourhood, or inherit housing from parents. Such social and demographic processes within the neighbourhoods might lead to neighbourhood socio-economic mixing in the initial phases of change. This is especially important in South European countries where spatial proximity of family members is still very common (Leal and Sorando 2016; Maloutas 2016; Petsimeris and Rimoldi 2016).

Comparative research on socio-economic residential segregation using recent data is missing for East European countries, with the exception of a study by Marcińczak *et al.* (2016) of five East European capital cities using data from the 2000 census. The results of this study reveal low levels of socio-economic segregation, reflecting the patterns of the late socialist period. Although social inequalities rose rapidly in the 1990s, they were not directly translated into urban space since residential mobility was still low at this time of institutional reforms and housing privatisation (Hegedüs 2013). This book uses the most recent data available from the 2011 census in many countries to investigate whether and how social inequalities, created mainly in the 1990s and persisting today, start to translate into urban space.

Contextual approach to residential segregation

Globalisation and economic restructuring, mediated by welfare regimes and housing systems, affect levels of socio-economic segregation. Yet, the association between structural factors and the level of segregation is not universal; it hinges on cultural differences, and on the historically developed institutional and spatial contexts of cities, where social divisions render spatial patterns in unique ways (Burgers and Musterd 2002; Maloutas 2012). Abstract models and universal factors simply fail to fully consider the rich reality of contemporary cities, with all their different historical layers and contemporary diversity in their key institutions – families, state and markets (Kazepov 2005; Häussermann and Haila 2005). Hence, making deductions from global megatrends to exact spatial patterns in the city should be done with great care.

What are the contextual factors that are important in shaping residential segregation, on top of and related to the welfare state and housing systems that we have already discussed? Musterd and Kovács (2013) refer to specific historically grown urban layers, while Maloutas (2012) refers to the spheres that characterise them. The economic layer pertains to labour market changes; the state layer has to do with the redistribution of public services; the social layer pertains to social and family networks; and the fourth layer is about specific local socio-spatial realities such as urban morphology. The institutional approach has made its way into the contextual understanding of segregation patterns, too, since the local institutional arrangements are much more complex and nuanced than the broad welfare regime types or housing systems, including various governance arrangements and other dimensions (Van Kempen and Murie 2009).

The local realities relate, in the first place, to historical pathways that city regions have taken and which have led to the contemporary diversity of urban morphology, housing stock, social class structures, etc. (Figure 1.3). Through most of the chapters in this book, the importance of historic pathways of city development in understanding contemporary segregation patterns is repeated. The historic layers are further coloured by the cultural diversity of Europe. For example, the family dimension is very important in the social and spatial relations of Southern European cities (Maloutas 2016; Leal and Sorando 2016; Petsimeris and Rimoldi 2016). Housing in Southern European cities is often more distant from market processes and embedded in family relations (Arbaci 2007). Even then, important differences emerge also between Southern European cities, for example when it comes to the effects of the last cycle of housing boom and bust and their spatial implications in the cities of Athens, Madrid and Milan as included in this book.

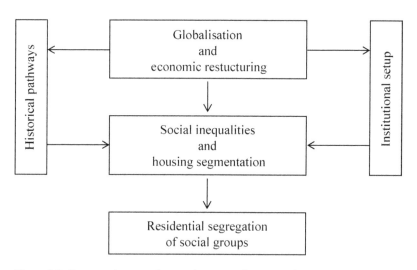

Figure 1.3 Contextual approach to socio-economic segregation.

The unique characteristics of place (the *genius loci*) are an important part of the historic development of the city. It includes, but is not restricted to, differences in attracting various economic activities, the functioning of the welfare regime and housing market, the match between demand and supply, quality of the built environment, the architecture, the urban layout and the state of the urban condition in general. These are all factors which are increasingly important assets that make a difference between cities (Musterd and Kovács 2013). All of these factors shift the attention away from generalised representation of national systems towards the unevenness of policy and capability associated with each city administration (Van Kempen and Murie 2009). The very same characteristics are also important at the intra-urban scale. The more diverse the historic layers of the city are, the greater is the housing and neighbourhood diversity, and the more 'opportunities' exist for different population groups to isolate themselves from other groups. Furthermore, the new urban reality, with less public involvement, could be characterised as a shift from government to governance. Various governance levels (state, region, city, neighbourhood) and other actors (private firms, inhabitants) work together in shaping the dynamics of the city and the milieus of the neighbourhoods in increasingly complex and diverse ways (Van Kempen and Murie 2009).

The advancement of the contextual approach to residential segregation thus allows us to pay due attention to the historic development and urbanisation pathways, city-specific policies, governance, planning practices and other factors unique to each city. Two of the four contributory factors discussed in previous sections – welfare and housing regimes – have more to do with the contextual factors than the more generic factors of globalisation and social inequalities. Therefore, each of the following chapters includes a section that discusses the context of the city under study. Still, by contrasting the evidence of thirteen cities across Europe, we want to seize the unique opportunity to shed some light on how the key structural factors potentially shape residential segregation. We therefore have developed a multi-factor framework for studying socio-economic segregation in European capital cities.

Multi-factor framework of the study

Our analytical framework for understanding social segregation in European capital cities includes four key contributory factors outlined above – socio-economic inequalities, welfare regime, housing regime and the global position of the city in the world economy – combined with a unique profile of each city. Using these factors as a starting point, we develop a theoretical model of levels of social segregation that allows us to predict segregation in each city under study. Following Marcińczak *et al.* (2016), and based on the literature review in the previous section, for each city we quantify the theoretical level of segregation by attaching one to three points to each factor that contributes to segregation (globalisation, Gini index, welfare regime, housing regime, share of higher occupations). This exercise may be overly simplistic, but it operationalises the conceptual framework underlying this book and, when viewed in a less deterministic way, allows us to advance the debate on how the various structural factors could be related to levels of socio-economic segregation.

The first factor that potentially has an important impact on levels of socio-economic segregation is globalisation. The best-known classification system groups cities into three main categories of Alpha, Beta and Gamma cities (Beaverstock *et al.* 2015). Alpha cities are the most important command-and-control centres in the global economy, and we attach the value 3 to them, indicating the highest expected level of segregation. The least global cities are Gamma cities and we attach the value of 1 to these, indicating the lowest expected segregation level (Table 1.1). Since we are studying capital cities, seven of our case study cities belong to the Alpha category (London, Amsterdam, Madrid, Milan, Prague, and Vienna) and only two to the Gamma category (Tallinn and Vilnius).

The second factor potentially shaping levels of socio-economic segregation pertains to socio-economic inequalities. At this point it is important to acknowledge that the five factors we use are not completely independent from each other. The first factor – globalisation – is an important source of socio-economic inequalities (Marcuse and Van Kempen 2000), but other factors shape inequalities, too, including the type of welfare regime, economic structure and many others. Thus, there is no one-to-one correspondence between the factors we use, and all of them uniquely contribute to segregation levels, as shown in the literature review in the previous sections. The most common indicator for characterising income-based socio-economic inequalities is the Gini index. The values of the index as used in Table 1.1 are obtained from around the year 2010, as is the case with the other variables (Eurostat 2015). The literature does not provide any guidance on which values of the Gini index could relate to high or low levels of segregation. Instead of focusing on the values of the index we therefore opt for a relative approach that contrasts our research cities with each other. We attach the value 3 to those cities where the Gini index is one standard deviation above the average of our thirteen cities, and we attach the value 1 to those cities where the value of the Gini index is one standard deviation below the average. All other cities get the value 2. This way, we classify London, Riga, Madrid and Athens as the most unequal cities, and Stockholm, Milan and Prague as the most equal cities (Table 1.1).

The link between socio-economic inequalities and socio-economic segregation is moderated by the type of the welfare regime. We use three main types of welfare regime (Esping-Andersen 1990), and we distinguish the South European or Mediterranean regime within the corporatist type. Arbaci (2007) shows that the liberal welfare regime tends to correlate with higher levels of residential segregation, while corporatist and social-democratic welfare types tend to relate to lower levels of segregation. Interestingly, she further argues that a corporatist (as well as Mediterranean) welfare regime could lead to a more mosaic type of urban spatial structure because of the large number and diversity of urban developers compared to the social-democratic welfare regime. As a consequence, Arbaci argues that the

Table 1.1 Key structural indicators that shape socio-economic segregation and their corresponding values

Indicators:	Globalisation	Gini index	Welfare regime	Housing regime	Higher occupations*	Lower occupations**
London	Alpha++	38	Liberal	Dual	33	10
Riga	Beta−	35	Liberal-PS***	Dual-PS	33	10
Vilnius	Gamma	34	Liberal-PS	Dual-PS	50	7
Madrid	Alpha	36	Mediterranean	Mediterranean	29	14
Tallinn	Gamma	32	Liberal-PS	Dual-PS	34	8
Milan	Alpha	21	Mediterranean	Mediterranean	32	15
Amsterdam	Alpha	30	Corporatist	Unitary	46	5
Budapest	Beta+	29	Corporatist-PS	Dual-PS	34	7
Oslo	Beta	27	Social Democratic	Dual	37	4
Athens	Beta+	35	Mediterranean	Mediterranean	26	9
Stockholm	Alpha−	24	Social Democratic	Unitary	33	6
Prague	Alpha−	27	Corporatist-PS	Unitary-PS	26	5
Vienna	Alpha−	28	Corporatist	Unitary	28	9

Indicator values:	Globalisation	Gini index	Welfare regime	Housing regime	Higher occupations*	Lower occupations**	Sum
London	3	3	3	3	2	2	16
Riga	2	3	3	3	2	2	15
Madrid	3	3	2	2	1	3	14
Vilnius	1	2	3	3	3	2	14
Milan	3	1	2	2	2	3	13
Tallinn	1	2	3	3	2	2	13
Amsterdam	3	2	1	1	3	2	12
Athens	2	3	1	2	1	2	11
Budapest	2	2	1	3	2	1	11
Oslo	2	1	2	3	2	2	11
Stockholm	3	1	2	1	2	2	11
Prague	3	1	1	1	1	2	9
Vienna	3	2	1	1	1	1	9

Notes:
* Share of managers and professionals in the workforce.
** Share of elementary occupations in the workforce.
*** Post-socialist.

lowest levels of segregation evolve under corporatist welfare regimes. We therefore expect that the welfare regime contributes to higher levels of segregation in London, Riga, Tallinn and Vilnius, and to lower levels of segregation in Amsterdam, Athens, Budapest, Milan, Madrid, Prague and Vienna.

The classification of the welfare regimes does not take into account the housing systems – a key element influencing segregation (Maloutas 2012). Socio-economic residential sorting is firmly shaped by the extent of income-based housing markets and policies (Reardon and Bischoff 2011). Although strongly linked, welfare regimes and housing regimes do not necessarily correspond with each other. The best examples in our pool of cities include Oslo and Stockholm. Although both represent a social-democratic welfare regime, the housing sector in Oslo (Wessel 2016) is much more market based compared to Stockholm (Andersson and Kährik 2016). Therefore, as the fourth key contributory factor, we introduce the housing regime into our analytical framework by assuming that marketisation of housing produces a stronger spatial separation of socio-economic groups (Marcińczak *et al.* 2015). As shown in the literature, the most important division line runs between dual and unitary housing systems (Kemeny 1995). Market-based residential sorting in the dual system can be expected to lead to stronger income-based residential segregation in cities such as Budapest, London, Oslo, Riga, Tallinn and Vilnius (Table 1.1). A lower level of marketisation and a tenure-neutral housing policy under the unitary housing system would lead to weaker income-based residential segregation in cities such as Amsterdam, Prague, Stockholm and Vienna. As with the welfare regimes, we distinguish a South European housing regime which sits in-between the two main types. Athens, Madrid and Milan represent such cities in our study.

The level of socio-economic segregation is also a function of the occupational structure of the city. The more socially polarised a city is, the higher the levels of expected segregation (Mollenkopf and Castells 1991) since both the higher-status and lower-status groups tend to be more segregated compared to middle-status groups (Duncan and Duncan 1955; Morgan 1980; Marcińczak *et al.* 2015). The share of managers and professionals has increased remarkably while the share of people working in elementary occupations (unskilled workers) has decreased to 15 per cent of the workforce or less in our research cities. We use both the share of managers and professionals, as well as the share of people working in elementary occupations to account for the effect of the occupational structure (Table 1.1). We do not prefer one group to another since in some of our case study cities, managers and professionals are the most segregated group while in other cities unskilled workers form the most segregated group. In Amsterdam and Vilnius, the share of managers and professionals is more than one standard deviation above the average, and we expect that this has a strong effect on segregation in those two cities. In the case of unskilled workers, this effect is strongest in Madrid and Milan. In Athens, Prague and Vienna, the share of managers and professionals is one standard deviation below the average, and we expect that this leads to the lowest levels of segregation. In the case of unskilled workers, this is true for Budapest, Oslo and Vienna.

As a final step, we calculate the sum of the indicator scores for each city in Table 1.1 (last column of the lower half of the table). We do not weight the various scores since the literature provides no guidance on how to weight each of them. The result of this exercise is a theoretical ranking of our thirteen case study cities based on the levels of socio-economic segregation. This ranking is obviously sensitive both to the number of factors/indicators included in the analytical framework, as well as to the scores attached to them. However, this is a first attempt to systematically contrast theoretical segregation levels across European capital cities and empirically test them (Marcińczak *et al.* 2016). The summation itself provides the following hypothetical ranking of cities included in this study (from most to least segregated): London (16 out of 18); Riga (15); Madrid and Vilnius (14); Milan and Tallinn (13); Amsterdam and Athens (12); Budapest, Oslo and Stockholm (11); Prague and Vienna (9). In order to facilitate our comparative study we next discuss data and methods that guide the analysis of the chapters included in this book.

Data and methods

In order to undertake a rigorous comparative analysis of socio-economic segregation in thirteen cities, the first task is to produce comparable datasets. This is not easy because of two major obstacles. First, different countries use different key indicators for socio-economic status. Second, different countries have different data policies when it comes to releasing data for small geographic areas, and use different aggregation levels of either socio-economic groups or spatial units/neighbourhoods. These obstacles are beyond our control, but we aimed at a high level of comparability and analytical detail within these two sets of limits.

The first data-related challenge pertains to the indicators of socio-economic status. We had to use three different variables for measuring socio-economic status in different cities: occupation, income and education. Occupation, but not income, is available at a detailed geographic resolution in those countries that undertake censuses. The analysis of Athens, Budapest, Madrid, Milan, London, Prague, Riga, Tallinn and Vilnius is thus based on occupational data. Income, but not occupation, is available at a detailed geographic resolution for cities in register-based countries: Amsterdam, Oslo and Stockholm. Finally, the study of Vienna is based on education as Austria switched from census to registers in 2010 with the unfortunate side effect that neither income nor occupation data is available at a detailed geographic resolution in this country for the 2001–2011 period.

We use the International Standard Classification of Occupations (ISCO) for defining the major occupational groups in chapters based on occupational data (ILO 2015), and income quintiles are used in chapters based on income data. We excluded two small occupational groups, agricultural workers and armed forces, from the ten major categories in the ISCO classification used in our analysis. This leaves us with the occupational ladder of eight major categories: managers, senior officials and legislators; professionals; technicians and associate professionals; clerks; service and sales workers; craft and related trades workers; plant and machine operators, and assemblers; and elementary occupations.

The ISCO classification is generally internationally comparable, although it should be noted that countries do make some minor modifications to the classifications. What is more important is that the classification itself changed between the 2001 and 2011 census rounds. ISCO-08 replaced the ISCO-88 for several reasons, mainly because the latter was seen to be seriously outdated, most notably due to developments in the field technology sectors (ILO 2007). Also, there was a need to better aggregate managerial occupations (ILO 2012). Most of the changes took place within the ten major categories, but some jobs were also shifted from one major category to another (detailed ISCO-88 and ISCO-08 correspondence tables can be found at ILO 2015). Most importantly, managers of small organisations without any sophisticated hierarchical structure, such as small shops, restaurants, cafes and similar establishments, were shifted from the first major group of managers to the fifth major group, service and sales workers. This had an especially important effect on cities with a large number of such small establishments, such as Southern European cities.

Occupation and income are strongly related to each other: the higher the job in the occupational ladder the higher the income, with managers and professionals earning the most (Table 1.2). The relationship is not directly linear, though. For example, service sector workers have the lowest income together with the elementary workers. Another general issue to consider is that the extent of the differences between occupational groups varies city by city. For example, differences in the wages between occupational groups are the smallest in Athens (for example, managers earn 2.2 times the salary of elementary workers) and Stockholm, and the largest in Prague, Budapest and Madrid. Despite those differences, it is still safe to

Table 1.2 Income of occupational groups relative to people working in elementary occupations (data from around 2010)

	Managers	Professionals	Technicians	Clerks	Service workers	Craft workers	Operators	Elementary workers
Amsterdam	3.3	2.5	2.3	1.5	1.1	1.6	1.5	1.0
Athens	2.2	2.3	2.0	1.6	1.4	1.3	1.6	1.0
Budapest	5.1	3.2	2.2	1.7	1.1	1.5	1.5	1.0
London	2.7	3.0	3.0	1.7	1.0	1.2	2.0	1.0
Madrid	4.6	2.6	2.2	1.5	1.2	1.6	1.6	1.0
Milan	3.8	1.9	1.6	1.4	1.1	1.1	1.2	1.0
Oslo	3.0	2.1	1.9	1.4	1.0	1.5	1.5	1.0
Prague	5.3	3.0	2.3	1.7	1.3	1.6	1.5	1.0
Riga	2.9	2.4	2.0	1.6	1.1	1.4	1.5	1.0
Stockholm	2.3	1.7	1.4	1.2	1.1	1.2	1.2	1.0
Tallinn	3.5	2.3	1.9	1.4	1.3	1.9	1.6	1.0
Vienna	3.0	2.1	1.8	1.5	1.1	1.5	1.4	1.0
Vilnius	3.1	2.3	1.8	1.5	1.1	1.4	1.5	1.0

Source: Statistical Offices of the countries.

argue that the two variables used in different case studies in this book – income and occupation – are clearly positively related to each other, allowing us to make broad comparisons between the findings. In Vienna, as noted, education has been used as a proxy for socio-economic status. This variable also correlates with income and professional categories, but again this is not a one-to-one relationship. Some caution is required when comparing this city with the others.

We used data from the 2000 and 2010 (or any other years close to these) census rounds. Some chapters also use data from the 1990 census round. We define cities as a continuous built-up area that forms a common housing market. In other words, the analysis is not confined to administrative city boundaries. Within this broad definition of a common housing market area, authors had to use different definitions. For example, cities that are more sprawling (many Western European cities without a communist past) adopt an extensive delimitation strategy of the city, while cities that are less sprawling (many East European cities) adopt a more restrictive delimitation strategy. Likewise, in some cities, data was available for the administrative unit only. Again, all these data limitations are beyond our control. Within the cities, the suggested smallest spatial unit of analysis is a neighbourhood of around a thousand inhabitants.

We apply the most well-known indices of segregation that measure the residential separation of population subgroups from each other, focusing either on their distributions across the neighbourhoods (evenness dimension) or on the potential to meet each other within each neighbourhood (exposure dimension). While studies of ethnic segregation tend to have a stronger interest towards the exposure dimension of segregation that characterises the potential for interaction between ethnic groups, in this book, our main focus is on the evenness dimension that allows us to understand how equally socio-economic groups are distributed across the neighbourhoods of European capital cities. Yet, we present both.

For analysing the evenness dimension, we calculate a dissimilarity index[5] (*D*) that compares the spatial distance between each occupational/income group, and the index of segregation[6] (*IS*) that compares the spatial distance of a given group from the rest of the workforce. Our main focus is on *D*. The values of the *D* range from 0 to 100, indicating what percentage of either one or the other group needs to change address across the neighbourhoods in order to achieve a similar residential distribution to the reference group. The *D* value 0 represents the completely equal distribution of the two groups across the neighbourhoods, while the *D* value 100 represents complete separation, with some neighbourhoods providing shelter to the members of a given group and other neighbourhoods to the other group. If the *D* value for the managers compared to professionals is 20, it means that either 20 per cent of managers or professionals have to redistribute in the city in order to achieve their equal distribution across neighbourhoods. In the context of ethnic segregation, index values of *D* below 30 are interpreted as low and *D* values above 60 are interpreted as high (Massey and Denton 1993). Since levels of socio-economic segregation tend to be lower than levels of ethnic segregation, Marcińczak *et al.* (2015) suggest that *D* values below 20 can be interpreted as low and D values above 40 can be interpreted as high.

Next, we capture the exposure dimension of segregation by calculating the index of isolation (*II*) and the modified index of isolation[7] (*MII*). The meeting potential it captures is important since previous literature argues that when lower socio-economic groups get isolated, they are cut off from important social networks and positive role models, thereby starting to hamper their other life careers (van Ham and Manley 2012). The *II* is sensitive to the relative sizes of the groups. If the given group is large in size, its probability for meeting members of the other groups in residential neighbourhoods is small, and if the group is small in size, its probability for meeting members of the other group in residential neighbourhoods is large, regardless of their even distribution across the neighbourhoods. Think of a group A of a thousand people and a group B of a hundred people who have a similar distribution across three neighbourhoods of a city, i.e. 50 per cent, 30 per cent and 20 per cent of the members of both groups live in neighbourhoods X, Y and Z, respectively. Because of differences in size, in each of these neighbourhoods X, Y and Z members of group A have a high potential to meet own-group members, while members of group B have a small potential to meet own-group members. When the group A increases in size, its isolation from the group B increases further, even when the distribution of both groups across the neighbourhoods remains the same.

This is exactly the case in cities that are undergoing a process of professionalisation – the share of managers and professionals increases in the urban workforce – which is typical for most of our research cities. Indices that measure the exposure dimension of segregation can thus change without changes taking place in indices that measure the evenness dimension of segregation. In order to also take into account the group size and its change, the modified index of isolation (*MII*) is used by subtracting the city-wide share of the group from *II*. We use both the *II* and *MII* for analysing the potential to meet members of the other socio-economic categories in their residential neighbourhood. The smaller the *MII* value, the less isolated the given group is from the rest of workforce and vice versa. For example, if the *MII* value for the managers is 20, it means that 20 out of the hundred people this person potentially meets within the neighbourhood of residence are also managers. In the context of ethnic segregation, the index values of *MII* below 30 are interpreted as low and *MII* values above 60 are interpreted as high (Massey and Denton 1993). Again, since levels of socio-economic segregation tend to be lower than levels of ethnic segregation, we interpret *MII* values below 20 as low and *MII* values above 40 as high.

This book compares residential distributions of all eight major occupational groups or five income groups to each other to find out how strongly socio-economic distance is related to spatial distance. All indices presented above are sensitive to the aggregation of workers into occupational/income groups, and the aggregation of addresses into residential neighbourhoods. As a rule of thumb, the larger the groups/neighbourhoods used are, the lower are the values of the dissimilarity index. When it comes aggregating addresses into neighbourhoods, we face zoning and scaling problems (see Flowerdew *et al.* 2008 on the modifiable area unit problem). The most common way of overcoming these is to define neighbourhoods as small and homogenous spatial units. Obviously, the aggregation of jobs into major occupational categories faces a similar problem. Here we follow the most common approach as explained above by using the standard major ISCO categories developed by the ILO (2015).

Finally, in order to also learn about the local geographies of segregation, we use location quotient[8] (*LQ*) maps that visualise the relative spatial concentration or dispersion of income/occupational groups in the neighbourhoods of the city. In essence, the *LQ* is a ratio between the share of a given group, such as managers, in a given spatial unit, and the city-wide share of this group. If the ratio is less than 1, the group is underrepresented in the given neighbourhood, and if it is more than 1, the group is overrepresented in the given neighbourhood.

These simple but well-known and widely used measures (*D*, *IS*, *II*, *MII*, *LQ*) are applied in all cities to 2001 and 2011 (census) data. In addition to this harmonised analysis, each chapter elaborates on the topics which are most relevant in the given city context for the understanding of changing levels and patterns of socio-economic segregation.

Main findings: introduction to the book chapters

The 13 cities brought together into this book represent different regions of Europe, as well as different degrees of globalisation, inequality, welfare and housing regimes, and occupational profiles (Table 1.1). The multi-factor approach resulted in the following theoretical ranking of cities with regard to their expected level of socio-economic segregation: London; Riga; Madrid and Vilnius; Milan and Tallinn; Amsterdam and Athens; Budapest, Oslo and Stockholm; and finally Prague and Vienna. The case studies presented in this book revealed a somewhat different ranking based on real data: Madrid and Milan; Tallinn; London; Stockholm; Vienna; Athens; Amsterdam; Budapest; Riga; Vilnius; Prague; and Oslo. Most importantly, Riga and Vilnius are actually much less segregated, while Stockholm and Vienna are much more segregated compared to what we predicted. We will elaborate further on the differences between the theoretical and actual rankings of cities in the conclusion of this book (Marcińczak *et al.* 2016). Next, we will briefly introduce each city and highlight the main findings from the contributions that follow in the rest of the book.

London, Amsterdam and Vienna represent West European cities. Based on factors outlined in Table 1.1, we hypothesised London to be highly segregated, Amsterdam moderately segregated and Vienna weakly segregated. The main findings confirm the hypothesis for London and Amsterdam but not for Vienna, which is highly segregated too. More specifically, the *D* value between top and bottom socio-economic groups is 42, 33 and 39 in these cities respectively. Also, by applying innovative multivariate extensions of traditional segregation indices for the first time, Manley *et al.* (2016) modelled occupational segregation in London. They found that although overall segregation decreased slightly in the 2000s, it was not statistically significant and there are still sharp divisions within the city landscape, with growing spatial distance between the top and bottom socio-economic groups. Amsterdam is the only one within our pool of cities where segregation between the top and bottom socio-economic groups decreased in the 2000s. This has happened at times of strong neo-liberalisation tendencies that included an increase in owner occupation and residualisation of social housing that contribute to forces that would increase segregation. Musterd and Van Gent (2016) argue that the still low level of segregation is probably related to the long tradition of a fairly equal income distribution in the Netherlands, but that the recent decrease must be attributed to the 2008 financial and economic crisis, which reduced residential mobility, and a temporary effect of new gentrification processes that initially causes more social mix and thus a decreasing level of segregation. Vienna has long been focused on policies of social equality, with the city constantly working to develop measures aimed at reducing social disparities. Contrary to Amsterdam, Vienna experienced a significant increase in socio-economic segregation in the 2000s. Hatz *et al.* (2016) link high levels of socio-economic segregation in Vienna with new immigration. There is also evidence that lower socio-economic groups have become more confined to public housing neighbourhoods.

Stockholm and Oslo represent North European cities. Based on the factors outlined in Table 1.1, we hypothesised Stockholm to be weakly and Oslo to be modestly segregated. The main findings do not confirm these hypotheses. More specifically, the *D* value between top and bottom socio-economic groups is as low as 24 in Oslo and as high as 40 in Stockholm. Quite unexpectedly, thus, the two cities with similarly low levels of social inequality are among the most and least segregated cities among our thirteen cities. This can partly be due to differences in measurement: the study of Stockholm is restricted to working age population while no such restriction was applied in Oslo. Still, the high level of segregation in Stockholm comes as a surprise. Andersson and Kährik (2016) argue that despite the long tradition of elaborate public policies in Sweden that have aimed towards neighbourhood social mix, the public sector started to cut back on housing subsidies in the 1990s. Wessel (2016) argues that the emerging pattern of socio-economic segregation in Oslo is a 'contingent outcome' of many structural factors rather than a simple reflection of economic transformation and globalisation. An especially generous welfare system due to the Norwegian revenues from natural resources is an important characteristic of Oslo above and beyond the strongly market-based housing system that allows the sustaining of relatively high levels of equality, at least in a comparative perspective.

Athens, Milan and Madrid represent South European cities. Based on the factors outlined in Table 1.1, we hypothesised Madrid to be the most segregated, followed by Milan and Athens. The main findings partly confirm these hypotheses. More specifically, the *D* value between top and bottom socio-economic groups is 49 in Madrid and Milan, and 35 in Athens. Madrid and Milan are also the most segregated cities in our pool of European capitals. Despite high levels of social inequality we find not only moderate levels and stable patterns of socio-economic segregation in Athens but even desegregation between some occupational groups. Maloutas (2016) explains this as a combination of stability in occupational structures, reduced immigration, high rates of homeownership and low levels of residential mobility at time of crisis, as well as vertical segregation within buildings. According to Leal and Sorando (2016), both professionalisation and residential entrapment of lower socio-economic groups are behind the dramatic growth in levels of segregation in Madrid. Furthermore, the authors argue that the invasion of professionals into new parts of the city, for example as a result of gentrification, as well as *in situ* inter-generational social mobility both actually exerted lowering effects on levels of segregation. In Milan, Petsimeris and Rimoldi (2016) indicate that some of the important mechanisms behind segregation include self-segregation of business owners into the most exclusive residential areas of the city; *in situ* intra- and inter-generational social mobility; and the purchase of apartments by working-class households under the right-to-buy schemes and a later selling of their properties to more affluent social groups.

In East Europe, we make a distinction between Visegrad and Baltic capitals; Budapest and Prague represent Visegrad cities. Based on the factors outlined in Table 1.1, we hypothesised Budapest to be moderately and Prague to be modestly segregated. The main findings confirm these hypotheses. More specifically, the *D* value between top and bottom socio-economic groups is as low as 26 in Prague and 32 in Budapest, with a slightly increasing trend in both cities. Budapest used to be the most segregated city in East Europe, but this is not the case anymore. Furthermore, instead of higher socio-economic groups, lower socio-economic groups became most segregated in the 2000s. Kovács and Szabó (2016) think that the most plausible reason for the decreasing segregation level of professionals is their more even distribution across neighbourhoods, triggered by new housing projects developed in the inner city and other areas with previously a high share of lower socio-economic groups. This is quite similar to what is taking place in Prague. Ouředníček *et al.* (2016) agree that low levels of socio-economic segregation are mainly a consequence of the location of new housing and in-migration of higher socio-economic groups into the formerly poorer neighbourhoods, often in the inner city of Prague. Such changes are common to many other cities included into our analysis beyond Eastern Europe. In other words, the increase of social inequalities often goes hand-in-hand with gentrification, which, at least initially, brings down levels of segregation as different social groups begin to mix in the inner city.

Riga, Vilnius and Tallinn represent Baltic cities in East Europe. They share a Soviet past and nation-building since regaining independence in 1991. Based on the factors outlined in Table 1.1, we hypothesised all of them to be highly segregated. The main findings confirm the hypothesis only for Tallinn. More specifically, the *D* value between top and bottom socio-economic groups is 31 in Riga and Vilnius, and 48 in Tallinn. Tallinn also witnessed the highest growth in socio-economic segregation among our case study cities in the 2000s, matching high social inequalities with high spatial inequalities, and becoming the most segregated East European city within the pool of our research cities. Neither in Riga nor in Vilnius has the combination of large social inequalities and a liberal society led to marked socio-economic divisions in urban space. Both Krišjāne *et al.* (2016) and Valatka *et al.* (2016) explain that gentrification has led to the increase of mixed neighbourhoods in the inner city of Vilnius similar to what has happened in Budapest and Prague. Krisjane *et al.* further argue that the ethnic dimension is more important than the socio-economic dimension in generating segregation in Riga, where the Russian-speaking population forms more than half of the city's population. Mixed neighbourhoods also characterised Tallinn in 2000. Tammaru *et al.* (2016) show that the residential relocation of higher socio-economic groups both to the inner city and outer city low-density areas is responsible for the increase in socio-economic segregation in the 2000s, replacing many earlier mixed neighbourhoods with more homogenous neighbourhoods. Thus it seems that gentrification processes have proceeded at a very rapid pace in Tallinn once the institutional transformations of the 1990s were completed. Privatisation in Tallinn was faster and the city is slightly wealthier compared to Riga and Vilnius (Tsenkova 2006), and less regulated and more unequal compared to Budapest and Prague. It remains to be seen whether other Baltic capitals that are as unequal but less segregated follow Tallinn.

Conclusions

This introductory chapter has outlined the multi-factor approach for the study of socio-economic segregation in thirteen European political and economic capital cities. Based on a literature review, we distinguished four important structural factors that could help us understand levels of socio-economic segregation: degree of globalisation, level of social inequalities, welfare regimes and housing regimes. As socio-economic segregation is closely related to the occupational structure of cities, a fifth additional factor is the share of managers and professionals. Our main findings show that socio-economic segregation grew across Europe in the 2000s (with the exception of Amsterdam). This provides evidence for a shift from a city of social classes to a city of socio-spatial groups as suggested by Kesteloot (2005), especially when it comes to the residential separation between the top and low socio-economic groups who are increasingly isolated from each other in urban space. There is no simple correlation between the main contributory factors to segregation and the actual levels of segregation; the levels of social inequalities and the levels of socio-economic segregation do not necessarily match up (compare Madrid and Milan). A unitary housing system along with elaborate public policies, as is the case in Stockholm and Vienna, is not a sufficient precondition for low levels of socio-economic segregation. Marketisation of housing does not necessarily lead to high levels of segregation as the case of Oslo shows – if placed into an otherwise generous welfare context.

The most common factor characterising highly segregated cities is the level of globalisation. In Western Europe, the most global city, London, is more segregated than Amsterdam and Vienna. In the South of Europe the more global cities of Madrid and Milan are more segregated than Athens despite the fact that social inequalities are much higher in Athens compared to Milan. The only distinct case is Tallinn, which is one of the least global but one of the most segregated cities in our pool of cities. All this leads to a clear message: universal structural factors, especially globalisation, are very important, but they also need to be combined with city-specific factors to fully understand the variations in the levels and patterns of socio-economic segregation in European capital cities. What follows in the rest of the book, therefore, is a detailed and context-sensitive analysis of each city, which, ultimately leads to a comprehensive synthetic account of our findings in the concluding chapter of the book.

Notes

1 We are very grateful to all the co-authors for their contribution to the book. Wouter Van Gent from the University of Amsterdam and Michael Gentile from the University of Helsinki provided invaluable comments to this introductory chapter. The research leading to the results presented in this chapter has received funding from the Estonian Research Council (Institutional Research Grant IUT no. 2–17 on Spatial Population Mobility and Geographical Changes in Urban Regions); European Research Council under the European Union's Seventh Framework Programme (FP/2007-2013) / ERC Grant Agreement no. 615159 (ERC Consolidator Grant DEPRIVEDHOODS, Socio-spatial Inequality, Deprived Neighbourhoods, and Neighbourhood Effects); and from the Marie Curie programme under the European Union's Seventh Framework Programme (FP/2007-2013) / Career Integration Grant no. PCIG10-GA-2011-303728 (CIG Grant NBHCHOICE, Neighbourhood Choice, Neighbourhood Sorting, and Neighbourhood Effects).
2 We use the term East Europe for countries that used to be part of the state socialist, centrally planned bloc of countries for the five decades after World War II (Czech Republic, Estonia, Hungary, Latvia and Lihtuania in this book), and West Europe for the rest of Europe (Austria, Greece, Italy, Netherlands, Norway, Spain, Sweden, and the United Kingdom in this book).
3 We should also recognise that besides polarisation processes, spatial and social mismatch processes may also occur and contribute to inequality and segregation (Wilson 1987). Mismatches between jobs supplied and jobs demanded will create unemployment (over the past decades more in former local economies dominated by manufacturing industries, and less in service oriented economies). This produces cleavages between employed and unemployed that will eventually also be reflected in segregation between these categories.
4 Figures 1.1 through 1.3 are inspired by work from Maloutas 2012.
5 We first use the index of dissimilarity (Duncan and Duncan 1955), which is calculated as follows:

$$D = \frac{1}{2} \sum_{i=1}^{n} \left(\frac{h_i}{H_T} - \frac{l_i}{L_T} \right),$$

where n is the number of spatial units/neighbourhoods; h_i is the number of members of one group (for example, highest socio-economic group) in neighbourhood i; H_T is the total number of this group members in the city; l_i is the number of the other group (for example. lowest socio-economic group) in neighbourhood i; and L_T is the total number of this group members in the city.
6 The index of segregation is a variant of the dissimilarity index and it is calculated as follows:

$$IS = \sum_{i=1}^{n} \left(\frac{x_i}{X_T} - \frac{t_i - x_i}{T - X} \right),$$

where n is the number of neighbourhoods; x_i is the number of people in the given group (for example highest socio-economic group) living in neighbourhood i; X_T is the total number of this group in the city; t_i is the number of all other groups' members (for example. the rest of the workforce) in the neighbourhood i; and T_T is the total number of them in the city. In other words, IS indicates how much the residential distribution of the given group, such as the highest socio-economic group, differs from residential distribution of the rest of the workforce across the neighbourhoods of a city.

7 The MII is calculated as follows:

$$MII = \left(\left(\sum_{i=1}^{n} \left(\frac{x_i}{x} \times \frac{x_i}{t_i} \right) - \frac{x_i}{t_i} \right) \right) \bigg/ \left(1 - \frac{x}{T} \right)$$

where n is the number of neighbourhoods; x_i is the number of people of a given group living in a neighbourhood i; X is the total number of people in this category; t_i is the total number of people living in a given neighbourhood i; and T is the total number of people living in the city. The equation reduces to II when we remove the group size correction from the MII equation.

8 The LQ is calculated as follows:

$$LQ = \left(x_i / t_i \right) / \left(X / T \right),$$

where x_i is the number of people of a given socio-economic group in the neighbourhood i; t_i is the total population of this neighbourhood i; X is the total number of the given socio-economic group in the city, and is the total population T (workforce) of a city. If the ratio is 1, the share of the given group in the given neighbourhood is exactly the same as her city-wide average.

References

Andersson, R and A Kährik 2016, 'Widening gaps: Segregation dynamics during two decades of economic and institutional change in Stockholm' in *Socio-Economic Segregation in European Capital Cities. East meets West*, eds T Tammaru, S Marcińczak, M van Ham and S Musterd, Routledge: London.

Arbaci, S 2007, 'Ethnic segregation, housing systems and welfare regimes in Europe' *International Journal of Housing Policy* 7(4), 401–433.

Beaverstock, J, Smith, R and Taylor, P 2015, *Global City Network*. http://www.lboro. ac.uk/gawc/ (last accessed 15 January 2015).

Berry, B and Kasarda, J 1977, *Contemporary Urban Ecology*. Macmillan: New York.

Bertaud, A and Renaud, B 1997, 'Socialist cities without land markets' *Journal of Urban Economics* 41(1), 137–151.

Bodnár, J, and Böröcz, J 1998, 'Housing advantages for the 1300 better connected? Institutional segmentation, settlement type, and social network effects in Hungary's late state socialist housing nequalities' *Social Forces* 76(4), 1275–1304.

Booth, C 1887, 'The inhabitants of Tower Hamlets (School Board Division), their condition and occupations' *Journal of the Royal Statistical Society* 50(2), 326–401.

Burgers, J and Musterd, S 2002, 'Understanding urban inequality: A model based on existing theories and an empirical illustration' *International Journal of Urban and Regional Research* 26(2), 403–413.

Dangschat, J 1987, 'Sociospatial disparities in a "socialist" city: The case of Warsaw at the end of the 1970s' *International Journal of Urban and Regional Research* 11(1), 37–60.

Deacon, B 2000, 'Eastern European welfare states: The impact of the politics of globalisation' *Journal of European Social Policy* 10(2), 146–161.

Dewilde, C and Lancee, B 2013, 'Income inequality and access to housing in Europe' *European Sociological Review* 29(6), 1189–1200.

Duncan, O and Duncan, B 1955, 'Residential distribution and occupational stratification' *American Journal of Sociology* 60(5), 493–503.

Esping-Andersen, G 1990, *The Three Worlds of Welfare Capitalism*, Polity Press: Cambridge.

European Commission 2010 *Why Socio-economic Inequalities Increase? Facts and Policy Responses in Europe*, Publication Office of the European Union: Luxembourg.

Eurostat 2015, 'Eurostat Electronic Database.' Luxembourg: European Commission. http://ec.europa.eu/eurostat/data/database. Last accessed 7 May 2015.

Fenger, H 2007, 'Welfare regimes in central and Eastern Europe: Incorporating post-communist countries in a welfare regime typology.' http://journal.ciiss.net/index.php/ciiss/article/viewPDFInterstitial/45/37 Last accessed 15 January 2015.

Flowerdew, R, Manley, D and Sabel, C 2008, 'Neighbourhood effects on health: Does it matter where you draw the boundaries?' *Social Science and Medicine* 66(6), 1241–1245

Fotheringham, A and Wong, D 1991, 'The modifiable areal unit problem in multivariate statistical analysis' *Environment and Planning A* 23(7) 1025–1044.

Gentile, M and Sjöberg, Ö 2013, 'Housing allocation under socialism: The Soviet case revisited' *Post-Soviet Affairs* 29(2), 173–195.

Gentile M, Tammaru, T and Van Kempen, R 2012, 'Heteropolitanization: Social and spatial change in Central and Eastern Europe' *Cities* 29(5), 291–299.

Hamnett, C 1994, 'Social polarisation in global cities: Theory and evidence' *Urban Studies* 31(3), 401–424.

Hatz, G, Kohlbacher, J and Reeger, U 2016, 'Socio-economic segregation in Vienna: A social-oriented approach to urban planning and housing' in *Socio-Economic Segregation in European Capital Cities. East meets West*, eds T Tammaru, S Marcińczak, M van Ham and S Musterd, Routledge: London.

Hirt, S 2103, 'Whatever happened to the (post) socialist city? *Cities* 32(1), 29–38.

Häussermann, H and Haila, A 2005, 'The European city: A conceptual framework and normative project' in *Cities of Europe: Changing Contexts, Local Arrangements, and the Challenge to Urban Cohesion*, ed. Y Kazepov, Blackwell Publishing: Oxford, pp. 43–64.

Hegedüs, J 2013, 'Housing privatisation and restitution' in *Social Housing in Transition Countries*, eds J Hegedüs, N Teller and M Lux, Routledge: New York, pp. 33–49.

Hochstenbach C, Musterd, S and Teernstra, A 2014, 'Gentrification in Amsterdam: Assessing the importance of context' *Population, Space and Place*. http://www.academia.edu/6873989/Gentrification_in_Amsterdam_assessing_the_importance_of_context_2014_with_S_Musterd_and_A_Teernstra_published_in_Population_Space_and_Place. Last accessed 16 April 2015.

ILO 2007, *Updating the International Standard Classification of Occupations (ISCO)*. International Labour Organization: Geneva.

ILO 2012, *International Standard Classification of Occupations*. International Labour Organization: Geneva.

ILO 2015, *International Labour Organization Webpage*. http://www.ilo.org/global/lang–en/index.htm. Last accessed 15 January 2015.

Janson, C-G 1980, 'Factorial social ecology: An attempt at summary and evaluation' *Annual Review of Sociology* 6, 433–456.

Jones, C and Murie, A 2006, *The Right to Buy*. Blackwell Publishing: Oxford.

Kährik, A and Tammaru, T 2010, 'Soviet prefabricated panel housing estates: Areas of continued social mix or decline? The case of Tallinn' *Housing Studies* 25(2), 201–219.

Kazepov, J 2005, 'Introduction', in *Cities of Europe: Changing Contexts, Local Arrangements, and the Challenge to Social Cohesion*, ed. Y Kazepov, Blackwell Publishing: Oxford, pp. 3–42.

Kemeny, J 1995 *From Public Housing to the Social Market: Rental Policy Strategies in Comparative Perspective*, London: Routledge.

Kesteloot, C 2005, 'Urban socio-spatial configurations and the future of European cities' in *Cities of Europe: Changing Contexts, Local Arrangements, and the Challenge to Urban Cohesion*, ed. Y. Kazepov, Blackwell Publishing: Oxford, pp 123–148.

Kish, L 1954, 'Differentiation in metropolitan areas' *American Sociological Review* 19(4), 388–398.

Kleinhans R and van Ham M 2013, 'Lessons learned from the largest tenure mix operation in the world: Right to buy in the United Kingdom' *Cityscape: A Journal of Policy Development and Research* 15(2), 101–118.

Kornai, J 1992, *The Socialist System: The Political Economy of Communism*, Princeton University Press: Princeton: NJ.

Kovács, Z 2009, 'Social and economic transformation of the historical neighbourhoods in Budapest' *Tijdschrift voor Economische en Sociale Geografie* 100(4), 399–416.

Kovács, Z and Herfert, G 2012, Development pathways of large housing estates in post-socialist cities: An international comparison *Housing Studies* 27(3), 324–342.

Kovács, Z and Szabó, B 2016, 'Urban restructuring and changing patterns of socio-economic segregation in Budapest' in *Socio-Economic Segregation in European Capital Cities: East Meets West*, eds T Tammaru, S Marcińczak, M van Ham and S Musterd, Routledge: London

Krišjāne, Z Bērziņš, M and Kratovitš, K 2016, 'Occupation and ethnicity: Patterns of residential segregation in Riga two decades after socialism' in *Socio-Economic Segregation in European Capital Cities: East Meets West*, eds T Tammaru, S Marcińczak, M van Ham and S Musterd, Routledge: London.

Ladányi J 1989, 'Changing patterns of residential segregation in Budapest' *International Journal of Urban and Regional Research* 13, 555–572.

Leal, J and Sorando D 2016, 'Economic crisis, social change and segregation processes in Madrid' in *Socio-Economic Segregation in European Capital Cities: East Meets West*, eds T Tammaru, S Marcińczak, M van Ham and S Musterd, Routledge: London.

Malmberg, B, Andersson, E, and Östh, J 2013, 'Segregation and urban unrest in Sweden' *Urban Geography* 34(7), 1031–1046.

Maloutas, T 2012, 'Introduction', in *Residential Segregation in Comparative Perspective. Making Sense of Contextual Diversity*, eds T Maloutas and K Fujita, City and Society Series, Ashgate: Farnham, UK, pp. 1–36.

Maloutas, T 2016, 'Socioeconomic segregation in Athens at the beginning of the 21st century' in *Socio-Economic Segregation in European Capital Cities: East Meets West*, eds T Tammaru, S Marcińczak, M van Ham and S Musterd, Routledge: London.

Manley, D and Johnston, R 2001, 'London: A dividing city, 2001–11?' *City* 18(6), 633–643.

Manley, D, van Ham M, Bailey N, Simpson L and Maclennan D eds 2013, *Neighbourhood Effects or Neighbourhood Based Problems? A Policy Context*, Springer: Dordrecht.

Manley, D, Johnston, R, Jones, K and Owen, D 2016, 'Occupational segregation in London: A multilevel framework for modelling segregation' in *Socio-Economic Segregation in European Capital Cities. East meets West*, eds T Tammaru, S Marcińczak, M van Ham and S Musterd, Routledge: London.

Marcińczak, S, Gentile, M, Rufat, S and Chelcea, L 2014, 'Urban geographies of hesitant transition: Tracing socio-economic segregation in post-Ceausescu Bucharest' *International Journal of Urban and Regional Research* 38(4), 1399–1417.

Marcińczak, S, Gentile, M and Stępniak, M 2013, 'Paradoxes of (post) socialist segregation: Metropolitan sociospatial divisions under socialism and after in Poland' *Urban Geography* 34(3), 327–352.

Marcińczak, S, Musterd, S, van Ham, M and Tammaru, T 2016, 'Inequality and rising levels of socio-economic segregation: Lessons from a pan-European comparative study' in *Socio-Economic Segregation in European Capital Cities: East Meets West*, eds T Tammaru, S Marcińczak, M van Ham and S Musterd, Routledge: London.

Marcińczak, S, Tammaru, T, Novák, J, Gentile, M, Kovács, Z, Temelová, J, Valatka, V, Kährik, A and Szabó, B 2015, 'Patterns of socioeconomic segregation in the capital cities of fast-track reforming postsocialist countries' *Annals of the American Association of Geographers* 105(1), 183–202.

Marcuse, P and Van Kempen, R 2000, 'Introduction' in *Globalizing Cities: A New Spatial Order?*, eds P Marcuse and R Van Kempen, Blackwell Publishing: Oxford, pp. 1–21.

Massey, D and Denton, N 1988, 'The dimensions of residential segregation' *Social Forces* 67(2), 281–315.

Massey, D and Denton, N 1993, *American Apartheid: Segregation and the Making of the Underclass*, Harvard University Press: Cambridge, MA.

Mollenkopf, J H and Castells, M eds 1991, *Dual City: Restructuring New York*. Russell Sage Foundation: New York.

Morgan, B 1975, 'The segregation of socio-economic groups in urban areas: A comparative analysis' *Urban Studies* 12(1), 47–60.

Morgan, B 1980, 'Occupational segregation in metropolitan areas in the United States, 1970' *Urban Studies* 17(1), 63–69.

Musil, J 1987, 'Housing policy and the socio-spatial structure of cities in a socialist country: The example of Prague' *International Journal of Urban and Regional Research* 11(1), 27–36.

Musterd, S 2005, 'Social and ethnic segregation in Europe: Levels, causes and effects' *Journal of Urban Affairs* 27(3), 331–348.

Musterd, S and Kovács, Z 2013, *Place-making and Policies for Competitive Cities*, Wiley-Blackwell: Oxford.

Musterd, S and W Ostendorf eds 1998, *Urban Segregation and the Welfare State: Inequality and Exclusion in Western Cities*, Routledge: London.

Musterd, S and van Gent, W 2016, 'Changing welfare context and income segregation in Amsterdam and its metropolitan area' in *Socio-Economic Segregation in European Capital Cities: East Meets West*, eds T Tammaru, S Marcińczak, M van Ham and S Musterd, Routledge: London.

Ouředníček, M, Pospíšilová, L, Špačková, P, Kopecká, Z and Novák, J 2016, 'The velvet and mild: Socio-spatial differentiation in Prague after transition' in *Socio-Economic Segregation in European Capital Cities: East Meets West*, eds T Tammaru, S Marcińczak, M van Ham and S Musterd, Routledge: London.

Park, E, Burgess, E and McKenzie, R 1925, *The City: Suggestions for Investigation of Human Behavior in the Urban Environment*, University of Chicago Press: Chicago.

Peach, C 2009, 'Slippery segregation: Discovering or manufacturing ghettos?' *Journal of Ethnic and Migration Studies* 35(9), 1381–1395.

Petsimeris, P and Rimoldi S 2016, 'Socio-economic divisions of space in Milan in the post-Fordist era' in *Socio-Economic Segregation in European Capital Cities: East*

Meets West, eds T Tammaru, S Marcińczak, M van Ham and S Musterd, Routledge: London.

Piketty, T 2013, *Capital in the Twenty-First Century*, Harvard University Press: Cambridge, MA.

Préteceille, E 2000, 'Segregation, class and politics in large cities' in *Cities in Contemporary Europe*, eds A Bagnasco and P Le Gales, Cambridge University Press: Cambridge, pp. 74–97.

Reardon, S and Bischoff, K 2011, 'Income inequality and income segregation' *American Journal of Sociology* 116(4), 1092–1153.

Rex, J and Moore R 1967, *Race, Community and Conflict*, Oxford University Press: Oxford.

Sachs, S 2012, *The Price of Civilization: Reawakening Virtue and Prosperity after the Economic Fall*, Vintage: London.

Sassen, S 1991, *The Global City: New York, London, Tokyo*, Princeton University Press: Princeton, NJ.

Sennnett, R 2003, *Respect in a World of Inequality*, WW Norton and Company: New York.

Słomczyński, K and Shabad G 1996, 'Systemic transformation and the salience of class structure in East-Central Europe' *East European Politics and Societies* 11(1), 155–189.

Smith, D 1996, 'The socialist city' in *Cities after Transition*, eds G Andrusz, M Harloe, and I Szelenyi, Blackwell: Oxford, pp. 70–99.

Smith, A and Timár, J 2010, 'Uneven transformations: Space, economy and society 20 years after the collapse of state socialism' *European Urban and Regional Studies* 17(2), 115–125.

Stanilov, K ed. 2007, *The Post-Socialist City: Urban Form and Space Transformations in Central and Eastern Europe after Socialism*, Springer: Dordrecht.

Sýkora, L 2009, 'Post-socialist cities' in *International Encyclopedia of Human Geography* eds R Kitchin and N Thrift, Elsevier: Oxford, pp. 387–395.

Sýkora, L and Bouzarovski, S 2012, 'Multiple transformations: Conceptualising the post-communist urban transition' *Urban Studies* 49(1), 43–60.

Szelényi, I 1996, 'Cities under socialism – and after' in *Cities after Socialism: Urban and Regional Change and Conflict in Post-Socialist Societies,* eds G Andrusz, M Harloe and I Szelényi, Blackwell Publishers: Oxford, pp. 286–317.

Sztompka, P 1996, 'Looking back: The year 1989 as a cultural and civilizational break' *Communist and Post-Communist Studies* 29(2), 115–129.

Tammaru, T 2001, 'Suburban growth and suburbanisation under central planning: The case of Soviet Estonia' *Urban Studies* 38(8), 1341–1357.

Tammaru, T, Kährik, A, Mägi, K Novák, J and Leetmaa, K 2016, 'The "market experiment": Increasing socio-economic segregation in the inherited bi-ethnic context of Tallinn' in *Socio-Economic Segregation in European Capital Cities: East Meets West*, eds T Tammaru, S Marcińczak, M van Ham and S Musterd, Routledge: London.

Tsenkova, S and Nedović-Budić, Z eds 2006, *The Urban Mosaic of Post-Socialist Cities*, Physica-Verlag Heidelberg: New York, pp. 21–50.

Tsenkova, S 2006, 'Beyond transitions: Understanding urban change in post-socialist cities' in *The Urban Mosaic of Post-Socialist Cities*, eds. S Tsenkova and Z Nedović-Budić, Physica-Verlag Heidelberg: New York, pp. 21–50.

Turkington, R, van Kempen, R and Wassenberg, F eds 2004, *High-Rise Housing in Europe: Current Trends and Future Prospects. Housing and Urban Policy Studies*, Delft University Press: Delft.

Valatka, V, Burneika, D and Ubarevičienė R, 2016, 'Large social inequalities and low levels of socio-economic segregation in Vilnius' in *Socio-Economic Segregation in*

European Capital Cities: East Meets West, eds T Tammaru, S Marcińczak, M van Ham and S Musterd, Routledge: London.

van Ham, M and Manley, D 2009, 'Social housing allocation, choice and neighbourhood ethnic mix in England' *Journal of Housing and the Built Environment* 24, 407–422.

van Ham, M and Manley, D 2012, 'Neighbourhood effects research at a crossroads: Ten challenges for future research' *Environment and Planning A* 44(12), 2787–2793.

van Kempen, R, and Murie, A 2009, 'The new divided city: Changing patterns in European Cities' *Tijdschrift voor Economische en Sociale Geografie* 100(4), 377–398.

Verdery, K 1996, *What Was Socialism and What Comes Next?* Cambridge University Press: Cambridge.

Węcławowicz, G 1979, 'The structure of socio-economic space in Warsaw in 1931 and 1970: A study in factorial ecology' in *The Socialist City: Spatial Structure and Urban Policy*, eds R French and F Hamilton, John Willey and Sons: Chichester, pp. 387–424.

Wessel, T 2016, 'Economic segregation in Oslo: polarisation as a contingent outcome' in *Socio-Economic Segregation in European Capital Cities. East meets West*, eds T Tammaru, S Marcińczak, M van Ham and S Musterd, Routledge: London.

Wilson, W J 1987, *The Truly Disadvantaged: The Inner City, the Underclass, and Public Policy*, University of Chicago Press: Chicago.

Wolpert, J 1965, 'Behavioral aspects of the decision to migrate' *Papers in Regional Science* 15(1), 159–169.

Wong, D 2003, 'Spatial decomposition of segregation indices: A framework toward measuring segregation at multiple levels' *Geographical Analysis* 35(3), 179–194.

2 Occupational segregation in London

A multilevel framework for modelling segregation

David Manley, Ron Johnston,
Kelvyn Jones and Dewi Owen

Abstract

London has a long and well-documented history as the seat of government for the United Kingdom and as one of the major world financial centres. The current spatial structure of the city is very much a function of this history and can be described using three central poles: the City, Westminster, and the port. We report on the current state of occupational segregation across London using data from both the 2001 and the 2011 Census. We supplement this with an exploration of a multilevel modelling framework through which segregation can be modelled and better understood. Using the occupational data from London we develop an approach showing segregation values complete with confidence intervals for significance testing. We also look back into the urban geography literature and suggest further potential for the modelling framework we introduce.

Introduction

London has for a long time been a tri-polar city, and its current spatial structure reflects that history. The first pole, the City, is the financial heart of the United Kingdom and a major centre of global finance. Its traditional focus at the eastern end of the original settlement is balanced by the second pole – initially the seat of the court and now the centre of government – centred now in the former settlement of Westminster on Whitehall and the Parliament buildings. Finally, there was the port, for many centuries just downriver from the Tower of London, where a multiplicity of docks, warehouses and port–related industries thrived. These have now gone, as the port functions have migrated downriver and the land they occupied redeveloped, in part to accommodate an expansion of the financial core (centred on Canary Wharf) and most of the remainder as major residential developments.

London has been central to the development of urban studies literature. Some of the first work seeking to characterise neighbourhood composition was undertaken in the city between 1886 and 1903 by philanthropist Charles Booth (1903) who, with a team of researchers, provided a comprehensive residential map depicting poverty throughout the city, one which still helps our understanding today.[1] Updating the analysis, Orford and colleagues (2002 and see also Dorling *et al.* 2000) demonstrated that the geography uncovered by Booth was still largely present some ninety years later. The sociologist Ruth Glass coined the term gentrification after observing the influx of middle classes and the squeezing out of the working-class communities in changing neighbourhoods in Islington (Glass 1964).

As a world city central to the financial and government functions of both the United Kingdom as well as further afield, London is one of the most diverse places in the country: the 2011 Census recorded over a hundred languages spoken in the capital including over 1.7 million people with a first spoken language other than English. The most diverse place in London is the borough of Hillingdon (see Figure 2.1 for location) where 107 languages were recorded. This hyperdiversity (Singh 2003) serves to create an urban environment that is unlike anywhere else in the UK. In such a diverse place it is no wonder that the 'right for space' is contested with accusations of class replacement and displacement writ large. For instance, Davidson and Wyly (2012) mapped the distribution of class groups within London and suggested that London was a firmly middle-class city, something contested by Hamnett and Butler (2013; see also Manley and Johnston 2014). Regardless, London has a constantly changing urban landscape, although it is one that has its history clearly visible throughout, as we explore below.

The rest of this chapter is organised as follows: the next section provides an overview of London, depicting it as a tri-polar city. Next, we provide the data and methods detailing including UK Census information and the innovative multilevel modelling techniques that we deploy in the second part of the chapter. We present an overview of changing occupational segregation in London between 2001 and 2011. This is complemented by the second substantive section of the chapter that uses the same data from the Census to provide empirical examples of our inferential and modelling framework. Finally, we highlight the potential of this approach to move the field of segregation studies forward from descriptive accounts to more nuanced modelled appreciations of the complex society in which we live. The focus of the chapter is first on the traditional measures of segregation followed by a new modelling framework to further or understanding of segregation and the wider processes of neighbourhood change.

Context: London the tri-polar city

The metropolitan area's residential pattern has developed around the three poles. Relatively high-status residential areas focused on the court-and-government core in Westminster (see area C, Figure 2.1) expanded outwards, mainly to the west, housing the increasing number of functionaries employed in the expanding public sector as the UK state grew in its functions and centralisation. Higher-status areas, housing many of the city's commercial elite – though in buildings and areas not quite as 'grand' as those serving the governing elite – developed to the north of

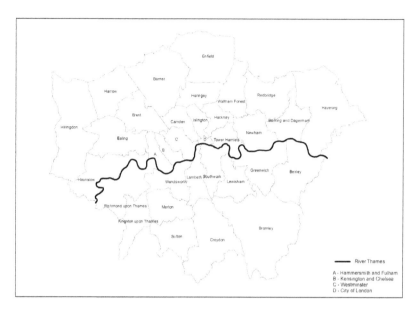

Figure 2.1 Local authority boroughs in London.

the city, stretching onto the higher areas that eventually merged with those extending north-west from Westminster. Between the two poles – in what is now central London (between Westminster Abbey at one end and St Paul's Cathedral at the other, areas C and D on the map) – was a high-density quarter housing the relatively poorly paid service workers who sustained the myriad small commercial and artisan operations on which the city's daily life depended. Finally, east of the financial centre a sector housing workers in the port and its associated industries extended downriver on its north bank (in the borough of Tower Hamlets, and the area labelled D, see Figure 2.1). This last area was socially more homogeneous than the other two, with very few areas catering for higher-status residents. Elsewhere, although the neighbourhoods were dominated by the emerging middle classes, dotted through them were, usually small, areas of lower status, higher-density housing – parts of which were the remnants of former villages engulfed by London's expansion and others specially constructed for workers who serviced the higher status homes.

All three parts of the emerging metropolitan area grew, with the 'great wen'[2] extending its tentacles outwards, first along the main roads and then, from the mid–nineteenth century onwards, along the new suburban rail lines and the various lines forming the underground network. Many of these new areas, engulfing formerly independent villages and small towns which became the suburban commercial cores, were focused on the expanding middle classes – white–collar workers who could afford to buy their own homes and commute in to the city centres. Much of the central residential fabric increasingly became home for the working classes.

Inner parts of that sector of the city were also the traditional destinations for some of the pre–twentieth-century large international migrations to London – such as the Huguenots and Jews – but there were pockets of recent migrants elsewhere, not least those colonised by the Irish and Welsh. Over time, the character of some of those areas changed as one migrant group succeeded another: parts of inner east London (in the current boroughs of Newham and Tower Hamlets, see Figure 2.1) became the major destination for Muslim migrants from South Asia, initially from one area of Bangladesh (then East Pakistan) which provided manual labour for the merchant shipping fleets trading through the Port of London but now from Pakistan more widely. Substantial development encompassing the villages south of the river came somewhat later, because of the few bridges until the last two centuries. As access became easier, so that area too was the scene of much estate building, focused largely on the middle class and higher echelons of the working classes.

The twentieth century saw the decline of many of London's traditional industries – both those based on artisan workshops and spread throughout the inner city fabric (but with local concentrations of particular occupations) and, from the 1960s on, the port-based industries along the Thames. These were replaced in part by new types of industries: some – notably the large Ford Motor Company complex at Dagenham – were heavy industries more typical of the country's northern regions, but most were modern 'light industries' housed in bespoke premises on trading estates, as on the approach roads in from the west. At the same time, the service sector expanded, comprising both a 'new middle class' in a wide range of professions plus large numbers undertaking relatively routine occupations in the retail, catering and hospitality sectors.

This changing occupational class structure was impressed on the existing residential fabric. Increasingly, the high-density areas of the inner city, on both sides of the river, became unattractive to the expanding middle classes as the housing and environmental quality deteriorated. Many of them were 'passed down' to the working class and expanding lower echelons of the new middle class, while at the same time in large areas of the highest density, lowest-quality housing was demolished in 'slum clearance' programmes. This resulted in many of the residents being moved out to large, public-sector social housing estates built by both the Greater London Council and – usually at a smaller scale – the various local governments of which until the 1960s there was a plethora. These estates ensured a social mix at one scale in parts of the ever-widening middle-class suburbia, although the clear separation of public and private meant that at a finer-grained scale there was residential separation: middle- and working-class households lived in adjacent areas through much of suburbia, but rarely in the same streets. Thus, in the nineteenth and twentieth centuries the housing stock of the current city was largely set. In 1900 the first council estate in England was built and substantial social housing programmes followed, with the greatest investment in the 1960s. However, after the mid-1970s there was a gradual erosion in the support (economic and political) for state-provided housing and through the 1980s the provision changed from being open to 'all' to being allocated to those in need.

The Conservative government led by Margaret Thatcher did not start the erosion of social housing, but through the Right to Buy (RTB) scheme they substantially quickened the pace with over 2.7million public-sector dwellings sold to sitting tenants (van Ham *et al.* 2013). In one of the largest housing estates in Europe, the Aylesbury Estate (located in Southwark, south London, see Figure 2.1), over 17 per cent were privately owned by 2010 as a result of RTB. The consequence of this move was that social housing in general become increasingly residualised, with the best properties and tenants leaving the sector. The stock of properties available to those in need was declining and little building was being undertaken to replace those lost through RTB policies. In to the 1990s and 2000s the Labour government embarked on a substantial and sustained regeneration programme under the rubric of 'mixed tenure' (see Manley *et al.* 2011) which further eroded the social stock by demolishing large swaths of social housing and replacing the previously high-rise, high-density developments with low-density often low-rise properties, only a fraction of which were for the social sector.

Alongside the social, economic and residential changes during the early post-World War II decades, the residential mosaic obtained a new dimension through extensive international migration to London. The first wave was dominated by migrants from British Commonwealth Caribbean islands, who congregated in particular parts of inner London – such as Brixton (in Lambeth, Figure 2.1) and Notting Hill (part of Kensington and Chelsea). As their numbers grew so the enclaves where they dominated the population expanded, increasing the outward pressure towards the suburbs. And new migrant groups resulted in new areas of concentration: black Africans in other parts of the inner city, for example, and Indians and Pakistanis with major congregations in the western suburbs north of Heathrow (the boroughs of Ealing, Hillingdon, Hounslow and Brent) as well as in the north-east. And then came the major migration streams from many parts of Europe, especially those from the former communist states of Eastern Europe after the Accession 8 countries joined the European Union in 2004 – with new separate enclaves and many increasingly mixed areas adding further complexity to the fractured residential mosaic. Parts of the higher-status residential neighbourhoods – especially to the east of the city centre in the boroughs of Westminster and Kensington and Chelsea – have retained their status and desirability throughout the twentieth century and the first decades of the twenty-first. Indeed, international entry into these neighbourhoods has enhanced their status as properties at the top end of London's housing market have become desirable for extremely rich overseas residents (from the Middle East and Russia, for example) as safe investments. Property prices there have boomed, with knock-on effects for the rest of London, making many parts of the capital too expensive for a wide range of occupational groups even to rent, let alone buy, homes there.

There are exceptions to this, however. Some areas with substantial housing formerly occupied by the middle classes had passed down the social scale in the early decades of the twentieth century. But as the city grew, more households preferred inner-city to suburban-living-cum-commuting so developers moved in to remove the lower-status residents and, after restoring the properties, sold them at substantial profits to those would-be 'inner-city-returners', along with other social groups (including several new 'demographics') to whom low-density family-centred estates associated with long (increasingly expensive and tiresome) commuting journeys were unattractive. Thus a number of neighbourhoods throughout inner London have been gentrified, adding a further element to the fine-grained differentiation that characterises much of contemporary inner London. And for those who cannot afford such areas and properties, much of the former Dockland area offers relatively high-quality housing – at a price – in both converted warehouses and industrial buildings as well as new, bespoke bijou estates (Imrie *et al.* 2009).

More recently, the social fabric of residential London has been threatened by the adoption of the policy formally known as the 'under-occupancy penalty' and more commonly referred to as the 'bedroom tax' whereby households in receipt of housing benefit[3] have their occupancy of their property assessed. The needs of a household are stated as one bedroom per adult (or couple), children under ten share a bedroom regardless of their gender. As an illustration, a household with two adults and two children under ten is 'allowed' to reside in a property with two bedrooms. If those children were of different genders, once one of them reached the age of ten or over then the bedroom allowance would increase to three. The tax component arises if the household has more bedrooms than 'allowed': payments are reduced by 14 per cent for one extra bedroom, and 25 per cent for two extra bedrooms. There has been little time for adjustment as the policy was introduced and there are few exemptions even for those with medical or mobility needs. As a result, the effect of this policy has been substantial: households experiencing arrears as a result of the loss of housing benefit are being evicted from their properties (see for instance Inside Housing 2013). It is clear that those being evicted are the most vulnerable, occupying the lower social grades. Ultimately, the loss to London will be one of diversity as it becomes a city only for those with the ability to pay their own way: the remaining households in social housing or in receipt of housing benefit are likely to be increasingly residualised into smaller properties, living at higher (person-per-room) densities in the cheaper parts of the city.

A final element is the scale of inward daily commuting swelling the city population from almost ten million people by a further four million (Eurostat 2012). These people, making up the daytime population, work daily within London but travel from well beyond the de jure boundaries of the city (defined here as the Greater London County, created in 1963 but without a separate elected government between 1986 and 2000). The commuting pull of the city ranges from the abutting counties of Essex and Kent to the east, Surrey, Buckinghamshire and Berkshire to the south and Wiltshire to the west. In practice, there are large population shifts from much of the south-east of England within a couple of hours' commuting time of the main London stations. The empirical section that follows is developed using data recording the residential 'nighttime' population within the Greater London county area, but these additional flows should be kept in mind.

London is a complex city with a long history and there are macro-, meso- and micro-scale components to London's social geography. At the macro-scale is the east–west divide that has been in place for centuries – although many of those who work in the east (in the City, Canary Wharf and their environs) live in the inner western areas, with more in exclusive estates in the outer suburbs and the separate commuter settlements (such as Beaconsfield, Radlett and Weybridge) in the cocktail belt[4] beyond the green belt[5] that contains the continuous built-up area. At the meso-scale are the large housing estates – both those dominated by detached and semi-detached houses occupied by the middle classes and those initially built by local authorities for social housing but, since the 1980s, with many of the more desirable properties sold to their renting occupants at substantial discounts – that characterise the suburban boroughs. Finally, at the micro-scale, there is the fine-grained variation, almost on a block-by-block grid, of neighbourhood characteristics reflecting recent redevelopment and gentrification across wide swathes of inner London. On top of which there is the complex, highly diverse cultural geography, reflecting the wide range of immigrants attracted to London and the various occupational niches they inhabit.

Data and methods

The data used in this chapter are drawn from the decennial UK Censuses for 2001 and 2011, focusing on Greater London County as defined in 1966.[6] The Census collects a wide range of individual-level information, but aside from some special licence datasets containing small samples the data are only available in aggregated form. The spatial units at the lowest level of aggregation available are known as Output Areas (OAs) comprising on average 135 people. One of the greatest challenges in analysing Census data over time is presented by changes in the aggregation structure – one that is defined post data collection to a compact geographical shape and social homogeneity (in terms of dwelling types – such as detached/semi-detached – and housing tenure – such as owner-occupied and private rented housing). For instance, when neighbourhoods have experienced a large increase (decrease) in population, OAs can become too large (too small) to be maintained between Censuses and must be split (or merged). While efforts are made to ensure that the OAs remain consistent, a little over 5 per cent of the OAs were either split or merged between the two Censuses. These changes can be dealt with by recombining those areas that were split in 2011 to replicate the 2001 boundaries, or by merging 2001 OAs to reflect the 2011 boundaries where mergers were made. There is an additional complication where some OAs have been split or merged into multiple surrounding OAs between the two periods. In practice, this process provided just over 24,000 OAs consistent for both 2001 and 2011.

The occupational variable used in all the analyses provides a classification for all usual residents in the OAs based on occupations given on Census day. The Standard Occupational Classification (SOC2000 for 2001 data and SOC2010 for 2011 data) is an indication of socio-economic position and is coded to align with international occupational classifications (see also the introduction of this book for more detail: Tammaru *et al.* 2016). The classification used is based on the response of the household reference person and their occupational title is combined with information about their employment status (employed, self-employed, if they supervise other employees) to create the code. The coding used in 2001 and 2011 is comparable, although there are small differences due to the way in which occupational classifications have changed between the Census periods, especially in the higher categories. Readers will note that the SOC is not identical to the ISCO classification. As is the case with many secondary data sources providing administrative data, there are trade-offs to be made between the resolution in terms of details released about individuals in the dataset and the spatial scale at which the data are geocoded. For the analysis presented in this chapter, we require fine-grained neighbourhoods (OAs) and because these are relatively small in terms of population size the occupational detail is coarse and recoding individuals from the SOC into the ISCO is not possible. Table 2.1 gives the descriptive information for the occupational categories, and also depicts the changing occupational structure in London. The greatest decline has been in the highest categories – the managers, the associated professionals and the administrative groups. In contrast the service classes have grown, in particular the personal service and sales and customer service groups. There has also been a decline in the proportion of the population in the bottom two categories that we speculate may be a consequence of the increasing cost of living in London.

Multilevel modelling for segregation

We do not dwell on the computation or definition of the traditional indices of segregation as these are covered elsewhere (see Duncan and Duncan 1955a; 1955b; Massey and Denton 1988). Instead we discuss the formation of the multilevel model (MLM) that we use as an alternative framework to model segregation. It could be suggested that, as segregation indices are based on full populations, the advantages of using an inferential modelling framework such as this are minimal. However, we are not seeking to generalise to the population and take a different approach to significance testing. We adopt an approach whereby we seek to 'draw conclusions about the relations and differences within that dataset' (see Johnston *et al.* 2014a). Thus, using a modelling framework is important as it allows the uncertainty around a parameter's value (in this case a measure of segregation) to be calculated and used as a means to determine the 'noisiness' of the data and signals that there is a degree of uncertainty around the size of the segregation parameter. What this enables the reader to gain is an insight into the amount of useful information contained within the analysis.

Table 2.1 Descriptive information for occupational classes (note groups will be referred to using the bold word)

	Mean OA %	
	2001	*2011*
Managers and Senior Officials	17.2	11.5
Professional Occupations	14.5	21.8
Associated Professional and Technical	17.6	15.9
Administrative and Secretarial	15.5	11.8
Skilled Trades	7.8	8.4
Personal Services	6.1	8.2
Sales and Customer Services	6.8	7.6
Process Plant and Machine Operatives	5.1	4.9
Elementary Occupations	9.5	9.9

To introduce the multilevel approach to the segregation literature we initially look back to the work of Kish (1954) who suggested that variance (the spread of the data) could provide a suitable measure through which it is possible to develop an understanding of segregation. Within the MLM, a variance term is available to describe the departure of the proportion of a group (such as an occupational class) within a unit (such as the OAs) from the mean proportion of that group across the whole of the urban space (London). For instance, if the variance value is (close to) zero, then each neighbourhood has the same underlying distribution as the whole of the urban space and we can conclude that there is no segregation. Conversely, where a large variance term is observed, then there is a substantial departure from the London average and we can conclude that there is over- or under-representation of the group, and that segregation is present. MLMs have been used previously to measure school segregation; however, we extend the approach into the residential literature using the example of occupational segregation.

For the model[7] we implement a two-level Poisson multilevel model (in its log-Normal form, see Rasbash *et al.* 2012) with class by year interaction is specified as:

$$O_{ij} \sim Poisson\left(\pi_{ij}\right)$$

$$Log_e\left(\pi_{ij}\right) = Log_e\left(E_{ij}\right) + \beta_{1j} Managers01_{ij} + \beta_{2j} Managers11_{ij} + \ldots + \beta_{18j} Element11_{ij}$$

$$\beta_{1j} = \beta_1 + u_{1j}$$

$$\beta_{2j} = \beta_2 + u_{2j}$$

$$\ldots$$

$$\beta_{18j} = \beta_{18} + u_{18j}$$

$$\begin{bmatrix} u_{1j} \\ u_{2j} \\ \vdots \\ u_{18j} \end{bmatrix} \sim N\left(0, \begin{bmatrix} \sigma_{u1}^2 & & & \\ o_{u1,2} & \sigma_{u2}^2 & & \\ \vdots & & \ddots & \\ o_{u1,18} & o_{u2,18} & \ldots & \sigma_{u18}^2 \end{bmatrix}\right)$$

$$Var\left(O_{ij} | \pi_{ij}\right) = \pi_{ij}$$

Where O_{ij} is the long stacked vector of the observed counts for each class separately for 2001 and 2011 which are assumed to come from a Poisson distribution so that underlying stochastic variance is given by the underlying mean occurrence (π_{ij}) where i represents groups of people and j represents areas. These are related by a log link to an offset of the expected count $-Log_e(Eij)$ – if each Output Area had the same proportion of people in that class in that year as the overall rate across London. The fixed terms (e.g. β_1) which are expected to be zero give the overall rate across London. The random departures from this (e.g. the u_{1j}) gives the Output Area's departure from this overall London rate for each class in each year. The variance term (e.g. σ_{u1}^2) summarises these departures and is the measure of segregation net of Poisson variation of dealing with counts. The covariances (eg $o_{u1,2}$) when standardized into a correlation give the 'similarity' of patterns for each group – when negative the groups are antagonistically located.

From the data description it is clear that we are using aggregated data, not individual level data. However, it is possible to include a 'pseudo' level where both i and j can be cells and the level 1 and level 2 units are the same. Although this may appear to be a contradictory set up, we can regard the level 2 counts as replications of the level 1 responses. All the data are included in the aggregated counts for the OAs, and because we include no further information about individuals in the OAs we could generate the complete individual level data from the OA level counts – all individual information has been retained at the aggregate level and vice versa. This enables what is known as 'extra Poisson dispersal' and allows the between area variation and the natural Poisson variation to be separated.

Occupational segregation in London: 2001 to 2011

The Gini coefficient depicts a city where segregation has been relatively static between 2001 and 2011 with values of 0.31 and 0.30 respectively. However, this measure index hides a vast amount of detail. Table 2.2 reports the outcomes of the Index of Segregation. The distribution of the index values takes on a 'U' shape with the occupational groups in the centre of the classification the least segregated (technicians and associated professionals the least segregated followed by the administrative and secretarial occupations). The most segregated groups are at the lower end of the classification (process, plant and machine operatives along with the elementary occupations). The middle occupational groups (skilled trades occupations along with the managers and senior officials and professional occupations) rank between these extremes. There is remarkably little change between 2001 and 2011, with the values of 2011 either matching those of 2001 or falling very close. The largest decline occurred for the personal service occupations and the elementary occupations while the administrative and managers and senior officials have become more segregated. The relative lack of substantial change in the index values for this is in contrast to the substantial shifts in the share of the workforce as an average across the city depicted in Table 2.1.

The second measure in Table 2.2 is the Isolation Index, which is a measure of exposure – of how much groups share common residential areas. Here the

Table 2.2 Segregation Index and Isolation Index for London 2001–2011

	Segregation Index			Isolation Index		
	2001	*2011*	*Change*	*2001*	*2011*	*Change*
Managerial	0.19	0.20	+	0.20	0.14	–
Professional	0.24	0.22	–	0.18	0.26	+
Associated	0.15	0.15		0.17	0.13	–
Admin	0.18	0.20	+	0.20	0.18	–
Skilled	0.25	0.23	–	0.10	0.10	
Personal	0.23	0.20	–	0.07	0.09	+
Sales	0.25	0.23	–	0.09	0.09	
Process	0.32	0.30	–	0.07	0.07	
Elementary	0.32	0.29	–	0.12	0.13	+

story changes and isolation declines as the occupational class status declines. The most segregated group are the managers and senior officials with the least segregated are the process, plant and machine operatives, with the elementary occupations being slightly higher than this group. Members of lower-status occupational groups are more likely to live in mixed residential areas than are those in the higher-status, better-paid groups. Again, the 2011 outcome matched the 2001 outcome closely, although the increases in isolation occur in the professional occupations, the personal service occupations and the elementary groups unlike in the Index of Segregation where all these groups experienced a fall in segregation. However, the changes in the values are relatively small.

The most widely used measure of evenness between groups in the segregation literature is the Index of Dissimilarity of which there are multiple versions, ranging from the standard paired index (presented below) to a multigroup adjustment (see Morgan 1975; Sakoda 1981) which provides a single value for the full group set. The multigroup Index of Dissimilarity for London in both 2001 and 2011 was 0.22. However, while the overall level of segregation may be the same, there are some differences that can be observed when the index is broken down into each occupational class.

Table 2.3 reports the Index of Dissimilarity between each pair of groups for 2001 and 2011 respectively (the former values are above the principal diagonal and the latter below it). From the 2001 table it is clear that the greater the occupational distance between two groups the greater their degree of spatial separation. For instance, in 2001 the most segregated pair were the professional occupations and the process, plant and machine operators (0.47). In 2011 this was also the case, although the value had fallen (to 0.42). This relatively high level of segregation is not surprising given the results highlighted in Table 2.2. There are substantial resource differences between these two occupational groups which, combined with the house price disparities that exist across the City, mean that

Table 2.3 Index of Dissimilarity 2001 (top) and 2011 (bottom) (shading denotes the lower value in the pairing. Where no value is shaded in either year, the values are the same)

2001 / 2011	Managerial	Professional	Associated	Admin	Skilled	Personal	Sales	Process	Elementary
Managerial		0.17	0.24	0.17	0.35	0.32	0.34	0.42	0.39
Professional	0.16		0.29	0.17	0.40	0.36	0.39	0.47	0.43
Associated	0.25	0.25		0.23	0.22	0.24	0.24	0.29	0.27
Admin	0.17	0.13	0.25		0.34	0.31	0.33	0.41	0.36
Skilled	0.35	0.35	0.20	0.34		0.27	0.26	0.27	0.27
Personal	0.32	0.32	0.20	0.31	0.20		0.28	0.32	0.27
Sales	0.35	0.35	0.23	0.34	0.21	0.20		0.30	0.26
Process	0.42	0.43	0.27	0.42	0.22	0.24	0.23		0.28
Elementary	0.41	0.40	0.29	0.39	0.23	0.21	0.20	0.23	

the lower of the two groups will struggle to access the professionals' areas. By contrast the professional occupations and the managers and senior officials record index values of 0.17 for 2001 declining to 0.13 in 2011, depicting occupational groups that are closely integrated in the residential space. Given the overlap in occupations, and especially salaries for these groups, it is not surprising that they are able to enter similar residential spaces.

Comparing the two time points more widely, there are two patterns emerging. First, between the professional occupations, skilled trades, personal service occupations and process, plant and macine operators segregation has fallen between 2001 and 2011. This is clearest for the professional group – with a relatively large change in the values of the index against all groups – with the largest single fall between the professional and the skilled (0.05). The converse is true for the managerial and senior occupations and the administrative occupations, who have experienced similar or greater segregation between 2001 and 2011 although the increases have been greater for the administrative group. The managerial group's index values are largely static between the two time periods. What these outcomes point to are some complex and competition processes that are operating behind the index values.

The final descriptive measure in this section is the Location Quotient (herein referred to as LQ). This measure describes how concentrated an occupational group is compared with the national (or in our case London) average. Values of 1 represent a neighbourhood whose OA has the same percentage of a given occupational group as the overall London average, while values below 1 represent a lower than average concentration and values above 1 the converse. Readers are reminded that Figure 2.1 at the start of this chapter will help place them as the discussion moves around the metropolitan area. Figures 2.2–2.4 report the LQ for the combined categories of the managers and senior occupations with the professional occupations, the hitherto neglected groups of the unemployed, the sales workers and those in elementary occupations. In each of the figures the choropleth is centred on the value of 1 (where the occupational group distribution of the OA matches that of London as a whole) with divisions of standard deviations either side of this point. The centre point of the distribution, 0.5 standard deviations either side of the value 1, is represented by the colour white, while under-representation is coloured light grey, and over-representation by the darker shades. Thus the maps show the under-representation and over-representation of the occupational groups relative to this equilibrium point for each occupational grouping year.

Figure 2.2 depicts the LQ for the managerial and senior occupations combined with the professional occupations. There is a clear concentration in the west-central area of London, extending westwards through Hammersmith and Fulham to Richmond upon Thames. The northern parts of Merton as well as the well-known neighbourhoods of Kensington and Chelsea, and the City of London, the latter of which represents largely the financial district within the City. It is no surprise that those boroughs are also the most expensive in terms of living costs (a recent BBC News article listed Kensington as the most expensive place to buy in the UK with an average house price in 2013 of £1.5 million followed by the City at £1.3million, BBC 2013). By contrast, the managers and professional class are under-represented, compared to the London average, in the north-west

42   *David Manley* et al.

(a)

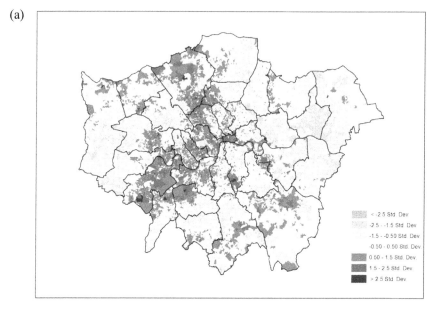

(b)

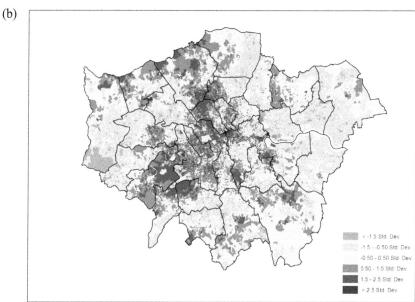

Figure 2.2a–b Higher managerial and professional occupations, 2001 and 2011.

(Hillingdon and Ealing) and the north-east of the city (Enfield and Havering). In the east of the city there is under-representation in Havering and the north of Bexley, while in the south of the city, in both north Croydon and Sutton, they are under-represented. Moving forward ten years to 2011, the pattern is similar. While London-wide segregation has decreased, there are clear demarcations between areas of high and low concentration in the north of the city. For instance, where there is low concentration in Waltham Forest abutting directly on to high concentration in Enfield, there is a much clearer boundary than in 2001. Similarly, the pockets of concentration in the south of London (Croydon and Bromley) have declined, with fewer OAs in the most concentrated category. This is not the case in the more centrally located areas, where concentration has increased: see for instance the south of Tower Hamlets where concentration has increased in the south of the borough at a time when there were high levels of gentrification recorded in the former dockland area (Davidson and Lees 2005; *Guardian* 2013). It is worth noting that the pattern of occupational segregation in London is long-established (as would be expected, see Meen *et al.* 2013). The current patterns that we observe are the result of the history outlined earlier in this chapter, with those areas close to the historical seat of government continually occupied by the wealthy and higher occupational groups. Similarly, the relative lack of higher occupational classes south of the river is a result of the later development there and the primary focus on working- and middle-class accommodation.

The second set of maps (Figure 2.3) refers to the sales and customer service occupations. In comparison to the managerial and professional workers, members of this group appear within the outer ring of the London conurbation, especially in 2001. The previous pattern of 'smoothed' changes between high and low concentrations now appears more 'stippled' with small pockets of concentrations in many areas. As such we suggest that in 2001 the areas in which these lower-middle-class workers were concentrated were less likely then to be found in substantial contiguous blocks. By 2011 the pattern had changed and, although the stippling was still apparent, many of the concentrated areas had been pushed outwards to the edges of the city in all directions but especially in the south-east (focusing on Bromley), leaving those areas in the centre of London more exclusive in their occupational composition. This suggests a process of removal of occupational groups from the central area as those environments become increasingly expensive to live within.

The spatial distribution of the elementary occupations is mapped in Figure 2.4. There are clear concentrations in the suburban edges of the city, with Hillingdon and Hounslow and Enfield and Waltham Forest being notable in the north while there are smaller concentrations in Bromley in the south. What is stark about the distribution in 2001 is the lack of concentration in the central areas as well as larger parts of the north and south. The 2011 map depicts concentrations in similar areas but has the appearance of being more 'smoothed'. Many of the smaller pockets of concentrations away from the larger clusters have declined or disappeared completely so that the central area as well as the northern boroughs of Barnet and Camden along with the southern boroughs of Richmond upon Thames and Bromley show substantial under concentrations. There have been some clear sorting effects across the city, with many in the elementary occupations clustering together even though the proportions of the population in this category in London has shown a small increase between 2001 and 2011 (see Table 2.1)

(a)

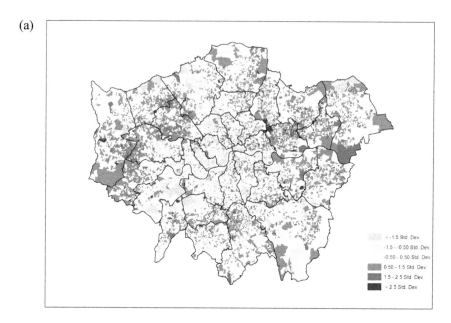

(b)

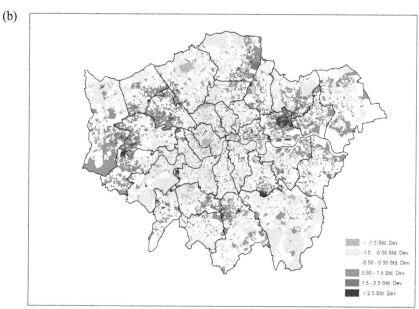

Figure 2.3a–b Sales and customer service occupations, 2001 and 2011.

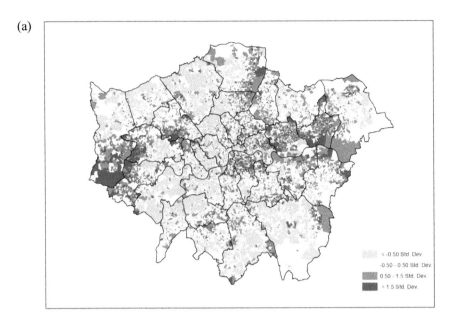

(a)

< -0.50 Std. Dev.
-0.50 - 0.50 Std. Dev.
0.50 - 1.5 Std. Dev.
> 1.5 Std. Dev.

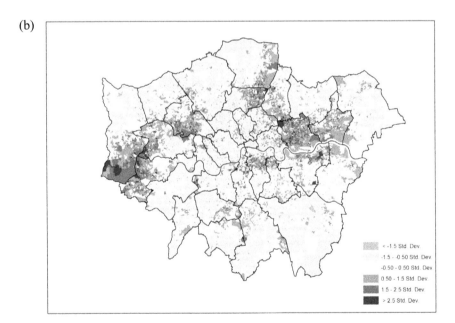

(b)

< -1.5 Std. Dev.
-1.5 - -0.50 Std. Dev.
-0.50 - 0.50 Std. Dev.
0.50 - 1.5 Std. Dev.
1.5 - 2.5 Std. Dev.
> 2.5 Std. Dev.

Figure 2.4a–b Elementary occupations, 2001 and 2011.

New approaches to segregation

Using an MLM we make two distinct contributions. The first is a methodological demonstration showing an alternative means through which segregation
can be understood. There have been many discussions about the best way to
measure segregation, the so-called 'index-wars' (Duncan and Duncan 1955a;
Massey and Denton 1988; Peach 1975) – but we do not seek to directly compare and contrast our approach with the indices. Rather, we are interested in
furthering our understanding of a highly complex process that shapes our urban
environments. The second contribution lies in the lack of information that the
descriptive indices provide about the change in segregation scores – when does
change matter and how much change is important? As has been demonstrated
in the first part of this chapter, the segregation scores for the occupational
groups have changed between 2001 and 2011. In none of the cases is it clear
whether there is a genuine difference in segregation or whether the change
could be considered within the 'natural variation' of population distribution,
given the small absolute counts of the numbers involved. In the remainder of
the chapter we adopt an alternative stance and suggest that measures of segregation should belong in the inferential statistical literature. In doing so, we aim
to move segregation analyses away from the approaches heavily influenced by
the American literature, and in particular the Chicago School, towards a better
understanding of population distributions.

MLM results

We present three sets of analysis using the results from the Multilevel Model
(MLM). The first analysis (Table 2.4) relates to the overall segregation of the
occupational groups. The second analysis uses the MLM results to investigate
which occupational groups are most likely to share neighbourhoods and vice versa
(Tables 2.5 and 2.6). The third analysis returns to one of the enduring themes of
urban research in London and uses Figure 2.6.

Table 2.4 has three key columns: the variance from the MLM estimated by
Monte Carlo Markov Chains (MCMC, see Browne 2012), and the upper and
lower Bayesian Credible Intervals (BCI). As with standard regression analysis we
can use the credible intervals to describe how different the distributions are from
each other. Thus if an occupation group has credible bounds (upper or lower) that
overlap with another occupational group, we conclude that there is no difference
in the segregation of these two groups. Conversely, where credible bounds do not
overlap, then there is a difference in the segregation of these two groups; similarly
we can compare the distribution of a group across two time periods to see if there
has been significant change in its segregation level. While the variance column is
clearly analogous to the measures of spatial separation reported above, these latter
columns contain additional information that is not available through traditional
descriptive measures of segregation. As a result we can, for the first time, discuss
the significance (or otherwise) of occupational segregation.

Table 2.4 Random part of the MLM – the variances (with Bayesian Credible Intervals)

Occupations	Year	Variance	Lower 95%	Higher 95%
Managerial	2001	0.125	0.122	0.128
Managerial	2011	0.159	0.155	0.163
Professional	2001	0.234	0.229	0.239
Professional	2011	0.150	0.147	0.153
Associated	2001	0.099	0.097	0.102
Associated	2011	0.129	0.126	0.132
Admin	2001	0.067	0.065	0.070
Admin	2011	0.068	0.066	0.071
Skilled	2001	0.307	0.299	0.315
Skilled	2011	0.249	0.243	0.255
Personal	2001	0.222	0.216	0.229
Personal	2011	0.158	0.154	0.163
Sales	2001	0.289	0.281	0.298
Sales	2011	0.224	0.219	0.231
Process	2001	0.589	0.572	0.605
Process	2011	0.489	0.477	0.502
Element	2001	0.429	0.418	0.439
Element	2011	0.405	0.396	0.415

There are two important findings in Table 2.4: first, for all the occupational groups there is a significant difference in the spatial separation of each from all others in London – this is consistent with the information gathered from the indices above. The second finding relates to the comparison between years. We have seen in the previous part of the analysis with the descriptive measures that segregation fell between 2001 and 2011. This is not the case in the modelled outcomes. For the groups professionals, skilled trades, personal services, sales and customer services, process and machine operatives and those in elementary occupations we do observe a fall in segregation, while for the groups managerial and associated and technical occupations we observe an increase, denoted by the higher non-overlapping variances. However, the most important finding from the table is for the administrative and secretarial occupations between 2001 and 2011. Here, although there is a difference in segregation, in line with the change reported by the descriptive measures, the BCI around the variance overlap. We cannot conclude, therefore, that there has been a change in segregation for this group between 2001 and 2011. This is new information only available because of the modelling environment and cannot be obtained from the indices presented above.

It is possible to plot the data from Table 2.4 (see Figure 2.5). There are three important pieces of information to note from this figure. First, and as in the tables, each variance is presented with its BCI. Those BCI are very 'tight' around the variances, demonstrating that the degree of segregation for each group is significantly different from the other groups and that they are different from each other both

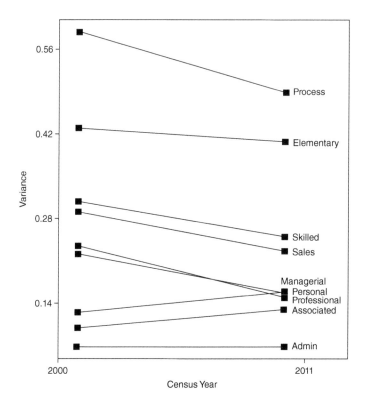

Figure 2.5 Occupational class variance, 2001 and 2011.

within each time period and between time periods (excepting the administrative group). Second, the occupational classes fall into four distinct groups. First the higher occupational classes (managerial, professional and associated) share similar levels of segregation. The administrative group have not only not experienced a change in segregation between the two time points but also have low segregation compared to all other groups. This is, perhaps, due to the nature of the occupations included in the category which will largely be jobs held by female members of the household. The third grouping sees the skilled, personal and sales categories together, while the fourth clearly shows that those in the process and elementary occupations are by far the most segregated in both time periods. The segregation decline for both occupational groups is clear in the chart. The overall conclusion from the modelled variances is that segregation has declined for most groups in London over the ten-year period, a finding in line with the ethnic segregation literature covering the same period (see Catney 2013; Johnston *et al.* 2014b).

Further information that can be obtained from the MLM is used for the second analysis. Table 2.5 reports the correlations from the model output for each occupational group for both 2001 and 2011. The information in this table can be read as you would read any correlations matrix – the higher the value the more similar the distribution of the occupational groups. The table demonstrates the simple underlying structure for both years whereby the managerial, professional and associated professions are located in similar areas while being located 'antagonistically' to the skilled, personal, sales, process and elementary groups who are also quite similarly located at both dates. In both time periods the administrative category tends to have a somewhat ambivalent position, not being in the same areas as the three higher groups but also not being strongly correlated with the five lower groups – with the exception of the skilled group.

It is also possible to correlate within the occupational group but between time points to understand how similar the OA distribution of the occupational classes has remained during the intervening ten years (see Table 2.6). Both the higher and lower occupational categories have remained in similar areas over the ten years, as shown by the correlation coefficients (0.89 for the managerial and 0.86 for the

Table 2.5 The OA correlations for occupational groups (2001 data on the top diagonal, 2011 in the bottom diagonal)

2001 / 2011	*Managerial*	*Professional*	*Associated*	*Admin*	*Skilled*	*Personal*	*Sales*	*Process*	*Elementary*
Managerial		0.67	0.52	−0.47	−0.66	−0.56	−0.67	−0.72	−0.81
Professional	0.66		0.67	−0.54	−0.74	−0.56	−0.63	−0.74	−0.73
Associated	0.66	0.79		−0.56	−0.67	−0.50	−0.64	−0.70	−0.63
Admin	−0.31	−0.43	−0.47		−0.59	0.23	0.40	0.50	0.30
Skilled	−0.72	−0.79	−0.79	0.59		0.43	0.55	0.68	0.56
Personal	−0.75	−0.80	−0.78	0.36	0.74		0.39	0.45	0.50
Sales	−0.79	−0.80	−0.81	0.36	0.71	0.72		0.57	0.59
Process	−0.75	−0.86	−0.87	0.54	0.85	0.79	0.82		0.64
Elementary	−0.85	−0.80	−0.76	0.13	0.70	0.76	0.82	0.79	

Table 2.6 Correlations between 2001 and 2011 for each occupational group

Occupation	*Correlation*
Managerial	0.89
Professional	0.87
Associated	0.81
Admin	0.81
Skilled	0.85
Personal	0.70
Sales	0.76
Process	0.86
Elementary	0.83

process groups for example). In comparison, the personal and the sales occupational groups (0.70 and 0.76 respectively) have experienced more locational shift, evidenced by a lower coefficient. While this cannot show if the individuals and households have remained static over the intercensal period, what it does highlight is that for the highest and lowest occupational groups there are processes of neighbourhood stasis, whereby even when mobility does take place the incomers replacing the outgoers are of similar occupational status (see Hedman *et al.* 2011; Meen *et al.* 2013).

Our third and final example from the MLM returns to the introduction of this chapter and recognises the contribution that the city has made to the gentrification literature. While some fifty years have passed since Ruth Glass first wrote about the changes in the city, they are undoubtedly still being written large within its social and economic fabric as gentrification proceeds apace. Here, then, we are interested in identifying areas where there has been a substantial increase in high-end professionals between 2001 and 2011 by combining the three highest occupational groups (the managers, professionals and associated occupations). Using the Poisson MLM, each OA has a modelled rate of incidence where a value of 1 means that the OA has the same rate of incidence for a given occupational grouping as London, above 1 evidences a higher than a London presence and vice versa for a rate below 1. By combining the rates we can create a ratio indicating change, with ratios above 1 for areas that have experienced an increase in the group of interest and ratios less than 1 for areas of decline. For the analysis we assume that an increase in high-end professions of over 50 per cent (ratio of 1.5) is indicative of an area that may be experiencing gentrification – areas not dominated by

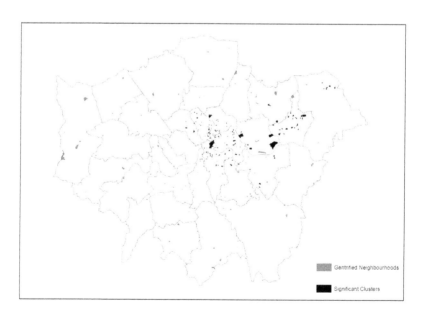

Figure 2.6 Clusters of OAs gentrifying between 2001 and 2011.

higher-social status residents in 2001 but that have become substantially higher in social status over the decade (here we are making an explicit reference to the work of Knox (1982) and Davidson (1976)). Additionally, the modelled rates are automatically shrunk back to the average when they are highly uncertain due to being based on small absolute numbers (see Jones *et al.* 2014). Using the ratios we ran a Local Moran's I (Anselin 1995) cluster analysis to search for clusters of gentrifying neighbourhoods to determine if there were any boroughs experiencing change clustered together. Figure 2.6 presents the results of this analysis, and it is clear that around the River Thames there are significant clusters of gentrification occurring. This is particularly the case in Hackney and Islington (the location of Glass's original analysis) as well as in the City area, Newham and Barking and Dagenham to the north of the river and in Southwark south of the river.

Discussions and further analysis

This chapter has presented segregation information for the city region of London, UK. For the first time occupational segregation has been modelled and the significance of that distribution assessed. Through the inferential statistical framework we were able to confirm many of the findings from the descriptive measures: namely that occupational segregation has declined between 2001 and 2011 and when combined with the ethnic segregation literature this suggests that London is becoming a more integrated city. However, we were also able to extend the analysis and demonstrate that the changes in segregation – namely for the associated professional and technical occupations – were not statistically significant and therefore should not be interpreted as a change in the degree of segregation experienced. Although segregation has declined overall, there are, however, still sharp divisions within the city landscape and these are brought to the fore by the location quotients that demonstrate the differing residential patterns within the city. This is reinforced by the correlations where the higher occupational groups are living apart from the lower groups, highlighting that while there may be integration between some groups there are still distinct divisions elsewhere.

The advancement of a modelling framework for segregation represents an important step for the segregation literature. It is possible, for the first time, to assess the degree of socio-economic segregation in an inferential framework and demonstrate that segregation is occurring above and beyond what would be expected due to random variations in the population distribution. While this may not surprise many the ability to do so should not be played down. Discussions about when and where we should be concerned about segregation can take on an additional dimension once we are able to discuss it in these terms: how much segregation matters is answerable in a robust way for the first time.

Once we have entered a modelling environment, there are, of course, many further analyses that can be considered. Two immediate gains strike us as useful. First, the maps demonstrated that the spatial scale of concentration for the elementary group was different from that of the higher managerial. As with all multilevel models, multiple scales of analysis can be added to determine if the segregation measure – the variation – is distributed equally at all scales or if it is concentrated at more local (for instance OAs) or more expansive neighbourhoods (such as lower super OAs, wards up to the borough level). While it is possible to construct all of the indices presented in this chapter at multiple spatial scales, it is not possible to do so controlling for the segregation contribution at the other scales of interest. Second, there is a substantial advantage to conducting the measurement of segregation in a MLM environment as is the possibility of including further variables to structure the segregation described. Although the data were not released at the OA level at the time of writing, tenure information could be included within the model presented above and conclusions drawn relating how much of the segregation was due to this structural factor as well as others, replicating the early discussions in Duncan and Duncan (1955b).

Acknowledgements

Some of David Manley's time working on the research reported in this chapter has been funded by the European Research Council under the European Union's Seventh Framework Programme (FP/2007–2013)/ERC Grant Agreement no. 615159 (ERC Consolidator Grant DEPRIVEDHOODS, Socio-spatial Inequality, Deprived Neighbourhoods, and Neighbourhood Effects).

Notes

1 The London School of Economics has placed all of Booth's maps online and examples can be viewed at http://booth.lse.ac.uk/
2 The great wen was a disparaging nickname for the City of London coined by journalist William Corbett in the 1820s.
3 A payment made by government to supplement or cover the housing costs for low income and unemployed households. Items taken into consideration when determining housing benefit include income, savings, how much you need to live on (as determined by the government), the number and ages of people in the house and if anyone is sick, disabled or a full-time carer.
4 The cocktail belt is an informal reference to the wealthier suburbs containing households employed in the central area of the city.
5 The green belt is a legally defined area of land surrounding London that has been denoted green belt and must remain largely unbuilt to preserve a less developed region around the heavily built up urban area.
6 This definition includes the thirty-two boroughs of Greater London, and although the first (City of London) is not technically a borough it is included here to avoid having a 'doughnut hole' in the centre of the city. The remaining thirty-one areas are: City of Westminster, Kensington and Chelsea, Hammersmith and Fulham, Wandsworth, Lambeth, Southwark, Tower Hamlets, Hackney, Islington, Camden, Brent, Ealing, Hounslow, Richmond upon Thames, Kingston upon Thames, Merton, Sutton, Croydon, Bromley, Lewisham, Greenwich, Bexley, Havering, Barking and Dagenham, Redbridge, Newham, Waltham Forest, Haringey, Enfield, Barnet, Harrow, Hillingdon. The boroughs are the principal authorities in the city with responsibility for running municipal services including education, social services, waste collection and infrastructure (roads). The public's representation in each borough is decided through local elections held once every four years.

7 We do not provide the full details of the MLM here due to space constraints. However, interested readers are directed to Jones *et al.* (2014) where the model is derived and the shrinkage described in detail.

References

Anselin, L 1995, 'Local indicators of spatial association – LISA' *Geographical Analysis* 27(2), 93–115.

BBC 2013, 'UK house prices: April to June 2013'. Available at http://news.bbc.co.uk/1/shared/spl/hi/in_depth/uk_house_prices/html/aw.stm. Last accessed 17 April 2015. Last accessed 17 April 2015.

Booth, C 1903, *Life and Labour of the People in London*, London, Macmillan and Company Ltd.

Browne, WJ 2012, *MCMC Estimation in MLwiN, v2.25*, Centre for Multilevel Modelling, University of Bristol.

Catney, G 2013, 'Has neighbourhood ethnic segregation decreased?' *ESRC Centre on Dynamics of Diversity*, Manchester. Available at http://www.ethnicity.ac.uk/census. Last accessed 17 April 2015.

Davidson, R N 1976, 'Social deprivation: an analysis of intercensal change' *Transactions, Institute of British Geographers* 1(1), 108–117.

Davidson, M and Lees, L 2005, 'New–build "gentrification" and London's riverside renaissance' *Environment and planning A* 37(7), 1165–1190.

Davidson, M and Wyly, E 2012, 'Class-ifying London: questioning social division and space claims in the post–industrial metropolis' *City* 16(4), 395–421.

Dorling, D, Mitchell, R, Shaw, M, Orford, S and Davey Smith, G 2000, 'The ghost of christmas past: health effects of poverty in London in 1896 and 1991' *BMJ* 7276 (23–30), 1547–1551.

Duncan, O D and Duncan, B 1955a, 'A methodological analysis of segregation indexes' *American Sociological Review* 20(2), 210–217.

Duncan, O D and Duncan, B 1955b, 'Residential distribution and occupational stratification' *American Journal of Sociology* 60(3), 493–503.

Eurostat 2012, 'Metropolitan area populations' *Eurostat*. 30 August 2012. http://ec.europa.eu/eurostat. Last accessed 4 October 2014.

Glass, R 1964, *London: Aspects of Change*, London, MacGibbon & Kee.

Guardian 2013, 'Regeneration in London has pushed poor families out'. Available at http://www.theguardian.com/local-government-network/2013/aug/29/mixed-communities-plan-government-regeneration. Last accessed 17 April 2015.

Hamnett, C and Butler, T 2013, 'Re-classifying London: middle class growth and growing inequality: a response to Davidson and Wyly' *City* 17(2), 197–208.

Hedman, L, van Ham, M and Manley, D 2011, 'Neighbourhood choice and neighbourhood reproduction' *Environment and Planning A* 43(6), 1381–1399.

Imrie, R, Lees, L and Raco, M (eds) 2009, *Regenerating London: Governance, Sustainability and Community in a Global City,* London, Routledge.

Inside Housing 2013, 'More than 50,000 council tenants at risk of eviction over bedroom tax' *Inside Housing*. Available at http://www.insidehousing.co.uk/more-than-50000-council-tenants-at-risk-of-eviction-over-bedroom-tax/6528646.article. Last accessed 17 April 2015.

Johnston, R, Jones, K, Harris, R and Manley, D 2014a, 'Statistical significance testing in the social sciences is invalid: a counter-argument' *The Psychology of Education Review*, 1–4.

Johnston, R J, Poulsen, M F and Forrest, J 2014b, 'Increasing diversity within increasing diversity: the changing ethnic composition of London's neighbourhoods, 2001–2011' *Population, Space and Place,* 21(1), 38–53.

Jones, K, Johnston, R, Owen, D, Forrest, J and Manley, D 2014, 'Modelling the occupational assimilation of immigrants by ancestry, age group and generational differences in Australia: a random effects approach to a large table of counts' *Quality and Quantity*, DOI 10.1007/s11135-014-0130-8.

Kish, L 1954, 'Differentiation in metropolitan areas' *American Sociological Review*, 19(4), 388–398.

Knox, P 1982, 'Regional inequality and the welfare state: convergence and divergence in levels of living in the United Kingdom, 1951–1971' *Social Indicators Research* 10(3), 319–335.

Manley, D, van Ham, M and Doherty, J 2011, 'Social mixing as a cure for negative neighbourhood effects: evidence based policy or urban myth?' in *Mixed Communities: Gentrification by Stealth*, eds G Bridge, T Butler and L Lees, Bristol, Policy Press, pp. 151–168.

Manley, D and Johnston, R 2014, 'London: a dividing city, 2001–11?' *City: Analysis of Urban Trends, Culture, Theory, Policy, Action* 18(6), 633–643.

Massey, D S and Denton, N A 1988, 'The dimensions of residential segregation' *Social Forces*, 67(2), 281–315.

Meen, G, Nygaard, C and Meen, J 2013, 'The causes of long-term neighbourhood change' in *Understanding Neighbourhood Dynamics*, eds M van Ham, D Manley, N Bailey, L Simpson and D Maclennan, Dordrecht, Springer, pp. 43–62.

Morgan, B S 1975, 'The segregation of socioeconomic groups in urban areas: a comparative analysis' *Urban Studies* 12(3), 47–60.

Orford, S, Dorling, D, Mitchell, R, Shaw, M and Davey-Smith, G 2002, 'Life and death of the people of London: a historical GIS of Charles Booth's inquiry' *Health and Place* 8(1), 25–35.

Peach, C 1975, *Urban Social Segregation*, Harlow, Longman.

Rasbash, J, Charlton, C, Jones, K and Pillinger, R 2012, *Manual Supplement to MLwiN v2.26*, Centre for Multilevel Modelling, University of Bristol.

Sakoda, J M 1981, 'A generalized Index of Dissimilarity' *Demography* 18(2), 269–290.

Singh, G 2003, 'Multiculturalism in contemporary Britain: reflections on the Leicester model' *International Journal on Multicultural Societies* 5(1), 40–54.

Tammaru, T, Musterd, S, van Ham, M and Marcińczak, S 2016, 'A multi-factor approach to understanding socio-economic segregation in European capital cities' in *Socio-Economic Segregation in European Capital Cities: East Meets West*, eds T Tammaru, S Marcińczak, M van Ham and S Musterd, London, Routledge.

van Ham, M, Williamson, L, Feijten, PM and Boyle, P 2013, 'Right to Buy . . . time to move? Investigating the moving behaviour of Right to Buy owners in the UK' *Journal of Housing and the Built Environment* 28(1), 129–146.

3 Changing welfare context and income segregation in Amsterdam and its metropolitan area

Sako Musterd and Wouter van Gent

Abstract

Segregation based on income differences is central to this chapter. We aim to understand the most recent (2004–2011) socio-economic segregation process in (metropolitan) Amsterdam, while connecting it to the changing Dutch welfare regime, which from around 1990 is moving in a liberal direction. The social rented sector and the 'regulated' parts of the private sector are under pressure, while owner-occupancy is growing. Social housing is increasingly accommodating only those who have a very low income. Since housing is not spatially distributed in an even way, this affects the level of socio-economic segregation.

Introduction

When it comes to spatial inequality in Western European cities, the need to address high concentrations of poverty has been a recurring political meme over time. While this is understandable from a socialist or social democratic point of view, it is also of concern for social and conservative liberals. The aversion to segregation among centre-right politicians, policy makers and commentators might appear surprising as their advocacy of a free market reign contradicts the notion of intervention and regulation to limit spatial inequality. A liberalised housing market inherently means more segregation based on wealth and income. It is important to consider this because over the past two decades Western Europe (and beyond) has clearly been confronted with a neo-liberal turn (Harvey 2005; Peck and Tickell 2002). Neo-liberalisation has placed the interest of capital over that of labour, resulting in a political project that seeks to restructure welfare state arrangements. To be clear, neo-liberalisation does not imply *less* state intervention but a rearrangement of state institutions, policies and public resources to serve market interests (Harvey 2005). As an important factor in current financial capitalism, housing and housing policy are key to this restructuring and may serve as a lever (Aalbers and Christophers 2014; Malpass 2008; Ronald 2008). Expanding owner-occupancy allows for cuts in health care and pensions, as growing housing equity and lower housing costs in later life are presumed to cover more of individual welfare expenses. Furthermore, in financially liberal countries, the expansion of owner-occupancy also serves the interests of financial actors and pension funds dealing in mortgage loans, derivatives and securities (Schwartz and Seabrooke 2008). So, the expansion of owner-occupancy is not only a symptom but also a cause of welfare state change.

Still, why would those who advocate free market capitalism also rally against segregation? One explanation is that politicians insufficiently define key concepts to leave room for manoeuvre in political discourse. They might have confused segregation with social inclusion and exclusion. Also, it may be that many do not fully grasp how socio-economic segregation comes about. In addition to political manoeuvring and ignorance, the practice of desegregation policies is also in line with the wish to expand owner-occupancy. In the last two decades, policies which seek to tackle segregation and poverty in European cities have come in the form of area-based interventions (van Gent *et al.* 2009). These interventions have sought to alter designated deprived areas' social compositions through renewal and housing market restructuring. This typically entails lowering the share of affordable and social rental dwellings in favour of more expensive and owner-occupancy housing to accommodate more middle-class dwellers. For this reason, gentrification scholars have cast social mixing policies as a form of state-led gentrification (Bridge *et al.* 2012; Lees 2008). Indeed, together with privatisation of social housing citywide and the lowering quotes for new-built social housing, social mixing policies are part of a policy which seeks to change the city's tenure and social composition, effectively reducing the number of low-income households (van Gent 2013).

Yet, explanations which rely on the political economy of capitalism, as has just been explained, are insufficient to fully understand the call for 'undivided cities' in the Netherlands and elsewhere in Western Europe. Here, anti-segregation policies are related to the issue of integration of immigrant communities (van Eijk 2010; van Kempen and Murie 2009; Uitermark 2014). While politicians and policy makers express the need to manage ethnic concentrations, anti-discrimination laws prohibit targeting ethnic groups directly. Instead, urban policies are formally targeting social-economic differences. Regardless, both political rhetoric and policy 'wisdom' assume a strong causal relation between 'social' and 'ethnic' segregation (Andersson 2006; van Gent *et al.* 2009). It seems irrelevant to them that this assumption can be challenged: first, because an increasing share of 'migrants' earns a middle or high income; and second, because the socio-economic position only explains 'ethnic' segregation to a limited extent (Peach 1999).

In this chapter we provide a recent description of social inequality (in particular income inequality) in the metropolitan area of Amsterdam and try to reach a better understanding of socio-economic segregation changes. We will also refer to spatial segregation of immigrants based on country of origin, broken down by income category, to investigate to what extent ethnic and income spatial inequality relate to each other in the Amsterdam context. We will analyse the spatial patterns and changes of levels of segregation for (grouped) income deciles and quintiles by applying standard indicators of evenness and isolation; this will be followed by a context-sensitive section in which we dig deeper in terms of analysing social spatial patterns of segregation of low-income households. Before turning to these empirical sections, we will first elaborate on a selection of the literature in which theories of socio-economic segregation and changes of patterns have been dealt with that may help to frame the empirical findings.

Framing the dynamics of socio-economic segregation

Studies on the explanation of segregation are rooted in different approaches to science. They include viewpoints developed in behavioural science, including those derived from human ecology and choice-based research (Clark 2009; Robson 1975); in structural theory, with reference to economic restructuring, globalisation and mismatch theory (Hamnett 1994; Wilson 1987); and in institutional theory, much inspired by Esping-Andersen's (1990) work, which also was the basis for a new understanding of urban social segregation (Musterd and Ostendorf 1998). Theories on segregation also refer to the impact of historically grown and path-dependent developments (Burgers and Musterd 2002).

Here we argue that individual households will try to realise some preferences based on lifestyle and, more importantly, income and wealth. However, they will be constrained by the opportunities that are available, by economic and other structures that have developed over time, and by rules, regulations and institutions that affect the development of specific social and physical spatial structures. These dimensions are not independent from each other. Welfare state restructuring and a reliance on owner-occupancy for welfare provision will influence the distribution of economic capital within and between generations, and will therefore influence the level of choice people have (McKee 2012). We argue especially that the type of welfare state is crucial, because this may change the attitudes, values, rules and opportunities; the type of welfare state also impacts on how economic restructuring and globally organised forces 'play out' in certain places. Effects may be cushioned through redistributions (through social and unemployment benefits, high-level minimum wages, collective pension systems and housing subsidies or individual rent subsidies) – as is common in universal types of welfare states. However, effects may also become more pronounced because the welfare state model at stake may amplify inequality. This seems to be more common in residual types of welfare states (Forrest and Murie 1988; Musterd and Ostendorf 1998).

Because we take the position that the type of welfare state takes on a special position in the social organisation of cities, a change in type is obviously regarded as a crucial dimension. As mentioned before, several Western European states, including the Dutch, are currently undergoing a neo-liberal turn (Peck and Tickell 2002). Welfare state restructuring will likely create more choice for the affluent but less opportunity for those with less economic capital (Kadi 2014). This is expressed by the Gini coefficient. In a recent study on income inequality in the Netherlands, Salverda *et al.* (2013) found that over a thirty-year period the Gini coefficient rose from 0.242 in 1977 to 0.284 in 2010 (p. 10). Much of the rise occurred just before 1990, followed by a new increase around 2001; in between these years and after 2001 the coefficient turned out to be fairly stable, between approximately 0.280 and 0.290. However, the authors showed that the tails of the distribution went further apart. Moreover, the upper income decile owns a fairly stable 70 per cent of total financial wealth (p. xi). The literature suggests that those who have a stronger economic position use that position to match their own characteristics as much as they can to the characteristics of the environment, resulting in higher levels of segregation, especially in liberalised housing markets (Boterman and van Gent 2014; Clark *et al.* 2013; Reardon and Bischoff 2011). This is helping the development and sustenance of socio-economically homogeneous residential environments (Sampson 2012). In a recent study, Musterd *et al.* (2015) found additional support for such types of dynamics. Based on large-scale data at the individual level for the entire population of the four largest urban regions of the Netherlands, they provided new evidence for the homogenisation that is currently evolving. They found that the larger the 'income distance' (positive or negative) between an individual and the median income of their residential neighbourhood, the higher the odds that the individual will move from that neighbourhood. Individuals who move tend to select destination neighbourhoods that reduce the social distance between themselves and the destination neighbourhood.

The liberalisation of urban housing markets has a particularly strong impact on the behaviour of middle-class and upper-class households. Compared to other households, they are more than others able to realise their wish for living in socio-economically homogeneous environments. Qualitative research has shown that middle-class households do not always directly refer to a wish to better match their own individual income with that of their residential environment, but use indirect arguments for such behaviour. Bridge (2006) and Boterman (2013) have shown that many middle-class households with children mention the quality of schools as among the prime reasons for moving into a homogeneous middle-class neighbourhood. The gentrification literature gives the core of its attention to this middle-class behaviour and politics, with a particular interest in the issue of displacement (Bridge *et al.* 2012; Lees 2008; Smith 1996). Whether the gentrification process would entail forced displacement has been disputed in some contexts, especially where households with relatively moderate socioe-conomic positions are more firmly protected by institutions and regulations (for example van Weesep and Musterd 1991). This was typically the case for the Netherlands and other states known for their regulated housing market and practices in support of households with relatively limited economic capital. This is not to say, however, that low-income households who are living in gentrification neighbourhoods will always stay at that level. Recent research has shown that many households with relatively low incomes rapidly realise social upward mobility after settling in such neighbourhoods (McKinnish *et al.* 2010; Teernstra 2014). Eventually, this may result in higher levels of homogeneity but ultimately in higher levels of segregation.

The demise of strong welfare states in which redistribution of affluence and social solidarity were key elements explains why ever firmer concepts are being used to describe the processes of segregation. When inequalities in society are increasing, this may ignite circular processes that further contribute to rising inequality. Social inequality is said to be related to negative developments in a range of spheres. Wilkinson and Pickett (2010) showed evidence that in more unequal contexts crime levels are higher, health conditions of part of the population are worse, housing opportunities for the poor more limited, etc. This may create more fear for 'the other', and further disaffiliation of the middle class from the rest of the population. As a result, we may see the development of so-called encapsulated homogeneous environments, insulated gated or semi-gated communities (Atkinson 2006). Boterman and Musterd (2014) suggest that this stretches beyond the residential sphere. They studied 'cocooning' behaviour and looked at segregation from the perspective of individuals who are exposed to diversity. They investigated levels of disaffiliation (withdrawing to one's own socially homogenous environment) of the middle class in residential, workplace and mobility spaces and concluded that in all of the domains higher-income natives are the most frequently cocooning population category. Obviously, when exit strategies in the form of living in gated communities, cocooning, disconnection or disaffiliation are taking extreme forms, such as in some North and South American metropolises, very negative processes of estrangement may occur, resulting in a rise of the number and size of no-go areas. This will eventually impact on the urban condition and result in a devaluation of life in urban settings (Atkinson and Blandy 2013). This will be harmful to the poor, especially those with poor and very local – primary ties – networks, as Marques (2012) has shown for São Paulo, but fear for certain urban spaces will also reduce the use of urban territory for the middle class itself.

So far, the experience in (continental) West European cities is different. Here, state intervention has been more extensive over a longer period of time, assuaging segregation levels. Even though these welfare states are changing, they still experience the legacies of a period of strong intervention. They continue to have institutions and practices that help to reduce difference and segregation and continue to create difference from contexts such as those of the United States (van Kempen and Murie 2009). It seems that irrespective of the wider societal changes and regime shifts, not all middle-class households develop firm disaffiliating behaviour. Based on a series of interviews, Andreotti *et al.* (2013) argue that even the upper middle class is applying only 'partial exit' strategies. They seem to be willing to share some dimensions of life with other social groups, while simultaneously searching for stronger separation in other domains of life. They conclude that 'The responses of our interviewees were consistently more nuanced and complex than any simplistic theory about a drive to free-ride or withdraw from society' (p. 594). Even under 'neo-liberalism' there may be limits to the extent people want to segregate themselves from others.

Overall, the discussion of the literature, combined with the perhaps somewhat special situation we are coping with in the Netherlands, more precisely Amsterdam, triggers the first question to be answered in this chapter:

To what extent do we (as expected) find strong and increasing segregation between social classes in the metropolitan area of Amsterdam?

The mechanisms that are producing segregation are not all operating at the same level. Individual preferences of those who are able to exert some choice may result in search processes in which a certain level of social homogeneity is aimed for; this will likely occur at small-area scale and become visible in segregation levels at that scale. However, when institutions at a state level play a significant role, this may not just have consequences for the local level of segregation; it may also imply that larger areas, such as the entire metropolitan area, are affected. In contrast, when due to liberalisation and decentralisation the implementation of uniform regulation principles is no longer obligatory, regional variation in levels of segregation within metropolitan areas may develop. Due to historically grown structures this may lead to sharper distinctions between the core city experiences (with a long and varied urban history) and the rest of the metropolitan region (with often shorter and less varied urban histories). Moreover, the core areas in larger Dutch cities have experienced long periods of social democratic governments. Although the local political arena has changed over the past decade, the welfare state legacy remains. Its lasting impact is noticeable in social housing and part of the private rental sector that are incorporated in the housing allocation system; in Amsterdam, in 2015, this still was way over 50 per cent. The city of Amsterdam also still owns almost 90 per cent of the land. This has effectively enabled the realisation of mixed housing programmes in small-scale neighbourhoods. Nevertheless, over recent years we see new discussion about land ownership with pleas for selling land to individual home owners. Social housing too is under considerable pressure (Boelhouwer and Priemus 2014). These trends reflect and accelerate a wider transformation process towards a more neo-liberal urban regime (van Gent 2013), which may already be manifest in new levels of segregation at certain scales. This results in the second question:

Is there a difference between levels of segregation at different levels of scale?

Apart from focusing on changing levels of income segregation, on individual level interactions between income and ethnicity, and on the geographical scales at which processes occur, segregation issues can also be approached in a different way if detailed spatial level data is available. In the second empirical section we will analyse micro-level data on the spatial distribution of households classified in terms of income. In that section we will particularly focus on the lowest-income category: households with a so-called minimum income (limits set by law), typically the very poorest households, and on the municipality of Amsterdam only. We will also be able to investigate to what extent the changing patterns of concentrations of minimum-income households are linked with the changing housing market structure. Two questions will be guiding that analysis:

To what extent are the lowest-income households increasingly marginalised spatially?

What are the housing-related factors that impact on the changing spatial pattern of low-income households in Amsterdam?

We will provide answers to these questions in two empirical sections (below), after a short introduction of the data and methods used.

Data and methods

For answering the first two questions we used data from the SSD, the Social Statistical Database of Statistics Netherlands. This is an individual-level longitudinal database (total population, no sample) that enabled us to calculate precise distributions of the disposable household income, to select only those who could, in principle, be employed (those between 25 and 65 years old), to combine income and country of origin information before aggregating the information to the neighbourhood level, to differentiate between calculation for the Amsterdam metropolitan region[1] (in short: region) and for the municipality of Amsterdam separately, and to select only those neighbourhoods that included at least 150 households (Figure 3.1). The average neighbourhood size was (in 2010) approximately 3,700 inhabitants, but in the city of Amsterdam almost double that size.

We used income deciles and income quintiles for mapping location quotients and for calculating the index of segregation (IS), dissimilarity indices (D), the index of isolation P*, and, taking into account changing sizes of income groups over time, also the (modified) index of isolation at the regional and municipal level on the basis of the income information, for 2004, 2008 and 2011 (see also the introduction of this book for more detail: Tammaru *et al.* 2016). This year-division

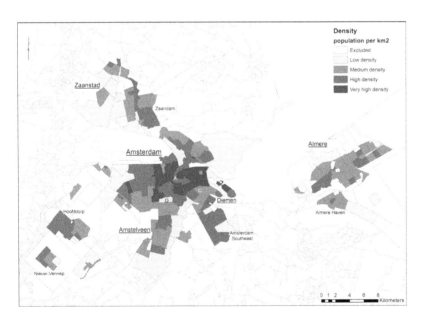

Figure 3.1 Amsterdam metropolitan region and the municipality of Amsterdam; A-Canal Belt, B-Eastern Docklands, C-Watergraafsmeer, D-South Axis.

enabled us to include the potential impact of the financial and economic crisis, which also hit the city and region of Amsterdam (Engelen and Musterd 2010). The income groups are based on national income distributions. This means that the groups may vary in size at the lower regional and municipal level between categories and over time. Changing sizes may be the result of uneven population growth as a result of gentrification in Amsterdam's city centre, urban renewal at the city's periphery and new housing developments in the city and region. Also, there may be an uneven spatial impact of the economic crisis at regional and lower levels after 2008. Indeed, Table 3.1 shows an increase of higher-income groups between 2004 and 2008, followed by stabilisation, and an increase of lower-income groups after 2008.

For answering the third and fourth questions we applied data provided by the Department of Research and Statistics of the municipality of Amsterdam. This covers six-digit postcode-level data in which, among other data, the number of people with a minimum income per postcode was available, for 2004 and 2012. Amsterdam has approximately 18,000 six-digit postcodes – with on average some 40 inhabitants. Detailed spatial concentrations of households with a minimum-income have been constructed with a GIS application that has been developed by Urban Geography of the University of Amsterdam, together with the Department of Research and Statistics of the municipality of Amsterdam.

Table 3.1 Distribution of income groups in % at regional and at municipal level; disposable household income per neighbourhood, 2004–2011

		Region			*Municipality*		
		2004	*2008*	*2011*	*2004*	*2008*	*2011*
Quintiles	1	20.3	20.1	21.9	25.0	24.7	26.4
	2	14.0	14.5	14.6	14.4	14.8	14.8
	3	17.5	17.5	17.1	16.1	15.9	15.8
	4	19.4	19.5	19.2	16.6	16.7	16.7
	5	23.0	23.7	23.8	20.8	21.9	22.2
Deciles	1	10.7	10.6	11.4	13.4	13.5	14.1
	2	9.6	9.4	10.5	11.6	11.2	12.3
	3	6.8	7.1	7.4	7.2	7.6	7.8
	4	7.1	7.5	7.2	7.1	7.4	7.0
	5	8.4	8.3	8.3	7.9	7.7	7.8
	6	9.2	9.1	8.9	8.2	8.2	8.1
	7	9.5	9.5	9.5	8.3	8.3	8.3
	8	9.8	9.9	9.8	8.3	8.5	8.4
	9	10.6	10.9	10.9	8.9	9.4	9.5
	10	12.7	12.9	12.9	11.8	12.6	12.7

Source: Statistics Netherlands; Social Statistical Database (SSD); authors' processing and analysis.

Note: Distributions do not add to 100 because of the category 'unknown'. This category represents households with missing income data.

Empirical section 1: questions 1 and 2

The income dimension only

Starting with the (modified) index of isolation (Tables 3.2a and 3.2b), we see that in each of the years of measurement households which find themselves in the lowest- and in the highest-income brackets (quintiles and deciles) are spatially relatively most isolated from the rest, whereas those who find themselves in the middle-income categories are least isolated. The most isolated category is the category with incomes in the highest decile. This general picture is rather similar for the Index of Isolation and for the Modified Index of Isolation (MI).

Table 3.2a Index of Isolation per income quintile and per income decile, at regional and at municipal level; disposable household income per neighbourhood, 2004–2011

		Region			Municipality		
		2004	*2008*	*2011*	*2004*	*2008*	*2011*
Quintiles	1	0.244	0.241	0.253	0.269	0.266	0.279
	2	0.150	0.157	0.157	0.153	0.159	0.159
	3	0.183	0.184	0.179	0.166	0.165	0.163
	4	0.206	0.207	0.203	0.172	0.172	0.171
	5	0.286	0.292	0.287	0.266	0.279	0.274
Deciles	1	0.132	0.132	0.136	0.144	0.145	0.149
	2	0.119	0.116	0.126	0.131	0.127	0.138
	3	0.075	0.078	0.081	0.078	0.082	0.084
	4	0.076	0.080	0.077	0.075	0.078	0.075
	5	0.088	0.088	0.087	0.082	0.081	0.081
	6	0.096	0.096	0.093	0.084	0.085	0.083
	7	0.101	0.101	0.099	0.086	0.085	0.085
	8	0.106	0.107	0.105	0.087	0.089	0.087
	9	0.120	0.122	0.121	0.098	0.103	0.103
	10	0.186	0.189	0.182	0.184	0.195	0.186

Source: Statistics Netherlands; Social Statistical Database (SSD); authors' processing and analysis.

Table 3.2b Modified Index of Isolation per income quintile and per income decile, at regional and at municipal level; disposable household income per neighbourhood, 2004–2011

		Region			Municipality		
		2004	*2008*	*2011*	*2004*	*2008*	*2011*
Quintile	1	0.041	0.040	0.034	0.019	0.019	0.015
	2	0.010	0.012	0.011	0.009	0.011	0.011
	3	0.008	0.009	0.008	0.005	0.006	0.005

(continued)

Table 3.2b (continued)

		Region			Municipality		
		2004	2008	2011	2004	2008	2011
	4	0.012	0.012	0.011	0.006	0.005	0.004
	5	0.056	0.055	0.049	0.058	0.060	0.052
Deciles	1	0.025	0.026	0.022	0.010	0.010	0.008
	2	0.023	0.022	0.021	0.015	0.015	0.015
	3	0.007	0.007	0.007	0.006	0.006	0.006
	4	0.005	0.005	0.005	0.004	0.004	0.005
	5	0.004	0.005	0.004	0.003	0.004	0.003
	6	0.004	0.005	0.004	0.002	0.003	0.002
	7	0.006	0.006	0.004	0.003	0.002	0.002
	8	0.008	0.008	0.007	0.004	0.004	0.003
	9	0.014	0.013	0.012	0.009	0.009	0.008
	10	0.059	0.060	0.053	0.066	0.069	0.059

Source: Statistics Netherlands; Social Statistical Database (SSD); authors' processing and analysis.

The difference between isolation levels in the region and in the municipality is limited, except for the lowest decile and lowest quintile when calculating the Modified Index. The general picture is that those who find themselves in the extreme categories of the income distribution are relatively most isolated; this holds for the regional and municipal levels. The one exception is the lowest decile at municipal level when calculated as a Modified Index. That decile shows a low level of segregation. This will likely be due to (older) students who are living in relatively mixed neighbourhoods in the core areas of the metropolis. Also, smaller clusters of social housing in relatively affluent neighbourhoods may play a role. We will return to these areas below. At municipal level those who are in the middle- and high-income categories (except for the very highest decile) are a bit less isolated than at regional level. The highest-income decile is most isolated at municipal level, both when calculated unmodified and modified.

Before the crisis started, levels of segregation defined as isolation were stable or slowly increasing for all income categories, while after the start of the crisis for most categories the level was stable or slightly decreasing, except for those with the lowest-income level (unmodified scores) who saw an increasing level. The pre-crisis experience seems to reflect the shift towards more neo-liberalisation, resulting in slightly higher levels of isolation. The limited drop in isolation of the poor may be a combined effect of the increasing share of the population in general that belonged to the poor and the policy of social mixing. The rising share of the poor after 2008 (unmodified) logically increases isolation, because the probability of encountering someone from one's own (low-income) category increases; when modified for the share in the region/municipality as a whole, the isolation in fact decreases (Table 3.2b). The policy of social mixing, which was particularly directed at neighbourhoods with the highest shares of low-income households, is expected to have a dampening effect. The post-crisis experience is characterised by postponing the social mix policy in poor neighbourhoods. Urban restructuring in these neighbourhoods used to rely on the demolition of a substantial volume of old social housing, while rebuilding on the spot new and more expensive ownership housing, thus forcing more social spatial mix. However, with the crisis this policy came to a halt. In the Amsterdam region, demolitions dropped to 75 per cent between 2007 and 2011; in the municipality of Amsterdam to even 78 per cent, according to Statistics Netherlands. These processes implied increasing segregation levels for those with the lowest incomes (unmodified), but decreasing segregation for that category when modified. For the middle- and higher-income categories the crisis implied a strong reduction of residential mobility. Difficulties in selling housing for pre-crisis prices or in obtaining new mortgage loans meant that residential adaptation strategies were put on hold. Also, job loss likely led to a drop in income levels of the entire pre-crisis working population, regardless of place of residence. These two developments would lead to moderately increasing 'spontaneous' income mix in the neighbourhoods they lived in. This is in support of findings of Bailey (2012, p. 718), who states that 'over time, the fit between individuals and their area weakens through social mobility. If people were not able to move, segregation would tend to fall as a result.'

In Table 3.3 we present the Index of Segregation for income quintiles and deciles. At regional and at municipal level, segregation levels for the lowest- and highest-income quintiles and deciles were almost stable before the crisis, and then

Table 3.3 Segregation Index for income quintiles and deciles, at regional and at municipal level; disposable household income per neighbourhood, 2004–2011

	Region			Municipality		
	2004	*2008*	*2011*	*2004*	*2008*	*2011*
Quintile 1 *vs* all others	0.249	0.245	0.221	0.151	0.149	0.133
Quintile 2 *vs* all others	0.131	0.139	0.135	0.125	0.135	0.132
Quintile 3 *vs* all others	0.097	0.104	0.101	0.076	0.084	0.085
Quintile 4 *vs* all others	0.137	0.134	0.126	0.083	0.078	0.071
Quintile 5 *vs* all others	0.260	0.255	0.240	0.269	0.272	0.255
Decile 1 *vs* all others	0.235	0.237	0.207	0.131	0.129	0.110
Decile 2 *vs* all others	0.234	0.227	0.214	0.171	0.177	0.172
Decile 3 *vs* all others	0.142	0.145	0.140	0.124	0.133	0.131
Decile 4 *vs* all others	0.111	0.120	0.116	0.107	0.119	0.115
Decile 5 *vs* all others	0.095	0.099	0.103	0.085	0.091	0.096
Decile 6 *vs* all others	0.094	0.100	0.093	0.063	0.071	0.069
Decile 7 *vs* all others	0.114	0.112	0.102	0.070	0.063	0.061
Decile 8 *vs* all others	0.138	0.135	0.128	0.092	0.089	0.080
Decile 9 *vs* all others	0.170	0.161	0.153	0.141	0.133	0.128
Decile 10 *vs* all others	0.301	0.298	0.284	0.329	0.329	0.309

Source: Statistics Netherlands; Social Statistical Database (SSD); authors' processing and analysis.

Table 3.4 Dissimilarity Index for selected income quintiles, at regional level; disposable
household income per neighbourhood, 2004–2011

D-Quintiles	2004	2008	2011
1–2	0.151	0.151	0.137
1–3	0.229	0.231	0.205
1–4	0.294	0.290	0.263
1–5	0.379	0.365	0.333
2–1	0.151	0.151	0.137
2–3	0.095	0.097	0.088
2–4	0.172	0.174	0.164
2–5	0.307	0.308	0.293
5–1	0.379	0.365	0.333
5–2	0.307	0.308	0.293
5–3	0.244	0.248	0.241
5–4	0.181	0.185	0.176

Source: Statistics Netherlands; Social Statistical Database (SSD); authors' processing and analysis.

dropping. The post-crisis postponement of residential migration clearly seems to
have had a desegregation effect.

Such an effect of the crisis is also clearly noticeable when we focus in some
greater detail at the dissimilarity levels between income quintiles for each of the
three years (Table 3.4). Segregation of the first quintile category, relative to each
of the other quintiles, is generally stable or in a downward direction before the
crisis and then further down during the crisis. For the second quintile the pre-post
crisis trend is stable, then down. For the fifth quintile we find that the rhythm is
generally up, then down. These dynamics are shown for the regional level, but are
similar for the municipal level.

Including the 'native–migrant' dimension

When the 'native–migrant' dimension is included in the analysis, a more
complicated picture emerges, showing that there is not a one-to-one relation
between income and the 'native–migrant' status. We confine the analysis to
comparing the first income quintile and the fifth income quintile within and
between 'native–migrant' categories, to allow for measuring effects of each
dimension separately and jointly. Figure 3.2 provides the graphs for the various combinations of dissimilarities between sub-categories, for the region and
the municipality.

In general, again a dampening effect of the crisis can be shown on levels
of segregation. Highest levels of dissimilarity can be found for the most affluent natives relative to the migrant poor. The indexes are much higher than
for the affluent natives relative to the native poor; and for the most affluent
migrants relative to the native poor. Lowest levels of segregation can be found

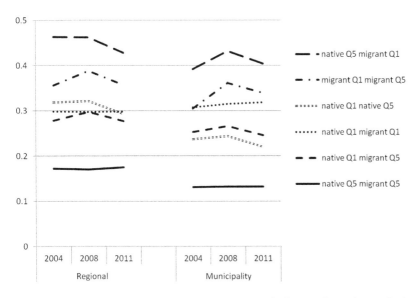

Figure 3.2 Dissimilarity Index for selected income quintiles (Q) for natives and migrants, at regional and municipal level; disposable household income per neighbourhood; 2004–2011.

Source: Statistics Netherlands; Social Statistical Database (SSD); authors' processing and analysis.

for affluent natives relative to affluent migrants. We also see an effect of the scale between regional and municipal. Whereas in the region the dissimilarity index for the first income quintile for natives and the first quintile for migrants is stable, we see a slight increase within the municipality of Amsterdam. In addition at regional level, D for the fifth-quintile natives and first- quintile migrants was stable and then going downwards before and during the crisis, while at municipal level the segregation between these two groups was first increasing and then going downwards before and during the crisis. The fact that the segregation between the first- and fifth-income quintile for migrant categories is much higher than between the first- and fifth-income quintile for natives seems to reflect the process which has been described by Wilson (1987) for the Chicago case: middle-class minorities were fleeing poor minority neighbourhoods, with – in the Chicago case – very negative effects on those who were left behind. Simultaneously, the middle-class migrants have been able to realise their housing ambitions.

The overall picture is that segregation in the municipality is generally a bit lower than at regional level, suggesting a stronger 'melting pot' at municipal level; however, just before the crisis started there was more often a tendency of increasing segregation at that level. This reflects the political changes whose social impacts seem to be more outspoken at municipal level than at the regional level.

Local patterns of three income categories, low-income migrants and high-income natives

The location quotients of low-, middle- and high-income categories are presented in Figures 3.3, 3.4 and 3.5. Relative to the share of low-income households in the metropolitan region, low-income households are still clearly overrepresented in much of the older parts of the core municipality of Amsterdam (the core of the metropolitan area) and in large sections of the post-war social housing-dominated neighbourhoods; with some exceptions they are vastly underrepresented in suburban areas (Figure 3.3). Middle-income households are overrepresented in suburban areas, and in large sections of the urban post-war neighbourhoods (Figure 3.4). The highest-income categories seem to have found their own 'niches' both in some of the older neighbourhoods in the inner city (including the Canal Belt) and some adjacent areas, and in specific suburban areas (Figure 3.5).

When income is (at individual level) combined with the 'native–migrant' dimension the patterns show a stronger contrast; these are almost 'complementary'. Low-income migrants are overrepresented in specific post-war neighbourhoods and in some of the older nineteenth-century neighbourhoods of the core city, and in a few neighbourhoods in more peripheral locations (Figure 3.6). High-income natives are overrepresented in four areas of the core city: the Canal Belt (A in Figure 3.1); the relatively new Eastern Docklands (B) neighbourhoods; the older inner-urban eastern neighbourhood Watergraafsmeer (C); and the south-western wedge from the inner-city Canal Belt to the most important economic area (South Axis) (D). In addition, some specific peripheral and suburban neighbourhoods show strong overrepresentation (Figure 3.7).

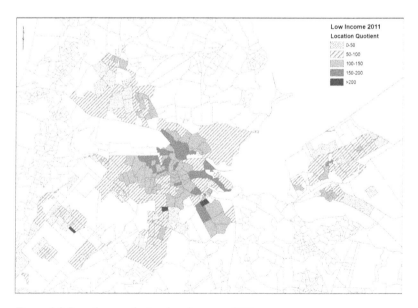

Figure 3.3 Location quotients – low incomes, 2011.

Source: Statistics Netherlands; Social Statistical Database (SSD); authors' processing and analysis.

Figure 3.4 Location quotients – middle incomes, 2011.

Source: Statistics Netherlands; Social Statistical Database (SSD); authors' processing and analysis.

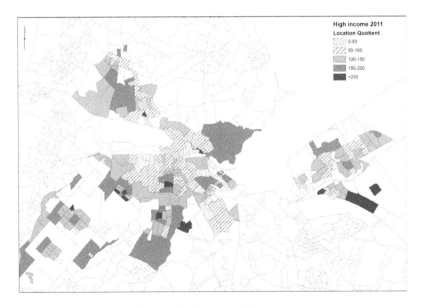

Figure 3.5 Location quotients – high incomes, 2011.

Source: Statistics Netherlands; Social Statistical Database (SSD); authors' processing and analysis.

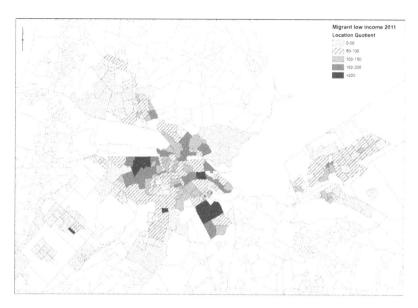

Figure 3.6 Location quotients – migrants with low incomes, 2011.

Source: Statistics Netherlands; Social Statistical Database (SSD); authors' processing and analysis.

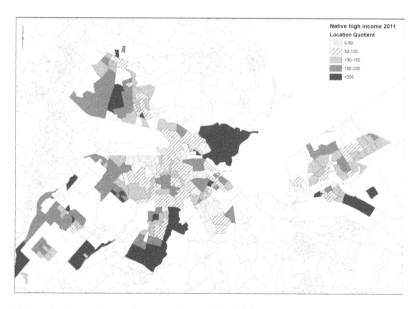

Figure 3.7 Location quotients – natives with high incomes, 2011.

Source: Statistics Netherlands; Social Statistical Database (SSD); authors' processing and analysis.

Empirical section 2: questions 3 and 4

The analyses of levels of segregation show that especially those households with a strong socio-economic position tend to be most strongly segregated from other socio-economic categories. These divisions are becoming even stronger when other dimensions of difference are added, such as belonging to the native population or to one of the migrant categories. The highest levels of segregation can be found between the highest-income natives and the lowest-income migrants. Because the most affluent have most choice, this may be interpreted as a disaffiliation of those with the strongest position from 'the other'. A key question is what this implies for 'the other'. In this empirical section we will provide some answers to that question, following the two questions (3 and 4) we formulated before. The focus will be on the position and spatial concentration of the lowest-income household category within the municipality of Amsterdam: those with a so-called minimum income. In 2012 the municipality of Amsterdam registered 72,261 households with a minimum income. This was 16.6 per cent of all households.[2] In absolute figures their number was increasing again from 2009 onwards, after a period of decline between 2005 and 2009. It is important to know whether the recent development also implies that minimum income households became increasingly marginalised spatially.

To provide an answer to that question we investigated the development of the concentrations of households with a minimum income between 2004 and 2012. We were able to perform such an analysis at the six-digit postcode level. We defined concentrations in various ways: as a clear concentration, where the share of households with a minimum income in an area is at least two standard deviations above the share in the city as a whole; and as a strong concentration, at least three standard deviations above the city level. Areas that fulfil the criteria and are adjacent to each other were taken together, thus forming larger spatial concentrations. For more detail, see Deurloo and Musterd (1998). We only considered concentrations with at least ten households on minimum income and only areas of at least 4,500 m². In Table 3.5 some core findings have been presented. Between 2004 and 2012, even though the relative share of (registered) households on minimum income dropped somewhat, we see a strong increase in the share of households on minimum income that lived in clear concentration areas of their own group (from 24.3 per cent to 29 per cent). For 2012, a respectively *strong* concentration was defined as an area with at least 31 per cent, respectively 38.9 per cent households with a minimum income. To make sure the increasing share of minimum income households living in concentrations of minimum income households was not just a result of decreasing concentration boundaries, we also present 2012 figures with 2004 boundaries. Increasing concentration is confirmed. We thus conclude that households who are the poorest in the city are increasingly spatially marginalised and deemed to live in concentrations with similarly income-deprived neighbourhoods.

Can we develop a better understanding of the reasons why such concentrations are developing? To get the beginning of an answer to that question we constructed

Table 3.5 Share of minimum income households in Amsterdam and in concentration neighbourhoods

Share of minimum income households in Amsterdam	Share of minimum income households in concentrations (2 st dev)	Share of minimum income households In strong concentrations (3 st dev)	(Avg) share of minimum income households in concentrations (2 st dev)	(Avg) share of minimum income households in strong concentrations (3 st dev)
2004 17.65%	24.3%	5.5%	39.0%	48.2%
2012 16.63%	29.0%	19.6%	39.3%	44.8%
2012* 16.63%	25.8%	15.0%	40.2%	46.3%

2012*, definitions 2004.

Source: Department of Research and Statistics, Municipality of Amsterdam; authors' processing and analysis.

a 'differences model' by performing an OLS regression analysis with the difference between the shares of households on minimum income per six-digit postcode in 2012 and 2004 as the dependent variable and a number of 'difference' variables for housing attributes as independent variables – these include real estate values of the dwellings and tenure information. The specification of a 'differences model' enables us to avoid potential spatial auto-correlation problems.[3]

Another issue is the assumption in OLS regression that the variability of the residuals is the same for all values of the dependent variable (homoscedasticity). While we expected a linear relationship between tenure change and social composition, preliminary analyses indicated a cubic trend. To avoid heteroscedasticity and to present an interpretable model, we recoded our change variables into categories, based on means, standard deviations and distribution (for example only one category for social housing increase despite a median and modus of zero percentage change). We only included postcodes in the analysis with at least twenty dwellings. Social housing, i.e. housing owned by social housing associations, decreased from 55 per cent in 2005 to 45 per cent in Amsterdam in 2012 (CBS 2014; van Gent 2013). From the descriptives (Table 3.6) we learn that only 5.2 per cent of the micro-neighbourhoods saw an increase in social housing.

The OLS model (Table 3.7) shows that housing-related factors are associated with the variation of the changing share of minimum income households. The model shows that decreases between 1 and 35 percentage points in social housing result in significant decreases in minimum income households compared to no change. An increase does not result in a significant increase in poor households however. This may be explained by the tendency of social housing associations during this period to build more expensive rental dwellings, some of which were not intended

Table 3.6 Descriptives of the variables used in the regression model presented in Table 3.7

		%	Average	Standard deviation
Change (difference 2012–2004) in minimum-income households (pp)			−0.24	9.1
Share social housing in 2004			17.08	21.84
Share owner occupancy 2004			6.65	12.27
Change in share of social housing in percentages points	Increase (> = 1pp)	5.2		
	No change (ref. cat.)	69.5		
	Decrease (> = −5 and < −1)	5.9		
	Decrease (> = −20 and < −5)	9.3		
	Decrease (> = −35 and < −20)	5.8		
	Decrease (< −35)	4.3		
Change in share of owner-occupancy in percentages points	Increase (> = 45)	2.1		
	Increase (> = 30 and < 45)	5.8		
	Increase (> = 15 and < 30)	14.4		
	Increase (> = 1 and < 15)	21.8		
	No change (ref. cat)	40.4		
	Decrease (> = −15 and < −1)	13.5		
	Decrease (< −15)	2.0		
Change in real estate tax value of all dwellings	Increase above 1 st. dev	15.2		
	Increase between mean and 1 st.dev. (ref.)	36.5		
	Decrease between mean and 1 st. dev below mean	40.3		
	Decrease more than 1 st. dev. below mean	8.0		

Source: Department of Research and Statistics, Municipality of Amsterdam; authors' processing and analysis.

for low-income households. As for ownership, we see that both an increase and decrease of owner-occupied dwellings result in a decrease in poor households. The negative effect of a decrease may seem odd but may be explained by the period after the start of the crisis when many owners would let their dwellings to cover expenses of a new dwelling. Because of this, the share of private rentals increased from 20 per cent to 27 per cent in the period 2005–2012 (CBS 2014; van Gent 2013). Finally, a strong increase in housing value also has a negative effect on the share of

Table 3.7 OLS regression analysis of the percentage point (pp) change in minimum-income households in six-digit postal code areas with at least 20 households and at least 20 dwellings in 2004 and 2012, without large additions or subtractions in housing stock (less than 20%), in Amsterdam, between 2004 and 2012.[a]

		B	Beta	Sign.
Constant		2.074		0.00
Share of social housing in % in 2004		0.038	0.092	0.00
Share owner-occupancy in % in 2004		−0.016	−0.022	0.17
Change in share of social housing in percentage points	Increase (> = 1 pp)	−0.711	−0.018	0.14
	No change (ref. cat.)			
	Decrease (> = −5 pp and < −1 pp)	−0.896	−0.029	0.03
	Decrease (> = −20 and < −5)	−2.555	−0.066	0.00
	Decrease (> = −35 and < −20)	−4.745	−0.106	0.00
	Decrease (< −35)	−0.145	−0.004	0.77
Change in share of owner occupancy in percentage points	Increase (> = 45)	−6.921	−0.109	0.00
	Increase (> = 30 and < 45)	−6.528	−0.168	0.00
	Increase (> = 15 and < 30)	−5.333	−0.207	0.00
	Increase (> = 1 and < 15)	−3.290	−0.150	0.00
	No change (ref. cat)			
	Decrease (> = −15 and < −1)	−2.314	−0.087	0.00
	Decrease (< −15)	−1.977	−0.031	0.02
Change in real estate tax value of all dwellings	Increase above 1 st. dev	−1.161	−0.046	0.04
	Increase between mean and 1 st.dev. above mean (ref.)			
	Decrease between mean and 1 st. dev. below mean	0.221	0.012	0.38
	Decrease more than 1 st. dev. below mean	0.886	0.027	0.87

N = 6264, Adj. R Square = 0.128

Source: Statistics Netherlands; Social Statistical Database (SSD); authors' processing and analysis.

Note:
[a] The average population of the analysed neighbourhoods is 59.3 persons and 33.7 households in 2004. There are 17,772 six-digit postal codes. This means that the model covers 35.2% of all postal codes. Most were excluded because of size restrictions in both years and changes in housing stock, which is mostly due to renewal in the post-war periphery and new construction in IJburg and Osdorp. Missing data meant that 310 cases were excluded.

minimum-income households compared to moderate increases in value. Neighbourhood downgrading does not seem to have an effect. This points to the complex relationship between social change and real estate values (Teernstra and van Gent 2012). The model's only significant positive effect is the share of social housing in 2004. These findings imply that concentrations of poverty are mainly forming in areas with existing social housing stock.

Discussion and conclusions

Answering the first research question (Is there increasing socio-economic segregation?) we can say that in the metropolitan area of Amsterdam segregation levels of most income categories are still rather modest. The spatial distinction between the lowest-income quintile and the second or even third income quintile is limited. In fact, these income categories are still mainly part of the same urban system. This is likely due to a long tradition of a fairly equal income distribution in the Netherlands in general. However, there are signals and threats of increasing segregation, increasing division and separation of sections of society. Especially before the economic crisis started, some income categories, such as the highest incomes, developed more isolation and segregation. They already show high levels of segregation relative to the lowest-income categories, but there is also a tendency to disconnect from other income strata. When we combine 'social class' with 'country of origin', fairly high levels of segregation can be found, often increasing (before the crisis); especially natives in the highest income quintile are rather vigorously separated from the lowest income quintile migrants. Remarkably, the segregation between the first and fifth income quintile for migrant categories turned out to be much higher than between the first and fifth income quintile for natives. This is pointing at turbulent processes, also within the migrant population.

We also found that even though the core city is raising its social level, low-income households are still predominantly overrepresented there. At the same time, the core city is a 'hot spot' for a segment of affluent households. However, overrepresentations of affluent households are also present in several selected suburban municipalities. The centre of gravity for middle-income households is still typically suburban.

The answer to the second research question (Is there a difference between levels of segregation at different levels of scale?) is that segregation levels appear to be slightly lower in the core city of the metropolitan area. This suggests a stronger 'melting pot' function of the core city. However, before the crisis started, increasing segregation could be shown, especially in the core city area. We expect that after the crisis segregation in the core area will continue to increase.

The third research question (Are the lowest income households increasingly marginalised spatially?) must be answered in the affirmative as well: households with a minimum income are increasingly found in concentrations of households like themselves. We interpret this process, which will ultimately show as increasing segregation and marginalisation of the poor, as a consequence of the segregation of those who who have the choice to segregate themselves from others, which are the middle and upper classes in society.

Answering the fourth research question (What are the housing-related factors that impact on the changing spatial pattern of low-income households in Amsterdam?) we found evidence that the existing stock of social housing is increasingly inhabited by the lowest (minimum-income) categories, and that the social housing distribution therefore increasingly predicts the spatial distribution of the poor. Less social housing and more expensive housing will negatively affect the share of minimum-income households.

The threats are that macro processes all point in the direction of growing inequality. Neo-liberalisation will stimulate inequality in society and thus also spatial inequality. Disaffiliation processes are therefore expected to continue. People may be misled by figures from the past half-decade, because this was a period of generally decreasing segregation. However, this is, as we have shown, very likely a consequence of the crisis. During economic crisis, residential mobility significantly drops. Economic uncertainty keeps people where they are, even if they are doing well. Also, financial and housing markets are hit hard by the crisis. New housing finance rules and residual mortgage debts have slowed demand and mobility. Meanwhile, low prices, increased taxation for housing associations and the credit crunch have slackened new housing construction and renovation. The general consequence is, as described in this chapter, a reduction of spatial inequality through larger social mix. However, this is likely just a temporary situation. The pre-crisis trends and processes are likely to be better predictors of what is to be expected than what we currently see.

The baseline seems to be the organisation of the welfare state. We are now in a phase of neo-liberalisation of state and market institutions that is inherently conducive to more (spatial) inequality, social polarisation, segregation, fragmentation and even cocooning behaviour. If such processes go so far as to reach disengagement and estrangement, then societies will be confronted with enormous costs to ensure individual safety and security. Experiences in the Americas and South Africa point to increasing budgetary and social burdens of ever-growing policing and penal policies. Additionally, when repressive policies fail, there is the risk of the development of states within the state. A debate on whether it would be more effective to turn the tide when this is still possible seems highly recommendable.

Notes

1 The region is including the municipality of Amsterdam.
2 The figures are minimum estimates, since these only refer to registered poverty, which appears to be underestimated; according to Statistics Netherlands, hidden poverty has increased during the research period.
3 In OLS regression models it is assumed that the outcomes that have been measured are independent from each other. In spatial analysis, however, the relative outcomes for the spatial units are often related to the distances between the units; there might be spatial auto-correlation. However, the distance between spatial units is constant over time and in our situation identical for 2004 and 2012. If we include the differences between these constant distances (which are all zero) as an independent variable that might impact on the difference between the shares of households on minimum income per postcode, the spatial auto-correlation problem does not apply.

References

Aalbers, M B and Christophers B 2014, 'Centring housing in political economy' *Housing, Theory and Society* 31(4), 373–394.

Andersson, R 2006, 'Breaking segregation – rhetorical construct or effective policy? The case of the metropolitan development initiative in Sweden' *Urban Studies* 43(4), 787–799.

Andreotti, A, Le Galès, P and Moreno Fuentes, F J 2013, 'Controlling the urban fabric: The complex game of distance and proximity in European upper-middle-class residential strategies' *International Journal of Urban and Regional Research* 37(2), 576–597.

Atkinson, R 2006, 'Padding the bunker: Strategies of middle-class disaffiliation and colonisation in the city' *Urban Studies* 43(4), 819–832.

Atkinson, R and Blandy, S (eds) 2013, *Gated communities: International perspectives*, London, Routledge.

Bailey, N 2012, 'How spatial segregation changes over time: Sorting out the sorting processes' *Environment and Planning A* 44, 705–722.

Boelhouwer, P and Priemus, H 2014, 'Demise of the Dutch social housing tradition: impact of budget cuts and political changes' *Journal of Housing and the Built Environment* 29 (2), 221–235.

Boterman, W R 2013, 'Dealing with diversity: Middle-class family households and the issue of "black" and "white" schools in Amsterdam' *Urban Studies* 50(5), 1130–1147.

Boterman, W R and van Gent, WPC 2014, 'Housing liberalisation and gentrification: The social effects of tenure conversions in Amsterdam' *Tijdschrift voor Economische en Sociale Geografie* 105(2), 140–160.

Boterman, W and Musterd, S 2014, 'Cocooning urban life: Household experiences with diversity in neighbourhoods, workplaces and mobility', paper presented at the 'Living in Enclave Cities' conference, Utrecht, 21–22 March 2014.

Bridge, G 2006, 'It's not just a question of taste: Gentrification, the neighbourhood and cultural capital' *Environment and Planning A* 38(10), 1965–1978.

Bridge, G, Butler, T and Lees, L (eds) 2012, *Mixed communities: Gentrification by Stealth?* Bristol, Policy Press.

Burgers, J and Musterd, S 2002, 'Understanding urban inequality: A model based on existing theories and an empirical illustration' *International Journal of Urban and Regional Research* 26(2), 403–413.

Centraal Bureau voor Statistiek (CBS) 2014, Statline databank. Available online: www.statline.cbs.nl

Clark, W A V 2009, 'Changing residential preferences across income, education, and age: Findings from the multi-city study of urban inequality' *Urban Affairs Review* 44(3), 334–355.

Clark, W A V, van Ham, M and Coulter, R 2013, 'Spatial mobility and social outcomes' *Journal of Housing and the Built Environment*. Available online: DOI 10.1007/s10901-013-9375-9380.

Deurloo, M C and Musterd, S 1998, 'Ethnic clusters in Amsterdam, 1994–96: A micro-area analysis' *Urban Studies* 35(3), 385–396.

Engelen, E and Musterd, S 2010, 'Amsterdam in crisis: How the (local) state buffers and suffers' *International Journal of Urban and Regional Research* 34(3), 701–708.

Esping-Andersen, G 1990, *The three worlds of welfare capitalism*, Cambridge, Polity Press.

Forrest, R and Murie, A 1988, *Selling the welfare state: The privatisation of public housing*, London, Routledge.

Hamnett, C 1994, 'Social polarization in global cities: theory and evidence' *Urban Studies,* 31, 401–425.

Harvey, D 2005, *A brief history of neoliberalism*, Oxford, Oxford University Press.

Johnston, R, Poulsen, M and Forrest, J 2005, 'On the measurement and meaning of residential segregation: A response to Simpson' *Urban Studies* 42(7), 1221–1227.

Kadi, J 2014, The neo-liberal restructuring of urban housing markets and the housing conditions of low-income households – An international comparison, PhD Dissertation, Amsterdam, University of Amsterdam.

Lees, L 2008, 'Gentrification and social mixing: Towards an inclusive urban renaissance?' *Urban Studies* 45(12), 2449–2470.

Malpass, P 2008, 'Housing and the new welfare state: Wobbly pillar or cornerstone' *Housing Studies* 23(1), 1–19.

Marques, E 2012, 'Social networks, segregation and poverty in Sao Paulo' *International Journal of Urban and Regional Research* 36(5), 958–979.

McKee, K 2012, 'Young people, homeownership and future welfare' *Housing Studies* 27(6), 853–862.

McKinnish, T, Walsh, R and White, T K 2010, 'Who gentrifies low-income neighborhoods?' *Journal of Urban Economics* 67, 180–193.

Musterd, S and Ostendorf, W (eds) 1998, *Urban segregation and the welfare state: Inequality and exclusion in western cities*, London, Routledge.

Musterd, S 2005, 'Social and ethnic segregation in Europe: Levels, causes, and effects' *Journal of Urban Affairs* 27(3), 331–348.

Musterd, S 2014 'Public housing in an era of neo-liberalism' *Housing Studies* 29(4), 467–484.

Musterd, S, van Gent, W P C, Das, M and Latten, J 2015, 'Adaptive behaviour in urban space: Residential mobility in response to social distance' *Urban Studies*. Available online: DOI: 10.1177/0042098014562344.

Peach, C 1999, 'London and New York: Contrasts in British and American models of segregation, with a comment by Nathan Glazer' *International Journal of Population Geography* 5(5), 319–347.

Peck, J and Tickell, A 2002, 'Neoliberalizing space' *Antipode* 34(3), 380–405.

Reardon, S F and Bischoff, K 2011, 'Income inequality and income segregation' *American Journal of Sociology* 116(4), 1092–1153.

Robson, B 1975, *Urban social areas,* London, Oxford University Press.

Ronald, R 2008, *The ideology of home ownership: Homeowner societies and the role of housing*, Basingstoke, Palgrave Macmillan.

Salverda, W, Haas, Chr, de Graaf-Zijl, M, Lancee, B, Notten, N and Ooms, T 2013, *Growing inequalities and their impacts in the Netherlands. Country Report for the Netherlands. GINI: Growing inequalities' impacts*. AIAS/EU-7th framework programme, Amsterdam. Available at http://gini-research.org/. Last accessed on 8 May 2015.

Sampson, RJ 2012, *Great American city: Chicago and the enduring neighbourhood effect,* Chicago, University of Chicago Press.

Sassen, S 1991, *The global city: New York, London, Tokyo*, Princeton, NJ, Princeton University Press.

Schwartz, H and Seabrooke, L 2008, 'Varieties of residential capitalism in the international political economy: Old welfare states and the new politics of housing' *Comparative European Politics* 6, 237–261.

Smith, N 1996, *The New urban frontier: Gentrification and the revanchist city,* Routledge, London.

Tammaru, T, Musterd, S, van Ham, M and Marcińczak, S, 2016, 'A multi-factor approach to understanding socio-economic segregation in European capital cities' in *Socio-economic segregation in European capital cities: East meets West*, eds T Tammaru, S Marcińczak, M van Ham and S Musterd, London: Routledge.

Teernstra, A 2014, 'Neighbourhood change, mobility and incumbent processes: exploring income patterns of in-migrants, out-migrants and non-migrants of neighbourhoods' *Urban Studies* 51(5), 978–999.

Teernstra, A B and van Gent, W P C 2012, 'Puzzling patterns in neighborhood change: Upgrading and downgrading in highly-regulated urban housing markets' *Urban Geography* 33(1), 91–119.

Uitermark, J 2014, 'Integration and control: The governing of urban marginality in Western Europe' *International Journal of Urban and Regional Research* 38(4), 1418–1436.

van Eijk, G 2010, 'Exclusionary policies are not just about the "neoliberal city": a critique on theories of urban revanchism and the case of Rotterdam' *International Journal of Urban and Regional Research* 34(4), 820–834.

van Gent, WPC 2013, 'Neo-liberalization, housing institutions and variegated gentrification: How the "third wave" broke in Amsterdam' *International Journal of Urban and Regional Research* 37(2), 503–522.

van Gent, W P C, Musterd, S and Ostendorf, W 2009, 'Disentangling neighbourhood problems: Area based interventions in Western European cities' *Urban Research & Practice* 2(1), 53–67.

van Kempen, R and Murie, A 2009, 'The new divided city: Changing patterns in European cities' *Tijdschrift voor Economische en Sociale Geografie* 100(4), 377–398.

van Weesep, J and Musterd, S (eds) 1991, *Urban housing for the better-off: Gentrification in Europe,* Utrecht, Stedelijke Netwerken.

Wilkinson, R. and Pickett, K 2010, *The spirit level; Why greater equality makes societies stronger*, New York, Bloomsbury Press.

Wilson, WJ 1987, *The truly disadvantaged,* Chicago, University of Chicago Press.

4 Socio-economic segregation in Vienna

A social-oriented approach to urban planning and housing

Gerhard Hatz, Josef Kohlbacher and Ursula Reeger

Abstract

Vienna is in a special position, characterised by a uniquely high proportion of old housing stock and communal housing. Typical for Vienna too is a policy of social equality, with the city constantly working to develop measures aimed at reducing social disparities. In Vienna socio-economic segregation is the result of a complex interplay between educational attainment, segmentation of the housing market and housing policies. This chapter analyses the processes of change in segregation patterns and tries to answer the question of how spatial polarisation processes are shaped under this 'special' social-oriented approach. Through mapping and factorial analysis it will be shown that socio-economic features have become more prominent in explaining patterns of socio-spatial segregation. Furthermore, a polarisation between public housing, where the lower qualified (with or without migration background) live, and the residential areas of the upper social strata has become obvious.

Introduction

Vienna has seen globalisation restructure urban society in terms of deindustrialisation, occupational change, migration and unemployment too. The city maintains the status of both a federal province and a municipality and is the only large metropolis in the country. It is Austria's economic and employment centre and an important economic link between Western and Central Europe. Over the past decades, the urban economy has seen a structural shift from manufacturing to business-related services, the backbone of which is formed by small and medium-sized enterprises (98 per cent).

Vienna is also the fastest growing city within the German-speaking countries, with an increase between 2001 and 2011 of 164,000 new residents. Population projections expect this growth to continue in the coming decades and see the city population increase to over two million in 2035.[1]

Typical for Vienna is its long tradition of social democracy, pursuing a policy of social equality. Nevertheless, neither Austria nor Vienna has been successful in preserving their status in the 1980s as the 'Island of the Blessed', as it was once called by Pope Paul VI. The municipality has tried to attract more external investments with institutional changes. These changes have included a restructuring of administration towards a more entrepreneurial model and the creation of new institutions to provide a better capacity to respond flexibly to new challenges following EU accession in 1995.

The housing policy of the Social-Democrat City Council is an important tool to combat social marginalisation. The Viennese housing market is characterised by a series of communal interventions (rental policies, housing promotion loans, a promotion policy of non-profit housing companies, etc.). The housing stock is determined by two factors: a considerable proportion of older stock and a uniquely high proportion of communal housing. More than 40,000 buildings containing 300,000 flats in Vienna were built during the 'Founders' Period' of the 1890s. With about 229,000 flats Vienna has the largest public housing stock in Europe. In Vienna, 31 per cent (in Austria about 10 per cent) of the population live in public sector housing. The municipality remained the most important building contractor until the 1970s and the City of Vienna is still Europe's biggest residential property owner. A system of housing subsidies provided the basis for this. The subsidy system not only promotes new construction but also renovation and housing improvements (Eigner *et al.* 1999). Notwithstanding the neoliberal trend for stronger market-orientation since the 1990s, low-income households are still supported by an elaborate housing benefit system (Matznetter 2002).

By means of the largest program of 'soft urban renewal' in Europe, the municipality succeeded in fighting urban decay. Nevertheless, unintended gentrification processes were a logical consequence. Recently, the growing dynamics of immigration has caused housing shortages and increasing rent costs. Social housing policies on eligibility and the city's withdrawal as a housing developer just as it was embarking on subsidised urban renewal have contributed to an accentuation of structural differences. The response of the public housing policy has come in the form of large new construction projects, not by the city itself but by housing associations.

On the labour market, restrictive wage policies and rising unemployment have led to an increase in socio-economically marginalised groups within the population. A certain degree of polarisation in spatial dimensions could not be prevented. These changes are challenged by increasing city competition, by the phenomena of urban sprawl and gentrification, and by the declared political goal of an equal spatial distribution of the socio-economically weak population.

Occupational changes, immigration and housing market developments are identified as the most relevant factors in the context of socio-economic segregation. Thus, we want to show the socio-spatial outcomes of a complex interplay between socio-economic structures, the building stock and housing market, and welfare interventions, all of which have their spatial implications. This study applies classic social area analysis and factorial ecology to identify the underlying dimensions in the formation of socio-spatial patterns in a context which is almost unique in Europe by its dominance of social housing and the cushion of segregation trends by social policy measures. The results of our analysis do not directly reveal a trend towards spatial polarisation but rather support the concept of emerging structural differentiations in a 'quartered city'.

Segregation research in Vienna

Most of the available segregation studies for Vienna are focused on ethnic residential segregation. The question of socio-economic segregation is not as prominent in a city with such an explicit socio-democratic tradition. Thus, when addressing socio-economic segregation, the older factorial-ecological survey of Lichtenberger *et al.* (1987) must be mentioned. In the 1990s Giffinger (1998) showed the influence of accessibility rules, market barriers and rent regulations on segregation of the population with Turkish and former Yugoslavian migration backgrounds. In 2002, Giffinger and Wimmer examined the complex interdependencies between spatial segregation and integration of the population with a migration background using two urban areas in Vienna as an example. Fassmann and Hatz (2004, 2007) asked if Vienna could be characterised as a fragmented city and underlined this question with detailed analyses of segregation patterns. Residential segregation patterns of Turkish and former Yugoslav guest workers were also investigated by Kohlbacher and Reeger (2007) who complemented their analyses (2008) with the outcome of naturalisation on residential patterns.

The transformation of society and patterns of segregation in Vienna, 2001–2011

General trends

Often neglected when examining socio-spatial polarisation, demographic changes and changes in household composition cannot be separated from the impact of labour force restructuring. Demographic shifts, changes in household or family structures, living arrangements or lifestyle choices may intersect with urban economic restructuring (Walks 2001: 440). The diversification of family types and household composition has led to a diversification of housing needs, forming specific demographic milieus (Musterd and van Kempen 2000). Since the 1970s, the demography in Vienna has been characterised by changes in the traditional family life cycle and a bifurcation due to increasing immigration.

According to the taxonomy of Esping-Andersen (1993: 27), Austria can be classified as a conservative, cooperative welfare state. Vienna therefore serves as an appropriate European example for examining the socio-spatial structural changes resulting from post-industrial restructuring and the changing role of welfare policies. As in other metropolitan areas, the urban society in Vienna has been transformed according to the notions of the 'global city hypothesis', in terms of deindustrialisation, occupational changes, immigration and high levels of structural unemployment.

The following analysis of the socio-spatial transformation is based on data gathered as part of the census in 2001 and the register-based[2] census of 2011 that allow a very detailed spatial differentiation and are analysed at the level of census districts, which are the smallest statistical units (165) available. The mean number of residents at the level of census districts has been calculated to be about 1,257. The first section of the analysis includes the identification of relevant indicators of the socio-spatial transformation in Vienna, whereas the single indicators are tested in their structural and spatial variation. A final – more conclusionary – section is dedicated to isolating the basic dimensions of social transformation and patterns of segregation by applying factor analysis.

Changing processes of the occupational structure

Since the 1990s, the globalisation and polarisation of society were the focus of analyses of the post-industrial restructuring of urban societies, resulting in increasing social inequalities and socio-spatial segregation. Based on Sassen's thesis, this polarisation is marked by the increase of a highly skilled, high-income labour force tied to the global economy and a new and growing urban underclass (see Sassen 1996: 148).

The analysis of the occupational structure only partially supports a shift according to the notions of a polarised society (see Table 4.1). The percentage of managers in the total work force in Vienna dropped from 9.3 per cent in 2001 to 5.3 per cent in 2011. However, what has to be considered as a

Table 4.1 Occupational structure and changes, 2001 and 2011

Occupation ISCO-08 Structure	2001		2011	
	In 1,000	In %	In 1,000	in %
Managers	69	9.3	43	5.3
Professionals	89	11.8	179	22.2
Technicians and associate professionals	163	20.0	155	19.2
Clerical support workers	113	13.5	89	11.0
Service and sales workers	107	13.2	156	19.3
Skilled agricultural, forestry and fishery workers	4	0.5	5	0.6
Craft and related trades workers	75	9.8	74	9.2
Plant and machine operators, assemblers	42	5.8	33	4.1
Elementary occupations	111	14.6	72	8.9
Armed forces occupations	6	0.6	1	0.0
First time job seekers	9	0.9	–	–
Total	790	100.0	807	100.0

Source: Statistics Austria, Census 2001 and Labour Force Survey 2011, own calculation.

striking shift is the increase in the professional – generally highly skilled – labour force. Even if a comparison between the data based on the population census of 2001 and the Labour Force Survey data for 2011 is limited, the number of professionals in Vienna has seemingly almost doubled within the last ten years, from 11.8 per cent in 2001 to 22.2 per cent in 2011. In contrast, the intermediate strata of technicians and associate professionals have only slightly decreased, just as the number of clerical support workers has reduced due to austerity programmes in public administration.

Seemingly in compliance with the concept of a polarisation of society, the labour market in Vienna shows a disproportional growth in service and sales workers. However, with respect to their educational level, this group cannot be classified as an unskilled workforce at all. Changes in occupational structures due to the globalised economy, paralleled with deindustrialisation, have become visible in the significant reduction of elementary occupations.

Since the 1970s, the proportion of non-Austrian citizens residing in the capital has increased from 16.4 per cent on 1 January 2002 to 21.2 per cent on 1 January 2011.[3] Most of these were migrants from the successor states of the former Yugoslavia and Turkey. In the labour market they have taken over positions vacated by low-skilled Austrians who had gained additional qualifications. In 2001, 41 per cent of the low or unskilled blue-collar labour force were immigrants. As immigration has become one of the major factors of socio-economic polarisation, a further analysis is provided later in the chapter.

By comparing occupational changes between 2001 and 2011 the following first conclusions can be drawn:

1   The occupational transformation of the work force in Vienna indicates a moderate trend towards a polarisation of urban society, marked by a disproportional growth rate of professionals, as well as service and sales workers.
2   The trend towards a polarisation of urban society in Vienna is modified by the overlapping cycle of deindustrialisation that has not yet been completed.
3   The transformation of the social stratification in Vienna is accompanied by a clear upward trend of educational attainment, which can be seen in the light of Hamnett's (2003) analyses of the interrelations between educational qualifications and labour market prospects.

Shifting educational structure

Educational attainment in Vienna, indicating the position of the individuals in the socio-economic hierarchy of the urban society, showed a clear upward socio-economic shift from 2001 to 2011. The share of the work force who had graduated from university increased from 13.5 per cent in 2001 to 21 per cent in 2011. However, the intermediate social strata indicated by skilled workers who count secondary education (thirteen or fourteen years of schooling, respectively K–13 or K–14 level) as their highest educational level, is the most significant of Vienna's social strata (see Table 4.2).

Table 4.2 Employed persons in Vienna by educational attainment, 2001 and 2011

Educational attainment	In %	In%	Index of segregation		Index of isolation		Modified index of isolation	
	2001	2011	2001	2011	2001	2011	2001	2011
University	13.5	21.0	33.7	31.8	0.21	0.29	0.08	0.10
College	2.9	3.4	19.8	16.7	0.04	0.04	0.01	0.01
High School (K–13. K–14)	16.4	20.5	14.8	11.3	0.18	0.22	0.02	0.01
Vocational school	10.6	11.2	13.1	13.9	0.12	0.12	0.01	0.01
Traineeship	29.7	23.3	19.0	19.9	0.33	0.26	0.05	0.04
Compulsory education (K–9)	26.9	20.6	21.1	25.0	0.31	0.25	0.05	0.06

Source: Statistics Austria, Census 2001 and Register-based Census 2011, own calculation.

The differentiation of educational groups is important for the study of changing spatial patterns (see Table 4.2). This is especially the case in Vienna as the data situation does not allow for the study of occupational segregation. It can be shown that spatial segregation for the highly skilled labour force has weakened slightly. The index of isolation points to the underlying societal changes in neighbourhoods dominated by a highly skilled labour force. Thus, the index of isolation – as with the modified index of isolation – shows a moderate increase from 0.21 in 2001 to 0.29 in 2011, suggesting that neighbourhoods preferred by the highly skilled labour force are becoming more 'homogenised' with regard to this social strata. The indices of segregation and isolation suggest a modest trend towards spatial polarisation. Social groups at the top and the end of social stratification are more segregated or isolated than those 'in the middle'.

For Vienna, social distance based on educational attainment is reflected in the patterns of socio-spatial distribution (see Table 4.3). The distance between the 'top' and the 'bottom' of the social ladder is mirrored in the indices of dissimilarity between members of the work force who completed university and the low-skilled work force (40.5) and also those having completed an apprenticeship (39.7). To a lesser extent, members of the labour force who have completed vocational school are segregated from the residential areas of the highly skilled work force. At the lower end of social stratification, the socio-spatial differentiation between the unskilled labour force and those who have completed an apprenticeship is one of the lowest and has decreased over the last ten years, seemingly indicating that those social groups are becoming more and more merged within the same neighbourhoods.

To conclude, the analysis reveals a slight trend towards polarisation but not a significant change in the patterns of socio-spatial segregation. It is interesting that housing areas of the highly skilled labour force are becoming more "homogenised" with regard to this social stratum, whereas groups at the bottom of the educational ladder have become more and more merged within the same areas.

Table 4.3 Indices of dissimilarity based on educational attainment, 2001 and 2011

Educational attainment	University		High School		Vocational school		Apprenticeship	
	2001	*2011*	*2001*	*2011*	*2001*	*2011*	*2001*	*2011*
High School	21.0	19.5						
Vocational school	34.1	34.2	15.1	16.3				
Apprenticeship	41.0	39.7	22.9	22.2	12.9	11.5		
Compulsory education	38.9	40.5	26.4	28.0	26.4	28.0	18.9	16.6

Source: Statistics Austria, Census 2001 and Register-based Census 2011, own calculation.

The housing market and the relevance of welfare interventions

In Vienna, housing market structures and housing and welfare policies are the dominant factors determining patterns of socio-economic segregation. Based on the demographic growth rates, the production of housing and the question of affordable housing will be one of the major challenges faced by urban planners and politicians. Housing legislation is primarily a federal responsibility, with an emphasis on tenant protection and regulation of the limited profit housing sector. The housing policy is predominantly supply-side oriented (Fassmann and Hatz 2007). For several decades it was also based on the corporatist principle of 'social partnership'. Since the 1980s, however it has been regionalised and became more market-oriented (Aufhauser *et al.* 1991). Since 2000 a liberalisation of national housing legislation has prevailed, accompanied by an implementation of a social-oriented approach to urban planning in Vienna, though a neoliberally influenced change in the understanding of the category 'social' could also be observed (Reinprecht and Levy-Vroelant 2008). From an international perspective, the Austrian model has been resilient in stabilising housing markets and delivering (new) quality housing (Czasny *et al.* 2004). It seems to be unique in Europe and deviates from dominant market provisioning which shapes the housing markets of most EU metropolises (Amann 2010).

The structure of the buildings and the segmentation of the housing market in Vienna defines the structural differentiation of the city and is a blueprint for socio-spatial patterns of segregation. Based on Lichtenberger *et al.* (1987), the urban form of Vienna consists of four major subdivisions that have developed historically since the mid-nineteenth century (the Founder's Period of 1860–1914). The inner city is marked by housing stock dating back to the time of industrialisation, when Vienna became a metropolis. The share of apartments built before 1914 in the Inner City in 2011 was 9.9 per cent, whereas in the outskirts the corresponding figure is just 2.2 per cent. The quantitative importance of the old housing stock is illustrated in Figure 4.1, showing the proportion of Founder's Period buildings in the city space. The city centre, as well as the surrounding fringe of inner districts (5th, 6th 7th, 8th and 9th), is dominated by this stock, reaching proportions of more than 50 per cent. This zone continues even into the working-class areas beyond the 'Gürtel' (Belt),[4] with concentrations of historical building substance of 25–50 per cent and sometimes even more. Similar concentrations can be found in the 2nd, 3rd and 20th districts adjacent to the city centre but also in some parts of the working-class 10th and 11th districts.

There is some conflict of interest in the districts built during this period with respect to preservation on one hand, and new social, economic and housing-related developments on the other. For the interpretation of the Viennese situation it is important to say that even throughout years of major social, technical and economic change these areas are still able to adapt easily to growing immigration, having a considerable integrative potential to being open for a mix of functions. Therefore, in Vienna the structures dating back to this era are treated with sensitivity despite the goal of eliminating any remaining substandard housing. In contrast to other European metropolises, infrastructure is generally speaking not bad in neighbourhoods with a high proportion of old stock. Public transport, for example, is well developed in most of these areas.

It is clear from Figure 4.1 that the urban form of Vienna is shaped by a concentric arrangement around a city centre, surrounded by a fringe of bourgeois inner districts, in turn surrounded by the densely populated area of the outer districts, once mainly

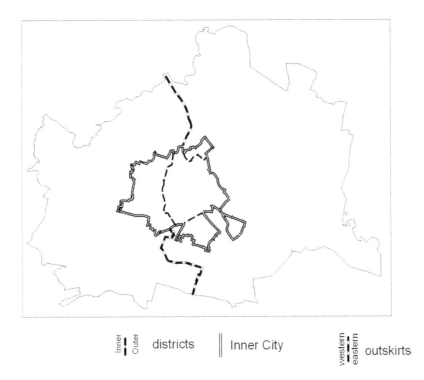

Figure 4.1 Vienna – urban form.

Source: based on Lichtenberger, Fassmann and Mühlgassner 1987; Geometry: WIGEOGIS, GEO ZID.

working-class residential areas dominated by nineteenth-century building stock. Both areas are clearly separated from each other, not only socio-economically but also spatially by the 'Belt'. The high proportion of green land ('Vienna Woods') in the western periphery is characteristic of that part of the city, which is made up of attractive residential areas at the slope of the Vienna Woods. Even at the turn of the nineteenth to the twentieth century, these areas were used by the upper class to build luxury villas and apartments. Continuing into the modern day, the western outskirts are dominated by low-density, single-family, semi-detached houses and high standard apartments. The eastern outskirts in their southern part include the working-class 10th and 11th districts and the extensive 21st and 22nd districts on the other side of River Danube. The eastern outskirts of the city came in the focus of modernist planning schemes through the construction of public housing complexes in the 1970s and still are dominated by them following the withdrawal of the city as a housing developer, increasingly supplemented by apartments built by housing associations.

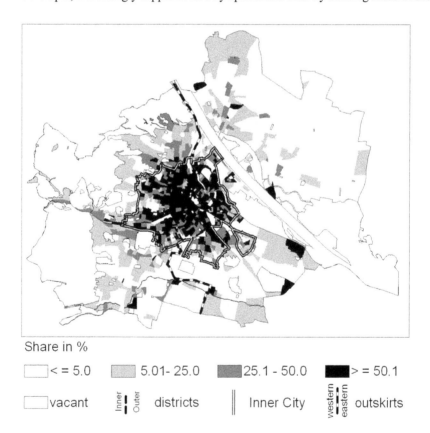

Share in %

☐ < = 5.0   ☐ 5.01- 25.0   ■ 25.1 - 50.0   ■ > = 50.1

☐ vacant   Inner | Outer districts   ‖ Inner City   western | eastern outskirts

Figure 4.2 Share of apartments built before 1919, 2011.

Source: Statistics Austria, Register-based Census 2011, own calculation; Geometry: WIGEOGIS, GEO ZID.

Note: Classification of values based on 'natural breaks'.

The quality of the apartments built in the inner city, however, cannot be considered a homogenous entity. The apartments in the inner districts were built for the bourgeois residents and met the criteria of high-quality apartments, even at the time when they were built. In contrast, the apartments on the outskirts of the inner city area were to provide housing for the working class adjacent to the industrial plants. These areas were characterised by small apartments of substandard quality. Even if the standard of these apartments has since been improved, these areas still show the highest share of low-quality apartments within the city. The nineteenth-century stock can also be found in the cottage areas but in lower percentages of 5–25 per cent. Of course, in these areas the residential stock is of a higher standard, providing larger housing units. The differentiation in terms of standard is mirrored in Figure 4.3, showing the strong division between the better-equipped old stock of the inner city and the fringe of substandard housing which was, until the 1980s and 1990s, a typical feature of the old stock in working-class districts. Even in 2011 there were still more than 10 per cent category D[5] flats in the areas adjacent to the 'Belt', in the 2nd, 3rd, 10th and 20th districts.

Everywhere else in Europe processes of change in the labour market are strongly interwoven with processes on the housing market and thus spatial aspects. Nevertheless, there are Viennese specifics which must be mentioned. Weak residential mobility in some segments of the housing market favours a considerable degree of stabilisation of residential patterns. Thanks to a fight against property speculation and a policy of supporting public housing (from the the council and recently in particular cooperative housing), Vienna was for a relatively long period untouched by problems typical of the housing sectors in other metropolises. Thus, 'ethnic ghettoisation' and large-scale socio-economic concentration are absent, as well as large, dilapidated urban quarters. Of course, spatial manifestations of socio-economic inequalities exist, but the patterns of residential segregation are spatially rather small scale and change relatively slowly. In some attractive parts of the urban space – certain areas of the 2nd district in the vicinity of the city centre are illustrative examples – gentrification trends can be seen but were slowed to some degree by a system of housing benefits. Recently, housing shortages have become an increasing problem, which is counterbalanced by a forced construction rate (for example Aspern in the 22nd district, Sonnwendviertel near the new Central Railway Station at the fringes of the 3rd and 10th districts) and loft conversions all over the urban space.

Substandard housing is no longer a fundamental problem. Between 1971 and 1991 the proportion of category D shrank from 40.3 per cent to 26.2 per cent in the densely built urban area. In the older housing areas (built up before 1919) there was a decrease from 56.4 per cent to 38.1 per cent during the same period (Schopper and Hansely 1999: 531). In 2001, it was only 8.3 per cent (for the whole city), further decreasing to 6 per cent by 2011 (without a toilet) and 3.1 per cent without a bathroom.[6] In the same year, roughly 90 per cent of Vienna's housing stock was in the top category, category A. This mirrors a process of upgrading of the whole stock due to targeted measures of soft urban renewal. Despite this positive development, it remains true that in certain districts (10, 11, 12, 15, 16, 17, 20) the share of flats with substandard infrastructure is still twice that of the overall city average (Stadtentwicklung Wien 2005: 103).

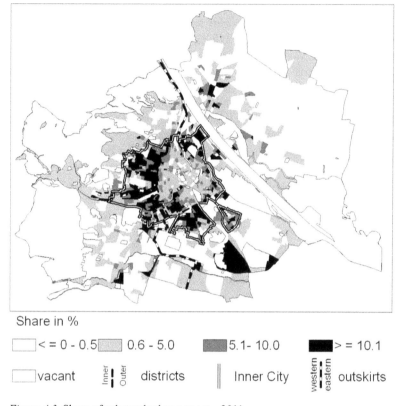

Share in %

☐ < = 0 - 0.5   ▨ 0.6 - 5.0   ▨ 5.1- 10.0   ■ > = 10.1

☐ vacant   Inner|Outer districts   ‖ Inner City   western|eastern outskirts

Figure 4.3 Share of substandard apartments, 2011.

Source: Statistics Austria, Register-based Census 2011, own calculation; Geometry: WIGEOGIS, GEO ZID.

Note: Classification of values based on 'natural breaks'.

The housing market in Vienna can be classified as a rental market. In 2011 only about one-fifth (21 per cent) of the entire housing stock was owner-occupied (2001: 20.2 per cent). Tenants in public housing have no right to buy and household incomes often mean that homeownership is not a viable option, thus the quantitative relation between owner-occupied apartments and rented apartments has not changed considerably between 2001 and 2011. Still, the differentiation between owner-occupied apartments and the rental market implies a selective distribution of social groups between these two segments of Vienna's housing market. The real estate market has been characterised by a dramatic increase in prices and thus ownership of apartments has become more and more socio-economically selective. However, in the past decades, owner-occupied apartments have been an option for the middle classes. Hence, owner-occupied apartments in Vienna encompass a heterogeneous ensemble of different social groups and income classes.

Although welfare interventions have changed over the past three decades, social housing policy is aimed at ameliorating the social mix in the city (Förster 2002). Socio-spatial inequalities and segregation are firmly related to the public housing segment and letting policies for social housing. Increasing segregation has meant an overrepresentation of people with lower social status in a residualised housing segment (Musterd 2014; van Kempen and Murie 2009). Figure 4.4 illustrates the spatial distribution of public housing. For the most part, public residences were built during early the twentieth century and are nowadays mostly multi-rehabilitated. The stock has an average standard and should be available for socially disadvantaged persons. Rents rise moderately after renovation activities but are usually lower than in the private rental sector. The city has become more reticent to undertake large-scale improvement works in older public housing developments in order to ensure the continued availability of a stock of cheap housing. There was a second public residential offensive starting during

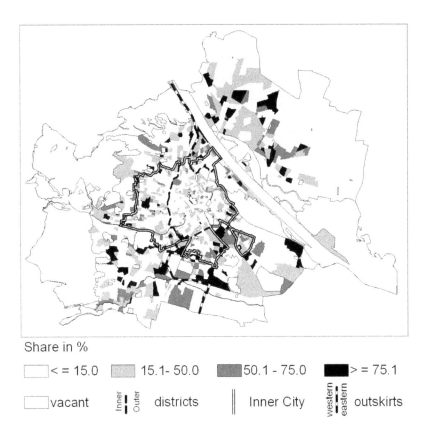

Share in %

☐ < = 15.0   ▦ 15.1- 50.0   ▓ 50.1 - 75.0   ■ > = 75.1

☐ vacant   Inner | Outer districts   ‖ Inner City   western | eastern outskirts

Figure 4.4 Share of public housing apartments, 2011.

Source: Statistics Austria, Register-based Census 2011, own calculation; Geometry: WIGEOGIS, GEO ZID.

Note: Classification of values based on 'natural breaks'.

the 1950s and in particular in the 1960s. Between 1961 and 1971 more than 105,000 new flats, mostly in the subsidised segment were built (Eigner *et al.* 1999: 52). During the 1970s and 1980s growth rates dropped when public stock was erected on vacant plots in the densely built-up districts but also on greenfield sites on the outskirts.

In contrast to other European cities, public housing in Vienna was never solely concentrated in working-class districts but was subject to a political strategy of also distributing the developments in better-off districts. This is why it is possible to find scattered council blocks in the more affluent residential areas of the 13th, 18th and 19th districts, too. The construction of new council housing blocks was finished in 2004, when the last genuine council block was erected in the 23rd district. More recently, council housing has partially lost its former importance compared to cooperative housing (Novy *et al.* 2001). Some developments, mainly in working-class districts, acquired a bad reputation because of an accumulation of socio-economically marginalised residents and rising numbers of inhabitants with a migration background. For counterbalancing a rising conflict potential, the mediation organisation Wohnpartner was entrusted to maintain professional conflict management.

The rental market is subdivided into different segments that might serve as an indicator of welfare interventions, just as the structural changes reveal not only changes in housing policies in Vienna but also the shift marked by the retreat of welfare interventions. Between 2001 and 2011 about 73,000 apartments were added to the housing stock, paralleling the additional 164,000 residents within the same time span. However, the structure of housing developers has changed. When the city took a step back from its role as housing developer, the number of public housing apartments stalled. Housing associations have taken over, constructing about 24,000 apartments within the last ten years. The slight commodification and privatisation of Vienna's housing market is indicated by 36,000 apartments having been built between 2001 and 2011 by the private sector. At the time of the register-based survey in 2011, 23 per cent of the entire housing stock in Vienna was public housing, and 15 per cent of the apartments were operated by housing associations. About 60 per cent of the apartments in Vienna belong to the private sector. In recent discourses on social inequalities in cities (see for example Musterd and Ostendorf 1998) privatisation and a withdrawal of the welfare state is associated with the right to buy and an increase of home ownership. For Vienna a respective restructuring of the housing market can only partially be confirmed. Even though it has featured in political discourse and is endorsed by the Conservative Party, the right to buy remains an option only available to tenants in housing complexes built by housing associations. Even if the total number of owner-occupied buildings has increased, the share in the entire housing stock has more or less remained the same. In relative figures an increase of home ownership cannot be confirmed between 2001 and 2011.

Welfare policies in Austria encompass a complex spectrum of individual benefits and interventions in the housing market. At the federal level, the changing role of the state since the 1970s was marked by lifting rent controls that had been in effect since 1917 for the old housing stock, and a 16 per cent cut of federal housing subsidies in the mid-1980s. However, the territorial fragmentation of social housing policies at the federal level of the nine provinces of Austria enabled the City of Vienna – which has had the legal status of a province since 1921 – to set its own criteria for housing policies (see Matznetter 2002). The following issues mark the city's welfare interventions in the housing market and changing housing policies:

- A strong public housing sector, of one-fifth of the housing stock, instigated the city's withdrawal as a housing developer in the 1980s. At the turn of the millennium, the ambitious public housing programme in Vienna silently faded out. The city handed this task over to private developers and housing associations, marking a political restructuring from corporatist urban governance to managerial governance and public–private partnerships. However, rent subsidies were retained and the construction of apartments is still subsidised by the city. Sixty per cent of all Viennese households live in subsidised apartments (public and cooperative sector) (Förster 2002) (see also above).
- Maintaining entitlements and letting policies for public housing: access to public housing apartments in Vienna is determined by income levels, the housing needs of families and citizenship. Residents are allowed to stay in their flats even after their income has increased considerably. Access to city-owned public housing apartments was limited to Austrian citizens between 1971 and 1991 and citizens of the EU-15 at the time of the census in 2001. However, in January 2006 foreign citizens were also granted admission.
- Subsidised urban renewal: in the mid-1980s, a specific model of 'soft' urban renewal was developed involving public–private partnerships. The goal was to maintain and improve the historic building fabric of the substandard working-class apartments through the creation of affordable, high-standard dwellings but inhibit any resulting gentrification. More than 210,000 apartments were renovated, about one-quarter of the entire apartment stock in the city.
- Steering market prices by enhancing the production of housing: faced with an increasing demand for housing, the city launched ambitious housing development projects in the inner city areas as well as on the outskirts of the city. These incentives are aimed at increasing the total number of apartments and to balance supply and demand in the housing sector, which eventually should mediate the increase of rents and market prices for owner-occupied apartments. However, due to the fiscal crisis, funding to support the construction of new homes has become scarce. The gap between housing supply and demand is widening.

Societal change and spatial developments in the context of immigration

Vienna's population is growing rapidly, whereby the largest contribution to this increase is made by immigration and there are strong interrelations between segregation by level of education and immigration. A considerable proportion of immigrants (for example, Turks, former Yugoslavs) are poorly educated. Migrants are no longer socio-economically marginal groups but constitute an essential element of the local population and the Viennese economy.

Table 4.4 shows how the growth rate for foreign-born Viennese has been very unequally distributed among the different groups of origin. The growth of EU-14 and EU-12 largely exceeds the increase rate among migrants from the two traditional

Table 4.4 Population in Vienna by place of birth, 2001 and 2011

Place of birth	2001 Abs.	In %	2011 Abs.	In %	Change in %
Total population	1,550,123	100.0	1,714,227	100.0	+9.6
Austria	1,183,834	76.4	1,189,808	69.4	+0.5
Foreign born total	366,239	23.6	524,419	30.6	+30.2
EU-14[a]	41,772	2.7	63,438	3.7	+34.2
EU-12[b]	81,466	5.3	117,218	6.8	+30.5
Former Yugoslavia	124,812	8.1	153,181	8.9	+18.5
Turkey	47,321	3.1	66,343	3.9	+28.7
Other	70,918	4.6	124,239	7.2	+42.9

Source: Statistics Austria, Census 2001 and Register-based Census 2011, own calculation.

Notes:
[a] Austria, Belgium, Denmark, Finland, France, Germany, Greece, Ireland, Italy, Luxembourg, Netherlands, Portugal, Spain, Sweden.
[b] Bulgaria, Cyprus, Czech Republic, Estonia, Hungary, Latvia, Lithuania, Malta, Poland, Romania, Slovenia, Slovak Republic.

sending countries former Yugoslavia and Turkey. However in absolute numbers it is still the former Yugoslavia which tops the list of the countries of origin.

The indices of dissimilarity reflect relevant changes in the uneven distribution of the migrant population between 2001 and 2011 (see Table 4.5). A distinctive steady state is mirrored in the case of the residents from former Yugoslavia and Turkey: this finding contrasts with the marked dissimilarity of these migrant groups compared with the native Austrian residents. Since 2001 the index rates for both groups have declined (more in the case of former Yugoslavs), reflecting a more equal distribution. The pronounced dissimilarity of EU-14 and Turkish immigration reflects the EU-14 as an immigration flow with a considerably better socio-economic position than is the case with Turkish immigrants.

Segregation indices have risen in the case of the population which moved from EU countries, reflecting their privileged status in the housing market (see Table 4.6). The largest decline of index values was recorded for former Yugoslavians. The main causal factor for this is eligibility for public housing (since 1 January 2006), which provided the chance to move from substandard housing in working-class districts into better-equipped housing stock. Public housing is more or less evenly distributed in Vienna's whole urban space and can even be found in so-called 'bourgeois' districts. Thus, the proportion of Turkish and former Yugoslav citizens in stock of municipal authorities grew strongly (see Statistik Austria 2014).

The residential patterns of the migrant population are strongly dependent on the structure and opportunities in the housing market and economic resources.

Table 4.5 Dissimilarity index on the level of census tracts, population by place of birth, 2001 and 2011

	EU-14	EU-12	Former Yugoslavia	Turkey	Other
2001					
Austria	23.8	15.7	37.0	42.3	23.9
EU-14	–	22.3	40.0	48.4	24.8
EU-12		–	29.7	37.5	17.4
Former Yugoslavia			–	21.7	30.8
Turkey				–	37.6
2011					
Austria	27.3	19.2	30.9	37.4	21.3
EU-14	–	26.4	38.8	48.8	26.2
EU-12		–	20.1	31.8	16.9
Former Yugoslavia			–	22.3	26.2
Turkey				–	33.3

Source: Statistics Austria, Census 2001 and Register-based Census 2011, own calculation.

Note: For reasons of comparability, data protection and in order to avoid biases, the analysis on the level of census tracts (maps, indices of segregation and dissimilarity) starts out from a data set that only includes spatial units with values for both points in time and a total population of more than 50 persons for both 2001 and 2011. This affects less than 1% of the total population.

1 Austria, Belgium, Denmark, Finland, France, Germany, Greece, Ireland, Italy, Luxembourg, Netherlands, Portugal, Spain, Sweden.
2 Bulgaria, Cyprus, Czech Republic, Estonia, Hungary, Latvia, Lithuania, Malta, Poland, Romania, Slovenia, Slovak Republic.

Table 4.6 Segregation index on the level of census tracts, population by place of birth, 2001 and 2011

	2001	2011
Austria	24.1	20.9
EU-14	23.2	26.6
EU-12	12.4	14.9
Former Yugoslavia	34.6	27.9
Turkey	39.1	34.3
Other	20.9	17.9

Source: Statistics Austria, Census 2001 and Register-based Census 2011, own calculation.

Housing integration also refers to recent economic and social trends and the ongoing deregulation of the labour and housing market. The mapping-based analyses show that market barriers and accessibility rules have an enormous influence on ethnic segregation.

The segregation patterns of EU-14 immigrants are an illustrative example of privileged immigration (see Figure 4.5). A characteristic feature of segregation in Vienna is that it is often concentrated in smaller spatial units (statistical areas or

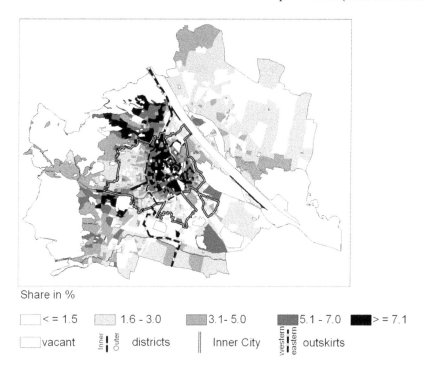

Share in %

| | <= 1.5   1.6 - 3.0   3.1- 5.0   5.1 - 7.0   > = 7.1

vacant   Inner / Outer districts   Inner City   western / eastern outskirts

Figure 4.5 Share of persons born in EU-14 in the total population, 2011.

Source: Statistics Austria, Register-based Census 2011, own calculation; Geometry: WIGEOGIS, GEO ZID.

Note: Classification of values based on 'natural breaks'.

groupings of them). Spatial large-scale segregation (ghettoisation) comparable to that found in UK or French cities is absent. The population is more or less mixed all over the whole urban space.

The majority of migrants from EU countries have settled in the classical 'bourgeois' housing areas in the inner districts (3, 4, 6, 7, 8, 9), as well as in the cottage areas of the north-west of Vienna's urban space and in the western parts of the 16th and 17th districts. The highest proportions can be found in the city centre, in Währing and Döbling and in the 2nd district, mainly in the centrally located and 'hip' Karmeliterviertel. Immigrants from 'old' EU member states still prefer a 'good address' in these western suburbs or directly in the historic old town.

The polarisation in Vienna's urban space is demonstrated by the segregation patterns of the former guest workers from the former Yugoslavian republics (see Figure 4.6). Settlement of these traditional guest workers can be seen in the working-class districts on both sides of the Belt. Many ex-Yugoslavians are residing in the western working-class districts (5, 12, 15, 16, 17) that directly border the middle-class neighbourhoods. Compared to a decade ago, the number of spatial units with higher proportions of former Yugoslavs has slightly decreased in the inner districts, whereas a diffusion process can be observed in the more peripheral parts of Vienna's western and southern districts, as well as in 21st and 22nd districts. This reflects the

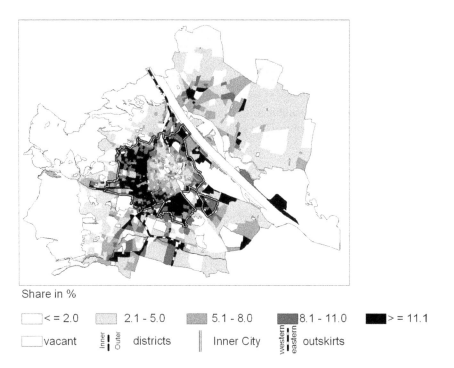

Share in %

☐ < = 2.0   ▨ 2.1 - 5.0   ▨ 5.1 - 8.0   ▨ 8.1 - 11.0   ■ > = 11.1

☐ vacant   Inner | Outer   districts   ‖ Inner City   western | eastern   outskirts

Figure 4.6 Share of persons born in former Yugoslavia in the total population, 2011.

Source: Statistics Austria, Register-based Census 2011, own calculation; Geometry: WIGEOGIS, GEO ZID.

Note: Classification of values based on 'natural breaks'.

movement of former Yugoslavs out of the private rental housing segment and into public and cooperative housing, which is more evenly distributed over the whole urban space. This is a consequence of the public housing sector becoming available to this group and their improved socio-economic position.

Structural differentiation of the city: factorial analysis

Data basis

The analysis is based on the 2001 census and the register-based census of 2011, allowing for a very detailed spatial differentiation. The smallest spatial unit in this analysis is the census district. The detailed analysis at this level implies limitations for the selection of indicators. Data reflecting the occupational structure according to ISCO classification are provided neither at the level of census district, nor at the level of municipal districts. For analysing socio-spatial differentiation the indicator of occupational structure had to be replaced by indicators of work force according to educational attainment (see Hatz 2009).

Selection of indicators

In order to identify structural differences between the areas of the city, a method is required that analyses the co-variation of relevant indicators that shape and reshape them, eliminates spurious correlations and identifies homogeneous areas as indicated by simultaneous variations of single-input variables. The first step in this analysis included the identification of relevant indicators characterising social inequality, the second step aimed to depict their spatial distribution and third, the individual features were combined to establish basic dimensions of segregation (see also the introduction of this book for more detail: Tammaru *et al.* 2016).

Factor analysis

Factor analysis was conducted for the data sets from 2001 and 2011, both at the level of census districts. For 2001, three dimensions were extracted and for 2011 four dimensions could be identified. The research design accounts for some limitations, primarily rooted in the availability of data provided by the censuses. Consequently, the selection of indicators was limited by the requirement for the dataset to have a common denominator, i.e. the availability of each of the indicators for both points in time. Overall, nineteen indicators referring to educational attainment, migration and features of the housing market were selected (see Table 4.7). The selection of the indicators, calculated as percentage values, was intended to avoid closed number relationships (see Hatz 2009).

The socio-economic dimension

In the last decade, socio-economic features have become more prominent in explaining patterns of socio-spatial segregation. Whereas in 2001 only 1.8 per cent

Table 4.7 Socio-economic dimension – factor loadings, 2001 and 2011

2001	2011
Explained variance: 1.8%	Explained variance: 24.3%
+ **Public housing**	+ **Public housing**
+ **Unemployed**	+ **Unemployed**
+ Unskilled workforce	+ **Unskilled workers**
	+ Apprentices
	+ Turkish origin
+ *Apprentices*	
	+ *Turkish citizens*
– Housing association	– *EU-14 citizens*
apartments	– *High school workers*
– *Vocational school*	– *Apartments built before 1919*
apprentices	
– Homeownership	EU-14 origin
– High school workforce	– **Highly skilled workers**

Factor loadings
positive (+): negative (–):
> = +**0.70** < = –**0.70**
< +0.70 – > = +0.50 > = –0.70 – < = –0.50
< +*0.50* – > = +*0.30* > = *0.50* – < = –*0.30*

Source: Data of Statistics Austria, Census 2001 and Register-based Census 2011, own calculation

of the variance of the included variables could be explained by the socio-economic dimension, in 2011 24.3 per cent of the variance of the variables could be explained by it. The factor identifying the socio-economic dimension is marked by a polarisation of neighbourhoods, characterised by a concentration of highly skilled workers indicated by negative factor loadings and neighbourhoods dominated by public housing. Within the last decade a clear accentuation of the features characterising the social mix of neighbourhoods dominated by public housing apartments can be identified. In 2001, unskilled workers and apprentices were loosely connected to public housing (see Figure 4.7). In 2011 those strata have become more confined to public housing neighbourhoods. As indicated by the indices of dissimilarity, the 'social' distance between the residential areas of highly skilled workers and of workers holding high school diplomas has decreased. Spatially they 'mix' with the highly skilled workers (see Figure 4.8). High negative factor values indicating the residential areas of the upper social strata show a clear sectoral pattern, stretching from the western inner-city districts to the western outskirts of the city, even though they have spread out of the inner-city districts and the nineteenth-century housing stock. Due to changes in the eligibility criteria, the number of immigrants from Turkey is definitely increasing in public housing neighbourhoods. As expected, neighbourhoods made up of public housing characterise the eastern and southern outskirts of the city.

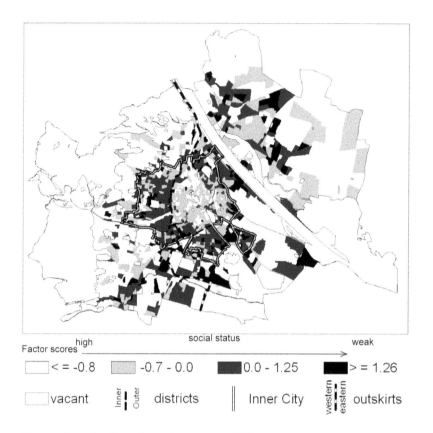

Figure 4.7 Social dimension – factor scores, 2001.

Source: Data of Statistics Austria, Census 2001, own calculation; Geometry: WIGEOGIS, GEO ZID.

Note: Classification of values based on 'natural breaks'.

The ethnic dimension

This factor describes the 'traditional' ethnic dimension and characterises census districts with above-average shares of substandard dwellings and residents from the former Yugoslavia and Turkey. Excluded from public housing until 2006, they were concentrated in residential areas dominated by affordable, substandard dwellings built before 1919 (see Figure 4.9). According to the notions of social area analysis, the spatial distribution shows a more clustered pattern. For 2001 this factor is characterised by high loadings of immigrants from former Yugoslavia and Turkey, who still concentrate in the former working-class substandard apartments in the outer districts of the inner city (see Table 4.8). Obviously due to the criteria regulating access to those apartments, these immigrants have to turn to the free rental market characteristic of the inner-city districts as indicated by high-factor values (see Figure 4.10).

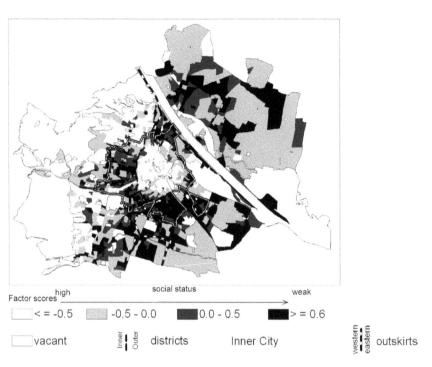

Factor scores

high ——————— social status ——————— weak

☐ < = -0.5   ☐ -0.5 - 0.0   ■ 0.0 - 0.5   ■ > = 0.6

☐ vacant   Inner | Outer districts   Inner City   western | eastern outskirts

Figure 4.8 Social dimension – factor scores, 2011.

Source: Data of Statistics Austria, Register-based Census 2011, own calculation; Geometry: WIGEOGIS, GEO ZID.

Note: Classification of values based on 'natural breaks'.

Table 4.8 Ethnic dimension – factor loadings, 2001 and 2011

2001	2011
Explained variance: 6.3%	Explained variance: 13.0%
+ **Substandard apartments**	+ **Substandard apartments**
+ **Ex-Yugoslavian origin**	+ **Ex-Yugoslavian origin**
+ **Ex-Yugoslavian citizens**	
+ **Turkish citizens**	
+ **Turkish origin**	
+ Unskilled workforce	
+ Apartments built before 1919	+ Apartments built before 1919
	+ *Ex-Yugoslavia-citizens*
– Public-housing apartments	– Public-housing apartments

Source: Data of Statistics Austria, Census 2001 and Register-based Census 2011, own calculation.

Notes: **Factor loadings**
positive (+): negative (–):
> = **+0.70** < = **–0.70**
< +0.70 – > = +0.50 > = –0.70 – < = –0.50
< +0.50 – > = +0.30 > = 0.50 – < = –0.30

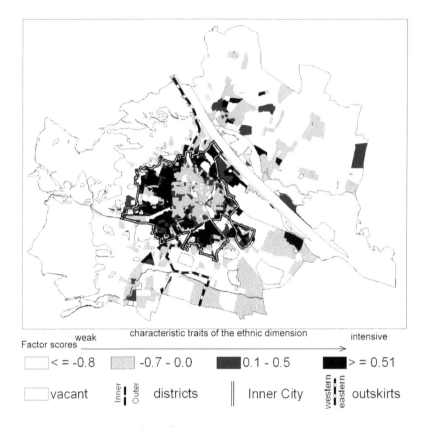

weak   characteristic traits of the ethnic dimension   intensive

Factor scores

☐ < = -0.8   ▨ -0.7 - 0.0   ◼ 0.1 - 0.5   ◼ > = 0.51

☐ vacant   Inner⎮Outer districts   ‖ Inner City   western⎮eastern outskirts

Figure 4.9 Ethnic dimension – factor scores, 2001.

Source: Data of Statistics Austria, Census 2001, own calculation; Geometry: WIGEOGIS, GEO ZID.

Note: Classification of values based on 'natural breaks'.

The dimension of EU immigration

This dimension is characterised by neighbourhoods preferred by newly arrived immigrants from the EU (see Table 4.9). Dwellings in the older stock of the inner-city obviously provide homes for immigrants from the EU. In this context the 'exclusionary' character of social housing for immigrants becomes visible. Recent immigrants have to turn to the private rental market characteristic of the inner-city districts (see Figure 4.11) as indicated by high factor values. In the decade 2001–2011 this dimension was split up due to new immigrants residing in the former working-class areas in the outer districts of the inner city, or concentrated in residential areas which are traditionally less typical of a population with an immigrant background (see Figure 4.12).

The preference for upscale, inner-district neighbourhoods by immigrants from the EU-12 is supported by the dimension of a 'new EU middle class' (see Table 4.10). It indicates a negative association between immigration from the EU to areas that have

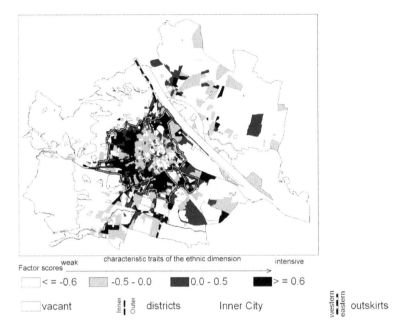

Factor scores weak   characteristic traits of the ethnic dimension   intensive

☐ < = -0.6   ▨ -0.5 - 0.0   ▨ 0.0 - 0.5   ■ > = 0.6

☐ vacant   Inner | Outer districts   Inner City   western | eastern outskirts

Figure 4.10 Ethnic dimension – factor scores, 2011.

Source: Data of Statistics Austria, Register-based Census 2011, own calculation; Geometry: WIGEOGIS, GEO ZID.

Note: Classification of values based on 'natural breaks'.

Table 4.9 EU immigration dimension – factor loadings, 2001 and 2011

2001	*2011*
explained variance: 4.6%	explained variance: 15.5%
+ **EU-14 origin**	+ **EU-12 citizens**
+ **EU-14 citizens**	+ **EU-14 citizens**
+ **Highly skilled workforce**	
	+ **Turkish citizens**
+ Apartments built before 1919	+ **Ex-Yugoslavian citizens**
+ *EU-12 origin*	
– Housing association apartments.	
– **Apprentices**	
– **Vocational school workforce**	

Source: Data of Statistics Austria, Census 2001 and Register-based Census 2011, own calculation.

Notes: **Factor loadings**
positive (+): negative (–):
> = **+0.70** < = **–0.70**
< +0.70 – > = +0.50 > = –0.70 – < = –0.50
< +0.50 – > = +0.30 > = 0.50 – < = –0.30

Table 4.10 Dimension of new EU-middle classes – factor loadings, 2011

2001	*2011*
Explained variance: 4.6%	Explained variance: 12.3%
+ EU-14 origin	+ EU-14 origin
+ EU-14 citizens	+ EU-12 origin
+ Highly skilled labor force	
+ Apartments built before 1919	+ Apartments built before 1919
	+ *Highly skilled workers*
+ EU-12 origin	
	– Vocational school workers
	– Housing association apartments
– Housing association apartments	
– Apprentices	
– Vocational school workforce	

Source: Data of Statistics Austria, Census 2001 and Register-based Census 2011, own calculation.

Notes: **Factor loadings**
positive (+):   negative (–):
> = +0.70   **< = –0.70**
< +0.70 – > = +0.50   > = –0.70 – < = –0.50
< +0.50 – > = +0.30   > = 0.50 – < = –0.30

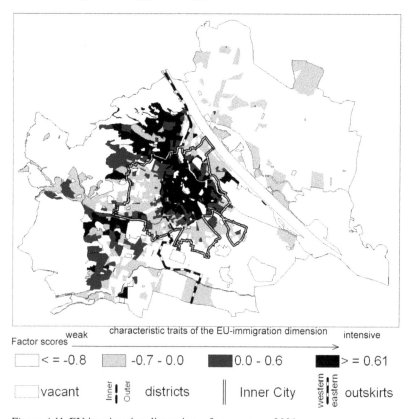

Figure 4.11 EU immigration dimension – factor scores, 2001.

Source: Data of Statistics Austria, Census 2001, own calculation; Geometry: WIGEOGIS, GEO ZID.

Note: Classification of values based on 'natural breaks'.

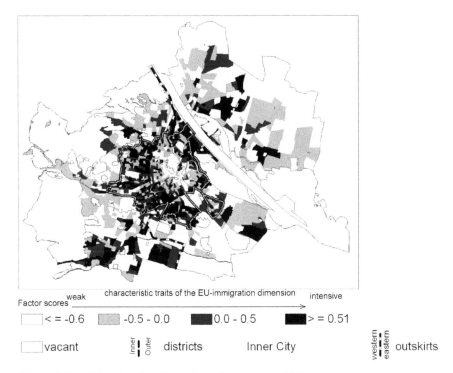

Factor scores weak characteristic traits of the EU-immigration dimension intensive

☐ < = -0.6   ☐ -0.5 - 0.0   ■ 0.0 - 0.5   ■ > = 0.51

☐ vacant   Inner | Outer districts   Inner City   western | eastern outskirts

Figure 4.12 EU immigration dimension – factor scores, 2011.

Source: Data of Statistics Austria, Register-based Census 2011, own calculation; Geometry: WIGEOGIS, GEO ZID.

Note: Classification of values based on 'natural breaks'.

a higher share of apartments built by housing associations, serving to underline the exclusionary character of these apartments for those migrant groups, who then turn to neighbourhoods with a higher social status (see Figure 4.13), as indicated by the association with highly skilled workers in these dimensions in 2001 and 2011.

In the context of socio-economic segregation, these dimensions reveal that even workers with vocational school qualifications are seemingly confined to neighbourhoods dominated by apartments built by housing associations. In contrast to the new immigrants from the EU, those having completed vocational school have not turned to inner-city neighbourhoods characterised by high numbers of highly skilled workers. These dimensions point to the modification of segregation by immigration, and respective criteria of accessibility to the social housing sector as a specific feature of socio-spatial patterns in Vienna.

Conclusion

The analyses of the structural differentiation of the Austrian capital were based on the four relevant indicators of occupational structure, education, immigration

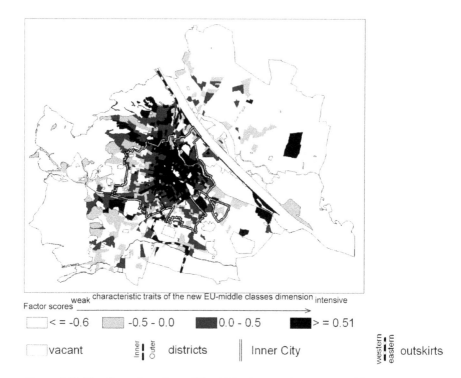

Figure 4.13 The dimension of new EU middle classes – factor scores, 2011.

Source: Data of Statistics Austria, Census 2001, own calculation; Geometry: WIGEOGIS, GEO ZID.

Note: Classification of values based on 'natural breaks'.

and housing and take into account the marked relevance of welfare interventions in Vienna. Although the occupational transformation indicates a disproportionate growth rate for professionals and service and sales workers, this only partially supports a shift to a polarised society. It is important to note that the trend towards polarisation is modified by the overlapping cycle of deindustrialisation that has not yet been completed in Vienna. A clear shift can be found in the number of professionals, nearly doubling in the last ten years. As the notions of a polarisation of urban societies are usually strongly related to a disproportional growth of unskilled workers, this generalised statement has to be modified in the Viennese case. Here the labour market shows a disproportional growth rate in service and sales workers between 2001 and 2011, but with respect to their educational skills, these groups cannot be classified as unskilled workers at all, as 68 per cent have attained specific educational skills.

In Vienna, housing market structures and welfare policies are dominant factors determining patterns of socio-economic segregation. From an international perspective, the Austrian model has been resilient in stabilising housing markets and delivering (new) quality housing, though rent levels have recently been rising rapidly. The dissimilarity index-based analyses reflect changes in the uneven distribution of the migrant population. The most pronounced dissimilarity concerns EU-14 immigration and the Turkish population. This reflects the EU-14 as a mainly socio-economic elite-dominated immigration flow with a better labour and housing market position than the former guest workers. Since 2001 the index rates have shown a growing equality in the distribution of the population from Turkey and former Yugoslavia. It can be noted that there was an ongoing process of moving out of working-class districts and a distribution over larger parts of the city space.

It has been shown that socio-economic features have become more prominent in explaining patterns of socio-spatial segregation. The change is marked by a polarisation of neighbourhoods and an accentuation of the features characterising the social mix of neighbourhoods dominated by public housing apartments. In 2011, people in the lower qualification strata had become more confined to public housing neighbourhoods, perhaps reflecting some kind of residualisation of this segment. Nevertheless, this sector takes on an important compensatory function which becomes increasingly significant in times of housing shortages and rapidly rising rents. The residential areas of the upper social strata show a clear sectoral pattern, stretching from the western inner-city districts to the western outskirts of the city, even though they have spread out of the inner-city districts and the nineteenth-century housing stock. New immigrants usually have to turn to the private rental market that is characteristic of the inner-city districts. In this context the almost 'exclusionary' impact of social housing in Vienna on immigrants after a longer stay (at least two years and varying time on a waiting list) becomes visible. In upper-class inner-city neighbourhoods, upper-class residents are supplemented by a new middle class made up of immigrants from the EU-12.

Notes

1 See http://www.statistik.at/web_de/statistiken/bevoelkerung/demographische_prognosen/bevoelkerungs.prognosen/.
2 The transition from traditional census to register data marked a fundamental change in Austrian statistics. The reasons for this shift were financial considerations, the faster availability of data and in shorter intervals between data collection which had previously been too long (ten years).
3 See http://www.statistik.at/web_de/statistiken/bevoelkerung/bevoelkerungsstruktur/bevoelkerung_nach_staatsangehoerigkeit_geburtsland/, accessed 05-11-2014.
4 The 'Gürtel' is a broad boulevard with an extremely high volume of traffic, air and noise pollution that is the clear border between the 'inner' and the 'outer' districts dominated by older private-owned apartment housing stock from the 'Founder's Period' and by social rental housing.
5 So-called 'substandard', without running water, toilet or bathroom.
6 See http://www.statistik.at/web_de/statistiken/wohnen_und_gebaeude/bestand_an_gebaeuden_und_wohnungen/wohnungen/index.html.

References

Amann, W 2010, *Lenkungseffekte der Wohnbauförderung* [Steering effects of housing subsidies], Presentation for the Symposium "Europäisches Sozialmodell – der österreichische Wohnbau als Best Practice?", 05-11-2010 [The European social model – the Austrian housing sector as best practice?]. Available online: http://www.fgw.at/aktuell/pdf/amann.pdf. Accessed 18 April 2015.

Aufhauser, E, Fischer, M M and Schöndorfer, E 1991, 'The Vienna housing market: Structure, problems, and politics' in *Housing market and institutions: An international comparison,* eds B Hårsman and J M Quigley, Kluwer, Boston, Dortrecht, London, pp. 235–281.

Czasny, K, Bständig, G and Hajek, J 2004, *Internationaler Vergleich wohnbezogener Transfers* [An international comparison of housing-related transfers], Studie der SRZ Stadt- und Regionalforschung im Rahmen der Bundeswohnbauforschung und der Wohnbauforschung des Landes Wien [Study of SRZ urban and regional research for federal housing research and Vienna housing research] SRZ, Vienna.

Eigner, P, Matis, H and Resch, A 1999, Sozialer Wohnbau in Wien: Eine historische Bestandsaufnahme [Subsidized housing construction in Vienna: A historical inventory] Jahrbuch des Vereins für die Geschichte der Stadt Wien 1999, 49–100. Available online: http://www.demokratiezentrum.org/fileadmin/media/pdf/matis_wohnbau.pdf. Accessed 18 April 2015

Esping-Andersen, G 1993, 'The comparative macro-sociology of welfare' in *Social exchange and welfare development,* ed. L Moreno, CSIC, Madrid, pp. 123–136.

Fainstein, S 2001, *The city builders: Property development in New York and London, 1980–2000.* Studies in Government and Public Policy, University Press of Kansas, Lawrence.

Fassmann, H and Hatz, G 2004, 'Fragmentiert Stadt? Sozialräumliche Struktur und Wandel in Wien 1991–2001' [Fragmented city? Socio-spatial structure and change in Vienna 1991–2001], *Mitteilungen der Österreichischen Geographischen Gesellschaft* (MIÖG) 146, 61–92.

Fassmann, H and Hatz, G 2007, 'The Austrian case study – Social inequalities in the Vienna metropolitan region' in *Social inequalities in urban areas and globalization: The case of central Europe,* ed. Hungarian Academy of Science, Centre of Regional Studies, Discussion Paper, based on the results of the project 'Urban areas, socio-spatial inequalities and conflicts – the socio-spatial factors of European competitiveness', Pecs, pp. 51–76.

Förster, W 2002, *Sozialer Wohnungsbau – innovative Architektur: Harry Seidler Wohnpark Neue Donau Wien* [Social housing – Innovative architecture: Harry Seidler housing park New Danube Vienna], Prestel, München.

Giffinger, R 1998, 'Segregation in Vienna: Impacts of market barriers and rent regulations' *Urban Studies* 35(10), 1791–1812.

Giffinger, R and Wimmer, H 2002, 'Segregation von ausländischer Wohnbevölkerung als Barriere der sozialen Integration?' [Segregation of foreign residential population as a barrier to social integration?] in *Zuwanderung und Segregation* [Immigration and Segregation], eds H Fassmann, J Kohlbacher and U Reeger, Drava, Klagenfurt, pp. 209–231.

Hamnett, C 2003, *Unequal city: London in the global arena,* Routledge, London.

Hatz, G 2009, 'Features and dynamics of socio-spatial differentiation in Vienna and the Vienna metropolitan region' *Tijdschrift voor Economische en Sociale Geografie* 100, 485–501.

Kohlbacher, J and Reeger, U 2007, 'Die Dynamik ethnischer Wohnviertel in Wien – Resultate einer Gebäudeerhebung 1981 und 2005' [The dynamics of ethnic housing areas in Vienna – results of a building-stock data collection 1981 and 2005], *Mitteilungen der Österreichischen Geographischen Gesellschaft* (MIÖG) 149, 7–28.

Kohlbacher, J and Reeger, U 2008, Staatsbürgerschaftsbonus beim Wohnen? Eine empirische Analyse der Unterschiede zwischen eingebürgerten und nichteingebürgerten Zuwanderern/-innen hinsichtlich ihrer Wohnsituation in Wien [Citizenship bonus in housing? An empirical analysis of the differences in the housing situation of naturalised and non-naturalised immigrants] ISR-Forschungsbericht 35, ÖAW Printing House, Vienna.

Lichtenberger, E, Fassmann H and Mühlgassner, D 1987, *Stadtentwicklung und dynamische Faktorialökologie* [Urban development and dynamic factorial ecology], Beiträge zur Stadt-und Regionalforschung 8, ÖAW Printing House, Vienna.

Matznetter, W 2002, 'Social housing policy in a conservative welfare state: Austria as an example' *Urban Studies* 39(2), 265–282.

Musterd, S 2014, 'Public housing for whom? Experiences in an era of mature neo-liberalism: The Netherlands and Amsterdam' *Housing Studies* 29(4), 467–484.

Musterd, S. and Ostendorf, W 1998b, 'Segregation, polarization and social exclusion in metropolitan areas' in *Urban segregation and the welfare state: Inequality and exclusion in western cities,* eds S Musterd and W Ostendorf, Routledge, Taylor & Francis Group, London and New York, pp. 1–14.

Musterd, S and Van Kempen, R 2000, *The spatial dimensions of urban social exclusion and integration: A European comparison,* Universiteit van Amsterdam, Amsterdam.

Novy, A V, Jäger J and Hamedinger A 2001, 'The end of Red Vienna. Recent ruptures and continuities in urban governance' *European Urban and Regional Studies* 8(2), 131–144.

Reinprecht, C and Levy-Vroelant, C 2008, 'Housing the poor in Paris and Vienna: The changing understanding of "social" ' in *Social Housing in Europe II: A review of policies and outcomes,* eds K Scanlon and C Whitehead, London School of Economics and Political Science, London, pp. 209–224.

Sassen, S 1996, *Metropolen des Weltmarkts. Die neue Rolle der Global Cities* [Metropolises of the global market. The new role of global cities], Campus Verlag, Frankfurt/Main.

Schopper, M and Hansely, H 1999, 'Wien im Aufbruch' *Geographische Rundschau* 10, 529–534. Available at http://www.demokratiezentrum.org/fileadmin/media/pdf/aufbruch_schopper_hansely.pdf. Accessed 9 May 2015.

Stadtentwicklung Wien (ed) 2005, *Stadtentwicklungsplan 2005 – STEP 05: Handlungsfelder der Stadtentwicklung: Wohnen* [Urban development plan 2005. STEP 05: Fields of action of Vienna's urban development]. Available at https://www.wien.gv.at/stadtent wicklung/strategien/step/step05/download/pdf/step-kapitel4-3.pdf. Accessed 18 April 2015.

Statistik Austria (ed.) 2014, *Registerbasierte Statistiken Wohnsituation (RS) Kalenderjahr 2014. Registerzählung 2011 – Gebäude und* Wohnungszählung [Register-based statistics housing situation (RS) 2014. Register census 2011 – building and housing census]. Schnellbericht 10.13, Vienna.

Tammaru, T, Musterd, S, van Ham, M and Marcińczak, S, 2016, 'A multi-factor approach to understanding socio-economic segregation in European capital cities' in *Socio-economic segregation in European capital cities: East meets West,* eds T Tammaru, S Marcińczak, M van Ham and S Musterd, Routledge, London.

van Kempen, R and Murie, A 2009, 'The new divided city: Changing patterns in European cities' *Tijdschrift voor economische en sociale geografie* 100(4), 377–398.

Walks, RA 2001, 'The social ecology of the post-fordist/global city? Economic restructuring and socio-spatial polarization in the Toronto urban region' *Urban Studies* 38(3), 407–447.

5 Widening gaps

Segregation dynamics during two decades of economic and institutional change in Stockholm

Roger Andersson and Anneli Kährik

Abstract

Sweden has had a long tradition in providing high-quality and affordable housing for all. From the early 1990s, Swedish housing policy has shifted radically: the housing market regulation was reduced and market principles were introduced, investment subsidies were mostly abolished and the percentage of municipality-owned public housing has dropped, especially in the Stockholm region. In the context of these profound changes, this chapter maps the residential socio-spatial outcomes of the structural changes in Swedish society in general and in the Stockholm housing market in particular. For the 1990–2010 period we study how long-term changes in social inequality, as well as neoliberal shifts in housing policy, have modified socio-spatial formations and residential segregation. We look both at the socio-economic and ethnic dimensions of this changing residential landscape by applying data from a complete set of individual longitudinal register-based data of all residents living in Stockholm. The results show that over the last two decades, socio-economic residential segregation has increased in Stockholm. Concentrations of low-income groups have become denser and such 'pockets of poverty' are located mostly in and around neighbourhoods that already displayed some social decline in 1990, mainly large housing estates from the 1960s and 1970s. We also found a 'double sorting' process whereby low-income natives tend to live in other areas than low-income non-Western immigrants.

Introduction

From the 1930s to the early 1990s in Sweden, public housing was a key element of the Social Democrats' plan to construct a housing system that would ensure high-quality, affordable housing for all (Elander 1991). Having traditionally strongly emphasized tenure neutrality, put into practice not least by substantial subsidies of housing investments of all tenure types, since the early 1990s, Swedish housing policy has shifted radically, first offering fewer and more targeted subsidies for specific groups and depressed residential areas (Whitehead and Turner 2002), and later offering almost no investment subsidies at all. In the early 1990s, substantial cuts in the state budget due to the unfolding deep economic crisis were believed necessary by almost all political parties in parliament. Liberalization trends in the housing markets of other European welfare states became paradigms for deregulating the housing sector in Sweden as well. Meanwhile, the earlier key role of public housing was contested, and its privileged position has been eroded in the wake of incremental changes in the regulatory system (Andersson 2014). Municipally owned public housing as a percentage of Swedish housing stock has declined from 23 per cent to 18 per cent over the 1990–2010 period, and the sector now caters to the housing needs of approximately 14 per cent of the population. This might not be viewed as a very dramatic decline, but, as we shall demonstrate later, the reduction has been much more profound in the capital region, Stockholm.

Although welfare state transfers still play an important role in housing allocation and residential outcomes, housing construction and distribution are now much more based on market principles. Housing policy per se is just one contextual factor that affects the housing market and households' disposable income development and hence their housing opportunities. Broader economic trends and labour market restructuring have affected income distributions as well as put pressure on state revenues and expenditures. This chapter maps the residential socio-spatial outcomes of the structural changes in Swedish society in general and in the Stockholm housing market in particular over the two decades from 1990 to 2010. Stockholm is a good example, illustrating the spatial manifestations of structural shifts in Swedish society for several reasons. Most housing tenure conversions have occurred in Sweden's biggest cities, and due to a growing population in Stockholm in recent decades, growing supply and demand imbalances in the housing market have speeded up the dynamics of the housing marketization process. The present analyses focus on Stockholm's built-up area, i.e., the continuously populated urban area, but we also include several municipalities functionally integrated into the capital city but formally outside a strict technical definition of the built-up area.[1] Although gradual changes in the housing policy had started even before 1990, the process accelerated in the early 1990s during times of economic crisis. The time span under investigation includes the period of social transformation during the economic depression of the early 1990s, as well as the later period of economic recovery and growth in the 2000s. Unlike in most other European countries, the recent financial crisis has so far had relatively minor effects on the Swedish economy.

The study has two unique features. First, we observe a long-term time horizon starting in 1990, the approximate start of the neoliberal reforms of housing and welfare policies (Hedin *et al.* 2012), and extending to 2010. We study how long-term changes in social inequality, as well as neoliberal shifts in housing policy, have modified socio-spatial formations by considering whether residential segregation has increased and, if so, how. We intend not only to describe the changes but also to understand structural processes that have affected the spatial pattern. Second, our focus on the socio-economic dimension of the changing residential landscape will be complemented by analysis of the ethnic dimension and of how these dimensions relate to each other. We use a complete set of individual longitudinal register-based data (taken from the national GeoSweden database at Uppsala University's Institute for Housing and Urban Research), in which all residents living in Stockholm in 1990 and/or 2000 and/or 2010 are included. We apply the small-area market statistics (SAMS) neighbourhood coding scheme as the geographical basis of our study, and use several index-based measures to characterize and summarize changes in residential pattern.

Underpinnings of residential segregation

Socio-spatial residential segregation refers to the relative separation of residential population categories from each other, characterizing the extent to which social groups are unevenly distributed across space. Researchers in the field normally focus on urban settings – in particular, on metropolitan cities. Residential sorting in urban space has been analysed by employing various categorizations of residential groups. Much research emphasizes the socio-economic dimension (*social class*), assuming that the sorting of households over neighbourhoods obviously occurs in a market in which economic resources strongly influence the housing choices that households can make. Another major body of literature is more occupied with *race* (more commonly in the USA) and/or *ethnicity* (more commonly in Europe). Here, the idea is traditionally that having shared attributes, such as language, religion and cultural habits, makes people identify with one another and form groups that become an important part of individuals' identity and sense of belonging. Over the last few decades, researchers have also stressed that groups can be constructed from outside, as a means to exclude certain categories and curtail their opportunities by stigmatization and discrimination. Finally, some segregation researchers identify sorting across family types and age as *demographic* segregation, but this aspect has received much less attention in empirical work. It is almost always the case that all three of the above dimensions interrelate so that, for example, what seems to be ethnic segregation need not have 'ethnic' explanations but could result from the variation in demographic and social class composition across ethnic categories (Andersson 2006, 2012; Finney and Simpson 2008). For example, recently arrived refugees are normally economically poor and predominantly young, giving them a subordinate position in the housing competition, with the result that they tend to be concentrated in less attractive parts of a city. We thus argue that all three dimensions should ideally be taken into account when trying to understand and explain segregation patterns and processes.

Spatial categorization is equally or perhaps even more problematic than is the grouping of population categories. How we divide space determines the patterns we can discern, and although segregation researchers are very aware of this, most have little choice but to accept the spatial categories used in official statistics, typically administrative units such as voting districts, postal code areas or larger administrative city districts. The range of geographies applied in empirical research also makes it difficult to compare levels of segregation across cities and countries (Musterd *et al.* 1998).

When presenting segregation dynamics over time, however, it is worth emphasizing that, while change in segregation patterns can be due to residential mobility across neighbourhoods, it can also be due to social mobility of *in situ* neighbourhood populations. Peoples' incomes do change over time, so income segregation can consequently change without migration. Other individual attributes, such as ethnicity, can of course also change in that self-identification can change, but the way we measure ethnicity in this study (using country-of-birth data) means that a neighbourhood's ethnic composition changes primarily due to migration to, from and within the region (see Andersson 2013).

Identifying segregation and change in segregation patterns thus relies on definitions of social categories and geographical space, but an important research question remains to be addressed: what produces segregation? One approach to understanding the processes influencing segregation dynamics could broadly be called 'structural' (or, sometimes, 'institutional'), as it pays attention to how a city is built and politically managed. Here, issues concerning the composition of housing types, housing tenure, housing costs and subsidies, accessibility, provision of services and other material aspects of neighbourhoods and housing are of key interest. These can change over time and are constantly affected by political decisions. The (neo)liberalization of the economy and of social welfare policy, including reduced public/social housing, reduced supply- and demand-side subsidies and widening wage and disposable income gaps (that have emerged, not least, in many formerly more regulated societies in Europe), can radically affect the social sorting and divisions in the housing market. Political decisions and urban/housing market transformations always vary between countries and localities and they must be seen as path dependent, embedded in specific national, regional and (historical) urban contexts (Arbaci 2007; Maloutas 2012).

In relation to our study of Stockholm, we should more specifically mention structural changes in the Stockholm economy that have resulted in important alterations in economic activities and in the income structure, as well as political decisions leading to the conversion of much of the public housing stock into private rental and cooperative housing (Andersson and Magnusson Turner 2014). Another example is the abolishment of rent subsidies for new housing construction. All in all, a series of central and local political decisions have given more freedom to market forces to shape housing allocation and new housing construction, but they have also increased the cost to the consumer of housing, and increasing costs of building new housing are inevitably accompanied by increasing rents.

Data, definitions and classifications

We first constructed a longitudinal dataset from the Geosweden datasets[2] covering all residents who lived in Stockholm County in 1990 and/or 2000 and/or 2010. The individual attribute data (i.e., demographic, socio-economic and housing characteristics) were added for all three time points. We then narrowed our geographical region by importing information from a Statistics Sweden dataset concerning the delimitation of the built-up area in 2010. In addition to the 'official' Stockholm built-up area definition (stretching across parts of thirteen municipalities) we included three municipalities which are functionally highly integrated into the Stockholm region, i.e., Lidingö (D in Figure 5.1), Täby (F) and Södertälje (J). While Lidingö and Täby are especially interesting from a socio-economic view-point, as they include many high-income residents, Södertälje is included because of its important role as a major destination for refugee immigrants.

We will apply a geographical definition that divides the Stockholm built-up area in 1990 into approximately 655 neighbourhoods with an average of 2,100 inhabitants each. The SAMS neighbourhood coding scheme was used to place individuals in neighbourhoods. The same coding scheme will also be used for 2000 and 2010.

In the next step, we classified neighbourhoods according to geographic location and dominant housing type, resulting in four neighbourhood types: two inner-city neighbourhood types, i.e., the historical inner city and the inner suburbs (existing before the post-World War II construction of the metro system), and two outer-city neighbourhood types, i.e., those dominated by multifamily dwellings built during or shortly after the 1965–1974 'Million Programme' era (housing at least two-thirds of residents) and either mixed neighbourhoods or those heavily dominated by

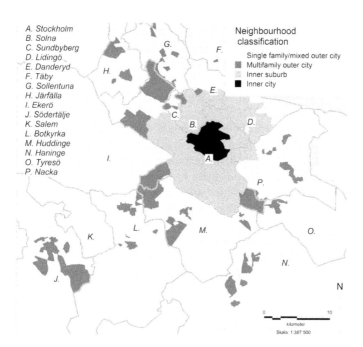

Figure 5.1 Stockholm built-up area map showing the locations of the four neighbourhood types.

Source: The Geosweden dataset, 2010. Map elements from Röda kartan (Lantmäteriverket) and shape file for SAMS areas (Statistics Sweden).

single-family housing – the latter having a dispersed settlement structure (see Figure 5.1). We use such a distinction as an analytical tool to let us better investigate and analyse the structural social and ethnic differences across urban space.

We construct socio-economic categories for measuring segregation based on the household based indicator 'equalised household disposable income'. Disposable income measures the effective demand that consumers can potentially exercise in various consumer markets. Disposable income is the sum of work income and the net value of positive (benefits/allowances) and negative (tax) transfers. Statistics Sweden offers an individualized breakdown of disposable household income, and we employ this individualized income measure when studying change in income segregation from 1990 to 2010.

Context for understanding change in residential segregation in Stockholm: population change, economic restructuring and policy shifts

Population change across neighbourhood segments

The total population of the Stockholm built-up area increased by 25 per cent, from about 1.4 million in 1990 to about 1.7 million by 2010. The inner suburbs and the single-family-housing-dominated outer-city areas are the most populous segments, having approximately 420,000 residents each in 1990, and adding another 131,000 and 111,100, respectively, by 2010. The two smaller segments also increased their populations but somewhat more slowly, meaning that the entire region under study has become more densely populated over the last twenty years. The proportion of foreign-born residents has increased in all four segments over the observation period, their overall share increasing from 16 per cent to 22 per cent. This in fact underestimates the ongoing 'visible' ethnic change: As all children born in the segments are registered as simply born in Sweden, much of the growth in the number of native-born Swedes comprises children of first-generation immigrants. Of all 0–19-year-olds living in the region in 2010 (i.e., added by birth since 1990), 27 per cent are either immigrants or children of immigrant parents.

The proportion of ethnic minorities obviously varies across the four neighbourhood types. It is by far highest in the outer-city multifamily housing segment, where the share increased from 27 per cent to 42 per cent from 1990 to 2010, and fairly similar and much lower in the three other segments, where it increased from 10 per cent to 20 per cent. Interestingly, the proportion of 'non-Western' immigrants, i.e., originating from countries outside of Europe, North America and Oceania, has increased markedly from 3.5 per cent to 9.4 per cent in the inner suburbs, where they account for almost half the population increase. Ethnic residential segregation is clearly an important feature of the region's population change, the influx of non-Western immigrants having affected all the segments. It should be noted, however, that the number of native-born Swedes in the multifamily outer-city segment has declined at the same time as the influx of new immigrants from non-Western countries continues to be high in this segment.

Economic restructuring and spatial inequalities

In many European countries, the recent financial crisis has had a large general impact on people's lives, not least in terms of employment and housing. In contrast, the recent crisis has not affected Sweden to the same extent, far less than did the crisis of the early 1990s, which led to a series of political decisions affecting housing costs and welfare systems. The economic crisis of the early 1990s clearly sparked the soon-to-come retrenchment of public spending on housing, but at the same time it negatively affected people's income and ability to spend money on housing. Importantly, it led to an increase in unemployment. The employment rate for people aged 20–64 years declined from 85 per cent in 1990 to 77 per cent in 2010, leaving more people dependent on social security systems that were tending to become less generous as a means to reduce state budget deficits. Unemployment quadrupled in less than two years, from 1991 to 1993, and has remained high ever since at approximately 8 per cent.

Stockholm's position in the European hierarchy of cities varies somewhat across different ranking criteria, and ranking institutes, but it is clear that the Swedish capital city is not part of the category of global cities but rather constitutes a second or third tier of larger European cities (Hall 2005). Like the rest of the Swedish economy, Stockholm's is strongly related to the global economy and has been growing faster than elsewhere in Sweden. Service production has long outweighed manufacturing, the latter accounting for about 10 per cent of total employment. Electronic industries, and firms associated with the 'new economy', play an essential role in the present industrial development, the telecommunication company Ericsson being the best-known example. As always, industrial restructuring has winners and losers and certain sectors have done more poorly than others. Most notable are the fast relative expansion of the financial sector (up from 17.6 to 26.1 percent of total employment) and the reduced importance of healthcare and social services (down from 18.7 per cent to 12.7 per cent). Noticeable is the growing gap in mean earnings between the sectors having the lowest and highest salaries (down from 93 per cent to 82 per cent of mean earnings for those employed in personal and cultural services and up from 126 per cent of mean earnings in 1990 to 140 per cent in 2010 for those working in the financial and business service sector).

The restructuring of the Stockholm economy is one factor underlying the increasing polarization across income groups. Not only is a smaller proportion of the workforce employed, leading to more people having very low levels of work income, but the income gap has increased even among those having a foothold in the labour market.

An important reason for this widening income gap is certainly labour market restructuring, but politically motivated tax decisions have also played an essential role. Sweden abolished the inheritance tax in 2005, and the change of government in 2006 resulted in a series of income tax cuts for working people and a radical property tax reform, in particular, reducing costs for homeowners of properties with high taxation assessments. In addition, the role of capital income has increased and high-income households in particular often have substantial revenues from invest-ment in stocks, housing market transactions, etc. (Statistics Sweden 2012b). Taken together, these changes have made the average Stockholm high-income earner richer and especially the non-working poor even poorer than before.

Income polarization naturally translates into spatial inequalities. Table 5.1 shows the work income quintile distribution across the four neighbourhood types presented above. Over time, the two poorest quintile groups have increased their concentration in the multifamily outer-city segment while losing ground in the inner city and, in the case of group 1, in the inner suburbs as well. The highest income groups are concentrated in the inner city and in the single family/mixed outer-city segments (though their presence in the latter has remained stable), while multifamily outer-city areas are clearly less favoured by them. The propor-tion of the highest-income group increased by 62 per cent in the inner city; the reverse occurred in the outer-city housing estates, where there was a substantial

Table 5.1 Work income quintile distribution across neighbourhood types, 1990, 2000 and 2010 (age 20–64 years)

Year	Work income quintile	Inner city	Inner suburb	Multifamily outer city	Single family/ mixed outer city	Total
1990	1	22.8	20.4	23.5	14.4	19.7
	2	18.5	19.7	22.5	19.2	20.0
	3	17.2	20.6	23.2	18.6	20.1
	4	19.3	20.2	19.4	20.8	20.1
	5	22.2	19.1	11.4	26.9	20.1
	Total	**100.0**	**100.0**	**100.0**	**100.0**	**100.0**
2000	1	19.1	19.2	28.3	14.3	19.8
	2	19.0	20.1	23.7	17.6	20.0
	3	15.7	20.1	22.8	20.5	20.0
	4	19.9	20.6	16.7	22.2	20.0
	5	26.3	20.0	8.4	25.3	20.1
	Total	**100.0**	**100.0**	**100.0**	**100.0**	**100.0**
2010	1	17.1	18.2	31.3	14.6	20.0
	2	18.8	20.2	24.6	16.8	20.0
	3	15.5	20.4	23.0	19.8	20.0
	4	20.9	21.1	14.8	22.3	20.0
	5	27.7	20.0	6.3	26.5	20.0
	Total	**100.0**	**100.0**	**100.0**	**100.0**	**100.0**
% of net change, 1990–2010	1	–2.1	27.5	55.8	18.1	28.1
	2	32.9	45.8	27.7	1.2	26.0
	3	17.0	41.6	15.8	23.9	26.0
	4	41.0	49.1	–11.1	24.2	25.9
	5	62.1	49.6	–35.5	14.2	25.8
	Total	**30.3**	**42.6**	**16.8**	**16.1**	**26.3**

Source: Geosweden datasets, 1990, 2000 and 2010.

increase (+56 per cent) in low-income residents and a reduction (−36 per cent) in the highest-income residents. Interestingly, when we compare these figures with distributions based on disposable income, the pattern remains largely the same, meaning that income redistribution due to the combined effect of tax and benefits seems to have a very limited effect on the housing allocation pattern across our roughly defined neighbourhood types.

Housing policy transformation and social segmentation

According to the broad institutional categorization applied in much comparative social research, Sweden is usually identified as the archetypical 'social-democratic' country, characterized by a high level of welfare intervention and relatively little social stratification (Esping-Andersen 1990). This has certainly affected urban development, housing construction and planning practices (see Barlow and Duncan 1992). Most of the planning in Stockholm is and has been carried out by the municipalities and the degree of spatial differentiation within the region has been affected by forms of land supply, forms of housing production and forms of housing promotion (see Arbaci 2007; Barlow and Duncan 1994), all factors that play out differently under different local political majorities. The regional coordination across municipalities is weak (except for health care and public transportation, which are controlled by the Stockholm County), and some municipalities tend to pursue a housing policy that attracts middle-class households while discouraging low-income renters to move in (by simply refraining from building affordable housing and in particular public rental housing).

Sweden's housing market has traditionally been characterized by a large public housing sector and a unitary rental system, with competition between providers and no substantial differences in rent levels between the private and public rental sectors, making the whole rental stock relatively open to socially deprived households (Kemeny 1995). Municipal housing companies have provided housing for less well-off households and immigrants but also for middle-income households (not least to attain socially mixed housing developments; see Bergsten and Holmqvist 2013; Elander 1991). No means testing occurs, or used to occur, in allocating public housing dwellings to applicants. A 'soft' rent control system has been applied, achieving market-like rents with certain restrictions, the same rent-setting procedure being applied in both the municipal and private sectors (Whitehead and Turner 2002). Until 2010, private rental companies had to adjust to the rent levels negotiated between the public housing companies and the tenants' organizations; after 2010, private landlords participated in these negotiations on equal terms. Striving for low residential segregation and attaining socially mixed neighbourhoods have long been important fundamentals of Swedish welfare policy (Holmqvist 2009). To achieve these goals, neutrality of tenure has been politically favoured in terms of investment subsidies to the housing sector (Lundqvist 1987).

Certain aspects of current housing policy, however, have tended to impede the attainment of this general goal. As indicated above, one result of the economic depression in the early 1990s was politically determined dramatic cutbacks in general (i.e., supply-side) housing subsidies, and a move towards, first, more targeted subsidies (Whitehead and Turner 2002) and, later, practically none at all (Christophers 2013). The reduction in general subsidies has resulted in an incremental increase in rent levels as landlords gained more freedom in rent-setting, with high market pressures to differentiate rent levels depending on the attractiveness of particular housing segments, especially in the private rental stock. In the owner-occupied and cooperative sectors, property prices in the Stockholm region have increased substantially, partly due to less subsidy of new construction, partly due to an increasing overall lack of housing and partly also due to low interest rates on mortgages over the past ten years. As a result, afford-ability has decreased for all lower-income categories but particularly affecting non-Western immigrants, who face major problems competing for jobs in the new Stockholm economy.

Municipal housing companies are now more than ever under financial pressure to act on market terms. As right-to-buy legislation was passed by the centre/right government in the early 1990s (Andersson and Magnusson Turner 2014), selling part of the municipal housing stock to sitting tenants who form a cooperative[3] has become common practice in many municipalities. Facing economic pressure, municipal housing companies are 'forced' to restructure rents, increasing them in more attractive parts of the city so that less attractive parts can retain stable rents (Whitehead and Turner 2002: 2014). The market influence is most obvious in attractive locations in the inner cities, leading to an intensified gentrification process (Andersson and Magnusson Turner 2014; Hedin *et al.* 2012).

Tenure conversions from public rental to private rental or cooperative tenure and from private rental to cooperative tenure have clear implications for house-holds' ability to access different housing segments. Over the 2000–2011 period, 155,000 public and private rental units in Sweden were converted to cooperative tenure. Of these, 112,000 were located in Stockholm County (which has about a quarter of the country's housing stock) and approximately 40 per cent of these were public rented dwellings (Statistics Sweden 2012a). Increasing numbers of poorer households, not least households of recently arrived refugees, now have to compete for fewer public rental dwellings in less attractive neighbourhoods, which on average tend to be more affordable or at least more accessible than any other combination of tenure and location. Table 5.2 summarizes the tenure structural change from 1990 to 2010, indicating the substantial total decline of the rental sector (from 50 per cent to 34 per cent) in Stockholm. Whereas the decrease in public rental housing supply has occurred almost proportionally in each city segment, the types of rental tenure conversions differ enormously between neigh-bourhood types. In the inner city and inner suburbs, much of the public and private rental sector has been converted into cooperative housing (Andersson and Magnusson 2014). However, in the outer-city housing estates, public housing has been converted into private rental housing and the cooperative sector has grown only slightly. Single family/mixed outer-city areas have been the least affected by tenure conversion.

Table 5.2 Change in tenure structure from 1990 to 2010 in neighbourhoods of different types

	Inner city		Inner suburb		Multifamily outer city		Single family/ mixed outer city		Total	
	1990	*2010*	*1990*	*2010*	*1990*	*2010*	*1990*	*2010*	*1990*	*2010*
Home ownership	0.0	0.0	22.4	19.7	6.1	5.5	75.9	77.9	31.3	31.1
Cooperative	26.2	63.4	16.3	43.2	23.1	29.7	11.0	13.9	17.8	34.4
Public rental	18.8	7.1	31.4	16.9	61.5	39.1	8.7	3.8	29.5	16.4
Private rental	54.2	29.2	29.3	19.9	8.6	25.5	2.3	3.8	20.3	17.7
Other	0.7	0.3	0.6	0.3	0.7	0.2	2.1	0.6	1.1	0.4
Total	**100**	**100**	**100**	**100**	**100**	**100**	**100**	**100**	**100**	**100**

Source: Geosweden datasets, 1990, 2000 and 2010.

Due to the high and rising price level of cooperative housing, the effect of conversions on affordability and accessibility is most dramatic in inner-city and inner-suburb neighbourhoods. In contrast, multifamily outer-city housing estates have remained more accessible to lower-income groups and immigrants. It would of course be surprising if the rapid expansion of housing distributed on market terms (i.e., cooperatives and home ownership) did not lead to stronger social segmentation across tenure types as well as increases in socio-economic segregation. Table 5.3 provides clear evidence: the lowest income category has rapidly become more dependent on and over-represented in the rental sector, in which the presence of the highest-income group is obviously reduced. Such a pattern of distribution is summarized in the dissimilarity index, based on disposable income categories, which indicates an increase from 0.3 to 0.4 over twenty years (see also the introduction of this book for more detail on segregation indexes used: Tammaru *et al.* 2016).

There is a distinct over- and under-representation of different ethnic categories across tenure types. A striking feature is the increasing rate of rental housing use by the Eastern European and non-Western immigrant population. This holds true for each of the four segments and in 1990 as well as 2010, meaning that we can expect ethnic segregation within each segment as well. This finding is, of course, in line with what other studies demonstrate for both Sweden and most other European countries (Brämå and Andersson 2010). Turkish immigrant households, for example, are less likely to move out of the municipal rental sector and have a higher probability of remaining in certain immigrant-dense areas of municipalities than do Swedish-born households (Andersson 1998; Magnusson and Özüekren 2002). Though socio-economic resources and length of residence in Sweden naturally greatly influence the outcome, studies have repeatedly demonstrated that such factors alone cannot account for ethnic differences in the housing market, at least not in Sweden or the other Nordic countries (Wessel *et al.* 2014). Note that Western European immigrants have a distribution that resembles that of the Swedish population.

Table 5.3 Over- and under-representation rates of the 1st and 5th income quintiles (of disposable income) across tenure types in the Stockholm region, 1990, 2000 and 2010

	Disp. income quintile	Home ownership	Cooperative	Public rental	Private rental	Other	Total
1990	1	81.4	84.8	121.7	110.5	109.1	100.0
	5	167.6	108.2	44.1	71.3	100.0	100.0
	Total	**100**	**100**	**100**	**100**	**100**	**100**
	***n* (1000s)**	**246**	**148**	**233**	**168**	**9**	**803**
2000	1	71.0	83.3	134.6	117.4	100.0	100.0
	5	158.4	121.8	38.2	68.4	120.0	100.0
	Total	**100**	**100**	**100**	**100**	**100**	**100**
	***n* (1000s)**	**266**	**217**	**212**	**229**	**4**	**927**
2010	1	67.3	81.4	150.0	137.4	133.3	100.0
	5	170.9	112.2	21.1	45.6	100.0	100.0
	Total	**100**	**100**	**100**	**100**	**100**	**100**
	***n* (1000s)**	**283**	**371**	**172**	**200**	**4**	**1030**

Source: Geosweden datasets, 1990, 2000 and 2010.

Change in segregation patterns

Below we report our empirical study of how the economic and institutional changes presented in the preceding contextual discussion have affected socio–spatial residential patterns in the Stockholm built-up area. The obvious question is whether residential segregation has increased over time and, if so, how.

We commence by charting the level of segregation by socio-economic categories, as measured by equalized household disposable income. Disposable income measures the effective demand that consumers can potentially exercise in various consumer markets. Figure 5.2 provides a preliminary account of the segregation levels and changes in them as measured by the segregation index for the more than 600 studied neighbourhoods (see note 1 for the formula). For each quintile of the disposable income distribution, we compare the extent to which quintile members live spatially integrated with or at greater distance from the other four quintile groups. As expected due to the market nature of housing provision, the level of segregation is less pronounced for the middle-income groups and more pronounced for those at the extremes. The most segregated category is quintile 5, i.e., those having the highest incomes. Of course, this population segment likely has the highest degree of freedom of housing choice, allowing them to self-segregate into high-income residential areas.

Furthermore, income segregation increases in magnitude over the period, doing so for all five groups; least affected by this development is the middle category, i.e., quintile 3. Interestingly, although quintile 4 still has a relatively low level of spatial separation from other income strata, it used to be the least segregated quintile in 1990 and 2000, though no longer in 2010.

Another way of displaying income segregation is to compute a dissimilarity index and an isolation index. With reference to Figure 5.2, we expect low- and high-income categories to live more segregated from each other, and the dissimilarity

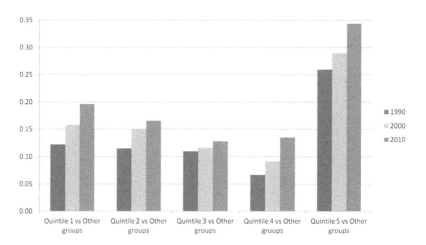

Figure 5.2 Segregation index by disposable income quintile group, 1990, 2000 and 2010.

Source: Geosweden datasets, 1990, 2000 and 2010.

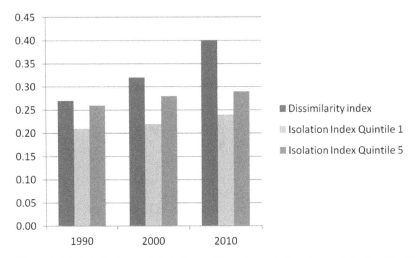

Figure 5.3 Dissimilarity and isolation indices for quintiles 1 and 5 in the Stockholm region, 1990, 2000 and 2010.

Source: Geosweden datasets, 1990, 2000 and 2010.

index indeed increases rapidly over both decades (1990: .27, 2000: .32, 2010: .40). As shown in Figure 5.3, both the quintile 1 and 5 income groups have also become more spatially isolated over time, although the high-income earners are the most persistently isolated (isolation index for quintile 1 (and 5) respectively up from .21 (.26) in 1990 to .24 (.29) in 2010).[4]

Figure 5.4 is a series of maps indicating the geographical pattern formed by quintile groups 1 and 5 in 2000 and 2010. The neighbourhood mean and standard deviation values are noted below each of the four maps and, as can be seen, mean values are higher for quintile 5, indicating many low-population neighbourhoods of these types. In 2010, a total of twenty-one neighbourhoods have an over-representation of quintile 5 residents amounting to more than two standard deviations above the mean value (up from ten neighbourhoods in 2000), i.e., the share of people in the highest income bracket is above 53 per cent in these neigh-bourhoods. This pattern was relatively similar ten and even twenty years earlier, but high-income households have since become even more concentrated in the north-east. Another ninety-four neighbourhoods have reached one to two standard deviations above the mean (39 per cent and 53 per cent, respectively). In contrast, the poorest neighbourhoods are fewer but have high concentrations of poor people. In 2010, eighteen neighbourhoods reached the two-standard-deviation threshold (at least 38.9 per cent in quintile 1) and another thirty-four have reached one to two standard deviations above the mean. Irrespective of whether we consider the narrower segment of very high over-representation of quintile 1 residents, or the broader segment having at least one standard deviation above the mean, many fewer poor neighbourhoods existed in 2000 and especially in 1990.

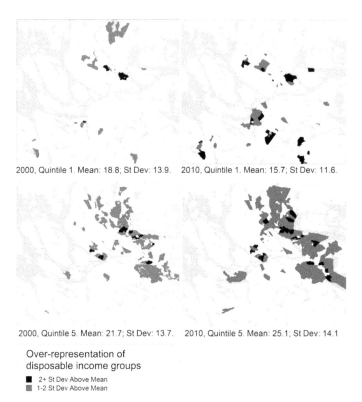

2000, Quintile 1. Mean: 18.8; St Dev: 13.9.   2010, Quintile 1. Mean: 15.7; St Dev: 11.6.

2000, Quintile 5. Mean: 21.7; St Dev: 13.7.   2010, Quintile 5. Mean: 25.1; St Dev: 14.1

Over-representation of
disposable income groups

■ 2+ St Dev Above Mean
▨ 1-2 St Dev Above Mean

Figure 5.4 Relative over-representation of disposable income groups, quintiles 1
and 5, 2000 and 2010.

Source: Geosweden datasets, 2000 and 2010.

We chose not to consider the distribution of the other three quintile groups;
however, in summary they display the following pattern. A pronounced over-
representation (two standard deviations above the mean) of quintile groups 2, 3 and 4
is much more unusual (in 2010, there were three such neighbourhoods for quintile 2,
four for quintile 3 and two for quintile 4). Close reading of the omitted maps also
reveals a fairly strong overlap between quintiles 1 and 2, indicating that these
population segments live concentrated in the same or adjacent neighbourhoods. In
terms of geography, only the highest quintile displays a relatively distinct overall
pattern of concentration, i.e., in the mixed/single-family outer area in the north-
east, while most other groups are scattered across the region, with the poorest
two quintiles found in the well-known housing estates on the urban periphery
(the 'multifamily outer city', cf. Figure 5.1 showing locations of the neighbourhood types). Most of these low-income large housing estates are found in a
handful of municipalities and stretched out along the main transportation routes
(E4, E18 and E20) in the north-western and south-western sections of the city
region (Sollentuna, Stockholm, Huddinge, Botkyrka, Södertälje). Interestingly,
the inner city and inner suburbs do not stand out as displaying concentrations of

any particular income group, thus representing areas of relatively mixed residential composition. The same applies to many of the mixed/single-family outer areas in the south and south-west, which are much more diverse than the more distinct high-income neighbourhoods in the north-east.

While politicians and planners have claimed to be striving to 'break segregation' (Andersson 2006), the past twenty years have brought about precisely the opposite: the Stockholm region is rapidly polarizing in terms of income and the spatial distribution of various income groups has become more uneven. Much of the political debate, including counter-segregation policies, has however more or less disregarded the social class dimension and instead focused on the ethnic segregation.

It is well documented that Sweden has a relatively pronounced segregation by ethnic origin (Andersson 1998, 2006; Bråmå 2006). The basic contours of the current geographical patterns emerged during and soon after the Million Programme (1965–1974). Much has happened since, and the rapidly increasing number of minority households since the 1970s has of course resulted in many more neighbourhoods having a high immigrant presence. The proportion of foreign-born residents in the working age population (20–64 years) stood at 20.3 per cent in 1990 and increased to 28.2 per cent by 2010. It is a persistent feature that (a) the poorest areas are immigrant-dense and vice versa, (b) immigrant-dense areas mostly expand by what could be called a 'spill-over effect', i.e., new concentrations tend to appear near existing ones, especially if neighbouring areas are similar in terms of housing types and tenure forms. It is well documented (Andersson 2013; Bråmå 2006; Molina 1997, 2000) that most immigrant arrivals tend to cluster in the rental segment and that many immigrants tend to remain there or move into cooperative dwellings in the same or adjacent areas.

Table 5.4 charts the development of the dissimilarity index over a range of 'eth-classes'. We are interested in whether different ethnic categories are homogeneous, or whether immigrant groups are internally differentiated. This issue relates to our second research question: to what extent is the socio-economic segregation related to the ethnic dimension? We compare low- and high-income groups within and across ethnic categories and for first- and second-generation immigrants (defined as born in Sweden having two parents from same regional category: Western, East European, non-Western). First, the increasing socio-economic segregation seems to hold true even within each ethnic category, meaning that even low-income natives have tended to become more segregated from high-income natives. This development is even more pronounced for non-Western immigrants, so it is clearly the case that class segregation has become more pronounced within this group as well.

In addition, however, low-income non-Western residents also live at a distance from low-income Swedes. It is only the Western immigrant low-income category that seems to have a residential pattern similar to that of native Swedes. Finally, the well-off segment of the non-Western immigrant category displays a tendency towards spatial integration with their Swedish counterparts, and their dissimilarity index drops from 0.46 in 1990 to a more modest 0.34 in 2010. The overall impression of the second-generation values is that they display similar

Table 5.4 Dissimilarity indices within and across income and ethnic categories, 1990–2010 (for working age population and by quintile groups of disposable income)

Groups compared	1990	2000	2010
Low-income Swedes vs. high-income Swedes	.22	.24	.29
Low-income Western vs. high-income Western	.32	.31	.33
Low-income Eastern Eur. vs. high-income Eastern Eur.	.36	.38	.44
Low-income non-Western vs. high-income non-Western	.27	.34	.43
Low-income Western vs. low-income Swedes	.22	.18	.16
Low-income 2nd gen. Western vs. low-income Swedes	.26	.31	.30
Low-income Eastern Eur. vs. low-income Swedes	.29	.32	.32
Low-income 2nd gen. Eastern Eur. vs. low-income Swedes	.36	.31	.30
Low-income non-Western vs. low-income Swedes	.50	.49	.46
Low-income 2nd gen. non-Western vs. low-income Swedes	NC	.62	.53
High-income Western vs. high-income Swedes	.16	.13	.12
High-income 2nd gen. Western vs. high-income Swedes	.27	.19	.18
High-income Eastern Eur. vs. high-income Swedes	.22	.25	.27
High-income 2nd gen. Eastern Eur. vs. high-income Swedes	.34	.25	.22
High-income non-Western vs. high-income Swedes	.46	.41	.34
High-income 2nd gen. non-Western vs. high-income Swedes	NC	.75	.53

Note: 'Western', 'Eastern Eur.', and 'non-Western' refer to categories of immigrants. NC=not calculated due to few 2nd generation immigrants age 20+ from non-Western countries in 1990. Values for 2nd generation non-Western high-income immigrants are high primarily because of small number of people (N ca. 100 in 2000 and ca. 700 in 2010).

or higher values than do the first generation. However, especially for second-generation non-Western immigrants, values should be interpreted with caution (very few above age 20 in this category, in particular with high income).

Discussion and conclusions

In this chapter, we have examined the spatial outcomes of the social restructuring that has occurred in Swedish society and in the Stockholm urban area in particular. This study focuses primarily on neighbourhood sorting, approached from a socio-economic perspective. Our stated purpose was to provide evidence of how residential segregation patterns have evolved and transformed over the two decades from 1990 to 2010 in the Stockholm built-up area. Besides emphasizing the importance of social class in understanding residential change, we have added the ethnic dimension of segregation and studied how these two dimensions are interrelated. Our approach to understanding change in segregation patterns is based on the structural–contextual approach, taking account of how the institutional set-up and other local specific factors have influenced residential patterning. Among the identified macro-trends, regional economic restructuring, reduced welfare state ambitions (especially in the housing sector) and high international in-migration have considerably influenced the structural development over the 1990–2010 period. Swedish politicians, including those in Stockholm, often claim that different socio-economic status groups should be mixed in urban settlements (Holmqvist 2009). Neighbourhoods with such a mix also seem to provide opportunities for successful educational and socio-economic careers for those growing up in them (Bergsten 2010), so such a normative position can also be justified on more objective grounds. However, empirical evidence on the outcome of long-term settlement pattern development tells another story: over the last two decades, socio-economic residential segregation has increased in Stockholm, and socio-spatial uneven distribution as measured by the dissimilarity index has increased, especially for the quintile 1 and 5 income groups. Concentrations of low-income groups have become denser and such 'pockets of poverty' are located mostly in and around neighbourhoods that already displayed some social decline in 1990. In terms of geography, these areas largely overlap what we call the outer-city multifamily housing segment – in other words, the large housing estates dating back to the late 1960s and the 1970s.

As is the case in many European countries, the role of the welfare state in Sweden is in decline, a process reflected in reduced levels of social insurance compensation, housing stock privatization and overall marketization tendencies in providing education and care for children and the elderly (Wessel *et al.* 2014). Income inequalities have increased both because of the economic restructuring process and because of lower income taxes and reduced property tax on home ownership since 2006. This has substantially increased the disposable income of homeowners in the Stockholm region. Another crucial factor contributing to the increase in residential segregation has doubtless been the tenure conversions that commenced at a large scale in the 1990s. These have resulted in a substantial decline of rental units and a very rapid expansion of market-based cooperative housing in the inner city and the inner suburbs. One might add that the neo-liberal turn has also affected the planning system as such, which now gives more room to private actors to influence planning and housing construction activity, and it seems more unlikely then twenty-five years ago that residential sorting along class and ethnic dimensions can be successfully combatted by public steering and pro-active planning.

Evidence clearly indicates that the observed intensified socio-economic segregation has led to an increasing concentration of high-income earners in the north-east. Those who possess sufficient resources to make a free choice in the housing market have obviously chosen to live in upper-middle-class areas, leaving formerly more income-mixed neighbourhoods less mixed. In addition, tenure conversions have also helped make the inner city in particular less socially mixed, strengthening the tendency for low-income residents to seek housing in a small set of rental-dominated housing estates on the urban periphery. The state and municipal levels have made many efforts to improve these estates via area-based urban interventions, notably the State's 'Metropolitan Development Initiative' and

Stockholm City's 'Outer City Initiative' (Palander 2006), but such interventions have limited capacity to counteract the ongoing social polarization and segregation process (Andersson 2006). Although the ethnic and socio-economic dimensions of segregation clearly overlap, neither can be reduced to the other. We see class segregation within the native population as well as within each broad category of immigrants. Immigrants originating from outside of Europe have a high but stable level of segregation, as measured by the dissimilarity index. However, the substantial annual influx of low-income non-Western immigrants tends to somewhat conceal the fact that many non-Western immigrants do well and move out of the large housing estates to less immigrant-dense neighbourhoods (Andersson 2013). Segregation by class increases within this category and within other ethnic categories, including that of the natives. A 'double sorting' is going on, whereby the level of disposable income predicts a certain housing location to a greater extent than before, and whereby low-income natives tend to live in other areas than do low-income non-Western immigrants.

International migration has definitely put pressure on the Stockholm housing market, with access to various submarkets becoming more limited over time for many newcomers to the metropolitan area. The liberalization of the housing market, which has led to a smaller supply of affordable housing, is making the situation even more challenging, especially for less resourceful immigrants. However, the constraints imposed by an increasing overall housing supply deficit and a reduced rental stock affect less wealthy native-born households as well. While the ethnic dimension of segregation was formerly seen as the most important political problem, the socio-economic aspect is adding an increasingly important layer of complexity to segregation in Stockholm. From this perspective, it would be particularly useful to examine more closely the housing trajectories of particular residential groups, for example, wealthy non-Western immigrants or lower-income native-born people. Such in-depth longitudinal studies, based on an 'eth-class' conception of the population, could enhance our understanding of the structural constraints and opportunities facing households of different types in the Stockholm housing market.

Acknowledgements

Roger Andersson's work was made possible due to generous funding from New York University, School of Law (Straus fellowship 2013–2014). Anneli Kährik was funded as a EU FP7 Marie Curie Fellow at the Institute for Housing and Urban Research, Uppsala University.

Notes

1 Statistics Sweden applies two criteria when delimiting a built-up area: (1) the distance between residential buildings should not exceed 200 meters and (2) any such agglomeration should have at least 200 residents. Irrespective of the low population threshold, one may easily question whether this formal definition produces relevant functional housing markets; however, in its defence, one might claim that this is not the underlying motive for delimiting urban agglomerations.

2 The Institute for Housing and Urban Research (IBF) at Uppsala University owns the Geosweden datasets. The datasets comprise population, educational, income, and real estate and property data from Statistics Sweden and cover all residents in Sweden annually from 1990 to 2010. Both workplace and housing information are geocoded into coordinates and administrative regions. The datasets can be merged into individual longitudinal datasets using a unique individual code that is used in all datasets.

3 Co-operative housing is (normally) multifamily housing collectively owned and managed by the residents. Each apartment is a market good in the sense that the right to live in and dispose of the apartment can be traded (normally in an open bidding process where the highest bid gets the contract). Costs for infrastructural re-investments (such as pipes, sewage, IT-solutions, cable TV, etc.) are covered by the co-operative while internal improvements (new kitchen and bathroom, wall paper, new floors etc.) of each apartment are covered by the apartment's contract holder. Each contract holder pays a monthly fee to the co-operative and the fee covers each household's share of the annual costs of running the property (including capital costs). Each co-operative has a democratically elected board (of contract holders) that takes care of running businesses, and all residents are invited to at least one annual meeting where budgets and other business are discussed and board elections take place. Normally, the contract holder needs a mortgage to purchase the contract and mortgage lenders are the same as those who finance home ownership. It is in practice not very different from a condominium system but ensures collective responsibility for development and maintenance of the property. Some co-operatives are large and comprise many buildings in a district and several hundred apartments; others have a small number of members.

4 The dissimilarity index is computed as follows:

Supposing

$Q1_i$ = the quintile 1 population of the ith areal unit, e.g., a SAMS area

$Q1_{tot}$ = the total quintile 1 population of the large geographic entity for which the index of dissimilarity is calculated (i.e., the Stockholm region)

$Q5_i$ = the quintile 5 population of the ith area unit, e.g., a SAMS area

$Q5_{tot}$ = the total quintile 5 population of the large geographic entity for which the index of dissimilarity is calculated (i.e., the Stockholm region),

then the index of dissimilarity measuring the segregation of quintile 1 from quintile 5 residents equals:

$(1/2) \times$ SUM $(Q1_i /Q1_{tot} - Q5_i/Q5_{tot})$.

The index of segregation follows the same logic but compares one group with all remaining groups in each area and then sums the difference.

The isolation index is computed as follows:

Supposing

$Q1_i$ = the quintile 1 population of a component part, for example, a SAMS area, of the larger geographic entity for which the isolation index is calculated

T_i = the total population of a component part of the larger geographic entity for which the isolation index is calculated

$Q1_{tot}$ = the total quintile 1 population of the larger geographic entity for which the isolation index is calculated,

then the isolation index for quintile 1 equals: SUM $(Q1_i / Q1_{tot}) \times (Q1_i / T_i)$.

References

Andersson, R 1998, 'Socio-spatial dynamics: Ethnic divisions of mobility and housing in post-Palme Sweden' *Urban Studies* 35, 397–428.

Andersson, R 2006, ' "Breaking segregation" – rhetorical construct or effective policy? The case of the metropolitan development initiative in Sweden' *Urban Studies* 43, 787–799.

Andersson, R 2012, 'Understanding ethnic minorities' settlement and geographical mobility patterns in Sweden using longitudinal data', in *Minority Internal Migration in Europe*, eds N Finney and G Catney, Ashgate, Farnham, Surrey, pp. 263–291.

Andersson, R 2013, 'Reproducing and reshaping ethnic residential segregation in Stockholm: The role of selective migration moves' *Geografiska Annaler Series B, Human Geography*, 95(2), 163–187.

Andersson, R 2014, 'Understanding variation in the size of the public housing sector across Swedish municipalities: The role of politics', in *The Future of Public Housing Ongoing Trends in the East and the West*, eds J Chen, M Stephens and Y Man, Springer-Verlag, Berlin, Heidelberg, pp. 261–280.

Andersson, R and Bråmå, Å 2004, 'Selective migration in Swedish distressed neighbourhoods: Can area-based urban policies counteract segregation processes?' *Housing Studies* 19(4), 517–539.

Andersson, R and Magnusson Turner, L 2014, 'Segregation, gentrification, and residualisation: From public housing to market driven housing allocation in inner city Stockholm' *International Journal of Housing Policy* 14(1), 3–29.

Arbaci, S 2007, 'Ethnic segregation, housing systems and welfare regimes in Europe' *European Journal of Housing Policy* 7(4), 401–433.

Barlow, J and Duncan, S 1992, 'Markets, states and housing provision: Four European growth regions compared' *Progress in Planning* 38, 93–177.

Barlow, J and Duncan, S 1994, *Success and Failure in Housing Provision: European Systems Compared*, Elsevier Science, Oxford.

Bergsten, Z 2010, *Bättre framtidsutsikter? Blandade bostadsområden och grannskapseffekter: En analys av visioner och effekter av blandat boende* [Better prospects through social mix? Mixed neighbourhoods and neighbourhood effects: An analysis of the purpose and effects of social mix policy]. Geografiska regionstudier 85, Department of Social and Economic Geography, Uppsala University, Uppsala.

Bergsten, Z And Holmqvist, E 2013, 'Possibilities of building a mixed city – evidence from Swedish cities' *International Journal of Housing Policy* 13(3), 288–311.

Bråmå, Å 2006, *Studies in the Dynamics of Residential Segregation*, Geografiska Regionstudier No 67, Dept. of Social and Economic Geography, Uppsala University, Uppsala.

Bråmå, Å and Andersson, R 2010, 'Who leaves rental housing? Examining possible explanations for ethnic housing segmentation in Uppsala, Sweden' *Journal of Housing and the Built Environment* 25(3), 331–352.

Christophers, B 2013, 'A monstrous hybrid: The political economy of housing in early twenty-first century Sweden' *New Political Economy* (January), 1–27.

Elander, I 1991, 'Good dwellings for all: The case of social rented housing in Sweden' *Housing Studies* 6(1), 29–43.

Esping-Andersen, G 1990, *The Three Worlds of Welfare Capitalism*, Princeton University Press, Princeton, NJ.

Finney, N and Simpson, L 2008, 'Internal migration and ethnic groups: Evidence for Britain from the 2001 census' *Population, Space and Place* 14, 63–83.

Gordon, M M 1964, *Assimilation in American life*, Oxford University Press, New York.

Gordon, M M 1978, *Human Nature, Class, and Ethnicity*, Oxford University Press, New York.

Hall, P 2005, 'The world's urban systems: A European perspective' *Global Urban Development* 1(1), 1–12.

Hedin, K, Clark, E, Lundholm, E and Malmberg, G 2012, 'Neoliberalization of housing in Sweden: Gentrification, filtering, and social polarization' *Annals of the Association of American Geographers* 102(2), 443–463.

Holmqvist, E 2009, *Politik och planering för ett blandat boende och minskad boendesegregation: ett mål utan medel?* [Policy and planning for social and housing mix and decreased housing segregation: a goal without means?] Geografiska regionstudier 79, Department of Social and Economic Geography, Uppsala University, Uppsala.

Kemeny, J 1995, *From Public Housing to the Social Market: Rental Policy Strategies in Comparative Perspective,* Routledge, London.

Lundqvist, L J 1987, 'Sweden's housing policy and the quest for tenure neutrality' *Scandinavian Housing and Planning Research* 4(2), 119–133.

Magnusson, L and Özüekren, A S 2002, 'The housing careers of Turkish households in middle-sized Swedish municipalities' *Housing Studies* 17(3), 465–486.

Maloutas, T 2012, 'Introduction: Residential segregation in context', in *Residential Segregation in Comparative Perspective: Making Sense of Contextual Diversity,* eds T Maloutas and K Fujita, Ashgate, Farnham, Surrey, pp. 1–36.

Molina, I 1997, *Stadens rasifiering: Etnisk boendesegregation i folkhemmet* [Racialization of the City: Ethnic residential segregation in the People's Home] Geografiska regionstudier Nr 32, Kulturgeografiska institutionen, Uppsala universitet, Uppsala.

Molina, I 2000, 'Bostadsrätten och det nya Sverige – en uppsats om etniska minoriteter på bostadsmarknaden' [Co-operative housing and the 'New Sweden' – An essay on ethnic minorities in the housing market], in *Bostadsrätten i ett nytt millennium,* eds B Malmberg and L Sommestad, Uppsala University, Institutet för bostadsforskning, Forskningsrapport 2000: 3, Uppsala, pp. 145–155.

Musterd, S, Ostendorf, W and Breebaart, M 1998, *Multi-Ethnic Metropolis: Patterns and Policies,* Kluwer Academic Publishers, Dordrecht.

Palander, C 2006, *Områdesbaserad politik för minskad segregation – En studie av den svenska storstadspolitiken* [Area-based policy to stop segregation: A study of the Swedish metropolitan policy], Geografiska regionstudier nr 66, Department of Social and Economic Geography, Uppsala University, Uppsala.

Statistics Sweden 2012a, Press release from Statistics Sweden, No 2012:760. Kalkylerat bostadsbestånd 2011 [Calculated housing stock 2011]. Available online: http://www.scb.se/Pages/PressRelease____335520.aspx

Statistics Sweden 2012b, Inkomstfördelningsundersökningen 2008 [Income distribution survey 2008], Sveriges officiella statistik, Statistiska Meddelanden. HE 21 SM 1001, korrigerad version, Stockholm, Statistics Sweden.

Tammaru, T, Musterd, S, van Ham, M and Marcińczak, S, 2016, 'A multi-factor approach to understanding socio-economic segregation in European capital cities' in *Socio-Economic Segregation in European Capital Cities: East Meets West,* eds T Tammaru, S Marcińczak, M van Ham and S Musterd, Routledge, London.

Wessel, T, Andersson, R, Kauppinen, T and Skifter Andersen, H, 2014, 'Spatial integration of immigrants in Nordic cities: The relevance of spatial assimilation theory in a welfare state context' Submitted to journal.

Whitehead, C and Turner, B 2002, 'Reducing housing subsidy: Swedish housing policy in an international context' *Urban Studies* 39(2), 201–217.

6 Economic segregation in Oslo

Polarisation as a contingent outcome

Terje Wessel

Abstract

The industrial structure of Oslo has changed dramatically over the last fifty years. Much of the change took place in the 1980s and 1990s, and led to increasing income inequality. The latest decade has seen a different development: stable income inequality and increasing economic segregation. This pattern implies that long-term effects of structural economic change fuse with influences of a shorter temporal length. The net result of many changes, including immigration, is geographical polarisation: increasing segregation of both poor and affluent groups. It is a 'contingent outcome', and not a simple reflection of economic transformation and globalisation.

Introduction

The city of Oslo has often been described as a remote and backward place. One of the more fascinating portraits is offered by the German author Hans Magnus Enzensberger. He made a revisit to Oslo in 1982, having stayed there twenty years earlier. What he found was a city with pre-modern structures in the midst of massive suburban expansion. The urban core, in particular, contained a large number of anachronistic activities, derelict buildings and shabby backyards. It was a city where 'modern city planning had suffered one humiliation after another' (Enzensberger 1987: 258).

Contemporary Oslo looks very different. Older structures do exist but have been transformed to accommodate specialist shops, restaurants and bars, galleries, museums and luxury apartments. The inner core has expanded along the seafront, with thousands of new dwellings, cultural institutions and public spaces for walking and recreation. One part of the seafront, Bjørvika, even contains a high-rise skyline, the Opera Quarter, which has become the new hub for financial and insurance enterprises. Further north, gentrification has made its way through parts of the traditional working-class areas, and has begun to affect the inner suburbs too. A large housing project, with the size of a small city, has appeared in a previous industrial area (Kværnerbyen), on the border between the core and the inner ring. Similar projects appear both in the inner ring (Skøyenbyen, Lørenbyen and

Fornebu) and the outer ring (Sandvika, Asker, Ski, Lillestrøm and Gardermoen). Outside these specific zones, a more familiar landscape of scattered houses and ribbon developments has continued to push the border of the built-up area. Many of these changes have occurred in response to industrial shift. The manufacturing sector in Oslo reached a peak in the mid-1960s, with 25 per cent of all employment. Some decades later, in 1990, the sector still accounted for 12 per cent of all jobs, most of which were catering to domestic consumption. The latest numbers, however, are not very comforting. As of 2011, only 5 per cent of all employees are working in the manufacturing and processing industries. Producer services (including finance, insurance and real estate activities) follow, not surprisingly, a completely opposite trajectory. These industries grew from 5 per cent in 1970 to 14 per cent in 1990 and to 24 per cent in 2011 (Rasmussen 1998; Statistics Norway 2014). Other activities that grew include information and communication, health and social services, accommodation, food services and personal services. In other words, Oslo has changed from a city with a mixed economic base, consisting of manufacturing industries and administration, to a quintessential post-industrial city.

It is in many ways a successful post-industrial city. Employment grew by 42 per cent, and population by 33 per cent, over the period 1994 to 2014. A recent assessment of 300 growth centres in Europe, The Regional European Growth Index, places Oslo in second place, mostly due to relative wealth (GDP per capita) and strong economic growth. As stated in the report, 'Oslo benefits from a diverse and dynamic economy; the city is the premier business centre in Norway and a key maritime centre in Europe' (Lasalle Investment Management 2014: 4).

Diversity is a key word in more than one respect. The immigrant population has grown from 3 per cent in 1970 to 9 per cent in 1990 and further to 24 per cent in 2014. What Enzenberger observed in 1982 was a city of emergent ethnic pluralism. Immigrants ('guest workers') from Pakistan, India, Turkey and North Africa made their imprint on the urban core but nowhere else. A visitor nowadays, by contrast, cannot avoid the impression of heterogeneity and complexity. The number of national backgrounds exceeds 200, with Poles, Swedes, Somalis and Pakistanis as the largest groups. Ethnic minorities are particularly visible in the municipality of Oslo, where the immigrant population of four out of fifteen townships is more than 40 per cent.

What happens to the social and residential composition of such a city? Is there increasing inequality in the distribution of incomes and wealth? How do changes at the city scale affect changes at the local scale – is there increasing economic segregation, and, if so, which parts of the distribution (the bottom, the middle, the top) does it affect? These questions underlie the first part of this chapter. The second part addresses the connection between demographic change and social change. I attempt to gauge whether immigration impinges on the spatial distribution of income and wealth. Does increasing differentiation within the immigrant population boost economic segregation in the population at large? Is there a large gap in economic segregation between native Norwegians and immigrants? How does the difference/gap develop over time – does it account for a growing part of all economic segregation?

An important premise behind the study is that social structure and spatial structure interact in extremely complex ways. One cannot 'read off' changes in the distribution of incomes and wealth from changes in the industrial structure. Nor is it wise to overlook intervening factors between individual inequality, household inequality and spatial inequality. Numerous studies show that housing policy and urban planning play a major role in the social transformation of cities (Arbaci 2007; Hamnett 1996; 2003; Kazepov 2005; Maloutas 2012; Murie 1998; Murie and Musterd 1996; Wessel 2000). Other potential influences include transportation policy, tax legislation, integration policy and the cultural atmosphere (for example the local acceptance of cultural diversity). And, also, changes in the urban landscape are often sluggish (Wyly 1998). Housing prices may reflect deep-seated symbolic values, and the sheer durability of urban environments ensures a large degree of continuity in the spatial distribution of social groups. These stabilizing forces imply that individual and spatial inequality may rise or fall in different periods. The Oslo case, as we shall see, is a prime example of such spatio-temporal complexity.

The chapter continues with a description of welfare policies, labour market changes, housing policies and housing market structure. I then turn to previous research, data and methods, results, and, finally, conclusions and implications.

Some comments on concepts are required. First, I have so far commented on 'Oslo' without due attention to geography. What I am referring to, throughout the chapter, is the Oslo region, which consists of two counties, Oslo and Akershus. The current population (2014) is 634,000 in Oslo and 576,000 in Akershus. Oslo, however, is just 8 per cent of the land area (Figure 6.1), which implies that changes in the inner city tend to disappear from regional maps. A key social division can be drawn between the western and the eastern part of the region, where the affluent west accounts for 37 per cent of the population and 7 per cent of the land. The east–west border cuts through the municipality of Oslo, with two municipalities on the western flank and twenty municipalities on the eastern flank. Second, 'economic segregation' is a collective term for segregation by income and wealth. Alternative indicators (for example occupation, education and employment) are not used in the analysis. Third, children of immigrant parents are counted as immigrants, in line with Norwegian statistical practice.

The analyses in this study stretch from 1993 to 2011, and are carried out at the census tract level. The average number of inhabitants, counting the total population, was 499 in 1993, 507 in 2001 and 594 in 2011.

The political context: welfare and housing

Norway has followed the rest of Europe in a move towards deregulation, privatization and competition policies. The scale of these reforms, however, tends to be smaller than elsewhere. Norway's natural revenues (oil, gas and fish) have made it possible to avoid large-scale cutbacks in the provision of services and benefits. A second idiosyncratic feature is a heavy government involvement in the banking sector. This policy was initiated early after World War II, and continues

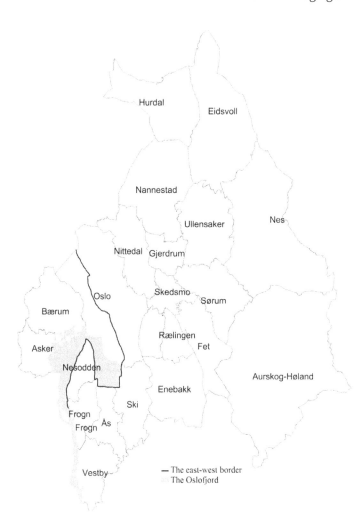

Figure 6.1 The Oslo region: 23 municipalities.

in the form of capital injection in private banks.[1] Equally important, and related to 'credit socialism',[2] is a perennial concern for autonomy and self-sufficiency. Norway is not only a rich nation with a complicated connection to Europe; it is also a nation of home-owners. Norwegian housing policy differs a lot from the standard conception of social-democratic housing policy. It is, or has become, a highly selective policy.

Several authors (Bengtsson 2006; Stamsø 2009; Torgersen 1987) emphasize the weak connection between the welfare regime and the housing system in Norway. This disconnection is evident when we look at recent political changes: the housing sector was deregulated in a sweeping operation in 1983–84, while changes in welfare programmes have occurred in fits and starts over several decades. One important welfare change is a new emphasis on work – labelled the 'workline'. A turning point can be traced to 1992–93, when the government introduced stricter qualifying conditions for unemployment and disability benefits, combined with extensive programmes for rehabilitation and vocational training. Later changes include reduction in the duration of benefits, options for re-entry to work and further restrictions in the eligibility criteria (applying to unemployment, disability, sickness and single-parent benefits). The level of benefits, on the other hand, has been extremely stable compared to other countries (Scruggs 2006; van Vliet and Caminada 2012).

It should be noted that provision of benefits (social insurance) is the preferred type of income protection in Norway. Social assistance is a last-resort support for people with no means of existence (Johansson and Hvinden 2007). A key point here is that benefits are financed through a combination of premiums, contributions and taxes. Social assistance, by contrast, is financed through taxes alone. Benefits are therefore more compatible with the workline (ibid.).

So, despite some changes in benefits and public spending, the welfare state model remains largely intact. A token of the stability is found in the Comparative Welfare Entitlements Dataset (CWED) (Scruggs 2006), which covers eighteen countries and includes annual information on replacement rates, coverage ratios, duration of benefits, eligibility criteria, employee/employer ratio of payroll taxes and take-up rates. The data are summarized in 'generosity scores', which represent each country's institutional commitment to welfare policy. An analysis of these scores for 1980 places Sweden at the top of the ranking, a small step ahead of Norway. Ten years later, the two countries figured side by side, but whereas Sweden moved to a lower level between 1990 and 2000, Norway obtained exactly the same score (Scruggs 2006; 2007). The same tendency is found in a broader analysis of four Nordic countries (Denmark, Finland, Norway and Sweden) for the period 2000–2008. Wessel *et al.* (2014) include more than 900 replacement rates pertaining to employment, added by data on sickness, disability benefits and paid leave. Again, Norway appears with the highest level of social insurance protection.[3]

Another parameter of the welfare state is the traditional co-operation between employees, employers and the government. This tradition was strengthened in the early 1990s in order to increase productivity and employment. The policy was formed around a treaty, called the 'solidarity pact', and brought many new jobs in the lower end of the labour market. It soon turned out, however, that high-skilled middle-class workers wanted a larger share of the pie. They also wanted a new set of rules, with larger emphasis on local bargaining and incentive pay. The formal co-operation continued, but there was no longer a firm commitment to solidarity between different fractions of the labour force. One part of the problem reflected the changing industrial structure (i.e. the growth of advanced services); another part reflected taxation policy: groups at the top had been able to profit from income shifting between wage income, profit income and personal income from business activities. A large reform in 2006 removed some of these loopholes, to the benefit of middle- and low-income earners.

The deregulation of the housing sector took place, as noted, in 1983–84. A series of reforms turned a system based on heavy government involvement into a residualist model. Virtually all price regulations on housing were lifted, accompanied by changes in the regulation of housing tenures, and corresponding changes in the credit system. A new legislation for condominiums (1983) spawned massive property speculation and, subsequently, a highly leveraged investor base. Households, too, had easy access to cheap credit. Many households with little or no equity seized the opportunity to buy a dwelling at a low rate of interest, added by generous tax deductions. Housing prices responded predictably, as we may sense from a 39 per cent price growth between 1985 and 1987. It was also predictable that prices would plunge, as they did between 1988 and 1992. These were dark years in Norwegian economy, with hardships, insecurity and declining trust in public institutions. The bottom was reached in late 1992, with the solidarity pact as the main vehicle for restored growth. Slowly, people regained trust in the banks, the politicians and each other. A valid indication of the new optimism can be found in the development of housing prices in the Oslo region: an increase by 460 per cent over twenty years, from 1992 to 2012, is hardly matched elsewhere in Western Europe. Only a minor slump in 2007, followed by a flat development in 2008, marks a deviation from the upward trend.

It is hard to appreciate all aspects of the long boom in housing prices. The major point here is that affordability has become a critical issue in the Oslo housing market. The ratio of prices to household income does not capture affordability properly, but it does give a clue about increasing housing costs. This ratio grew by 33 per cent in the decade from 2001 to 2011.[4] What has not changed is the structure of the housing market. Public housing accounted for 4 per cent in 1990, in 2001 and in 2011. Private rented housing grew from 18 per cent in 1990 to 21 per cent in 2001, and remained at 21 per cent in 2011.[5] The composition of these tenures is obviously different, with a larger social diversity in the private sector, but both of them are viewed as inferior options. Public housing is strictly reserved for households with large and complex problems. The private rented sector has a broader recruitment base but suffers from instability and resource deficits. The main aim for young households, accordingly, is to head for home ownership as soon as possible.

The promotion of home ownership in Oslo has been facilitated by a fragmented system of housing provision. Land supply was privatised in the early 1980s, and the traditional agency of social housing production (OBOS) adopted a private market strategy from 1985 onwards. The scale of production, and the importance of large firms, was different forty or fifty years ago, but the industrial approach to housing provision was always contested, and so were many plans for development and redevelopment. Oslo, in other words, is not a showcase for homogeneous urban expansion.

Table 6.1 summarises the presented features, both from this and the former section. The largest changes concern housing prices, population size, population diversity, economic prosperity and industrial structure. Housing policy and housing market structure are the most stable features, whereas welfare policies and employment/unemployment have undergone minor changes.

Table 6.1 Key features of the Oslo region during the observation period, 1993–2011

Feature	Change/stability
Housing policy	Stable: market-oriented
Housing market structure	Stable: ownership bias
Housing provision	Stable: fragmented
Housing prices	Spiralling upwards
Welfare benefits	Stable, but stricter qualifying conditions
Social assistance	Small/shrinking part of income security provision
Population size	Increasing through positive net migration and natural growth
Population diversity	Increasing through immigration and natural growth
Employment/unemployment	Fairly stable
GDP per capita	Growth
Industrial structure	Deindustrialisation, growth in business services

Spatial differences in socio-economic status: debate and research

The interest in socio-economic segregation in Oslo and Norway has fluctuated over time. Much of the debate has revolved around a division between poor areas in Oslo east and rich areas in Oslo west. This division was formed in the 1840s and further strengthened during the growth of manufacturing industries in the nineteenth and twentieth century. Urban development after World War II made each part of the city, each 'lifeworld', much larger.

The new suburbs were at the same time different, and many people felt that the east had been suitably compensated with modern housing and green environments. A newspaper debate in 1958 shows the new mentality very clearly. Several participants in the debate were furious over the content in a radio programme on social changes. What they reacted to was a suggestion, made by a teenage girl, that old geographies remained intact: east was still east, and west was still west. The debate was so intense that an office manager in the municipality of Oslo conducted an analysis of Oslo's social geography. His conclusion gave more support to the girl than to her critics: the new satellite towns contributed to a mixed social geography, but the east–west divide had not been bridged. As he put it, 'the girl was not so naive after all' (Østberg 1958: 6).

A totally different debate played out two decades later. The context this time was social research on living conditions in Norway. A report on urban living conditions (Aase and Dale 1978) laid the foundation for new political initiatives (NOU 1979: 5; St.meld. 16 1979–80), followed by new urban research. One of the main messages in the report was that socio-economic segregation remained a significant challenge due to three structural factors: competition for space, concentration of public goods and the commercial character of big cities.

The next phase commenced in the early 1990s. Several commentators, including researchers, politicians and public officers, suggested that Oslo had become increasingly divided as a result of globalisation and privatisation policies. Even the local branch of the Conservative Party expressed an intention to combat increasing spatial differences in well-being. Others utilised the new polarisation metaphor: the east–west divide had never been deeper, to the extent that Oslo had acquired a new socio-spatial form. The problem, however, was that no-one had presented comparative-historical data. Some reports showed large spatial differences in socio-economic status, for example in educational level, but these reports were based on synchronic analysis. A more relevant dataset was produced in the mid-1990s, after a reconstruction of old townships. The ensuing analysis provided no support to the polarisation argument: socio-spatial differences between townships remained stable during the period 1970 to 1990/1995. A more gloomy part of the picture was that household inequality had increased distinctly between 1986 and 1996, which implied a striking mismatch between social indicators at different spatial levels. The explanation, according to the author, could be found in a change from modernist to post-modernist urban development. A local conservative government had introduced small-scale housing and functional mixture as the new development approach in Oslo. This choice emerged from aesthetic ideals, and not from a preoccupation with social policy and segregation. An effect, nevertheless, was that poor, disadvantaged or newly urbanized districts received a larger proportion of middle-income households (Wessel 2000).

Later research found similar patterns at a lower spatial level (Vatne Pettersen 2003), and a marked growth at the top of the income distribution (Wessel 2001). Looking behind the changes, there were no signs of increasing premiums on education (Wessel 2005). Almost all increasing inequality in market income could be attributed to increasing inequality within the business services, and even within social groups in the business services (Wessel 2013).

The latest research explores segregation of social classes, covering 1970, 1980 and 2003 (Ljunggren and Andersen 2014). Social class is defined partly in vertical terms, between the upper class and the working class, and partly in horizontal terms, between economic and cultural class factions. The analysis documents increasing segregation between the upper class and the working class between 1980 and 2003. It also shows increasing segregation between the economic fraction of the upper/upper middle class and the remainder of the population (Ljunggren and Andersen 2014). However, since the middle class is excluded from the analysis, one cannot conclude anything about socio-economic segregation at large.[6]

A rough impression of the presented evidence is that globalisation, immigration and changes in the industrial structure have brought substantial changes to the Oslo region. The most important impact concerns the ability of different groups to exercise residential choice. Upward social mobility and redistribution of income have given high-income households the upper hand in the competition for urban space. Another impression is that spatial forms display a high degree of continuity. Some parts of the city have gained a larger social mix, but the major geographical divisions remain intact. But these patterns are, admittedly, somewhat dated. A key question is whether economic segregation has been affected in the longer run.

Data and methods

The data in the analysis are retrieved from a database with 100 per cent population coverage. The database was created in the project 'Neighbourhoods at risk', which is part of the programme 'Welfare, Working Life and Migration' (Norwegian Research Council). Individuals are the primary units in the database, with added information on families and households. All data derive originally from registers and censuses at Statistics Norway.

A major concern with selection bias has guided the empirical approach. Much of the reviewed research is not sufficiently broad to address the intertwining influences of economic change and intra-urban mobility. It has been usual, for instance, to focus on the core municipality instead of the Oslo region (see Brevik 2001; Ljunggren and Andersen 2014; Wessel 2000, 2001). The urban area expands far beyond the borders of the core municipality, both in functional and visual terms. Choosing the Oslo region increases the possibility of capturing neutralising changes in different areas: east and west, north and south, inner and outer city. A similar logic applies to the selection of population groups. It is tempting to pick particular cohorts or particular sections of the labour force, for example people in full employment. These choices reduce the confusing effect of population structure; however, they also increase the risk of hasty generalisation. The scale of residential change can easily be over- or underestimated when labour income, taxes and transfers are unevenly distributed across sections of the population. An option, which is chosen here, is to combine a narrow and a wide age span. The narrow analysis in this case covers individuals between thirty-five and forty-nine years of age, as a trade-off between increasing population size and decreasing demographic complexity. The wide analysis attempts to reduce selection bias as much as possible, and includes adults aged twenty or more.

Four indicator variables are used: market income, income after tax, gross wealth and net wealth. Market income includes wages, income from self-employment and capital income. It is a concept that, despite some noise, is well-suited in analyses of advanced service economies, as recently noted by Thomas Piketty (2014). Income after tax (or disposable personal income) is a broader concept, since it builds on gross income. The deductions include all assessed taxes and negative transfers. Gross wealth is defined as the tax-assessed value of property and finance capital. This concept is useful because it reflects accumulation of capital in the past. It should be noted, however, that property is taxed at a fraction of its true value. A measurement of true values would probably boost some of the estimates, particularly for the richest groups. Net wealth is even more 'polluted', since a large section of the population can deduct all their mortgages. The main aim here, therefore, is to look at net wealth as a secondary source of information, i.e. as a complement to gross wealth.

A further complication concerns the relationship between personal income and corporate income. Rich people tend to channel a part of their income through joint-stock companies or personal businesses. It is hard to speculate whether the distorting effect of such practice is significant. What we can say for sure is that rich people have incomes and assets that escape proper registration.

Income and wealth are nevertheless acceptable indicators in the Norwegian context. Occupation appears to have variable reliability over time, and education has been seriously devalued over the last decades. The increasing proportion of university graduates has affected relative wages, which in turn yields a distorted picture of socio-economic segregation. This became evident after an empirical test: none of the changes that appear in this study were captured by a variable for educational attainment.

One problem is hard to avoid: Norway did not have a proper income register prior to 1993. It would be possible to utilise census data, for instance from 1980, but not without comparability issues.

Measures of inequality and segregation

The first empirical section shows changes in individual and household inequality, measured by the Gini index (G) (see also the introduction of this book for more detail: Tammaru *et al.* 2016). One formal representation of G is

$$G = \frac{2}{n^2 \mu} \sum_{i=1}^{n} i\left(y_{i\_} \mu\right)$$

where n is the number of income units, i is the position in the distribution and y_i are individual incomes ranked from the lowest to the highest. I have chosen to multiply index values by 100, which gives a range between 0 and 100.

The second section explores segregation by income and wealth. Segregation in the current context implies uneven distribution of population groups, defined as income/wealth quintiles. I rely mostly on the segregation index (IS) but will also apply the dissimilarity index (D) and the isolation index (P*), all of which vary between 0 and 100. IS and P* can be represented as

$$IS = \frac{\sum_{i=1}^{n}(X_i - Y_i)/2}{1 - \sum_{i=1}^{n} Y_i / \sum_{i=1}^{n} X_i}$$

$$P* = \sum_{i=1}^{n}\left(\frac{Y_i}{\sum Y_i}\right)\left(\frac{Y_i}{\sum X_i}\right)$$

where X is the total population and Y a subgroup in each area (i). $\sum Y_i$ is the total number of the subgroup in the city. $\sum X_i$ is the total population of the city. D, which is the numerator of IS, is used instead of IS when one subgroup is measured against another subgroup.

The third section contains a decomposition of economic segregation on natives and immigrants. The methodology here builds on average income/wealth for each group, not on the representation of income/wealth brackets in each subarea. The measure I use, mean log deviation (MLD), allows a decomposition into segregation within and between the two groups. The formula can be written, before decomposition, as

$$MLD = \frac{\sum\limits_{i=1}^{n} \log\left(\dfrac{\mu}{y_i}\right)}{n}$$

where n is the total population, μ is mean income for all subareas, y_i is average income/wealth in each subarea. MLD varies between 0 and infinity, and gives particular weight to changes at the bottom of the neighbourhood hierarchy, i.e. between poor and somewhat less poor areas. This feature is particularly suitable in an analysis of natives and immigrants, since immigrants tend to advance at the bottom of the hierarchy. MLD decomposes as

$$MLD = \sum\limits_{k=1}^{k} MLD_k \left(\frac{n_k}{n}\right) + \sum\limits_{k=1}^{k} \left(\frac{n_k}{n}\right) \log\left(\frac{\mu}{\mu_k}\right)$$

where k represents the two groups, with n_k individuals in each group, and (n_k/n) is a statistical weight (reflecting group size). The decomposition shows how three types of change contribute to overall change in economic segregation: (1) the level of economic segregation among natives/immigrants, (2) the change in the size of the two subgroups (natives/immigrants), (3) change in economic segregation between natives and immigrants.

Individual and household inequality

Economic structure is often considered as the raw material of socio-economic segregation. There are good reasons for this view, as amply demonstrated by Allen Scott (1988). Individuals and groups tend to be sorted into particular districts according to income, occupation and workplace. Yet, while economic structure has a logical primacy, it should never be framed as a deterministic association. The referred evidence from Oslo is just one example of complex relationships between economic and socio-spatial change. Two studies from London bring home the same point: Buck *et al.* (2002) and Hamnett (2003) observe stability in the pattern and level of socio-economic segregation despite major increases in earnings inequality. Buck *et al.* even conclude that all social classes except for manual workers became less segregated during the decade from 1981 to 1991.

It is therefore useful to start with a brief overview of economic inequality. Table 6.2 shows, first, an upward trajectory of earnings inequality (market income). The change over the whole period is quite pronounced for the age-group thirty-five to forty-nine, but even the wider age group experienced growing inequality from 2001 to 2011. The picture is very different, however, when we look at income after tax. This indicator does not move upwards but downwards. The measures for gross wealth show a similar tendency in the second period, but not in the first. It is fascinating to see the fluctuating index value for the narrow age span: it jumps markedly from 1993 to 2001 but falls back even more from 2001 to 2011. A similar but less distinct change applies to the wider age span.

How can we account for the apparent contradictions in Table 6.2? One sensible interpretation is that taxes and transfers counterweight changes in the distribution of labour market earnings. In other words: there may be 'stretching' in earnings, but the net effect on welfare is moderated by distributive policies. It is hard to say how strong the counterweighting forces are – whether the regressive market change is completely neutralized. One might get the impression of effective government policies, given the figures for income after tax and wealth. But, as noted, registered personal income and registered personal property may not capture privileges at the top. There have been changes in the way rich people organize their lives that suggest an increasing gulf between this group and the rest of society. A provisional conclusion can therefore be drawn: Table 6.2 suggests an increasing potential for segregation of wealthy people.

The development of household inequality is presented in Table 6.3. These data stretch over a longer period, from 1986 to 2010, and are based on income surveys.

Table 6.2 Income and wealth inequality for individuals in the Oslo region, measured by the Gini coefficient 1993, 2001 and 2011 (register data)

	1993	*2001*	*2011*
Individuals aged 35–49			
Market incomes	36.0	37.2	39.5
Income after tax	31.4	30.8	29.9
Gross wealth	67.7	72.5	67.4
Net wealth[a]	91.4	90.1	89.9
Individuals 20 years plus			
Market incomes	52.3	51.6	53.8
Income after tax	34.0	32.1	32.9
Gross wealth	70.1	72.1	70.1
Net wealth[a]	88.1	90.7	86.0

Note: [a] Negative net wealth is set to zero.

Table 6.3 Income inequality for households in the municipality of Oslo and the whole of Norway, measured by the Gini coefficient 1986, 1996, 2000 and 2010 (income surveys)

	1986	*1996*	*2000*	*2008*	*2012*
The municipality of Oslo	22.8	32.1	32.2	31.4	30.4
Norway	21.0	24.4	26.1	24.7	24.9

The geographical scope is the municipality of Oslo (see Figure 6.1), which is compared to the whole of Norway. All sources of income, from all members of the household, are included. Following the norm, some members of the household count more than others, in accordance with the EU scale.[7]

The changes may be summarised in three points. First, household inequality in Oslo reached a high in the mid-1990s, and has declined slightly in recent years. Second, a sharp increase in inequality occurred in the 1980s and early 1990s. The registered jump in the Gini coefficient between 1986 and 1996, 9.3 percentage points, may be complemented by some figures for the highest and lowest decile: the former group increased its share of all incomes by 10 percentage points, compared to a decrease by 1 percentage point for the lowest decile (Wessel 2001). These are clearly dramatic changes, almost a nightmare, for an egalitarian society. Third, Oslo and Norway have to some extent split part. The difference in the Gini coefficient between the two entities is now three times higher than twenty-five years ago. An obvious explanation for the disparity is the position of Oslo as the chief business centre in Norway. This role has been strengthened since the mid-1980s.

Economic segregation

The connection between household inequality and spatial inequality may require a certain time-lapse to materialise. Symbolic values do not change over night, nor do housing prices in various parts of the city, nor the urban fabric for that matter. The complexity is further affected by the social profile of winners and losers. A development that benefits people at the top involves two unpredictable factors: first, price signals have to trickle down the market before all adjustments have taken place; second, housing consumption in the local area, i.e. in Oslo, is bound to compete with other investments (for example house purchases abroad), expensive leisure activities and luxury goods. A challenging question therefore arises: does the social landscape of Oslo reflect redistributive changes in the 1980s and 1990s?

Table 6.4 contains two sets of indices of segregation, IS and P*, and two definitions of income, market income and income after tax, for the wider age span. All measurements show increasing segregation for the fifth quintile, whereas the lowest quintile has declining segregation in one measurement (market income) and increasing segregation in the other one (income after tax). The overall impression, when all quintiles are included, is a tiny decrease in segregation between 1993 and 2001, and a tiny increase between 2001 and 2011. We further note that IS values for the fifth quintile have changed more than P* values. This might indicate that neighbourhoods with a high proportion of the fifth quintile have remained fairly stable in population size, i.e. that urban infill and redevelopments have occurred in other places.

A more detailed picture of the changes between 2001 and 2011 is given in Table 6.5. All five quintiles are here contrasted against each other, with 2001 and 2011 in the upper and lower halves of the table, respectively. A surprising feature is that quintile 2 and quintile 5 are more segregated from each other than quintile 1 and quintile 5. One obvious reason for the pattern is gentrification in the inner

Table 6.4 Segregation by income: individuals aged 20 years or more in the Oslo region, measured by the segregation and isolation indexes at the census tract level

	1993	2001	2011	1993	2001	2011
	Segregation index			Isolation index		
Market income						
Quintile 1	18.8	17.2	17.3	23.1	22.5	22.6
Quintile 2	9.0	8.2	8.6	20.7	20.6	20.7
Quintile 3	10.8	11.3	12.5	19.6	21.0	21.2
Quintile 4	10.5	9.8	11.7	20.9	20.8	21.1
Quintile 5	20.9	20.6	23.1	23.3	23.2	23.9
Average all quintiles	14.0	13.4	14.6	21.5	21.6	21.9
Income after tax						
Quintile 1	10.1	9.9	12.1	21.1	21.0	21.6
Quintile 2	13.8	11.9	13.8	21.6	21.2	21.5
Quintile 3	9.6	8.9	10.3	20.8	20.7	20.8
Quintile 4	9.2	8.3	9.3	20.7	20.6	20.7
Quintile 5	22.4	21.7	24.1	23.8	23.6	24.3
Average all quintiles	13.0	12.1	13.9	21.6	21.4	21.8

Table 6.5 Segregation by income: individuals aged 20 years or more in the Oslo region, measured by D at the census tract level: matrix between quintiles in 2001 and 2011

		2001				
		Quintile 1	Quintile 2	Quintile 3	Quintile 4	Quintile 5
2011	Quintile 1		9.9	11.4	13.2	22.2
	Quintile 2	13.4		8.7	14.3	25.8
	Quintile 3	14.1	8.7		8.2	23.0
	Quintile 4	15.5	14.2	9.4		18.9
	Quintile 5	24.3	29.2	25.7	20.7	

Table 6.6 Segregation by wealth: individuals aged 20 years or more in the Oslo region, measured by the segregation index at the census tract level

	1993	2001	2011
Gross wealth[a]			
Quintile 1	14.5	18.2	21.0
Quintile 2	13.6	15.0	15.2
Quintile 3	19.3	15.4	19.9
Quintile 4	15.1	14.2	13.3
Quintile 5	27.7	27.0	32.3
Average all quintiles	17.6	17.9	20.3

(continued)

Table 6.6 (continued)

	1993	*2001*	*2011*
Net wealth[b]			
Quintile 1	17.6	19.8	22.9
Quintile 2	11.8	13.4	15.7
Quintile 3	11.5	11.4	16.2
Quintile 4	10.9	12.1	13.9
Quintile 5	26.2	25.9	30.3
Average all quintiles	15.6	16.5	19.8

Notes:
[a] Includes individuals with zero wealth.
[b] Individuals with negative net wealth are excluded.

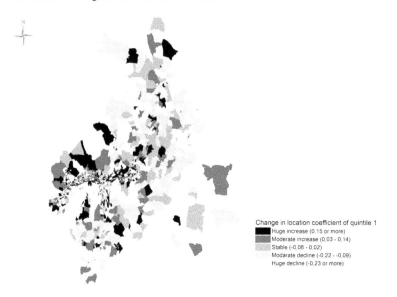

Figure 6.2 Changes in the location coefficient of quintile 1 over the period 2001 to 2011, measured by income after tax for individuals aged 20 plus.

city, where low-income and high-income groups have become close neighbours. A related reason concerns the structure of the housing market. Many immigrants with fairly low incomes, typically in quintile 2, have bought co-operative flats in satellite towns from the 1960s, 1970s and 1980s. These places do not attract high-income households and individuals, partly because of the housing stock, partly because of the location (east) and partly because of the changing population composition. A fourth reason is a fluctuating tendency to establish rental property in single-family-homes. There are many landlords among high-income households in the western part of the city, as we may sense from Figure 6.2. There has been a

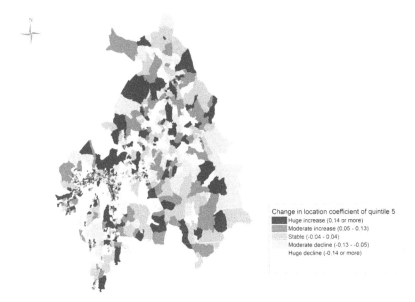

Change in location coefficient of quintile 5
■ Huge increase (0.14 or more)
■ Moderate increase (0.05 - 0.13)
▨ Stable (-0.04 - 0.04)
Moderate decline (-0.13 - -0.05)
Huge decline (-0.14 or more)

Figure 6.3 Changes in the location coefficient of quintile 5 over the period 2001 to 2011, measured by income after tax for individuals aged 20 plus.

distinct increase in quintile 1 in western areas, and it is not far-fetched to assume that this change is connected to rental activities. Quintile 5, by contrast, shows a more scattered pattern of change, with relative increases in the inner city, northern/ eastern areas and parts of Oslo west (Figure 6.3). A more narrow definition of affluent groups would have shown a larger change in the centre of the region, i.e. in the municipality of Oslo.

The evidence pertaining to gross wealth is easier to summarise and comprehend. Table 6.6 (upper panel) shows a clear tendency towards polarisation, with increased segregation for quintile 1 and quintile 5. There have been changes at the middle as well, but these are smaller and less systematic. A further look at net wealth (lower panel) confirms the impression for the fifth quintile. Several alternative definitions of net wealth, with variable cut-points at the bottom, produce basically the same result for the top. Net wealth at the lower end, on the other hand, is difficult to measure, given the large proportion of individuals with large debt.

The analyses above are challenged by the variable balance between earnings, taxes and public transfers at different stages of life. Let us therefore look at the narrow age span, individuals aged thirty-five to forty-nine. Table 6.7 follows the same logic as Table 6.4, with market income in the upper panel and income after tax in the lower panel. Only IS values are shown, since P* provides little additional information.

What we see in Table 6.7 is a picture which closely resembles polarisation, with stability at the middle and increasing segregation at each end of the distribution. Another interesting feature is the sharp tendency towards separation at the

Table 6.7 Segregation by income: individuals aged 35–49 in the Oslo region, measured by the segregation index at the census tract level

	1993	2001	2011
Market income			
Quintile 1	14.0	17.5	18.8
Quintile 2	13.7	15.5	16.8
Quintile 3	13.0	11.8	13.0
Quintile 4	11.3	11.8	12.3
Quintile 5	27.3	30.1	30.6
Average all quintiles	15.8	17.3	18.3
Income after tax			
Quintile 1	15.4	17.6	20.6
Quintile 2	14.5	15.6	17.1
Quintile 3	12.9	13.3	13.3
Quintile 4	11.8	11.9	13.1
Quintile 5	27.5	30.1	31.1
Average all quintiles	16.4	17.7	19.0

top. Similar observations abound in the segregation literature, but it is nevertheless surprising that values for the fifth quintile in Oslo exceed 30. This is a higher level than Musterd (2005) reports for Amsterdam, Rotterdam and Copenhagen. A closer look at different parts of the fifth quintile shows some significant internal differences. The richest percentile had an index value around 60–61 in 1993, which dropped to 57–58 in 2011. A similar tendency applies to all the following analyses. In other words: the very top has not become more segregated.

Table 6.8 measures segregation according to wealth, still limited to people between thirty-five and forty-nine. Here, the impression of polarisation is even stronger. The lowest quintile of wealth holders (gross wealth) displays a stunning increase in the index value, from 16.4 in 1993 to 27.6 in 2011. There is also increasing segregation at the top, whereas the middle has smaller changes. It might be objected that net wealth (the lower panel) shows a reduction in segregation at the bottom, but, as noted, this indicator does not provide reliable information at the lower end.

It is clear from the analyses so far that Oslo has developed along different lines than twenty or twenty-five years ago. The combination of increasing inequality in household income and stable socio-economic segregation is now reversed: the latest period is marked by stable economic inequality and increasing social/economic segregation. Using wealth as a supplementary indicator strengthens the impression of a lagged effect. A current tendency towards increasing inequality in the distribution of market incomes may be moving in the same direction.

Then there is the population factor. The immigrant population, including descendants, has almost tripled from 1993 to 2011. It is well known that immigrants lag behind native Norwegians on most measures of economic well-being. A recent study is particularly relevant since it covers the period from 1993 to 2011. The

Table 6.8 Segregation by wealth: individuals aged 35–49 in the Oslo region, measured by the segregation index at the census tract level

	1993	2001	2011
Gross wealth[a]			
Quintile 1	16.4	24.9	27.6
Quintile 2	14.0	19.2	25.8
Quintile 3	23.8	17.9	22.3
Quintile 4	19.0	18.6	18.3
Quintile 5	29.7	29.3	33.6
Average all quintiles	20.6	22.0	25.5
Highest percentile	60.9	61.0	58.7
Net wealth[b]			
Quintile 1	16.5	13.4	13.1
Quintile 2	13.7	15.1	14.3
Quintile 3	12.8	19.2	21.4
Quintile 4	12.7	12.3	14.0
Quintile 5	19.5	24.6	27.7
Average all quintiles	15.0	16.9	18.1

Notes:
[a] Includes individuals with zero wealth.
[b] Individuals with negative net wealth are excluded.

conclusion here (Bhuller and Brandsås 2014) is that all but one immigrant group (immigrants from Eastern Europe) have a stable level of poverty. This suggests that economic segregation may be driven from two fronts: partly from incomes and wealth at the top, and partly from population change and poverty at the bottom.

Immigration and economic segregation

The connection between population change and economic segregation involves many mechanisms and levels of causation. What follows is a first attempt to explore how much each of two groups, natives and immigrants, contributes to separation in economic terms. The main aim is to provide a direction for further research.

Table 6.9 contains a full decomposition of segregation by market income and income after tax. The upper part of the table reports results for the narrow age span, and the lower part for the wider age span. Each section includes three types of information: first, index values for each group; second, a division of total segregation on segregation within and between groups; and third, an estimation of how much each group contributes to segregation within groups. The index values show the degree of segregation by income independent of group size. Total segregation is self-explanatory – this is the level of segregation for the aggregate population (i.e. natives plus immigrants). Segregation between and within groups depends on two factors: the gap between index values and the relative size of the two groups.

Table 6.9 Segregation by income: MLD decomposition of natives and immigrants, measured at the census tract level

	Individuals aged 35–49			Individuals aged 20 plus		
	1993	*2001*	*2011*	*1993*	*2001*	*2011*
Market income						
Index values for natives	0.042	0.050	0.061	0.072	0.050	0.067
Index values for immigrants	0.138	0.092	0.087	0.179	0.093	0.059
Segregation between groups	0.002	0.003	0.012	0.002	0.003	0.004
Segregation within groups	0.050	0.056	0.067	0.080	0.055	0.065
Total segregation	0.052	0.059	0.079	0.082	0.058	0.069
Native share of within-group segregation	76.4%	77.8%	70.9%	83.4%	80.3%	82.7%
Immigrant share of within-group segregation	23.6%	22.2%	29.1%	16.6%	19.7%	17.3%
Income after tax						
Index values for natives	0.035	0.034	0.032	0.028	0.025	0.022
Index values for immigrants	0.078	0.055	0.046	0.064	0.036	0.041
Segregation between groups	0.003	0.005	0.013	0.003	0.006	0.010
Segregation within groups	0.039	0.037	0.035	0.031	0.026	0.026
Total segregation	0.042	0.042	0.049	0.034	0.032	0.036
Native share of within-group segregation	79.9%	77.8%	69.2%	82.4%	80.7%	67,4%
Immigrant share of within-group segregation	20.1%	22.2%	30.8%	17.6%	19.3%	32,6%

The first point to note is that immigrants are not becoming more but less segregated in terms of income. MLD for the narrow age span drops by 37 and 41 per cent, and by 67 and 36 per cent for the wider age span. Natives, for their part, display a combination of increasing, stable and slightly declining segregation. One section of the group, those between thirty-five and forty-nine, became more segregated according to market income but not according to income after tax. The wider age span has a more coherent pattern, with a trifling reduction in segregation by income.

Declining differentiation among immigrants leads, logically, to a smaller gap in economic segregation between the two groups. The significance of this gap, however, increases considerably over time. Segregation between groups is boosted simply because immigrants make up an increasing share of the total population. It is also interesting to see that between-group segregation lies at a higher level for income after tax than for market income. This difference is particularly large in relative terms, i.e. as a proportion of total segregation. One obvious reason for the outcome is that immigrants have a lower labour market participation than natives. Segregation between the two groups counts for little when we confine the analysis to people with earnings.

The greater proportion of segregation can be viewed as 'residual' – i.e. a rest-variation that occurs within the two groups. Immigrants have increased their share of such variation in all but one instance. The exception is segregation by market income for the wider age span. Here, we observe a lower level of segregation in 2011 among immigrants than among natives. Income after tax, by contrast, yields very different figures for the same age span. The reason, again, is the gap in segregation levels, plus the compression of differences that occurs through population mix (for example the presence of middle-income elderly people) and public policies. It may be difficult to fully grasp the content and implications of Table 6.9. One way to simplify the picture is to compare two sets of figures. The first one is immigrants' contribution to within-group segregation, the second is immigrants' contribution to the total population. Looking at the wider age span and income after tax, these figures are 32.6 and 20.6 per cent. In other words: immigrants contribute more to income segregation than their share of the population would imply. The same conclusion holds for 11 out of 12 calculations in Table 6.9.

Poverty among immigrants is therefore bound to affect the level of economic segregation. It is, needless to say, important to avoid all sorts of blaming games. Immigrants contribute significantly to the growing economy, and to the development of an exciting multi-cultural city. The new flavour of Asia, Africa and Latin America lies atop of older chaotic layers, and makes Oslo a colourful place, even if urban planning continues to suffer one humiliation after another.

Conclusion

Oslo has been transformed to a rich, post-industrial city over the last three decades. Growth in advanced business services has made the city and its surrounding areas more unequal, but most of these changes took place in the late 1980s and early 1990s. The same period was marked by a housing market collapse, due to a combination of domestic policies and the general economic crisis. Later in the 1990s, Norway benefited vastly from abundant natural resources but also from traditional tripartite politics. The prosperous economy gave Norway an advantage compared to neighbouring Sweden and Denmark, and made it possible to retain a higher level of social insurance protection.

This background sheds important light on the development of economic segregation in Oslo. We may separate two periods, one with increasing income inequality and stable economic segregation, and one with stable income inequality and increasing economic segregation. The link between growth in advanced business services and growth in income inequality has been firmly established, and suggests increasing segregation of affluent groups. So far, we have no overview of all structural impacts, but we do know that affluent groups are becoming more segregated. The change is quite substantial, and obtains for all indicators: market income, income after tax, gross wealth and net wealth. Contrary to some other results, it makes no difference whether the analysis is carried out for a narrow or a wide age span.

There is also increasing segregation of poor groups. The lowest quintile in the age-span thirty-five to forty-nine experienced a substantial increase in segregation from 1993 to 2011, amounting to 11 percentage points in one measurement (gross wealth). A decomposition of economic segregation between and within two groups, natives and immigrants, brought further evidence to the fore. Both types of difference (between/within groups) indicate a causal connection between population diversity and polarisation of the social landscape. A comforting part of the picture, though, is that immigrants are becoming less segregated in economic terms.[8] Equally important is the fact that immigrants in Oslo have easy access to credit, which is reflected in housing statistics: 68 per cent of all immigrants in Oslo are home owners.[9]

Finally a word on theory: should we view the results as a confirmation of polarisation theory? The answer is not straightforward, since the growth of advanced business services has led to increasing economic inequality, in line with the social polarisation thesis (Sassen 1991). Other aspects of polarisation theory receive less support. The changes in Oslo do not reveal massive deprivation at the bottom of the social hierarchy. A more suitable perspective is polarisation as a product of different coinciding processes. A celebrated term from the 1980s, 'contingent outcome', is highly applicable. There appears to be a drift towards increasing economic inequality, where top earners increase their wages and benefits at the expense of all others. This can be seen as a core dynamic, a relentless force at the centre of the capitalist economy. Another dynamic is immigration and growth of ethnic diversity. The influx of migrants and refugees is obviously affected by economic growth and redistribution of incomes and wealth. Nothing, however, points towards a strong functional relationship, where economic needs determine the size and composition of migrant flows. The relationship, hence, is much looser and less predictable than suggested in the global city framework. Immigration may be seen, instead, as a factor with a similar status as welfare politics – neither generic nor specific but something in between: a syndrome of causes and outcomes that lends itself to typological theorising. The final factor comprises urban planning, housing policy, housing provision and housing market structure. These latter influences appear to have a surprisingly independent basis, as recognized in recent studies (Kazepov 2005; Arbaci 2007; Maloutas 2012). What many studies fail to recognise is the complicated relationship between income, wealth and housing market provision. It may take years before distributive changes affect the structure of market signals, and when these signals are firmly expressed, there is still a time lag before residential replacements and accretions emerge. This, I believe, is the most important lesson from the Oslo case.

Acknowledgement

This chapter is based on research funded by the Norwegian Research Council [grant number 217210/H2]. Many thanks to Lena Magnusson Turner for constructing the maps in this study.

Notes

1 The state-centred development approach was to a large extent abandoned in the early 1980s. A collapse in the banking sector in 1987–91 led to new engagement, with state-injected capital in crisis-stricken banks.
2 This term was coined by Lars Mjøseth in 1986.

3 None of the mentioned studies include social assistance. This part of the welfare system is highly important, but it is too small to change the big picture. Social assistance in Norway accounts for approximately 5 per cent of all income security provision (Johansson and Hvinden 2007).

4 The measurement is based on average house prices and median income after tax. Prices are from Norwegian Association of Real Estate Agents and income data from Statistics Norway (Table 04452 in Statbank). Average income after tax for households is not available at the county level.

5 The numbers for 2001 and 2011 are from Statbank. The 1990 numbers are calculated from the 1990 housing census and Table 7 in Holm and Dyb 2001.

6 Another complicating factor concerns the population sample: it is restricted to parents of children aged thirteen to fifteen at each observation point.

7 The weights are: 1.0 for the first adult, 0.5 for the second adult and each subsequent person aged seventeen and over, and 0.3 for children aged under seventeen.

8 An explanation for the shrinking gap in segregation levels is the fact that descendants make up an increasing proportion of the immigrant population. One might argue that descendants are not immigrants, but the concept 'immigrants' may nevertheless suffice as a stenographic shorthand. Unfortunately, it was not possible to conduct the analysis with descendants as a separate category: there were too few members of this group in 1993.

9 Source: the database in 'Neighbourhoods at risk'.

References

Aase, A and Dale, B 1978, *Levekår i storby* [Level of living in major cities], Universitetsforlaget, Oslo.

Arbaci, S 2007, 'Ethnic segregation, housing systems and welfare regimes in Europe' *International Journal of Housing Policy* 8, 401–433.

Bengtsson, B 2006, 'Varför så olika? Om en nordisk gåta och hur den kan lösas' [Why so different? A Nordic puzzle and how to solve it] in *Varför så olika? Nordisk bostadpolitik i jämförande ljus* [Why so different? Nordic housing policy in a comparative historical light], eds B Bengtsson, E Annaniassen, L Jensen, H Ruonavaara and J R Sveinsson, Égalité, Malmö, pp. 11–44.

Bhuller, M and Brandsås, E 2014, 'Fattig i fjor – fattig i år? Tilstandsavhengighet i innvandrefattigdom' [Poor last year – poor this year? Continuous poverty among immigrants] *Søkelys på arbeidsmarkedet* 31, 209–22.

Brevik, I 2001, 'Income inequalities and socio-economic segregation in Oslo. Governance by the market' in *Governing European cities: Social fragmentation, social exclusion and governance*, eds H T Andersen and R van Kempen, Ashgate, Aldershot, pp. 211–232.

Buck, N, Gordon, I, Hall, P, Harloe, M and Kleinman, M 2002 (eds), *Working capital: Life and labour in contemporary London*, Routledge, London and New York.

Enzensberger, HM 1987, *Akk Europa,* Universitetsforlaget, Oslo.

Hagen, K, Djuve, A B and Vogt, P 1994, *Oslo – den delte byen?* [Oslo – the divided city?] Fafo–rapport 161, Oslo.

Hamnett, C 1996, 'Social polarisation, economic restructuring and welfare state regimes' *Urban Studies* 33, 1407–1430.

Hamnett, C 2003, *Unequal city: London in the global arena*, Routledge, London and New York.

Holm, A and Dyb, E 2001, *Boliger for vanskeligstilte* [Housing for disadvantaged groups], Norges Byggforskningsinstitutt, Oslo.

Johansson, H and Hvinden, B 2007, 'Re-activating the Nordic welfare states: Do we find a distinct universalistic model?' *International Journal of Sociology and Social Policy* 27, 334–346.

Kazepov, Y 2005, 'Introduction' in *Cities of Europe: Changing contexts, local arrangements, and the challenge to urban cohesion*, ed. Y Kazepov, Blackwell, Oxford, pp. 3–42.

Lasalle Investment Management 2013, *European Regional Economic Growth Index (E-regi) 2013*. Available online: http://www.lasalle.com/Pages/default.aspx. Accessed 9 May 2014.

Ljunggren, J and Andersen, P 2014, 'Spatial class divisions? Residential segregation in Oslo 1970–2003' *International Journal of Urban and Regional Research*, Article first published online: 22 DEC 2014 DOI: 10.1111/1468-2427.12167

Maloutas, T 2012, 'Introduction: Residential segregation in context' in *Residential segregation in comparative perspective: Making sense of contextual diversity*, eds T Maloutas and K. Fujita, Ashgate, Farnham, pp. 1–36.

Murie, A 1998, 'Segregation, exclusion and housing in the divided city' in *Urban segregation and the welfare State: Inequality and exclusion in Western cities*, eds S Musterd and W Ostendorf, Routledge, London, pp. 110–125.

Murie, A and Musterd, S 1996, 'Social segregation, housing tenure and social change in Dutch cities in the late 1980s' *Urban Studies* 33, 495–516.

Musterd, S 2005, 'Social and ethnic segregation in Europe: Levels, causes and effects' *Journal of Urban Affairs* 27, 331–348.

NOU 1979: 5 *Bypolitikk* [Urban Policy]. Universitetsforlaget ,Oslo.

Østberg, E 1958, 'Øst og vest i Oslo: naivitet eller sosial og økonomisk realitet' [East and west in Oslo: Naitivity or economic reality?] *Sosialøkonomen* 5, 4–6.

Piketty, T 2014, *Capital in the twenty-first century*, Harvard University Press, Cambridge, MA;

Rasmussen, T F 1998, *Norsk industri 1900–1992: distriktsnæring eller storbylokalisering?* [Norwegian manufacturing industries: Regional or urban location?], NIBRs plusserie (98), Oslo.

Sassen, S 1991, *The global city: New York, London, Tokyo*, Princeton University Press, Princeton and Oxford.

Scott, A J 1988, *Metropolis: From the division of labor to urban form,* University of California Press, Los Angeles.

Scruggs, L 2006, 'Welfare state decommodification in 18 OECD countries: A replication and revision' *Journal of European Social Policy* 16, 55–72.

Scruggs, L 2007, 'Welfare state generosity across space and time' in *Investigating welfare state change: The "dependent variable problem" in comparative analysis*, eds J Clasen and N A Sigel, Edward Elgar Publishing Limited, Cheltenham, pp. 133–165.

St.meld. 16 1979–80, *Om bedre nærmiljø* [On the improvement of local communities] (White paper).

Stamsø, M 2009, 'Housing and the welfare state in Norway' *Scandinavian Political Studies* 32, 195–220.

Statistics Norway 2014, *Historical statistics*. Available online: http://www.ssb.no/a/histstat/. Accessed 21 April 2015.

Tammaru, T, Musterd, S, van Ham, M and Marcińczak, S, 2016, 'A multi-factor approach to understanding socio-economic segregation in European capital cities' in *Socio-economic segregation in European capital cities: East meets West*, eds T Tammaru, S Marcińczak, M van Ham and S Musterd, Routledge, London.

Torgersen, U 1987, 'Housing: The wobbly pillar under the welfare state' in *Between state and market: Housing in the post-industrial era*, eds B Turner, J Kemeny and L J Lundqvist, Almqvust & Wiksell International, Göteborg, pp. 116–126.

van Vliet, O and Caminada, K 2012, *Unemployment replacement rates dataset among 34 welfare states, 1971–2009. An update, modification and extension of the Scruggs welfare states entitlements data set.* Available online: http://papers.ssrn.com/sol3/papers.cfm?abstract_id=1991214. Accessed 21 April 2015.

Vatne Pettersen, S 2003, *Bosettingsmønster og segregasjon i storbyregionen* [Settlement and segregation in major urban regions], Statistics Norway, Notater 2003/33, Oslo.

Wessel, T 2000, 'Social polarisation and socioeconomic segregation in a welfare state: The case of Oslo' *Urban Studies* 37, 1947–1967.

Wessel, T 2001, 'Losing control? Inequality and social divisions in Oslo' *European Planning Studies* 9, 889–906.

Wessel, T 2005, 'Industrial shift, skills mismatch and income inequality: A decomposition analysis of changing distributions in the Oslo region' *Urban Studies* 42, 1549–1568.

Wessel, T 2013, 'Economic change and rising income inequality in the Oslo region' *Regional Studies* 47, 1082–1094.

Wessel, T, Andersson, R, Kauppinen, T and Skifter Andersen, H (2014) 'Spatial integtration of immigrants in Nordic cities: The relevance of spatial assimilation theory in a welfare state context'. Submitted to international journal.

Wildavsky, A 1979 *Speaking truth to power: The art and craft of policy analysis*, Little, Brown & Co, Boston, MA.

Wyly, E K 1998, 'Continuity and change in the restless urban landscape' *Economic Geography* 75, 309–338.

7 Socio-economic segregation in Athens at the beginning of the twenty-first century

Thomas Maloutas

Abstract

This chapter provides evidence for the relatively moderate level of durable patterns and socio-economic segregation in Athens. The level of segregation remained stable, only slightly decreasing during the last two decades, while the patterns of social division were more clearly demarcated in space. Although the level of socio-economic inequality is relatively high, its translation to spatial division continues to be obstructed by a host of parameters – such as the high rate of home ownership and the low rate of residential mobility – inscribed in the residual local welfare state. The segregating impact of the sovereign debt crisis has also been curtailed following the collapse of housing demand.

Introduction

Socio-economic segregation is an expression of urban social inequalities that is either mitigated or exacerbated by the type of social regulation regime. At the same time, segregation usually affects social reproduction by emphasizing disadvantage and/or by enhancing privilege through neighbourhood effects. Following authors such as Friedmann and Wolff (1982), Sassen (2001) or Mollenkopf and Castells (1992), globalization has impacted on urban social division by intensifying the segregation process through social polarization, especially in world/global cities.

However, segregation outcomes cannot simply be inferred from globalization. Unless capitalist globalization is taken as an unavoidable economic necessity and not as the political project it in fact is, there is ample evidence of intended or indirect resistance to segregation in different parts of the urban world. Hamnett (1996), Musterd and Ostendorf (1998) and Murie and Musterd (2004) pinpointed the importance of the European welfare state in producing different outcomes from those theoretically expected in terms of social polarization and residential segregation. If the traditional European welfare state intentionally counteracted the growth of inequalities and segregation, other modes of social regulation also produced relatively low levels of inequality and segregation in different ways. The developmental state of the Far East (Fujita 2003; Hill and Kim 2000) generated a similar effect as a by-product of the endeavour to make a socially unifying national cause out of development targets. In southern Europe, residual welfare states and clientelist political regimes impeded the growth of segregation by respectively encouraging family-centred social relations (Allen *et al*. 2004) and by providing 'concessions' to a broad range of social groups against electoral support.

Different political *rapports des forces*, welfare regimes, institutional structures and arrangements, ideological orientations and shapes of the built environment and of the social relations that animate it constitute the main contextual parameters that mitigate or exacerbate the impact of global forces on urban inequalities and segregation (Maloutas 2012). The domination of neoliberal policies during the last three decades has undoubtedly contributed towards growing inequality, but the actual segregation outcomes proved to be more complex than what was theoretically expected. An analysis of socio-economic segregation in Athens during the 2000s is a showcase of this complexity.

Athens: an overview of urbanization and social geography in the post-war period

Population and labour market dynamics

Athens grew very fast during the three first post-war decades following population movement towards the cities produced by the civil war (1946–49) and the stagnation of the rural economy. This growth greatly declined as internal migration decreased in the 1980s and has remained at a low level ever since (Figure 7.1); the small growth during the last two decades was sustained by the immigrant inflow that started in the early 1990s. Moreover, birth rates declined impressively since the 1980s following the same trend in Italy and Spain, and the population of Athens underwent a process of precipitous ageing counterbalanced only by the young age of immigrants.

During the early post-World War II period, Athens was arguably the archetype of south European urbanization (Leontidou 1996; Salvati 2014). Characterized by a much larger population increase than its anaemic industrial development could induce, the growth of the Greek capital city – which led the country's intense urbanization – occurred in parallel with an equally strong trend of emigration to Fordist labour markets in Western Europe and overseas (Maloutas *et al.* 2012). Push rather than pull factors were behind this strong urbanization trend in the first three post-war decades (1950–80), affecting the ways migrants from the countryside and small cities were socially and spatially integrated in the rapidly growing capital (Allen *et al.* 2004: ch. 3).

The occupational structure in Athens developed reflecting the city's weak international/regional economic influence but also its absolutely dominant position within the Greek national economic space (Economou *et al.* 2001). The city's economy was deeply influenced by its own rapid growth with the housebuilding sector in a prominent position and leading industrial growth in related sectors (building materials, housing equipment etc.) rather than being led by broader

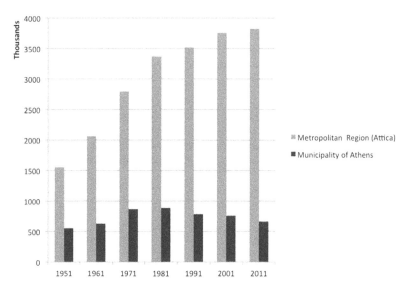

Figure 7.1 Population growth in the Athens metropolitan area and the Municipality of Athens, 1951–2011.

industrial growth. For most of the first three post-war decades, housebuilding activity was the economic barometer as well as the lever used to heat or cool the economy as a whole (Economou 1987 and 1988).

A host of factors formed an occupational structure with three main features: first, a very high rate of self-employment – Greece presents the highest rate of self-employment among OECD countries (UNECE 2003) – comprising mostly employers in small family businesses and self-employed without employees in a broad range of professions; second, a relatively small and 'fluid' working class which was constituted mainly by newcomers from rural areas rather than being internally reproduced (see Leiulfsrud *et al*. 2002) on the comparative weakness of the Greek working class in the European context); and third, a strong upward mobility throughout the occupational hierarchy which led to a process of professionalization. Professionalization, in this case, should not be understood as a process led mainly by jobs related to large corporate firms. It was led by a comparatively wide social distribution of access to the independent practice of medicine, law and engineering; it was also led since the 1980s by the rapid growth of hiring of higher education graduates by the public sector. The status of these professionals eventually declined following the impressive growth of their numbers. Similar trends have been observed in other south European countries as well: the decline of status for professionals in Spain is depicted by Domingeuz *et al.* (2012) following the comparative stagnation of their income during the decade before the 2008 crisis.

The large wave of immigration to Athens since the early 1990s changed the trend in the evolution of the occupational structure from professionalization to polarization. Immigrants have fuelled the growth of the lower occupational pole, while natives continued to be almost exclusively responsible for the growth of the upper pole. However, this polarization has not led to more segregation since the socio-economic content of the upper pole includes important differences from what might be expected according to the global city model (i.e. it does not comprise any considerable number of members of the global corporate elite that could induce segregation through gentrification, compared to the local occupational elite which is impeded from doing so by its integration into traditional family networks and property structures, and by much lower economic resources). Moreover, the structure of the housing market and the relatively even spatial distribution of different types and quality of housing have further prevented the increase of segregation by facilitating urban social mix, especially in central areas (Maloutas 2007).

Housing systems have deeply affected segregation levels and patterns following the pivotal role of housing in the south European urbanization model (Allen *et al.* 2004). The way housing systems affected segregation in Athens is discussed in the next section.

Housing structures and residential segregation

The meagre development of industry and the abundance of workers with respect to actual jobs resulted in large waves of emigration from southern Europe during the early post-war period. They also resulted – in tandem with the authoritarian regimes in most of the countries in the region – in establishing weak welfare states with opaque procedures that facilitated the operation of clientelism, bringing together populist party systems and family-centred electorates. The development of residual welfare states in southern Europe (Andreotti *et al.* 2001; Ferrera 1996; Mingione 1995) affected all areas of social reproduction but had a major impact on housing (Allen *et al.* 2004), thereby affecting the form and intensity of urban segregation throughout the region.

The absence of strong industrial development and the residual character of the welfare state made housing a pivotal process for urban integration during the first post-war period throughout southern Europe (Allen *et al.* 2004). During that period of workforce abundance, emigration and rapid urbanization, housing policies in Greece turned away from rented social housing and opted rather for home ownership in laissez-faire ways that involved the initiative of settlers themselves. This room for initiative was, in fact, a protected terrain where the mutual interests of petty landownership and small builders were regulated in ways that resulted in low-cost home ownership for a broad social spectrum of old and new city residents (Economou 1988). Home-owner households in Athens were 54.4 per cent of all households in 1958, 57.0 per cent in 1982 (Maloutas 1990: 123) and have climbed to over 65 per cent since 1991 (EKKE–ELSTAT 2014). The project to increase home ownership was, at the time, a major element of political stability, begun within the clientelist confines of authoritarian democracy in the turbulent post-civil war (1946–49) decades. Thus, the profile of residential segregation in

Athens has been structured mainly through the two dominant housing production and allocation systems, i.e. the self-promotion of substandard and often illegally built individual housing in the urban periphery (Leontidou 1990; Maloutas 1990) and the massive production of modern apartment buildings in very wide areas around the city centre (i.e. the central municipality and a few adjacent ones) that eventually became very densely built (Antonopoulou 1991). These two systems produced most of the city's current housing stock and affected segregation trends in specific – and sometimes contradictory – ways.

The first system (self-promotion) provided housing for hundreds of thousands of new residents who had moved from rural areas to the city's periphery – especially the western periphery, where most of the industry and the working class were located. This system reinforced both the east (bourgeois)/west (working class) divide in the city as well as the divide between the affluent centre and the poor periphery (Leontidou 1990; Prévélakis 2000; Maloutas 2003). The second system (*antiparohi*) provided massively low-cost modern apartment housing in the 1960s and the 1970s (Antonopoulou 1991) in the areas around the centre. Operations were small scale, as they entailed the joint venture of a small land-owner and a small builder who shared the apartments produced according to an initial contract. The popularity of this system was due to generous tax relief that made any other form of condominium production uncompetitive. Almost 35.000 units of five floors or higher were produced between 1950 and 1980 in a city that, before that period, had fewer than a thousand such buildings (Maloutas and Karadimitriou 2001). *Antiparochi* brought an impressive increase of residential space in central areas through the massive production of new apartment buildings and led to their rapid densification.

Eventually, it also led to the degradation of living conditions in the areas most affected by congestion through overbuilding, i.e. of most areas around the centre. As a result, since the mid-1970s, affluent households gradually started migrating to the suburbs, following the trend of 'belated' suburbanization in southern Europe. However, this trend exhibits important internal differences as demonstrated in work on urban sprawl in Athens, Barcelona and Rome (Salvati and De Rosa 2014; Salvati and Morelli 2014). The suburbanization process in Athens is still ongoing and has radically changed the centre/periphery social divide by producing new homogenous middle-class residential areas in the north-eastern and southern suburbs; by creating deeper internal social divisions among central neighbourhoods and by lowering the average social status of the centre's inhabitants. Since the 1970s, many suburbs have come closer to the centre as the city expanded rapidly and eventually constituted a large semi-peripheral buffer within the centre–periphery continuum.

During the 1970s and 1980s, the central municipality lost a very large part of the city's higher occupational categories since its share was reduced from 62 per cent in 1971 to 27 per cent in 1991 (Maloutas 1997). However, this loss was much more the outcome of new households belonging to higher social categories who chose to settle in the periphery than of the literal outward movement of established households.

Social segregation in the 1990s

Before the 1990s, residential segregation in Athens existed only in terms of class – apart from the long-lasting segregation of Roma groups who continue to suffer a high level of social and spatial marginalization. The higher occupational categories traditionally resided in and around the city centre, while the working class was mainly located at the periphery, and especially in the western part. Since the mid-1970s, the geography of social segregation in Athens has started to change (Maloutas 2000). The new generations of the numerically expanding higher and upper-middle occupational groups opted for residence in the north-eastern and south-eastern suburbs; this suburbanization trend has continued during the first decade of the twenty-first century. At the same time, the shrinking native working class has been residentially much less mobile and has remained increasingly within traditional working-class strongholds (i.e. the working-class suburbs in the western part of the metropolis) (Maloutas 2004).

Maloutas *et al.* (2012) assessed the trend of residential segregation in terms of class during the 1990s by comparing indices of segregation for major occupational categories in 1991 and 2001. Due to important changes in the occupational categories used by the Greek census of 1991 and 2001, common subcategories were necessarily used and eventually major categories were only partly recomposed through them. The indices of segregation were rather low and remained stable or decreased during the 1990s. The few exceptions (small employers and skilled workers) consist of numerically shrinking and ageing categories that usually tended to regroup in spaces where their presence was already high. Higher occupational categories presented the highest indices, followed by the working class, while intermediate categories and lower-intermediate positions in the services were the least segregated (index of segregation around 35 for high-status professionals, 25 for workers in building trades, skilled workers in industry, unskilled workers in several sectors and much lower for office clerks, sales persons in shops, managing proprietors of small businesses, etc.). Very low segregation levels characterized the unemployed, indicating that unemployment was less related to space than it was to class.

In the same paper, dissimilarity indices were calculated for each pair of major occupational categories in 1991 and 2001. The higher and upper-intermediate categories increased their mutual spatial distance and the distance from all other categories except the skilled workers in building trades and the unskilled workers, who had reduced their distance from all other categories. The overall tendency during the 1990s was, therefore, fuelled by the combination of more segregation among the higher and upper-intermediate categories with desegregation among the lower occupational categories.

The explanation of this desegregation trend affecting the lower categories of unskilled workers and skilled workers in building trades was based on the large percentage of immigrants that became part of these occupational categories during the 1990s. De-segregation resulted from the fact that most immigrants have not found residence in the city's traditional working-class areas since the latter were mainly spaces of owner-occupation with limited supply of rented accommodation. Immigrants were attracted mainly by the small and affordable low-quality apartments privately rented around the city centre where they mixed with lower- and middle middle-class native Greeks who remained in the centre in spite of the suburbanization of middle-class groups since the 1970s. Evidence from other south European cities confirms this parallel growth of immigrant populations with the decrease of class and ethnic segregation levels that should be mainly attributed to the profile of the region's housing systems (Arbaci 2008; Arbaci and Malheiros 2010).

Occupational data and spatial units

The area constituting the metropolis of Athens comprises fifty-eight munici-palities on the continental part of the Attiki Region (Figure 7.A1 in appendix). Municipalities form a rather loose union at the regional level as a very weak substitute for metropolitan government. Recent changes have merged munici-palities and transferred responsibilities, but the latter are still intricately divided among municipal, regional and central governments, with local authorities' tasks and funding, in particular, remaining curtailed (Chrianopoulos *et al.* 2010; Chorianopoulos 2012).

The detailed data from the 2011 Census make it possible to work on the new segregation patterns and the trends for 2001–11. Depicting the patterns of social segregation for 2011 in Athens in a compatible way with other European capital cities is immediately possible since the occupational categories used in the last cen-sus are those of ISCO08 (International Standard Classification of Occupations). Indices of segregation are also comparable for the same reason, as well as for being calculated on the basis of 2.835 Urban Analysis Units (URANU), which are either individual census tracts or groups of census tracts with a minimum of 900, a maximum of 3.000 and an average of 1.200 residents. Census tracts are defined by the Greek Statistical Authority (ELSTAT), while the regrouping in URANUs was produced by the project 'Dynamic management and mapping of social data' conducted by the National Centre for Social Research (EKKE) in the course of preparing an Internet application to access and map Greek census data (EKKE–ELSTAT 2014).

Important difficulties appear in terms of the comparison with the 2001 Census data and, therefore, for determining social segregation trends in Athens for the last decade. These difficulties result from the change in the occupational catego-rization used by the two censuses (ISCO 88 for 2001 and ISCO 08 for 2011). Additional difficulties result from the fact that ISCO 88 was modified by the Greek Statistical Authority, producing a slightly different categorization under the name STEP92 (ELSTAT 1995). This categorization, which was founded on ISCO 88, provided much more detail for occupations considered closer and more relevant for the local context (mainly in agriculture) and aggregated others that seemed less important. As a result, several categories have been merged in new ensembles that blurred their socio-economic identity and skill level; international comparison has also obviously become harder. A similar problem is discussed in a recent publication dealing with segregation trends in Athens during the 1990s (Maloutas *et al.* 2012). Occupational categories also changed between 1991 and 2001 (from ISCO 68 to ISCO 88) and were both altered by the Greek Statistical Authority, making comparison even harder.

In this chapter, the strategy of using more detailed categories is not possible since it would create comparability issues with the other cases discussed in the book (see also the introduction of this book for more detail: Tammaru *et al.* 2016). Thus we are using the major occupational categories of the two censuses and will try to make cautious assumptions when categories – often carrying the same name – have different content in 2001 and 2011.

There is a long list of important changes from ISCO 88 to ISCO 08 (ILO 2012). The major ones can be summarized as follows: the stricter redefinition of managers; the reappearance of supervisors and the clearer and more autonomous definition of IT-related occupations. As a result, large numbers of small business owners, previously coded as managers, are no longer part of this category. In a country with very large numbers of small employers and self-employed individuals without employees, the removal of small business owners from managerial positions has provoked a substantial change in both the category they were removed from (managers) and those they were transferred to (mainly service and sales workers). The other two major changes had a lesser impact as fewer numbers were affected in the Athenian context.

Social segregation in the 2000s

Segregation indices

The changes between 2001 and 2011 in ISCO categories do not permit reliable assumptions about their evolution during this period, nor do they permit meaningful comparisons of the segregation indices between the two dates. The data presented in the following should, therefore, be considered for each census separately, and the comparisons will be presented very cautiously as tentative and indicative.

The profile of the major occupational categories (one-digit ISCO codes) in Athens is presented in Table 7.1. The big reduction in the number of managers is mainly due to the transfer of managing owners of small businesses to category 5 (service and sales workers). The growth in the number of professionals is almost entirely due to the real growth of this category, whose status is declining (partly due to its own growth). The category of technicians and associate professionals has received all those with supervising tasks from working-class categories and some categories with IT-related tasks previously designated as clerical jobs. The growth of technicians, therefore, may be entirely related to these recategorizations. Clerical support workers have decreased after losing numbers both to technicians and associate professionals and to service and sales workers. Their reduction is, therefore, probably due to these recategorizations rather than to effective losses.

Service and sales workers have received subcategories, both from managers and from elementary occupations, but the extent of their growth must also comprise some increase in the numbers of sub-categories added to their old definition. Craftsmen and plant and machine operators have long been stagnating categories, while elementary occupations lost some subcategories to sales, and probably also lost the vitality of their growth following the reduction of immigrant inflows that sustained their significant growth during the 1990s.

Table 7.2 shows segregation indices for the same occupational categories during the same period. Indices are low, with categories at the extremes of the occupational scale scoring around 0.2 and those in the middle scoring around 0.1. In spite of the low level of segregation, the tendency – keeping in mind the caution needed to assess it – seems to be more towards desegregation than the opposite. Managers and elementary occupations are the only two categories showing a considerable increase of segregation; however, they both lost a part of their previous sub-categories which makes them more homogenous by more clearly

Table 7.1 Composition of the active population by major occupational category, 2001 and 2011 (%)

	2001	2011
Managers	9.2	5.8
Professionals	14.2	20.1
Technicians and associate professionals	9.9	11.1
Clerical support workers	13.0	10.6
Service and sales workers	14.0	21.6
Skilled agricultural, forestry and fishery workers	1.1	1.1
Craft and related trades workers	14.8	12.8
Plant and machine operators, and assemblers	6.8	6.3
Elementary occupations	12.7	9.3

Source: ELSTAT. Detailed census data at census-tract level for 2001 and 2011.

Table 7.2 Segregation indices for major occupational categories in the Athens metropolitan area calculated at Urban Analysis Units (URANU) level, 2001 and 2011

	2001	2011
Managers	16.5	18.6
Professionals	22.5	19.3
Technicians and associate professionals	12.7	9.9
Clerical support workers	9.7	8.4
Service and sales workers	9.5	8.6
Craft and related trades workers	15.4	15.7
Plant and machine operators, and assemblers	20.5	20.1
Elementary occupations	20.0	21.0

Source: ELSTAT, Detailed census data at census-tract level for 2001 and 2011.

marking either their higher (managers) or their lower-unskilled profile (elementary occupations).

Indices of dissimilarity among major occupational categories show that higher distances are observed between extreme categories, with the professionals and the plant and machine operators presenting the more dissimilar spatial distribution (Table 7.3). Indices over 30 (bold in Table 7.3) are limited to couples of opposite extreme categories. Categories 1 to 4 present some similarities in spatial distribution and the same is also true for categories 5 to 9. Categories closer to the social middle in the two groups (3, 4 and 5) have relatively low dissimilarity indices even when coupled with categories that do not belong to their own group. The general trend between 2001 and 2011 seems to lean towards desegregation, with a few exceptions (italicized for 2011 in Table 7.3), although assumptions about trends are questionable due to the changes in the content of major occupational categories mentioned earlier. All increasing dissimilarity indices are related to categories 1 (managers) and 9 (elementary occupations). We can reasonably claim, therefore, that this increase in segregation is probably due to the redefinition of the content of these two categories – which eventually became more homogenous – rather than to a more segregated redistribution of the common subcategories they contained in both census years.

Isolation indices (Table 7.4) show that the major social categories are not isolated much more than their percentage in the active population suggests. Corroborating the pattern of segregation indices, isolation tends to be higher for categories at the extremes of the occupational hierarchy, and especially for professionals whose modified index of isolation supersedes their percentage by almost 60 per cent.

Segregation patterns

Social segregation patterns in Athens have been changing steadily since the 1970s when the upper-middle and middle strata started migrating towards the periphery following the rapid densification of the centre and the ensuing decline in living conditions. This persistent movement of affluent households towards the periphery has reduced the opposition between the bourgeois centre and the working-class periphery. This division was substantially reinforced by the settlement of 250,000 destitute refugees from Asia Minor during the 1920s in new satellite quarters (*synoikies*) outside the city's perimeter (see map in Philippides 2005).

On the other hand, the traditional social division between east and west in Athens started quite early and has shaped the metropolis since the nineteenth century (Bournova and Dimitropoulou forthcoming). The initial plans for the city centre in the 1830s and the decision about the location of the king's palace on its eastern side was the foundation for shaping the city's social geography (Kallivretakis 2009). Industrial activities were situated mainly in the western part of the city, from the port of Piraeus and the bay of Eleusis along the northbound highway [the sector limit linking *Piraeus* to *Acharnes*, map in appendix] up to the

Table 7.3 Dissimilarity indices by couples of major occupational categories in the Athens metropolitan area calculated at URANU level, 2001 and 2011

	(1)	(2)	(3)	(4)	(5)	(7)	(8)	(9)	2001
(1) Managers		18.0	16.9	18.1	23.3	30.2	32.8	33.0	
(2) Professionals	15.2		18.8	23.0	28.7	36.9	41.3	36.4	
(3) Technicians and associate professionals	16.1	15.1		14.4	17.6	25.6	29.7	28.2	
(4) Clerical support workers	19.6	19.9	10.2		12.3	20.4	24.2	26.9	
(5) Service and sales workers	25.1	26.6	15.8	11.8		14.3	19.0	22.6	
(7) Craft and related trades workers	31.4	34.1	23.7	19.2	12.3		14.1	21.1	
(8) Plant and machine operators, and assemblers	33.6	37.2	26.3	21.8	15.9	13.9		26.3	
(9) Elementary occupations	35.1	35.3	28.9	25.7	20.1	17.1	23.0		
2011									

Source: ELSTAT, Detailed census data at census-tract level for 2001 and 2011.

Table 7.4 Isolation indices for major occupational categories in the Athens metropolitan area calculated at URANU level, 2001 and 2011

	2001		2011	
	index of isolation	*modified index of isolation*	*index of isolation*	*modified index of isolation*
Managers	10.8	11.8	7.3	7.7
Professionals	18.8	21.7	25.2	31.5
Technicians and associate professionals	11.1	12.2	11.9	13.3
Clerical support workers	14.2	16.2	11.3	12.5
Service and sales workers	15.2	17.5	22.7	28.7
Craft and related trades workers	17.0	19.8	14.5	16.4
Plant and machine operators, and assemblers	8.6	9.1	7.8	8.3
Elementary occupations	17.5	19.9	12.2	13.3

Source: ELSTAT, Detailed census data at census tract level for 2001 and 2011

actual industrial zone developed just outside the regional limits of Attiki as the unexpected outcome of decentralization incentives.

Since the 1970s, the city's social geography has been changing in terms of one of the two traditional divisions, following the outward movement of the affluent strata and the ensuing suburban growth, especially in the eastern periphery (the sector comprising *Kifisia* as well as areas farther eastward, see map in appendix; see also relevant maps in Maloutas (2000) and Spyrellis (2013)). The city's most socially homogenous residential areas have been increasingly formed in the eastern periphery (especially towards the north-east and the south along the coast), while the population of the city centre decreased and became increasingly socially mixed. In the western (working-class) part of the metropolis, socio-spatial changes have been comparatively mitigated since population changes have also been moderate. An increasing internal division appeared, however, between traditional working-class areas [the sector comprising *Peristeri* and *Chaidari* as well as municipalities around *Piraeus*; see map in appendix], where lower middle-class presence has been increasing, and new working-class areas farther to the west, where the concentration of lower occupational categories is very high. The clearer formation of internal divisions within the broad divisions of east/south and centre/periphery is a feature of the city's social geography that has been developing since the 1980s and continued in the 2000s, as we will see in the next sections, through the changing patterns of residential location for a number of major occupational categories and for the unemployed.

The following maps depict segregation patterns for managers and professionals, elementary occupations, service and sales workers and the unemployed; they were produced using the mean percentage of each category in the city as the central division point and two further subdivision points at one standard deviation above and below the mean. The darkest areas in each map denote the spaces where the variables' percentages are higher than one standard deviation above the mean.

Managers and professionals

The spatial distribution of managers and professionals in the metropolis shows the outcome of the outbound movement of affluent categories towards the north-east and the south (Figure 7.2). The change during the 2000s seems to be a further consolidation of the areas of high concentration in these categories (like *Kifisia*, *Psychico* or *Ekali*) and of their expansion in other areas in the north-east (like *Amarousio*, *Chalandri* or *Aghia Paraskevi*; see map in appendix). Their major pole in the north-east has been expanding to in-between and adjacent spaces; the central pole has been expanding in a process of embourgeoisement of adjacent spaces rather than through gentrification (Maloutas and Alexandri forthcoming; Maloutas *et al.* 2012), while the pole in the south has remained relatively stable. Once again, I should stress that caution is needed regarding the comparison between the two dates as the category of managers has been redefined, mainly by the removal of managing owners of small businesses. A similar pattern would appear, however, if maps were limited to professionals only (not presented due to lack of space) who were not affected significantly by ISCO redefinitions.

(a)

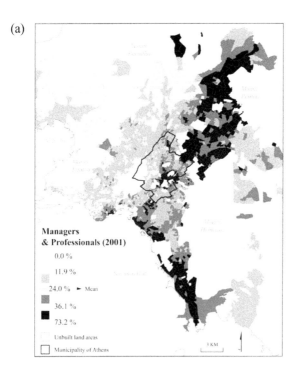

Managers
& Professionals (2001)

0.0 %

11.9 %

24.0 %   ▶ Mean

36.1 %

73.2 %

Unbuilt land areas

Municipality of Athens

1 KM

(b)

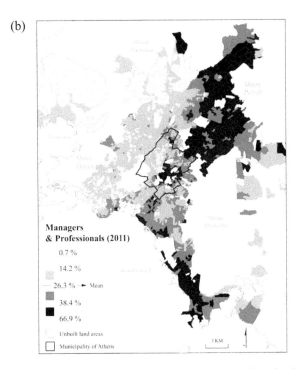

Managers
& Professionals (2011)

0.7 %

14.2 %

26.3 % → Mean

38.4 %

66.9 %

Unbuilt land areas

Municipality of Athens

3 KM

Figure 7.2a–b Spatial distribution of managers and professionals by URANU in the
Athens metropolitan area, 2001 and 2011.

Elementary occupations

Elementary occupations have also been redefined to some extent between 2001
and 2011 by the removal of certain categories (for example door-to-door sales and
telephone centre operators) that were transferred to sales and services. However,
the difference between the two maps is probably not only the outcome of the category's redefinition but also of a tendency of the lowest occupational categories
to be more concentrated in space (Figure 7.3). There are two major observations
in this case: (1) working-class spaces in the outer western periphery are becoming marked by the increased share of occupations that require the lowest level
of skills; and (2) a large space of highly concentrated elementary occupations
is becoming increasingly important within the central municipality. At the same
time, the presence of this category seems to decrease wherever it was already
rather limited and/or spatially dispersed.

Sales and service workers

The category of sales and service workers has been affected by the inclusion in
2011 of sub-categories coming both from higher (for example managing owners

(a)

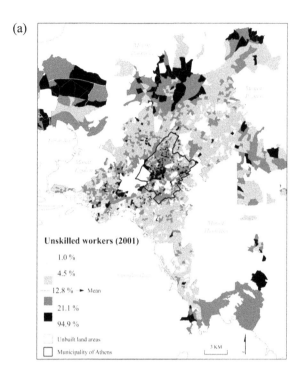

Unskilled workers (2001)

1.0 %

4.5 %

12.8 % ► Mean

21.1 %

94.9 %

Unbuilt land areas

Municipality of Athens

3 KM

(b)

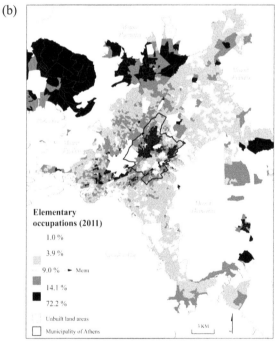

Elementary
occupations (2011)

1.0 %

3.9 %

9.0 % ► Mean

14.1 %

72.2 %

Unbuilt land areas

Municipality of Athens

3 KM

Figure 7.3a–b Spatial distribution of elementary occupations by URANU in the Athens metropolitan area, 2001 and 2011.

(a)

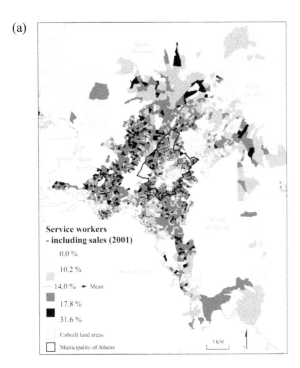

Service workers
- including sales (2001)

  0.0 %

  10.2 %

  14.0 % ► Mean

  17.8 %

  31.6 %

  Unbuilt land areas

  Municipality of Athens   3 KM

(b)

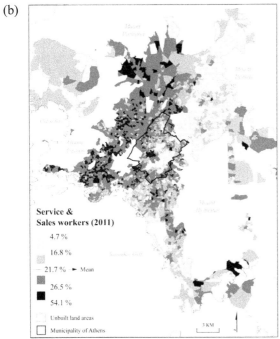

Service &
Sales workers (2011)

  4.7 %

  16.8 %

  21.7 % ► Mean

  26.5 %

  54.1 %

  Unbuilt land areas

  Municipality of Athens   3 KM

Figure 7.4a–b Spatial distribution of service and sales workers by URANU in the
Athens metropolitan area, 2001 and 2011.

of small businesses from category 1) and lower categories (for example. door-to-door salespersons from category 9). In spite of these changes and the limitations they entail for significant comparison, the 2011 pattern seems more concentrated in the broad space of working-class areas in the western part of the metropolis but without producing poles of strong concentration (Figure 7.4).

Unemployed

Unemployment has been rising dramatically in Greece since 2009, eventually climbing to 28 per cent in 2013; during the last census (May 2011) it was measured at 18 per cent in Athens. The spatial distribution of unemployment seems to have changed considerably in parallel with its rapid growth. Figure 7.5 shows a much more hierarchical socio-spatial distribution of the unemployed for 2011 since they are clearly concentrated in the working-class part of the city and, in particular, in areas where the lowest occupational categories are also concentrated. The fact that very high levels of unemployment do not appear in the areas of the central municipality, where elementary occupations are also highly concentrated, is probably due to the ethnic composition of the latter. In these areas there is a high rate of immigrant groups who are seldom eligible for unemployment benefits and are, therefore, poorly registered as such.

The spatial redistribution of unemployment between 2001 and 2011, which occurred in ways that make it much more related to social/occupational hierarchy, is also clearly revealed by the change in its correlation coefficients with the spatial distribution of the higher occupational categories (managers and professionals) and the lower ones (elementary occupations). In 2001, these coefficients were -0.46 and 0.23, while in 2011 they increased to -0.75 and 0.59 respectively, revealing the much stronger correlation of unemployment (negative in the case of managers and professionals) with both social extremes.

Another indication that supports some growth in segregation is provided by the growing percentage of occupational categories – especially those at social extremes – in the areas where they are most concentrated (i.e. where their percentage is over one standard deviation above the mean). Table 7.5 shows an increase for all categories, except service and sales workers. This is partly in contradiction with Tables 7.2 and 7.3 where the dominant trend was towards desegregation. However, at the same time, Table 7.5 offers an indication in the opposite sense: all categories have increased their percentage in areas where they are least represented as well. This means that all the categories considered tend to increase their presence in areas where they are both highly over- and underrepresented, having a contradictory effect on segregation measures. The sociological interpretation of this contradictory tendency requires further investigation. It could be the outcome of occupational categories' internal social differentiation or of changes in residential areas' attributes and profiles, or most likely of both. However, once more the measures used are not completely reliable due to changes in the composition of

(a)

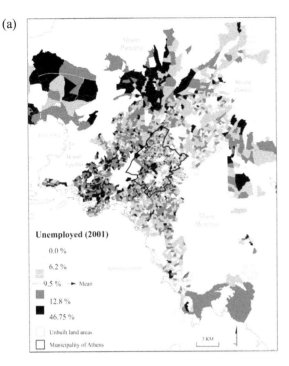

Unemployed (2001)

0.0 %

6.2 %

9.5 % ➤ Mean

12.8 %

46.75 %

Unbuilt land areas

Municipality of Athens

3 KM

(b)

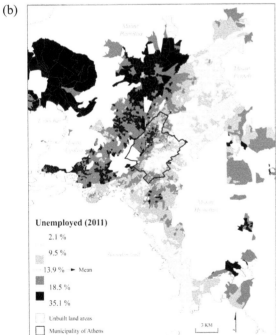

Unemployed (2011)

2.1 %

9.5 %

13.9 % ➤ Mean

18.5 %

35.1 %

Unbuilt land areas

Municipality of Athens

3 KM

Figure 7.5a–b Spatial distribution of the unemployed by URANU in the Athens metropolitan area, 2001 and 2011.

categories between the two dates. The only exceptions are the unemployed, not affected by these changes, and the elementary occupations, whose increasing rate of concentration in the areas where they are highly concentrated is too great to be explained only by their redefinition.

Another way of reading Table 7.5 is to consider that even though almost all the categories displayed have increased their shares in the spaces where they are both most and least represented, their largest part continues to reside in areas where their percentage is close to the mean. Managers are the category least present in areas close to their mean, and yet 63 per cent of this category's members reside in such areas. The same applies to 63.8 per cent of professionals, 67.9 per cent of elementary occupations and 73.7 per cent of service and sales workers. These figures corroborate the low levels of segregation indices (Tables 7.2 and 7.3).

On the other hand, what we observe on the maps as a spatial consolidation of areas where the extreme occupational categories and unemployment are overrepresented is corroborated by the increase of autocorrelation indices (Table 7.6) that does not have to go together with increased segregation. When taking into account the confusing effect of the categories' redefinition between the two dates, this parallel increase of area consolidation of high scores with a stable or decreasing level of segregation is something that requires further investigation.

Table 7.5 Members of selected occupational categories residing in areas where their category is most concentrated and least concentrated (over or under one standard deviation above or below the mean), 2001 and 2011 (%)

	2001	*2011*
Managers and Professionals		
+ 1 stdev	28.8	31.5
− 1 stdev	4.1	4.9
Managers		
+ 1 stdev	26.8	30.8
− 1 stdev	5.3	6.4
Professionals		
+ 1 stdev	30.2	31.7
− 1 stdev	3.3	4.5
Service and sales workers		
+ 1 stdev	18.3	16.2
− 1 stdev	7.7	10.2
Elementary occupations		
+ 1 stdev	20.1	29.2
− 1 stdev	1.3	2.9
Unemployed		
+ 1 stdev	21.0	23.1
− 1 stdev	2.1	3.7

Source: ELSTAT, Detailed census data at the census-tract level for 2001 and 2011.

Table 7.6 Moran's I for major occupational categories in the Athens metropolitan area calculated at URANU level, 2001 and 2011

	2001	2011
Managers	0.247	0.293
Professionals	0.371	0.451
Managers and professionals	0.299	0.429
Service and sales workers	0.167	0.327
Craft and related trades workers, and plant and machine operators and assemblers	0.348	0.450
Elementary occupations	0.137	0.500

Source: ELSTAT, Detailed census data at the census-tract level for 2001 and 2011.

Context-related segregation forms

There are two specific forms of residential segregation in Athens that contribute to lowering the city's overall level of neighbourhood segregation. The first is vertical segregation (Maloutas and Karadimitriou 2001; Maloutas forthcoming), which reduces segregation indices due to interclass cohabitation in the same areas, and even in the same buildings. The process was instigated by the densification of the central municipality following 'overbuilding' and congestion that led to the decline of living conditions and the progressive outflow of affluent social groups. This decline especially affected the apartments on the lower floors of apartment buildings which, apart from being systematically smaller, also became darker, noisier and dirtier after the densification and the increase of air pollution that occurred during the same period. These smaller apartments on lower floors – usually rented rather than owner-occupied – were, as a result, increasingly abandoned by middle-class tenants. The latter were replaced by lower-status tenants or remained empty. The process of vertical segregation reached full swing in the 1990s when immigrants started arriving in large numbers and found no other housing options beyond this downgraded part of the private rented sector. Thus, immigrants – usually joining the lower occupational categories – were housed in apartments literally beneath those of middle-class native Greek households rather than in working-class areas, where no housing options existed for them. As a result, immigration in the 1990s led to the decrease of class segregation (Maloutas 2007).

In recent years, there have been claims that vertical segregation declined following the wholesale downgrading of areas where migrants settled, marked by the ensuing 'white flight' of native Greek middle-class households (Region of Attica 2012: 81). Although the outflow of middle-class households has occurred steadily since the 1970s, vertical segregation is still present in the densely built areas around the city centre. A recent survey – which was conducted as part of the research project 'Socioeconomic class, social position and urban consumption: Stratification, mobility and consumption in Athens (SECSTACON)'[1] carried out by the National Centre for Social Research (EKKE) – has corroborated this presence within the central areas of the metropolis.

The analysis of 435 questionnaires from households within the central municipality confirmed, first of all, the clear social stratification by floor. Figure 7.6 shows that higher occupational categories, higher educational level and higher income are markedly over-represented in upper floors (fifth and above), while lower occupational categories, education level and income are overrepresented in basements and ground floors. Intermediate floors (first to fourth) appear mixed. with a slight tendency of higher categories to be on the upper-intermediate rather than the lower-intermediate floors.

(a)

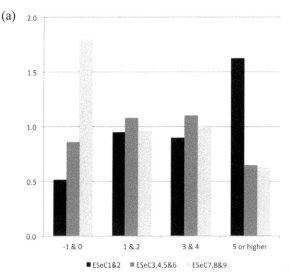

(b)

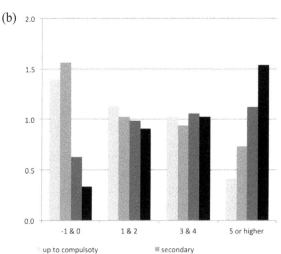

(c)

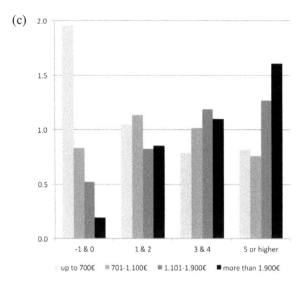

Figure 7.6a–c Distribution of respondents by floor of residence and by (a) socio-economic category (ESeC), (b) education level and (c) household income (2013). Location quotients

Source: SECSTACON database (2013).

Note: ESeC – European socio-economic classes (Rose and Harrison 2009). ESeC 1: Higher professionals and administrators/managers, including large employers, ESeC 9: Routine occupations.

Figure 7.7 shows that stratification by floor is also related to citizenship. Immigrant presence is considerably stronger on lower floors and decreases gradually on the way up, while native Greeks present an opposite but smoother curve. Floor is also important in terms of tenure. Tenants are overrepresented in lower floors, while owner-occupants are over-represented in the upper ones.

The second context-related segregation pattern refers to the spatial 'entrapment' of social mobility in traditional working-class areas of Athens. Between 1971 and 1991, the distribution of the higher occupational categories in the three major types of residential areas (the centre, the bourgeois suburbs and the traditional working-class suburbs) changed considerably. In the centre [Municipality of Athens], the share of higher categories diminished dramatically (from 62 to 27 per cent), while it tripled in the bourgeois suburbs (from 10 to 30 per cent) located mainly in the sector comprising *Kifisia* and expanding farther to the east (see Figure 7.A1 in the appendix). The intriguing part of these changes was that these categories almost doubled their percentage distribution (from 12.5 to 23 per cent) in working-class suburbs (Maloutas 1997: 3; Maloutas and Karadimitriou 2001: 713).

The increase of the share of higher occupational categories in the bourgeois and upper-intermediate suburbs in the north-eastern and southern periphery of the city comes as no surprise following the wave of suburbanization towards these areas

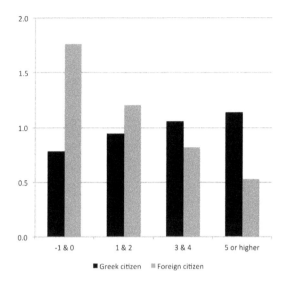

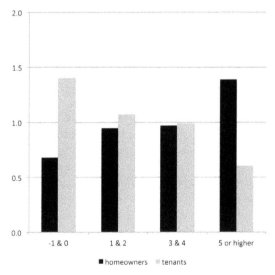

Figure 7.7 Distribution of respondents by floor of residence and by (a) citizenship
and (b) tenure, 2013. Location quotients.

Source: SECSTACON database (2013).

since the mid-1970s. The substantial increase of higher occupational categories in
working-class suburbs, on the contrary, is the outcome of a less obvious process:
these suburbs remained relatively stable during the first part of the same period
and substantially decreased their population weight in the metropolis during the
last twenty years (34.3 per cent in 1971, 33.9 in 1991 and 26.6 in 2011), while no

tendency was registered for households belonging to the higher social categories to relocate to working-class suburbs from other parts of the city.

This phenomenon is explored in some detail in Maloutas *et al.*'s study (2006). In the early 2000s, a special research project was designed to address this and a number of related issues. It was eventually proved that the increase of higher occupational categories in working-class suburbs is, in fact, an endogenous process that has nothing to do with exogenous processes like gentrification or embourgeoisement. The increased presence of higher categories ensued from their endogenous growth, which was the product of a high social mobility period having positively affected most social groups; in traditional working-class suburbs the socially mobile younger generations remained 'entrapped', to a large extent, in their parental residential areas (Maloutas 2004; see also Leal (2004) for a discussion of the same process in Madrid).

Further evidence about this phenomenon was provided by the survey in the SECSTACON project mentioned earlier. Using this new material, it was possible to contrast the profile of higher occupational categories located in working-class suburbs to those in middle- and upper-middle class ones that were the main receivers of the 'white flight' from the centre. Eventually, it was possible to provide evidence of their distinctive profile and substantiate the scenario of their endogenous generation (Maloutas forthcoming).

Thus, it became clear that although this group's members share the same socio-economic classification label, they also exhibit important and systematic dissimilarities when their different residential locations are considered. It seems that members of this higher occupational category that live in working-class suburbs are of a more recent intergenerational mobility cohort; although the members of higher occupational categories in working-class suburbs seem to have similar jobs and income as their counterparts in other parts of the city, they definitely lack property and broader family wealth.

Eventually, the spatial 'entrapment' of socially mobile categories originating from a working-class background seems to be the product of a number of reasons. First, family solidarity networks are (still) very important within the context of a poorly developed welfare state, even for young households that are socially mobile, especially since the educational passports for this mobility are not immediately convertible to employment conditions and income levels that can compensate for the lack of daily family support.

Second, working-class parental households cannot monetize their solidarity and, therefore, spatial proximity remains crucial for the practical ways they can offer their help (for example keeping the children while parents work, helping with domestic chores, etc.).

Third, whatever property belongs to the parental household that could be used as housing by the young household is usually in the vicinity of the parental house or is limited to the parental house itself, following the rationale of housing provision systems that dominated in previous decades (Maloutas 1990). Therefore, whatever property is transferred to the new household, by inheritance or otherwise, tends to be located in the same area. Taking into account that, whenever possible, a house for owner-occupation is provided by the parents to the young couple when the latter is formed (usually by marriage), access to owner-occupation occurs too early for the new household to make choices based on its expected rather than its actual, and relatively poor, financial means. This argument is further reinforced by the traditionally limited social diffusion of housing loans, due to very high interest rates until the mid-1990s (Emmanuel 2004 and 2006) and the standstill in transactions since the crisis of 2010 (Balampanides *et al.* 2013). But even in the decade of rapidly growing housing credit, young adults would usually have to use family patrimony or some other collateral, making residential location to some extent more of a family affair than an independent decision.

Fourth, there has been increasing provision of housing with higher than average local standards – by private, small-scale, apartment-building operations through the progressive peripheralization of *antiparochi* – that could accommodate *in situ* the upwardly mobile part of the younger generation; thus the on-going entrapment of social mobility in working-class traditional suburbs was made a less unsatisfying option.

Both processes briefly sketched above (i.e. vertical segregation and the spatial entrapment of social mobility in working-class areas) contribute to mitigating residential segregation in Athens and should be informing the analysis of segregation data for this city. High rates of home ownership which enable low rates of residential mobility to accommodate families' solidarity networks have been a long-standing feature of the housing market in Athens that has not been seriously undermined by the current economic crisis (Emmanuel 2014). High unemployment induced further dependency on family solidarity and the collapse of housing demand led to even lower rates of residential mobility.

Concluding remarks

In this chapter, through the analysis of 2001 and 2011 Census data, we witnessed the relative stability of low segregation indices and some ambivalent trends leading more to de-segregation than to its opposite. We found lower segregation indices for the higher and middle occupational categories that expanded during the 2000s, while indices were more or less unchanged for lower categories whose numbers remained stable or decreased. Increases in segregation appeared only for categories whose content changed between the two dates, making these increases an unreliable indicator of segregation trends. Stability was also observed in terms of segregation patterns. More importantly, stability of distribution patterns was accompanied by the clear spatial consolidation of areas where the socially extreme categories are highly overrepresented. This consolidation, however, was also followed by growth of the same categories in areas where they were highly underrepresented.

The underlying parameters of stability in segregation levels and patterns can be attributed to several factors, including the relative stability of the occupational structure; the reduced inflow of immigrants after the mid-2000s; the stability of the housing market (deriving from the high rate of home ownership and the low rate of residential mobility) and the context-specific processes of vertical segregation and spatial entrapment of social mobility in working-class areas.

The analysis of segregation tendencies in this chapter was founded on very broad occupational categories that probably aggregate – and therefore dissimulate – a number of important and mutually neutralized lower-level tendencies. This task has to be undertaken using much more detailed occupational categories and it should eventually clarify the uncertainty produced in our results by the change of content for broad occupational categories that led to their reduced comparability.

Athens is a lower-tier metropolis in the global urban network whose social structure has not been under enormous pressure from globalization for some time. Its rather low segregation indices may be partly attributed to this comparative lack of pressure, i.e. to the fact that global economic processes have not put local segregating mechanisms in motion on a massive scale. More effective pressure from globalization was probably exercised in higher-order metropolises in the region, such as Madrid or Milan. However, low segregation levels and ambivalent trends in those cities as well indicate that more inequality and social polarization may not be enough to increase segregation. Cities in the the European south have been socio-spatially organized for a long time with respect to residual welfare states and family-centred processes of social reproduction, relying on spatial proximity, wide social access to home ownership and reduced residential mobility. These features, in spite of important differences among cities in the region, constituted eventually effective barriers in converting inequality to segregation.

Since the 1970s, the city's social structure followed a steady trend of professionalization as the service economy developed, higher education was becoming accessible to a broader social audience and substantial hiring by the public sector sustained the high rate of social mobility. In the 1990s, the trend turned to polarization due to the growth of the lower occupational pole following the large waves of immigration. This effect of globalization was not, however, followed by similar development in the higher pole. The number of managers and professionals increased, but this was not induced by the growth of members of the international corporate elite since Athens never became a hub for important functions of multinational corporations and, thus, of advanced producer services. As a result, the growth of the higher occupational pole in Athens – which remained almost entirely of local origin – did not bring the important reshuffling for both the labour and the housing markets that the presence of a large international elite group would entail. During the last decade these broad parameters had not changed until globalization pressure was introduced with unprecedented force through the sovereign debt crisis.

However, segregation remains stable, or even slightly negative, in spite of the extreme conditions of the current crisis and the docile and complacent policies of Greek governments that increased inequalities and marginalized large numbers of people through unemployment. Social relations embedded in urban structures continue to mitigate segregation trends in Athens, offering possibilities that may contribute to alternative political futures from those prescribed by dominant European policies and the IMF.

Appendix

Figure 7.A1 Municipalities and sectors of the prefecture of Attiki, 2014.

Acknowledgements

Thanks to Stavros N. Spyrellis for the design of the maps.

Note

1 The project SECSTACON (http://www.ekke.gr/secstacon/) is headed by Dimitris Emmanuel as Principal Investigator and is part of the action 'Excellence' (ARISTEIA) of the General Secretariat for Research & Technology (GSRT) funded by Greece and the European Union (Operational Programme *Education and Lifelong Training*, NSRF 2007–2013).

References

Allen, J, Barlow, J, Leal, J, Maloutas, T and Padovani, L 2004, *Housing and welfare in Southern Europe*, Blackwell, Oxford.

Andreotti, A, Garcia, S M and Gomez, A 2001, 'Does a southern European model exist?' *Journal of European Area Studies* 9(1), 43–62.

Antonopoulou, S 1991, *Postwar transformation of the Greek economy and the residential phenomenon*, Papazisis, Athens [in Greek].

Arbaci, S 2008, '(Re)viewing ethnic residential segregation in Southern European cities: Housing and urban regimes as mechanisms of marginalisation' *Housing Studies* 23(4), 589–613.

Arbaci, S and Malheiros, J 2010, 'De-segregation, peripheralisation and the social exclusion of immigrants: southern european cities in the 1990s' *Journal of Ethnic and Migration Studies* 36(2), 227–255.

Balampanides, D, Patatouka, E and Siatitsa, D 2013, 'The right to housing within the crisis in Greece' *Geographies* 22, 31–44 [in Greek].

Bournova, E and Dimitropoulou, M forthcoming, 'The social geography of Athens in the late 19th and early 20th century' in *Atlas of the social geography of Athens*, ed. T Maloutas and S N Spyrellis.

Chorianopoulos, I, Pagonis, T, Koukoulas, S and Drymoniti, S 2010, 'Planning, competitiveness and sprawl in the Mediterranean city: The case of Athens' *Cities* 27(4), 249–259.

Chorianopoulos, I 2012, 'State spatial restructuring in Greece: Forced rescaling, unresponsive localities' *European Urban and Regional Studies* 19(4), 331–348.

Dominguez, M, Leal, J and Martinez Goytre, E 2012, 'The limits of segregation as an expression of socioeconomic inequality: The Madrid case' in *Residential Segregation in Comparative Perspective* eds T Maloutas and K Fujita, Ashgate, Farnham, pp. 217–236.

Economou, D 1987, 'Housing policy in post war Greece' *The Greek Review of Social Research* 64, 56–129 [in Greek].

Economou, D 1988, 'Land and housing system in post-war Greece: Functional equivalents to the Keynesian welfare and state' in *Problems in the development of the Greek welfare* state, eds D Economou and T Maloutas, Paratiritis, Thessaloniki, pp. 57–113.

Economou, D, Getimis, P, Demathas, Z, Petrakos, G and Pyrgiotis, J 2001, *The international role of Athens*, The University of Thessaly Press, Volos [in Greek].

EKKE (National Centre for Social Research)–ELSTAT (Greek Statistical Authority) (2014) *Panorama of Greek Census Data 1991–2011. Internet Application for Accessing and Mapping Census Data.* Available online at http://panorama.statistics.gr/en/about-panorama/

ELSTAT (Greek Statistical Authority) 1995, *Statistical classification of occupations STEP-92* Available at http://dlib.statistics.gr/portal/page/portal/ESYE/categoryyears?p_cat=10007372&p_topic=10008097. Accessed 27 April 2015.

Emmanuel, D 2004, 'Socio-economic inequalities and housing in Athens: impacts of the monetary revolution of the 1990s' *The Greek Review of Social Research*, 113(A), 121–43.

Emmanuel, D 2006, 'Social housing policy in Greece: Dimensions of an absence' *The Greek Review of Social Research* 120, 3–35 [in Greek].

Emmanuel, D 2014, 'The Greek system of home ownership and the post-2008 crisis: Class aspects of structure and change in Athens' *Region et Development* 39, 167–182. Available at http://region-developpement.univ-tln.fr/en/pdf/R39/8-Emmanuel.pdf. Accessed 9 May 2015.

Ferrera, M 1996, 'The "southern model" of welfare in social Europe' *Journal of European Social Policy* 6(1), 17–37.

Friedmann, J and Wolff, G 1982, 'World city formation: An agenda for research and action' *International Journal of Urban and Regional Research* 6(3), 309–344.

Fujita, K 2003, 'Neo-industrial Tokyo: Urban development and globalization in Japan's state-centered developmental capitalism' *Urban Studies* 40(2), 249–281.

Hamnett, C 1996, 'Social polarisation, economic restructuring and welfare state regimes' *Urban Studies* 33(8), 1407–1430.

Hill, R C and Kim, J W 2000, 'Global cities and developmental states' *Urban Studies* 37(12), 2167–2198.

ILO 2012, *International standard classification of occupations,* International Labour Office, Geneva (1), pp. 1–433.

Kallivretakis, L 2009, 'Athens in the 19th century: From regional town of the Ottoman empire to capital of the Kingdom of Greece' in *Archaeology of the City of Athens*, National Foundation of Research, Athens. Available at http://www.eie.gr/archaeologia/En/Index.aspx. Accessed 21 April 2015.

Leal, J 2004, 'Segregation and social change in Madrid metropolitan region' *The Greek Review of Social Research* 113(A), 81–104.

Leiulfsrud, H, Bison, I and Jensberg, H 2002, *Social class in Europe: European social survey 2002/03*, Università degli Studi di Trento. Available online: http://is.muni.cz/el/1423/jaro2006/SOC772/um/ESS1SocialClassReport.pdf. Accessed 21 April 2015.

Leontidou, L 1990, *The Mediterranean city in transition: Social change and urban development*, Cambridge University Press, Cambridge.

Leontidou, L 1996, 'Alternatives to modernism in (southern) urban theory: Exploring in-between spaces' *International Journal of Urban and Regional Research* 20(2), 178–195.

Maloutas, T 1990, *Housing and family in Athens: An analysis of postwar housing practices*, Exandas, Athens [in Greek].

Maloutas, T 1997, 'La ségrégation sociale à Athènes' *Mappemonde* 1(4), 1–4.

Maloutas, T (ed) 2000, *Social and economic atlas of Greece: The cities*, EKKE-University of Thessaly Press, Athens and Volos [in Greek].

Maloutas, T 2003, 'La vivienda auto-promovida: Soluciones de posguerra en Atenas' *Ciudad Y Territorio: Estudios Territoriales,* 136–137, 335–345.

Maloutas, T 2004, 'Segregation and residential mobility: Spatially entrapped social mobility and its impact on segregation in Athens' *European Urban and Regional Studies* 11(3), 195–211.

Maloutas, T 2007, 'Segregation, social polarization and immigration in Athens during the 1990s: Theoretical expectations and contextual difference' *International Journal of Urban and Regional Research* 31(4), 733–758.

Maloutas, T 2012, 'Introduction: Residential segregation in context' in *Residential segregation in comparative perspective*, eds T Maloutas and K. Fujita, Ashgate, Farnham, pp. 1–36.

Maloutas, T 'Enclaves and mobility: Vertical segregation, spatial entrapment and residential relocation in Athens'. Available at http://www.academia.edu/4380189/Segregation_and_Residential_MobilitySpatially_Entrapped_Social_Mobility_and_its_Impact_on_Segregation_in_Athens. Accessed 9 May 2015.

Maloutas, T and Alexandri, G forthcoming, 'La gentrification dans des villes non gentrifiables? Rénovation urbaine et changement des structures sociales dans le centre d'Athènes' in *Gentrification, transformations des quartiers populaires et couches moyennes; notion unique, processus pluriels*, eds C Rhein and E Préteceille, Anthropos, Paris.

Maloutas, T, Arapoglou, V P, Kandylis, G and Sayas J 2012, 'Social polarization and de-segregation in Athens' in *Residential segregation in comparative perspective*, eds T Maloutas and K. Fujita, Ashgate, Farnham, pp. 257–283.

Maloutas, T, Emmanuel, D, Pantelidou-Malouta, M 2006, *Athens. Social structures, practices and perceptions: new parameters and trends 1980–2000*, EKKE, Athens [in Greek].

Maloutas, T, and Karadimitriou, N 2001, 'Vertical social differentiation in Athens: Alternative or complement to community segregation?' *International Journal of Urban and Regional Research* 25(4), 699–716.

Mingione, E 1995, 'Labour market segmentation and informal work in southern Europe' *European Urban and Regional Studies* 2(2), 121–143.

Mollenkopf, J H and Castells, M 1992, *Dual city: Restructuring New York*, Russel Sage Foundation, New York.

Murie, A and Musterd, S 2004, 'Social exclusion and opportunity structures in European cities and neighbourhoods' *Urban Studies* 41(8), 1441–1459.

Musterd, S and Ostendorf, W 1998, *Urban segregation and the welfare state: Inequality and exclusion in western cities*, Routledge, London.

Philippides, D 2005, *Urban planning in Greece*. Available online: http://www.greekarchitects. gr/gr/αρχιτεκτονικες-ματιες/η-πολεοδομία-στην-ελλάδα-id65 [in Greek]. Accessed 21 April 2015.

Prévélakis, G 2000, *Athènes. Urbanisme, culture et politique*, L'Harmattan, Paris.

Region of Attica 2012, *Strategic positions and priorities of the Region of Attica for the programming period 2014–2020: "Attica 2020+"*. Available online: http://www.pepattikis. gr/home/wp-content/uploads/2013/02/strathgikes_proteraiothtes_20142020.pdf, [in Greek]. Accessed 21 April 2015.

Rose, D and Harrison, E (eds) 2009, *Social class in Europe: An introduction to the European socio-economic classification*, Routledge, London.

Salvati, L 2014, 'Neither ordinary nor global: a reflection on the "extraordinary" expansion of Athens' *Urban, Planning and Transport Research: An Open Access Journal*, 10.1080/21650020.2014.898571

Salvati, L and De Rosa, S 2014, '"Hidden polycentrism" or "subtle dispersion"? Urban growth and long-term sub-centre dynamics in three Mediterranean cities' *Land Use Policy*. Available at http://dx.doi.org/10.1016/j.landusepol.2014.02.012

Salvati, L, and Gargiulo Morelli, V 2014, 'Unveiling urban sprawl in the Mediterranean region: Towards a latent urban transformation?' *International Journal of Urban and Regional Research*. Available at http://onlinelibrary.wiley.com/doi/10.1111/1468-2427. 12135/Abstract. Accessed 21 April 2015.

Sassen, S 2001, *The global city: New York, London, Tokyo*, Princeton University Press, Princeton, NJ.

Spyrellis, S N 2013, *Division sociale de l'espace métropolitain d'Athènes: Facteurs économiques et enjeux scolaires*, PhD Thesis, University Paris.

Tammaru, T, Musterd, S, van Ham, M and Marcińczak, S, 2016, 'A multi-factor approach to understanding socio-economic segregation in European capital cities' in *Socio-economic segregation in European capital cities: East meets West*, eds T Tammaru, S Marcińczak, M van Ham and S Musterd, Routledge, London.

UNECE 2003, *Trends in Europe and North America: The statistical yearbook of the Economic Commission of Europe 2003*, ch. 4.

8 Socio-economic divisions of space in Milan in the post-Fordist era

Petros Petsimeris and Stefania Rimoldi

Abstract

This chapter examines new forms of social segregation in Italy's economic capital, Milan. Over the last three decades, processes of deindustrialisation and urban regeneration associated with the arrival of large inflows of migrants have been the most dynamic trends, and the largest contributors to recent territorial and demographic changes. During this period important qualitative and quantitative population changes have occurred in Milan's urban region, particularly in terms of the characteristics and directions of migratory flows, and the ethnic and social structuration of metropolitan areas. In this chapter, segregation in the city of Milan is addressed using segregation indices, dissimilarity indices, indices of relative concentration, indices of isolation and a factor analysis. Special emphasis is given to the relationship between urbanisation and the social division of space, and the relationship between ethnic and social segregation for the period 1991–2011. As a tentative conclusion we provide a number of explanatory hypotheses concerning the changing nature of segregation in Milan.

Introduction

Studies of the social polarisation and residential segregation of world cities are now well established (Fainstein *et al.* 1992; Kantrovitz 1973; Massey 1990; Sassen 1991). However, far less attention has been given to disparities within middle-ranking cities, with populations of between 1 and 2 million. In this chapter we focus on the socio-economic segregation of one such city, Milan (Italy), with a population of 1.3 million. Our aim is to analyse patterns of and changes in residential segregation during the period 1991–2011. While there have been allusions to segregation and a number of social area analyses of Italian cities, this study aims to redress the lack of detailed quantitative analysis of segregation in Italy (Petsimeris 1998).

Even if Rome is Italy's capital, Milan has had – and continues to have – an important role as the economic capital of the country (Dalmasso 1971). In the period of the economic boom of the 1960s, together with Turin and Genoa, Milan formed one of the three vertices of the Italian industrial triangle. Milan constitutes the most important urban area in the national settlement system of Italy, and satisfies each of the key characteristics of a metropolitan area in terms of size, density, ethnic and social heterogeneity (Wirth 1938), and by means of possessing a network of firms with high degrees of specialisation in the domains of finance, fashion, trade, research and development, media and the arts. Milan's functional structure dominates a vast area that extends beyond regional and national scales. The metropolitan area of Milan is comprised of a huge conurbation that incudes the city itself, the Province of Milan and part of the region (Lombardy) bordering on the contiguous areas of Novara (Piedmont region), Piacenza (Emilia Romagna region) and Veneto. The city's degree of functional interdependence with Switzerland is also high. Brunet's European megalopolis iconography, known as the 'blue banana', places Milan at the southern limit of the European metropolis that extends to London in the north (Brunet 1989). Freedman (1995) considers Milan as an international city in Europe, along with Paris, London and Madrid.

At the core of the metropolitan area is the city of Milan, which is characterised by a concentric ring pattern. The city is formed by the zone of Navigli (a ring of canals which have been covered) that constitutes the historic centre of the city, characterised by the location of prestigious institutions, firms and residences of the elite. The second ring is delimited by the Spanish walls. The outer part of the city is the result of annexations in 1873 of Corpi Santi, Greco Milanese and Turro Milanese, and of a further twelve municipalities in 1923. The internal core of the city represents 4.5 per cent of the total area of the city, and the extensions of 1873 and 1923 36 per cent and 60 per cent respectively. It is mainly in the outer rings that the rapid processes of urbanisation and industrialisation have occurred, and where large numbers of immigrants were housed in collective housing and in *autocostruzione* (self-construction) developments in the 1950s and 1960s (Cerasi and Ferraresi 1974).

More recently, processes of industrialisation associated with financial activities have reinforced the economic basis of Milan and the incomes of its population. These have in turn attracted domestic and international migration flows, which have left their impression on the form of the city. This study focuses on the changes that have occurred at intra-metropolitan level, with particular focus on the socio-economic and spatial differentiation of the core city during the post-Fordist period. In order to analyse the socio-economic and ethnic structuration of a metropolitan space as complex as that of Milan, we examine the evolution of the population, the distribution of socio-economic groups in intra-urban space, the degree of heterogeneity of the population and the levels of segregation. The evolution of the structure and location of socio-economic groups are analysed using census data for 1991, 2001 and 2011. Special emphasis is given to the relationships between deurbanisation, reurbanization and social polarisation, and new forms of distribution of socio-economic groups in intra-urban space.

Over the last three decades the economic bases of Milan have undergone strong processes of deindustrialisation and deurbanisation that have in turn impacted on the structure of society, the land uses and the material space of this city. Our principal hypothesis is that the new international division of labour has had an impact on processes of deurbanisation and deindustrialisation, and that, within this context, the general expansion of the service sector has led to a socio-spatial reorganisation at regional and intra-metropolitan levels. Analysis of these changes at the intra-urban level uncovers the effects of the new international division of labour and the geopolitical processes that fuel international migration, such as EU enlargement and globalisation. This is because the intra-urban level crystalises aspects of social polarisation and residential segregation, and more particularly their materiality in terms of urban landscapes. A number of questions are posed that will be developed in the following paragraphs:

• How has the transition from Fordism to post-Fordism affected the socio-economic structure of the city?
• Has socio-economic segregation in Milan decreased or increased over the period?
• Which is the most appropriate scale at which to read the social and economic division of intra-urban space at municipality level?

In this chapter we will present the study area, and the methodology for the synchronic and diachronic analyses of the socio-economic division of space in Milan. We will then go on to present the results of our analyses, before concluding with the main characteristics of socio-economic segregation in Milan.

Socio-demographic profile of Milan

With more than 1.242 million people, Milan is the second city in Italy (Table 8.1). It includes almost 41 per cent of the population of its province, and represents nearly 13 per cent of the Lombardy region. The economic structure of Milan (Table 8.2) has a broad-based economy. During the period 1991–2011 employment increased in both the city of Milan and the Lombardy region by 11.3 per cent and 19.3 per cent respectively, while falling by minus 4.6 per cent in the province of Milan. An analysis of employment change by sector shows that the most important loses concerned the manufacturing sector, which fell from 148,000 in 1991 to 60,000 in 2011 (minus 59 per cent) in Milan. When comparing manufacturing with other sectors of the economy, manufacturing lost two-thirds of its share, passing from 22.8 per cent of Milan's total employment to only 7.8 per cent in the last Census. We have to underline that this process continues a trend that started in the 1970s (Petsimeris 1998), and which may be anticipated to have worsened since the last Census as the crisis deepened in manufacturing and in some other sectors such as construction, transportation and retail. In terms of the impact on the socio-economic structure, it means that the reduction in employment among manual labourers has been continuous, which has in turn impacted on the distribution of socio-economic groups. We can therefore anticipate that processes of social mix will have been affected by these changes in employment structure, and possibly to a greater extent than any offsetting effects of public policies. Changes in employment structure have also had an impact on the urban landscape, with many areas formerly occupied by industries having been taken up by other uses (commercial, residential, education, museums).

Table 8.1 Milan: population growth rates for city, adjacent municipalities and other municipalities of the province, 1971–2011[a]

	Population	Growth rate (per 1,000)			
	Census 2011	1971–81	1981–91	1991–2001	2001–11
Milan	1,242,123	−7.6	−15.7	−8.6	−1.1
Adjacent municipalities	604,568	15.6	2.0	−1.6	1.4
Other municipalities of the province	1,191,729	11.8	8.4	5.1	9.1
Total province	3,038,420	2.0	−4.6	−2.3	3.3
Italy	59,344,794	4.4	0.4	0.4	4.2

Note: [a] Population at Census.

Source: Authors' calculation on Istat (Italian Institute of Statistics) data.

During the last forty years, the city underwent demographic development reflecting the decentralisation of the production activities to the peripheral areas previously concentrated in the urban areas of the 'industrial triangle' of north-west Italy. The post-war years were characterised by intense population growth, due to impressive immigration flows from the south and rural areas. While the surrounding territories continued to experience population growth rates, starting from the beginning of the 1970s the city showed a considerable decrease (minus 8 per thousand annually), peaking between 1981 and 1991 (minus 15 per thousand annually). In addition, the change in direction of the migration dynamics caused a progressive reduction of the internal natural resources of the population (i.e. the births), resulting in an older population structure. Since the 1990s this negative trend has been slowing down but still quite high negative rates are observed. In the framework of an apparent overall increase in the population of Italy, the current century has begun with population growth in the province and a halt in the population drain of the city.

Much of the change over the last two decades is mainly due to foreign immigration, primarily with its direct impact on urban population and secondly with its indirect effect on fertility as the immigrant population begins to settle and start families (Figure 8.1). With regard to the impact on population, it is important to note how foreign immigration in Milan – that was about 27,000 units in the early 1980s (only 13 per cent coming from high migratory pressure countries) – more than doubled only ten years later (Blangiardo and Terzera 1997). At the beginning of the 1990s the foreigners' share of overall resident population was just 2 per cent (Table 8.3). In the following decade, 2001–2011, the trend halts: the pace of foreign population growth slowed down sharply in the centre as well as in other non-adjacent municipalities and in the 'belt' surrounding the centre where such a population maintains high rhythms of growth. Foreign immigration is still the engine of population in the north of Italy, where – based on 2011 census data – two out of three foreigners reside (35 per cent

Table 8.2 Enterprises, local units and persons employed in local units. City of Milan, its province and region, 1991–2011

	1991			2001			2011		
	Enterprises	Local units	Persons employed in local units	Enterprises	Local units	Persons employed in local units	Enterprises	Local units	Persons employed in local units
	(thousands)								
Lombardy Region	574	634	3,141	752	810	3,382	812	883	3,496
Province	227	251	1,462	273	292	1,310	296	321	1,394
Milan	98	109	648	156	166	688	174	186	774
	(% of Milan totals)								
– manufacturing	13.0	13.0	22.8	6.9	7.2	11.5	5.2	5.4	7.8
– construction	4.3	4.5	4.6	6.1	5.9	4.4	6.1	6.0	4.5
– wholesale and retail trade	36.4	36.5	23.5	20.9	21.5	17.3	17.3	17.9	16.3
– transportation and storage	4.1	4.4	8.9	3.5	3.7	7.2	5.8	3.2	7.6
– accommodation and food service activities	5.4	5.4	4.8	4.1	4.2	5.2	4.5	4.8	6.6
– Other	36.8	36.2	35.5	58.5	57.5	54.4	61.2	62.7	57.1

Source: Authors' elaborations on Industry and Services Censuses (Istat), 1991–2011.

Table 8.3 Foreigners resident at Census, 1991–2011

	Foreigners: share of total population (%)			Av. Annual growth rate (per 1,000)	
	1991	*2001*	*2011*	*1991–2001*	*2001–2011*
Milan	1.9	7.0	14.2	126.7	72.5
Adjacent municipalities	0.8	3.1	8.6	138.7	111.3
Other municipalities of the province	0.9	3.8	7.6	166.8	140.0
Total province[a]	1.3	5.0	9.9	138.1	100.2

Note: [a]For comparison, 2011 data for Milan include the municipalities of the province of *Monza e Brianza*, created in 2004 as separate from Milan.

Source: Authors' calculations on Census data.

in the north-west region). In Milan, foreign residents are nearly 176,000, representing 14 per cent of overall population. Finally, looking at the more recent data, direct effects of immigration on population structure can be highlighted. Based on population registers (data for 1 January 2012)[1] more than 1 in 5 residents aged 22–37 years is a foreigner. The direct contribution of foreigners to population by age reaches 26–28 per cent between the ages of 27 and 31. This is particularly true for the female population, in which foreigners account for 1 in 3 female residents aged 28–31.

The indirect effect of immigration on the overall population fertility level coincides with the phase of maturity in the immigration process that combines normally with a wildfire spreading out of the city cores, where the early immigrants normally arrive ('the Duomo is the first thing the immigrants go to see when they arrive, even before looking for a place to sleep', Pezzoni 2013). This may help to explain why the effect on natural balance appears quite dimmed in the urban area. Although the natural balance (i.e. the difference between births and deaths) has increased between 1991 and 2011, it still remains negative (Figure 8.1).

The net migration rate with other Italian municipalities is negative, although it has approached close to zero in the very recent years, while the net migration rate with other countries is positive. Furthermore, during the decade 2001–2011, these two components have shown opposite trends, revealing how the illusory renewed charm of the city seems to be addressed almost exclusively towards foreign immigrants. In this regard, the peaks of net foreign migration in the middle of the 2000s and after must be mostly attributed to legislative measures directed towards legalising immigrants already illegally present in Italy.

Transformations dating back to the 1970s have caused a sharp increase in population ageing. The ageing index started to grow very steeply from 1981. This trend lasted until 2001 when intense immigration from other countries began to influence the population structure. The recent structural improvements in the urban populations are not to be attributed to a decrease in the number of elderly people, which in fact continues to increase in relative terms (their share of total population reached almost 25 per cent at Census 2011). Rather it should be ascribed to the major rise in

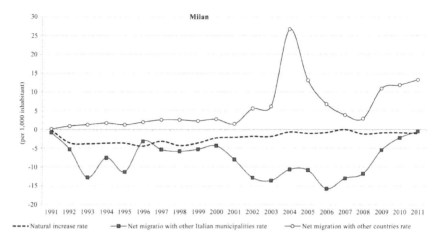

Figure 8.1 Natural increase and net migration rates, 1991–2011.

Source: Authors' calculations on Istat data.

the number of young people, whose share has nearly doubled during the last decade. The segment of population that has reduced is the active population: its share having reduced from nearly 71 per cent in 2001 to 62 per cent in 2011. The intense ageing process includes both the centres and the peripheries: it seems to be spreading out from the city.

In order to detect their socio-economic stratification, these populations need to be analysed by their work status (Figure 8.2). The classification of population by work status[2] indicates that the groups that are increasing their share during the period 1971–2011 consist of business owners, professionals and independent workers (plus 10 per cent), while the medium/high-skilled workers, managers, executives, and white-collar workers show a sharp decrease (minus 11 percentage points), and the share of other dependent workers also drops down by 20 percentage points to reach 21 per cent of working population in 2011.

Throughout the second half of the last century the number of households remained broadly stable (around 600,000 units). The new century began with an increase in the overall number of families (plus 4 per cent) and a continuous decline in their mean size: from 2.11 to 1.99. Since 1971 the most important change has been the increase in single-person households, particularly since 1991 when they have grown at a soaring rate (and particulary during the last decade). By the 2011 census they represented 45 per cent of households in Milan. By contrast, the share of five-person or more households, which at the 1971 census was about 11–12 per cent, has decreased to less than 3 per cent over the past forty years. With regard to housing by tenure status,[3] the increase of share of ownership status (up to 78 per cent in 2001 for the other municipalities of the province of Milan) is similar in all the areas considered (Figure 8.3). Observing the distribution of dwelling by age of construction a significantly more dynamic trend can be noticed for Milan recently, where the rate of renewal of housing stock was more intense during the last decade

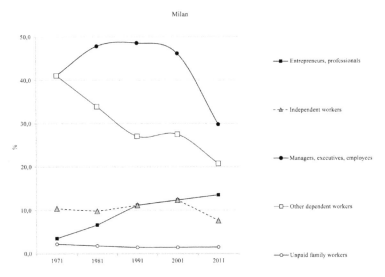

Figure 8.2 Working population by work status, 1971–2011*

Source: Authors' calculations on census data.

Note: *As regards the dependent workers, data for 2001 and 2011 are partially estimated in order to be compared to previous censuses.

for which data are available, 1991–2001. This not only occurs for the very old buildings (built before 1919), for which the rate of renewal is 17 per cent, but also for the relatively more recent constructions (1961–1981), for which it is 4 per cent.

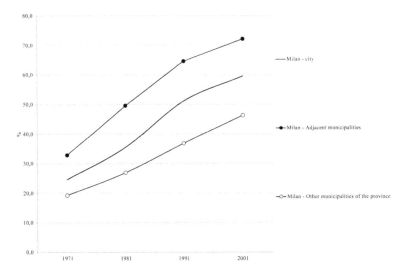

Figure 8.3 Owner occupied conventional dwelling, 1971–2001 (%).

Source: Authors' calculations on census data.

Finally, addresing inequality from the point of view of welfare, it seems interesting to question whether and how the slowing down of the economic primacy of Milan – following the transition towards a post-Fordist economy – reverberates on social morphology. The correlation between inequality and segregation is particularly apparent at the urban level, where high density leads to human capital polarisation (Glaeser *et al*. 2008).

Although based on different sources of data,[4] there is a general agreement that some milestones in the evolution of income distribution in Italy have been reached (Acciari and Mocetti 2013). The 'egalitarian' phase, strictly connected to the industrial economic structure, lasted until the early 1980s, when income distribution began to diverge. The economic crisis at the beginning of the 1990s signalled a marked increase in inequalities, up to the levels of the 1980s (Brandolini 2009). The decade 1990–2000 is characterised by a moderate increase in inequalities of personal incomes in Italy. The Gini coefficient for Milan follows an analogous trend, but 5–8 points above the average for Italy: estimates based on fiscal data[5] for 1998 report 0.397 for Milan versus 0.346 for Italy when equivalent family income is considered, and 0.487 versus 0.404 when individual income is considered (Bono and Checchi 2001). However, it is worth emphasising that these differences must be evaluated in the light of an income average for Milan that was nearly twice the national average. The Gini index appears to continue to increase also during the 2000s: calculations on aggregated fiscal data show 0.305 in 2004 up to 0.311 in 2006, indicating a higher polarisation (Percopo 2009). The income distribution points to a greater incidence of the highest-income groups for Milan compared to other Italian cities (D'Ovidio 2009): in Milan the richest 10 per cent of population account for 40 per cent of overall income, while the poorest 10 per cent account for only 2 per cent.

In conclusion, the process of tertiarisation affecting the economic structure of Milan since the 1980s seems to have provoked a higher social polarisation (Zajczyk 2003), with a shrinkage of the middle class in favour of the upper social class.

Data and methods

In order to analyse the social structure of the population in the city of Milan, two sources of data are employed: the population census and the population register. A set of 31 indicators (Table 8.4) drawn from the 1991 and 2001 population censuses is calculated at census tract level. The set covers the thematic areas of population structure by sex, age, citizenship, education level, economic activity status and work status, household size and finally dwelling. Based on census tract data, a factor analysis (using the principal component extraction method) has been carried out for both 1991 and 2001.[6] In order to detect the possible segregation of the socio-economic categories, the dissimilarity index and the isolation index were computed (see also the introduction of this book for more detail: Tammaru *et al.* 2016). Finally, to locate the tendency towards segregation, the location quotients for selected groups have been shown. The dynamic analysis of location quotients, referring to the two consecutive censuses of 1991 and 2001 (Table 8.5), allows us to detect the trends over the decade towards decline, potential decline, potential increase and finally an increase in each subarea.

Table 8.4 Population Census indicators by thematic area

Thematic area	Indicators	
Sex	Females (% of total population)	
Age	Population less than 15 years old (% of total pop.)	
	Aging index (%)	
Education	Graduates (% of pop. 5 years old or more)	
Citizenship	Foreigners (% of total pop.)	
	EU citizens (% of foreigners resident)	
	Asians (% of foreigners resident)	
	Africans (% of foreigners resident)	
	Americans (% of foreigners resident)	
	Others (% of foreigners resident)	
Work	Unemployment rate	
status[a]	Employment rate	
	Employed (% of 15–64 years old or more)	
	Seeking work (% of labour force)	
	Housekeepers (% of active females 14 years old or more)	
	Retired (% of inactive pop. 14 years old or more)	
	ISTAT classification	ISCO08 major groups
	Business owners and professionals	I and II
	(% of total employed)	
	Independent workers (% of total employed)	
	Co-operators[b] (% of total employed)	
	Managers/executives (% of total employed)	
	White-collar workers	III, IV and V
	Other employed (% of total employed)	VI, VII, VIII, IX, X
	Average household size	
	Singles (% of total households)	
	Households of more than 4 (% of total households)	
	Owner-occupied housings (% of total housings)	
	Built before 1961 (% of total housings)	
	Built during 1962 to 1981 (% of total housings)	
	Built after 1981 (% of total housings)	
1991 only	Small dwellings (< 50 sq.m.) (% of total housings)	
1991 only	Medium dwellings (50–120 sq.m.) (% of total housings)	
1991 only	Large dwellings (> 120 sq.m.) (% of total housings)	
2001 only	Average housing size (sq.m)	

Population (spanning Sex through Households of more than 4)
Households
Dwelling[c] (spanning the dwelling rows)

Notes: [a]With reference to 2001 Census, the work status is partially estimated in order to separate the white–collar workers from 'other employed' (both included in the 'other dependent workers'), based upon the occupational classification (ISCO88). Since the ISCO categories are not available at the tract level for the 1991 Census, a broader classification of occupations has been adopted.
[b]Co-operators are members of a cooperative society.
[c]Housing surface is a continuous variable in 2001 (average surface in sq. m.) and categorical in 1991 (houses by class of surface), due to differences in the original data sets for the two censuses.

With regard to the geographical data, four geographical levels are considered (Tables 8.6 and 8.7, Figure 8.4): census tracts, census areas (*ACE*), districts[7] (*Circoscrizioni*) and finally the present administrative districts (*Zone di decentramento*).

Table 8.5 Dynamic analysis of location quotients

	$LQ_{(2001)} \leq 1$	$LQ_{(2001)} > 1$
$LQ_{(2001)} - LQ_{(1991)} \leq 0$	Decline	Potential decline
$LQ_{(2001)} - LQ_{(1991)} > 0$	Potential increase	Increase

Table 8.6 Geographical levels

	Units	Average population
Tracts[a]		
1991	5,565	246
2001	5,746	219
ACE		
1991	85 (+6)[b]	16,109
2001	85 (+6)[b]	14,778
Circoscrizioni		
1991	20	68,462
2001	20	62,811
Zone		
1991	9	152,137
2001	9	139,579

Notes:
[a] Uninhabited tracts excluded.
[b] Residuals.

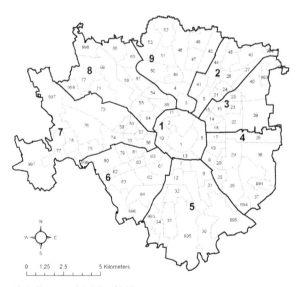

Figure 8.4 Zone and ACE of Milan.

Table 8.7 Zone and ACE of Milan

Areas 'Zone'		ACE[a]
1	Centro storico	1. Duomo, 2. Brera, 6.Guastalla, 10.Magenta-San Vittore, 11.Sempione, 13.Conca del naviglio
2	Stazione Centrale, Gorla, Turro, Greco, Crescenzago	5.Centrale, 21.Loreto, 24.Turro, 26.Padova, 27.Crescenzago, 41.Maggiolina, 43.Adriano, 44.Greco, 45.Viale Monza
3	Città Studi, Lambrate, Venezia	14.Venezia, 15.Buenos Aires, 16.Bacone, 18.Dei Mille, 22. Città Studi, 23.Porpora, 25.Casoretto, 39.Lambrate, 40.Parco Lambro-Cimiano
4	Vittoria, Forlanini	9.Libia, 17.Dateo, 19.XXII Marzo, 20.Viale Umbria, 28.Parco Forlanini-Ortica, 29.Corsica-Ortomercato, 35. Lodi, 36.Corvetto, 37.Rogoredo-Mecenate, 38. Parco Monluè-Ponte Lambro
5	Vigentino, Chiaravalle, Gratosoglio	7.Vigentina, 8.Porta Romana, 12.Tibaldi, 30.Ex OM Morivione-Ripamonti, 31.Scalo Romana, 32.Stadera, 33.Missaglia-Ticinello, 34.Torretta-Gratosoglio
6	Barona, Lorenteggio	60.Tortona, 61.Navigli, 62.San Cristoforo, 63.Ronchetto sul Naviglio, 64.Barona, 79.Primaticcio, 80. Lorenteggio, 81.Bande Nere, 82.Giambellino, 83.Piazza Napoli
7	Baggio, De Angeli, San Siro	56.Washington, 57.Monte Rosa, 58.Selinunte, 59.De Angeli-Brescia, 70.Siena, 73.San Siro, 74.Forze Armate, 75.Bisceglie, 76.Quinto Romano/Quarto Cagnino, 77.Muggiano-Olmi
8	Fiera, Gallaratese, Quarto Oggiaro	54.Ghisolfa, 55.Portello, 65.Quarto Oggiaro, 66.Sacco-Vialba, 67.Villapizzone, 68.Accursio, 69.Musocco-QT8, 71.Gallaratese, 72.Trenno, 78.Baggio, 84.Tre Torri, 85.Sarpi
9	Stazione Garibaldi, Niguarda	3.Garibaldi-Isola, 4.Farini, 42.Bicocca, 46.Maciachini-Parco Nord, 47.Cà Granda, 48.Niguarda, 49.Dergano, 50.Bovisa, 51.Affori, 52.Bruzzano, 53.Comasina-Bovisasca

Notes: [a] 992–998 codes refer to residual ACE.

It is well known that the geographical level of analysis captures a considerable variation in results, and sometimes leads to different conclusions. Still far from resolution, the problem (Openshaw 1984) consists in finding the best compromise between the endogenous and the exogenous variability of the indicators. Therefore we suggest taking into account both of them, exploring the phenomena at different scales, from the detailed census tracts to the largest districts.

Results

Factor analyses from censuses

In order to study the socio-economic structure of the population of Milan, taking into account the socio-demographic characteristics, housing types and material space, we effectuated a factor analysis based on the set of 31 indicators computed at the finest territorial level (census tracts), separately for the 1991 and 2001 censuses. Table 8.8 provides a synthesis of these analyses in terms of number of variables selected for each city, the variance explained and some descriptive statistic tests. The five factors extracted are: 'elite', 'singles', 'lowest social status and large households', 'ageing' and 'ethnicity'. These factors have different weights in each period.

The 'elite' represents the first factor: it explains respectively 22 per cent and 19 per cent of the variance for 1991 and 2001, and it is characterised by high positive correlations with its share of graduates, business owners, professionals and managers and by strong negative correlations with other employed groups and its unemployment rate. It also presents a positive correlation with the presence of larger dwellings occupied by owners. This component identifies the upper social class of population. The second factor is 'singles' (16 per cent of variance in 1991 and 17 per cent in 2001). It is characterised by high values with single-person households, small dwellings built before 1961, a high employment rate and the female population and it is negatively correlated with recent housing, large families and with the average family size. The third factor is 'lowest social status and large households' (12 per cent of variance in 1991 and 10 per cent in 2001).

Table 8.8 Factorial analyses: descriptive statistics

	Milan	
	1991	*2001*
N. variables used	24	24
Factors	5	5
% Variance exp.	63%	65%
KMO test[a]	0.6	0.6
Bartlett test[b]	sign.	sign.

Notes:
[a] The Keiser Meyer Olkin test (>0.6) measures the sampling adequacy.
[b] Bartlett's test of sphericity tests if the correlation matrix is an identity matrix, which would indicate an inappropriate factor model.

It is characterised by remarkable negative correlations with white-collar workers, retired people and home ownership, but positive correlations with the share of foreign population, large families and large dwellings in the peripheral estates with high levels of cohabitation. The fourth factor, 'ageing' accounts for 7 per cent of variance in 1991 and 13 per cent in 2001; it is characterised by high positive coefficients in the old age index, female population and housewives, while it is negatively correlated with the employment rate. The last component, 'ethnicity' (6 per cent of variance in 1991 and 7 per cent in 2001), mainly describes the ethnic composition of the population: it is highly positively correlated with the Asian population (slightly less with Americans – mostly Latin Americans) and negatively with the European population.

Between 1991 and 2001 some important changes occurred. One of the most important was the sharpening of demographic ageing and therefore the increasing role of factor 4 (i.e. 'ageing'). A second change refers to the emergence of immigration as a driver for population: from the negative role (loading minus 0.57) in describing factor 1 ('elite') in 1991 to the positive contribution (loading plus 0.54) in defining factor 3, 'the lowest social status and households' in 2001. Figure 8.5 shows increasing segregation levels between 1991 and 2001. The first factor ('elite') tends to concentrate in the city core (*Zona 1*) and in the residential areas situated on the routes to the 'Lakes' (north-west) and 'Monza' (north-east)

Milan – 1991

Factors scores

Elite

  Less than –1

  –1 to 0

  0 to 1

  Greater than 1

  "Zone" boundaries

Figure 8.5 (Continued)

Milan – 1991

Factors scores

Lowest social status and large households

☐ Less than –1

☐ –1 to 0

▨ 0 to 1

■ Greater than 1

☐ "Zone" boundaries

Milan – 2001

Factor scores

Elite

☐ Less than –1

☐ –1 to 0

▨ 0 to 1

■ Greater than 1

☐ "Zone" boundaries

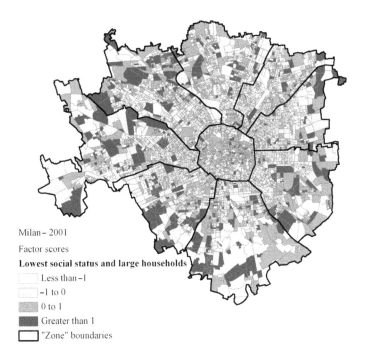

Milan - 2001

Factor scores

Lowest social status and large households

▢ Less than -1

▢ -1 to 0

▨ 0 to 1

■ Greater than 1

▢ "Zone" boundaries

Figure 8.5 Factor scores at census tracts* level. Selected factors: Milan, 1991 and 2001.

Source: Authors' calculations on Istat data.

Note: *Uninhabited tracts have been given the lowest factor score.

that were among the most industrialised areas of Italy. In contrast, the 'lowest social status and large households' factor mainly characterises the very peripheral belt, especially in the east and south: the neighbourhood of *Ponte Lambro (Zona 4)* in the east, with a landscape of working-class hamlets built to face the massive internal post-Second World War immigration; while those of *Stadera (Zona 5)* and *Barona (Zona 6)* in the south are the historical neighbourhoods hosting the first immigration streams since the 1920s. The relationship core–periphery is subject to constant change, with some centre elitist functions (i.e. leadership in public administration offices and shopping facilities) spreading out from the centre to some more peripheral areas like the neighbourhoods of *Garibaldi-Isola (Zona 9)* or *Navigli (Zona 6)* and with the inclusion in the urban areas of some very external neighbourhoods like *San Siro (Zona 7)*. At the same time, and as shown by the fifth factor ('ethnicity'), more recent foreign immigration flows are rapidly changing the appearance of the centre. The immigrant population that was concentrated at the first stage of arrival in peripheral areas has since moved towards the core of the city, often living at the place of work as many are employed in domestic services, nursery and personal care (Zanfrini 2013).

Segregation, dissimilarity, isolation indices and location quotients

The geographical scale of analysis captures a great deal of variability in the results, such that different levels of analysis may lead to different conclusions (Boal 1976; Wood 1976; Peach 1996; Petsimeris 1998). For this reason we explore the phenomenon of segregation at different scales, from the the largest districts to detailed census tracts. We measure the segregation of the various subgroups by means of the segregation index, the dissimilarity index and the isolation index at various levels. Observing the indices at the tracts level (Table 8.9), the synchronic analysis shows that the most segregated groups are the ones that are sittuated at the extremes of the social hierarchy (business owners, professionals and the working class), while the least segregated are the white-collar workers and the independent workers. The general tendency concerning the dynamic of the vari-ous occupational categories within the social structure of the city is an increase of the groups situated at the top of the social hierarchy (managers increase by 5.9 points), a decrease of the groups situated at the middle and a dramatic decrease of the working class that loses 5.4 points.

The diachronic analysis shows that the segregation of almost all occupational categories (covering 86 per cent of those employed) appears to decrease between 1991 and 2001, except for business owners (plus 4.6 points) and unpaid family workers (plus 3.3). The highest decreases are observed for managers and executives (minus 9.8 points) and the working class (minus 5.8). Nevertheless, the hierarchy of segregation hasn't changed significantly between the two censuses. Finally, the group of unemployed (versus total employed) remains stable at 30.2 per cent.

Table 8.9 Segregation index for occupational groups[*]. Milan, tracts level, 1991 and 2001

	1991		2001	
	Segregation	*Share %[(c)]*	*Segregation*	*Share %[(b)]*
Business owners	32.9	4.2	37.5	2.9
Professionals	34.4	7.4	33.6	9.5
Managers/executives	30.2	12.5	20.4	18.4
White-collar workers	17.0	38.0	16.1	35.4
Self-employed	16.1	11.2	14.7	12.4
Working class	33.2	23.5	27.4	18.0
Co-operators	54.2	0.5	39.2	1.5
Unpaid family workers	36.0	1.5	42.1	1.3
Unemployed	30.2	5.1	30.2	5.7

Source: Authors' calculations on census data.

Note: [*] Segregation for Armed Forces group is not considered since its values depend on the military sectors' locations.

Table 8.10 Dissimilarity index for occupational groups*. Milan, tracts level, 1991 and 2001

	Business owners	Professionals	Managers/ executives	White collars	Self-employed	Working class	Co-operators	Unpaid family workers	Unemployed vs total employed
Business owners		25.2	26.3	36.1	33.4	49.3	63.1	43.0	27.1
Professionals	28.9		22.0	36.6	34.1	51.2	63.2	44.2	
Managers/ executives	31.9	22.8		29.1	30.3	49.1	61.3	41.9	
White-collar workers	42.8	38.3	23.5		18.3	28.7	54.2	37.7	
Self-employed	36.1	30.8	20.4	18.7		29.6	54.6	34.9	
Working class	51.7	48.7	36.7	21.7	28.0		54.4	45.2	
Co-operators	60.1	57.7	49.3	41.7	44.0	37.4		81.9	
Unpaid family workers	48.8	46.5	42.1	41.9	38.8	44.1	51.5		
Unemployed vs total employed	26.7								

1991 values above diagonal; 2001 values below diagonal.

Source: Authors' calculations on census data.

Note: *Segregation for Armed Forces is not considered since its values depend on the military sector's locations.

By analysing the values of the index of dissimilarity (Table 8.10), one can observe that there is a strong differenciation between the top and the bottom of the social hierarchy. The lowest dissimilarity index is recorded between the groups situated at the middle: white-collar workers and independent workers, both in 1991 and in 2001 (18.7 in 1991 and 18.3 in 2001). The diachronic analysis shows that there is a tendency towards the diminution of dissimilarity but with two very significant exceptions:

1   the increases of dissimilarity of business owners with all the other social groups. For instance the index with the working class increases from 49.3 in 1991 to 51.7 in 2001;
2   the increase to a lesser degree of dissimilarity between the upper and the middle parts of the social hierarchy (i.e. white-collar workers with professionals, managers with business owners).

Among the groups that decrease their dissimilarity, it is important to underline the case of managers and the working class (from 41.9 to 36.7) and managers and white-collar workers (from 29.1 to 23.6). The working class group decreases its indices of dissimilarity with all social groups (except the business owners and family workers) and records the most significant decreases with the managers and the white-collar workers. The reasons underlying these trends can be found in five possible explanations:

1   the location of the business owners in the most exclusive residential areas of the city of Milan and within the metropolitan region that increases their level of segregation and dissimilarity with all the other social groups;
2   the substitution *in situ* of the working class by managers and white-collar workers, in terms of invasion and succession (Petsimeris 1998) that became more intense and diffused in the following decades;
3   the purchase by working-class households, under right-to-buy schemes introduced in the 1980s (Padovani 1996; Tosi 1994), of properties which may subsequently be sold to more affluent social groups such as white-collar workers and managers;
4   the upgrading through inheritance, where a white-collar son or daughter inherits a house from his or her working-class parents; and
5   the tendency for self-employed households on modest incomes to settle in working-class peripheral areas of the city, where attractively priced public and state-subsidised housing is located.

These five possible explanations work together to produce a new geography of social settlement in Milan. With regard to the isolation index (Table 8.11), which shows the tendency of a group of people to live close together in the same areas (census tracts, in this case), one can observe that the most isolated groups are the working class, professionals and managers, both in 1991 (9.5, 5.0 and 5.2, respectively, looking at the modified index) and in 2001 (5.8, 5.5 and 3.1).

Table 8.11 Isolation index for occupational groups. Milan, tracts level, 1991 and 2001

	1991		2001	
	Isolation	Modified isolation	Isolation	Modified isolation
Business owners	7.5	3.2	5.9	3.0
Professionals	12.4	5.0	15.0	5.5
Managers/executives	17.7	5.2	21.5	3.1
White-collar workers	40.7	2.7	38.0	2.6
Self-employed	12.8	1.7	13.9	1.5
Working class	33.0	9.5	23.8	5.8
Co-operators	1.9	1.4	3.2	1.9
Unpaid family workers	3.5	2.0	3.4	2.0
Unemployed vs total empl.	8.6	3.5	10.1	4.3

Source: Authors' calculations on census data.

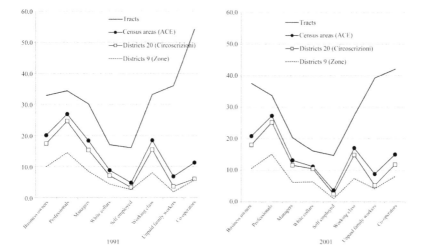

Figure 8.6 Ponderated segregation for occupational categories at different geographical levels, 1991 and 2001.

Source: Authors' calculations on census data.

However, while the working-class values have decreased over time, the values for professionals have increased. A sharp decrease can also be noticed for managers/ executives which can be attributed to the increasing share of this group in the population, as testified by the increasing value of the isolation index.

By comparing segregation of occupational categories at different geographical levels (Figure 8.6), it is clear that segregation increases broadly in line with increasing levels of spatial disagregation, in both 1991 and in 2001. It is also the case that differences in the degrees of segregation are greatest for those groups situated at either end of the social hierarchy. In terms of difference by spatial scale, we find a large difference between the Zone (macro level) and Circoscrizioni and ACE (meso levels), and between the meso levels and the tracts level (micro level). Segregation indices at the tracts level have a 'U' shape that indicates higher levels of segregation for the groups situated at the extremes of the social hierarchy (business owners, the working class, unpaid family workers and co-operators). The groups situated in the middle of the social hierarchy (white-collar workers and self employed) record very low levels of segregation at the macro and meso levels, and slightly higher at the micro level.

Based on what emerged from previous analyses, the Location Quotients (LQ) in 1991 and 2001 are computed at the tracts level (Figure 8.7). Hereafter, maps for the smallest scale (tracts) are examined, accompanied by a dynamic analysis of trends between 1991 and 2001. The highest LQs (2.2) for business owners and professionals both in 1991 and in 2001 are recorded in District 1: *Centro Storico* (especially in *Brera, Sempione* and *Guastalla* neighbourhoods). The self-employed and managers record their highest LQs in the areas of *Porpora* and *Piazzale Bacone*, that are respectively in the region of 1.5 in 1991 and 1.3 in 2001. The same groups also have high concerntrations in *Zona 3* (*Città Studi, Lambrate, Venezia*). Managers show the lowest concentration (and the lowest of all groups) in *Zona 9* (*Stazione Garibaldi, Niguarda*). The co-operators show an increase in their LQs in *Zona 9*, from 1.0 to 1.3 between 1991 and 2001. The white-collar workers, when comparing the two time periods, have a slighly higher concentration in *Zonas 8* and *9* in the north-western part of the city, spreading to *Zona 6* (*Barona, Lorenteggio*) in 2001.

Milan 1991

Location Quotients: tracts

High skilled: managers + professionals – business owners

  0.0 – 0.5
  0.6 – 1.0
  1.1 – 1.5
  > 1.5
  Zone boundaries

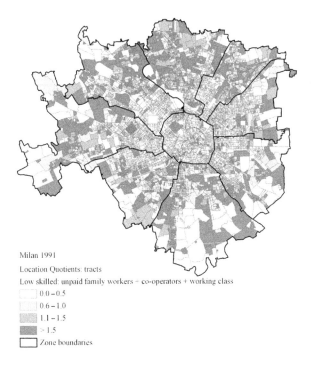

Milan 1991

Location Quotients: tracts

Low skilled: unpaid family workers – co-operators + working class

☐ 0.0 – 0.5
☐ 0.6 – 1.0
▨ 1.1 – 1.5
■ > 1.5
☐ Zone boundaries

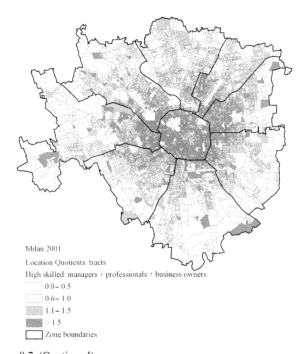

Milan 2001

Location Quotients: tracts

High skilled: managers + professionals + business owners

☐ 0.0 – 0.5
☐ 0.6 – 1.0
▨ 1.1 – 1.5
■ > 1.5
☐ Zone boundaries

Figure 8.7 (Continued)

Milan 2001

Location Quotients: tracts

Low skilled: unpaid family workers + co-operators + working class

☐ 0.0 – 0.5
☐ 0.6 – 1.0
▨ 1.1 – 1.5
▧ > 1.5
☐ Zone boundaries

Figure 8.7 Location quotients for selected categories. Milan, tracts, 1991 and 2001.

Source: Authors' calculations on census data.

The working class has its highest levels of concentration (LQ 1.2) in *Zona 9* and especially in the adjacent census tracts 65 and 66, corresponding to *Quarto Oggiaro* and *Sacco, Vialba* neighbourhoods. This group is also concentrated in the eastern part of the city, in *Circoscrizione Forlanini, Taliedo*. By jointly analysing the location quotients for the censuses of 1991 and 2001, it is possible to clas-sify the various areas of the city according to the different stages of potential and actual growth or decline in the concentration of a particular group. Values for the most recent location quotients are compared with those for the previous period. By using the ACE scale – which thus ensures both greater detail with respect to districts and areas of decentralisation and a sufficient degree of uniformity and homogeneity of areal units – the dynamic analysis of the location quotients leads to the following results (Table 8.12).

Both business owners and professionals increased their relative concentrations in nearly 50 per cent of the sub-areas of *ACE*. These increases mainly concern the areas in *Zona 7* (*Monte Rosa* and *San Siro* neighbourhoods) and *Zona 8* (*Tre Torri, Sarpi* and *Portello*) in the western part of the city, in *Zona 2* (*Centrale*), *Zona 3* (*Venezia, Buenos Aires, Bacone* and *Dei Mille*) and parts of *Zona 4* (*Libia, Dateo* and *XXII Marzo*) in the east, in addition to the whole *Centro Storico*.

Table 8.12 Dynamic analysis of location quotients. Milan, 1991–2001: *ACE**

	Decline		Potential decline		Potential increase		Increase	
	n.	*% of ACE*	*n.*	*% of ACE*	*n.*	*% of ACE*	*n.*	*% of ACE*
Business owners	40	*43,5*	12	*13,0*	25	*27,2*	15	*16,3*
Professionals	34	*37,0*	17	*18,5*	25	*27,2*	16	*17,4*
Managers/executives	12	*13,0*	29	*31,5*	40	*43,5*	11	*12,0*
White-collar workers	33	*35,9*	18	*19,6*	5	*5,4*	36	*39,1*
Self-employed	28	*30,4*	21	*22,8*	21	*22,8*	22	*23,9*
Working class	22	*23,9*	22	*23,9*	18	*19,6*	30	*32,6*
Co-operators	36	*39,1*	13	*14,1*	12	*13,0*	31	*33,7*
Unpaid family workers	40	*43,5*	11	*12,0*	10	*10,9*	31	*33,7*

Note: *Residual *ACE* areas are included.

Source: Authors' calculations on census data.

Managers increased their concentration in 60 per cent of areas, especially in *Zona 3* (*Porpora* and *Parco Lambro, Cimiano*), *Zona 4 (XXII Marzo), Zona 5 (Vigentina* and *Porta Romana), Zona 6 (Navigli* and *Piazza Napoli), Zona 7 (Forze Armate), Zona 8 (Sarpi)* and *Zona 9 (Garibaldi, Isola)*. White-collar workers increased their concentration in 25 per cent of the subareas of *ACE* located in *Zonas 5, 6, 8* and, especially, *Zona 9* (*Bicocca, Ca-Granda, Niguarda, Bovisa, Affori, Bruzzano* and *Comasina, Bovisasca*). Finally, the working class reduced its concentration in *Zonas 7* and *8*, due to the restructuring and gentrification of the zones of *Portello* and *Fiera* that attracted managers and business owners. On the other hand, they increased their already high concentrations in the very peripheral areas of the city, especially in the north-western part in *Zona 9* (*Farini, Maciachini, Ca-Granda, Niguarda, Dergano, Bovisa* and *Affori*) and in *Zona 8* (*Quarto Oggiaro, Sacco, Vialba, Villapizzone* and *Accursio*) and in the north-eastern part in *Zona 2* (*Padova, Crescenzago, Greco* and *Viale Monza*).

The dynamic analysis for the period 1991–2001 reveals a general increase in the level of concentration of the categories that were originally most segregated. There has been a polarisation process leading to higher levels of segregation of the more wealthy classes (business owners, professionals) and the lowest social status categories (working class and unpaid family workers). The process of ejection out of the core of the city of the woking class by the elite, already in progress in 1991, was reinforced over the decade. There are also signs of this process extending to the displacement of white-collar workers by the elite.

Conclusions

This chapter's analysis of the socio-economic structures of Milan has shown that the city is undertaking a transition from a late-industrial to a post-industrial city, as marked by substantial population declines in its cores and suburbanisation. These trends are mirrored in the urban fabric in terms of the large-scale production of residential and office space on vacant areas of land in the peri-central and peripheral areas. After decades of decline, the city records positive net migration, which rejuvenates its senescent demographic structures while also reshaping its social structures in terms of ethnic segregation. The indices of segregation for the most segregated ethnic groups are multiples of those for the most segregated socio-economic groups.

Socio-economic segregation is difficult to analyse because of the difficulty in comparing socio-economic groups. It is easier to comment on the segregation levels of the elite groups rather than the levels of segregation of the working class. Despite these difficulties, a number of phenomena emerge that point to a parallel process of social polarisation and, in many cases, a diminution of the social division of space. Important among these are:

- a further increase in high levels of segregation for business owners and professionals, and in intermediate levels of segregation for the working class at all scales;
- a significant decline in the levels of segregation for managers and executives;
- a decrease in the high levels of segregation for graduates that still remain high. This is also due to the location of a part of this group in working-class areas where there are processes of gentrification;
- a decrease in the very high levels of ethnic segregation that despite their decline still remain high, in the region of 50. Even if Latin American and African migrants have a tendency to disperse, Asian migrants have a pattern of further concentration in a number of subareas.

In Milan, despite a decrease in levels of segregation for some groups, there is a tendency to increase the selectivity of certain socio-economic groups that is translated spatially into the auto-segregation of the elites. From the factor analysis it emerges that the most important changes between 1991 and 2001 concern the increasing importance of the factor 'ageing' (from 6 per cent to 13 per cent) in explaining the overall variability. Other structural factors, 'single' and 'ethnicity', also increase their share while, on the contrary, the factors 'elite' and 'lowest social status and large households' show a lower weight. This means that the evolutionary path towards lower segregation is mainly driven by the demographic structural change that occurred in Milan between 1991 and 2001. In addition, the tendency towards lower segregation can be explained by the decrease of the working class in the city.

In summary, the picture of Milan shows a changing relationship between the centre and the periphery. The former boundaries are dissolving in favour of a polycentric pattern, in which the social-periphery is now inside the core of the city (Bonomi 2010). Among the distinctive traits of this new relationship are the following:

- an increasing concentration in the urban core of a quite large proportion of the marginalised population, leading to the establishment of a new lower class characterised by a social, ethnic and cultural mix for which a unique description is impossible (Blangiardo and Rimoldi 2013; Magatti and De Benedittis 2006);

- an increase in the social vulnerability of the middle class, due to higher levels of exposure to accidental events (job loss, threats to health status or family dissolution) that can lead to poverty;
- the traditional lower social class appears to be marked by a sense of economic insecurity, enhanced by the weakening of both community safety nets and institutional presence, such that the economic vulnerability of the lower classes (which were historically protected by the welfare system) becomes more acute.

When taken together, these factors mean that Milan does not have just one single concentration of marginalised population, but rather a number of niches of marginality and decay distributed here and there (Zajczyk 2005). The results of the 2011 census will allow us to test the validity of this working hypothesis.

Notes

1 Data for foreign population by age from registers should be considered as temporary, as census data at local levels are not available at the moment.
2 The working population is usually classified by work status. In this classification employers are distinguished from employees and from workers on own account or independent workers. The latter do not employ labour for pay, but they, as well as employers, may be assisted by unpaid family workers or family helpers who are usually distinguished as a separate group (see http://en-ii.demopaedia.org/wiki/35#350). The category of 'other dependent workers' includes the major ISCO08 groups VI-skilled agricultural, forestry and fishery workers, VII-craft and related trades workers, VIII-plant and machine operators and assemblers, IX-elementary occupations and X-armed forces.
3 Data for 2011 are unavailable at the current time.
4 Comparisons between different sources are not possible since they differ, starting from the definition of income (family or personal income) and the equivalence scale adopted to ending with the calculus on individual or aggregated data.
5 The Gini Index is based on the income definition of Banca d'Italia.
6 Data for 2011 census tracts are unavailable at the current time.
7 The twenty administrative districts were effective until 1999 when they were reduced to nine.

References

Acciari, P and Mocetti, S 2013, 'Una mappa della disuguaglianza del reddito in Italia' [A map of income inequality in Italy] *Questioni di Economia e Finanza* n. 208, Banca d'Italia.

Blangiardo, G C and Rimoldi, S 2013, 'Atlante statistico della povertà materiale' [Statistical atlas of material poverty] in *L'esclusione sociale in Lombardia: quarto rapporto 2011*, ed Eupolis, Eupolis Lombardia, Milano, pp. 15–36.

Blangiardo, G C and Terzera, L 1997, *L'immigrazione straniera nell'area milanese. Rapporto statistico dell'Osservatorio Cariplo ISMU. Anno 1996* [Foreign immigration in the Milanese area. Statistical Report by Cariplo–ISMU Observatory. Year 1996] Quaderni ISMU N. 4, Milano.

Boal, F W 1976, 'Ethnic residential segregation, ethnic mixing and resource conflict: A study in Belfast, Northern Ireland' in *Ethnic segregation in cities*, eds C Peach, V Robinson and S Smith, Croom Helm, London.

Bono, G and Checchi, D 2001, *La disuguaglianza a Milano negli anni '90* [Inequality in Milan during the 1990s], Research report, Ufficio Studi Camera di Commercio di Milano.

Bonomi, A 2010, *La città che sente e che pensa: Creatività e piattaforme produttive nella città infinita* [The city that feels and thinks: Creativity and production platforms in the infinite city], Mondadori Electa, Milano.

Brandolini, A 2009, 'La disuguaglianza dei redditi personali: perché l'Italia somiglia più agli Stati Uniti che alla Germania?' [Personal income inequality: Why does Italy look more to the USA than to Germany ?] in *La fatica di cambiare. Rapporto sulla società italiana*, eds R Catanzaro and G Sciortino, Il Mulino, Bologna.

Brunet, R 1989, *Les villes "européennes"* [European cities], La Documentation française, Datar–Reclus, Montpellier-Paris.

Cerasi, M and Ferraresi, G 1974, *La residenza operaia a Milano* [Working class housing in Milan], Officina Edizioni, Roma.

Dalmasso, E 1971, *Milan Capitale économique de l'Italie* [Milan, economic capital of Italy], Orphys, Paris.

D'Ovidio, M 2009, 'Milano città duale?' [Milan dual city?] in *I limiti sociali della crescita: Milano e le città d'Europa, tra competitività e disuguaglianze. Secondo Rapporto su Milano Sociale*, ed C Ranci, Maggioli, Milano.

Fainstein, S, Gordon, I and Harloe, M 1992, *Divided cities; New York and London in the contemporary world*, Blackwell, Oxford.

Friedmann, J 1995, 'The world city hypothesis' in *World cities in a world system*, eds P L Knox and P J Taylor, Cambridge University Press, Cambridge, pp. 317–331.

Glaeser, E L, Resseger, M G and Tobio, K 2008, 'Urban inequality', *NBER working paper* 14419, Cambridge.

Kantrowitz, N 1973, 'Ethnic and social segregation in New York metropolis'. *American Journal of Sociology* 74, 186–203.

Magatti, M and De Benedittis, M 2006, *I nuovi ceti popolari* [The new working class], Feltrinelli, Milano.

Massey, D 1990, 'American apartheid: Segregation and the American underclass', *American Journal of Sociology* 96, 329–357.

Openshaw, S 1984, *The modifiable areal unit problem*, CATMOG 38. Geo Abstracts. Norwich. Available online: http://qmrg.org.uk/files/2008/11/38–maup–openshaw.pdf. Accessed 22 April 2015

Padovani, L 1996, 'Italy' in *Housing policy in Europe,* ed P Balchin, Routledge, London, pp. 188–209.

Peach, C 1996, 'Does Britain have ghettos?', *Transactions of the Institute of British Geographers*, New series 21(1), 216–235. Available online: https://www.ucl.ac.uk/celsius/research-outputs/abstract-peach-1996. Accessed 22 April 2015.

Percopo, M 2009, 'La distribuzione del reddito in Lombardia' [Income distribution in Lombardy] in *Rapporto di legislatura*, ed. IReR, Guerini e Associati, Milano.

Petsimeris, P 1998, 'Urban decline and the new social and ethnic divisions in the core cities of the Italian industrial triangle'*Urban Studies* 35(3), 449–466.

Pezzoni, N 2013, *La città sradicata: Geografie dell'abitare contemporaneo. I migranti mappano Milano* [The city eradicated: Geographies of contemporary living. Migrants map of Milan], O barra O Edizioni, Milano.

Sassen, S 1991, *The global city; New York, London, Tokyo*, Princeton University Press, Princeton, NJ.

Tammaru, T, Musterd, S, van Ham, M and Marcińczak, S, 2016, 'A multi-factor approach to understanding socio-economic segregation in European capital cities' in *Socio-economic segregation in European capital cities: East meets West*, eds T Tammaru, S Marcińczak, M van Ham and S Musterd, Routledge, London.

Tosi, A 1994, *Abitanti. Le nuove strategie dell'azione abitativa* [New strategies of housing], Il Mulino, Bologna.

Wirth, L 1938, 'Urbanism as a way of life' *American Journal of Sociology* 44(1), 1–24.

Wood, R 1976, 'Aspects of the scale problem in the calculation of segregation indices: London and Birmingham, 1961 and 1971' *Tijdschrift voor Economische en Sociale Geografie* 67(3), 169–174.

Zajczyk, F (ed) 2003, *La povertà a Milano* [Poverty in Milan], Franco Angeli, Milano.

Zajczyk, F 2005, 'Segregazione spaziale e condizione abitativa' [Spatial segregation and housing conditions], in *La povertà come condizione e come percezione*, ed. D Benassi, Franco Angeli, Milano, pp. 53–88.

Zanfrini, L 2013, 'Immigration and labour market', in *Migration: a picture from Italy*, ed. V Cesareo, Fondazione ISMU, Milano, pp. 39–55.

9 Economic crisis, social change and segregation processes in Madrid

Jesús Leal and Daniel Sorando

Abstract

Both the growth and the crisis stages of urban society in Madrid have produced dramatic transformations to its social structure. As a consequence, the intensity of residential segregation within this territory had a remarkable increase between 2001 and 2011. On the one hand, the expansion of professionals has led to a wide process of spatial segregation rather than a step towards socio-spatial integration. Whereas, on the other hand, the great rise of unemployment during the economic crisis has exclusively affected manual workers. As a result, the traditional peripheries in which these categories used to live have become the place where precariousness is concentrated.

Introduction

At the beginning of the twenty-first century, during the period between the two censuses, from 2001 to 2011, Madrid experienced many changes, which serve to explain not only the relationship between social change and segregation, but also between the latter and processes of social inequality. These transformations include the effects of the huge growth of both its population and its home-building activity throughout the metropolitan area that caused a remarkable increase in the stock of housing units. However, this increase has not met the social needs of significant numbers of the population, who are experiencing dramatic changes related to the contemporary economic crisis as well as a restructuring of the relationship between centre and periphery.

If segregation is taken to be a concrete social fact, it is possible to compare the segregation characteristics of different cities. Furthermore, research on southern European cities has stressed some of the particular mechanisms by which great social inequality does not automatically translate to an equivalent residential segregation. Explanations for this apparent paradox relate to the particular history of these urban societies, basically marked successively by a massive suburbanisation, some considerable migration processes at the beginning of the century and the recent economic crisis. Finally, and most importantly, in southern European cities this series of events has occurred within the context of undeveloped welfare systems. Thus, this chapter considers segregation as a social fact that is tied to the ways a society occupies urban territory and aims to show the forms and processes of segregation in Madrid over the last few years, in direct relation to its socio-labour structure and recent transformation.

Social effects of the expansion and bursting of the housing bubble

Madrid has experienced a dramatic change in the first decade of the twenty-first century. From being one of the greatest European cities with the highest rates of economic and population growth, it has gone on to suffer among the highest percentages of unemployment and population loss because of the financial crisis. The following pages will attempt to explore how the great changes experienced in Madrid's population and production systems influenced the increase of social inequalities and segregation in these years. Regional and local policies and national urban and housing laws also influenced this disparity. In order to understand changes in the distribution of the various socio-economic categories in urban spaces, the importance of two specific categories must be highlighted. On the one hand we have the expansion of the group consisting of professionals and highly skilled trades, both waged and freelance. On the other hand, we have the elevated and continued abundance of foreign workers over the period in question who are often either unemployed or employed within the category of service and sales workers.

Moreover, the change in the social balance over the last few years has shown some differences with other European cities. Overall, this is due to the lessened impact of the availability of contaminated funds in Spanish banks. However, it is also due to the bigger impact of the housing market crisis, which, in addition to the international credit crunch, was the principal factor behind the rise in unemployment. As a result of these trends, during the years of the crisis social inequality has grown in Spain far above the European standards: according to Eurostat, the Gini coefficient shows that Spain went from 31.2 in 2008 to 35 in 2012 (33.2 in the Urban Region of Madrid), whereas the European Union average remained at 30.6 during the same period.

Population growth and economic change

The Urban Region of Madrid has grown considerably over the last few years, in a dissimilar way to any other European capital, with a total increase of 27.5 per cent in the period 1998–2012. This rapid growth is the result of a migration process, involving some people who gained Spanish nationality. Over this period, the number of foreign residents multiplied by 6.3, going from 3.2 per cent to 16.5 per cent of the population. According to the Population Register, in January 2011, the most numerous foreigners in the Urban Region of Madrid were Americans (north and south), followed by Europeans, Africans and Asians. Yet, at the same time the November 2011 census shows that of a total of 310,649 Spanish nationals born abroad, the majority could be considered to be immigrants who obtained Spanish nationality or were citizens with dual nationality – over 35 per cent of the residents born in American countries have Spanish nationality.

In this regard, the total number of immigrants living in Madrid, counting those nationalised and those not, exceeds 1.2 million inhabitants out of a total population of 6.4 million according to the 2011 census. Thus, although foreign nationals represent 14.7 per cent of the population in real terms, the total of immigrants, including those nationalised, exceeds 18.5 per cent. This entire population has played a decisive role in the growth of the population of the entire region and in the change of its social structure. The increase in the foreign population combined with a relevant change in the size of households, from 2.89 in 2001 to 2.57 in 2011, resulted in a greater demand for housing. This demand, in turn, resulted in an increase in home-building activity that caused an increase of more than half a million units between 2001 and 2011, representing an increase in stock of 20.3 per cent. The construction of these housing units over the decade in question, and especially over the period 2003–2007, also implies an increase in related activities, for example in industry, finance, commerce, etc.

Such a high level of growth over such a short period of time could not be achieved without generating high levels of both public and private debt, leading to the economic stagnation or even collapse of many households and companies. This fact explains part of the reason for the transformation of the city; immersed in a spiral in which the previous housing market growth meant the attraction of workers, which themselves constituted an important element of the overall growth, followed by a subsequent fall in construction activities that led to a large proportion of unemployment and the subsequent negative migratory balance.

The crisis

The economic crisis of recent years has had very different effects on the economic categories. In the four years between the second quarter of 2008 and that of 2012, 3,008,000 jobs were lost in Spain, representing a decrease of 15 per cent of the employed across the country. At the same time, in the urban region of Madrid, there have been 286,000 job losses, 9.5 per cent of those working in 2008, the year that marks the highest peak of employment for a decade.

One of the main explanations for the economic growth and decline can be found in the housing market and the credit facilities, which enabled inclusion in the Euro zone. Thus, the housing sector is a key cause of the economic crisis in the case of Spain, and especially in that of Madrid, which added to the financial crisis provoked by the sinking of the market on a global level. The fatigue in the real estate production sector, which strongly knocked the Spanish economy, started to manifest itself in mid-2007, one year before the fall of Lehman Brothers in the United States. This found form in the deflation of demand and the decrease in the prices of housing and office space.

The fall of the entire international financial sector seriously aggravated a crisis rooted in a completely unbalanced sector, in which there was a clear overproduction of housing. Since the 1990s, public authorities had worked on the liberalisation of the land market so as to promote it as the driving force of the Spanish economy. Moreover, new housing stock built during the following years has been characterised by the commodification of the sector and the minor role of public housing (Figure 9.1). In this regard, the increase in the weight of subsidised housing after the bursting of the bubble has been due to the fall of market housing, not as a result of a rise in public housing.

Although most of this stock has been produced for home ownership (in the Urban Region of Madrid, the percentage of home owners who had a mortgage grew from 29.7 per cent in 2001 to 37.9 per cent in 2011), rentals have increased due to the demand of affordable housing by the economic immigrants during the first decade of the century: 64.9 per cent of the immigrants lived in a rented flat in the Urban Region of Madrid, contrasting with 10.2 per cent of the native locals, according to the 2011 census. As a result, old central districts received immigrants in the first moments of their trajectory since they offer affordable rental dwellings and mutual support networks. However, with the development of their trajectory, foreign migrants begin to live in specific peripheral neighbourhoods where they can find this kind of dwelling, as a result of the saturation of rental housing in the urban centres. This sprawl coincided with that of many Spanish households who chose to live in different sorts of peripheral neighbourhoods, newly built with homogeneous communities, taking advantage of the facilitated mortgages available during the years of the housing bubble (1997–2007).

The demand for housing, which abruptly collapsed in mid-2007, was followed by the removal of the possibility of obtaining funding from the financial entities affected by the crisis. Despite the sharp fall in demand for housing, the buildings

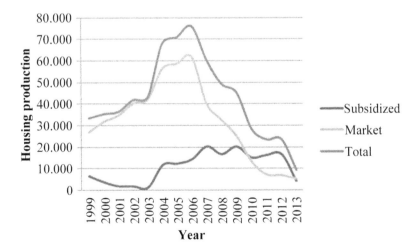

Figure 9.1 Housing productions in the Urban Region of Madrid by type of promotion.

that had already been started during the expansion phase had to be completed, meaning that unemployment in the sector increased slowly over a period of two years. The imbalance of demand and supply, which had started two years previously, in 2011, left an unsold housing stock that can be measured at around 70,000 units in the case of Madrid. Despite the crisis, in 2011, there were 350,000 more people employed in Madrid than in 2001. But this suggests an unequal distribution, given that while there was an increase in jobs of 490,000 in the service sector in absolute terms, all the other sectors lost jobs: 60,000 in industry and 63,000 in construction. Furthermore, these figures hide a large variation over the whole decade in which there were big variations in employment, characterised by a general increase in the first seven years followed by a sharp fall later.

In the last twenty years a process of change in occupational distribution has been taking place, with different characteristics in each of the periods mentioned earlier (growth and recession). Meanwhile, over these periods the socio-economic structure has undergone a profound change with a considerable growth in the middle categories, especially the upper middle ones; whereas a rapid decline in the traditional working categories has given way to new forms of relationships among industrial workers and service-sector workers.

Upper-category proximity, not overlap

The upper socio-economic categories, formed by businessmen, directors and managers of companies, have also seen a notable increase, from 5.1 per cent to 7.9 per cent of the working population over the period 2005–2012. This growth has meant that the traditional living areas for these categories are overflowing, and are expanding towards the outskirts. In these areas large individual mansions were constructed, generally positioned in private housing estates with contracted security personnel, albeit with legal constraints that prevent an exclusive appropriation of public spaces. Furthermore, some central districts of Madrid that were previously the typical living areas of these groups have been maintained by those who inherited or succeeded the prior inhabitants, generally in certain large apartments in the city centre. These groups do not share the typical middle categories' dialectic between centre and periphery as they rarely conquest spaces occupied by other socio-economic categories. Instead, they just enlarge the pre-eminent places in which they previously settled. These places are located in the north-west (Pozuelo de Alarcón, Majadahonda, Boadilla del Monte) and the north (Alcobendas) of the Metropolitan Area, whereas large apartments in the city centre are situated within Chamartín, Salamanca and Ciudad Lineal districts.

The leading category of professionals

Through all of these recent changes, the middle socio-economic categories have been the major protagonist owing to two important facts. First, as a result of the general rise in the level of professional training because of easy access to higher education for young people, the total number of workers with a higher education diploma has grown by 400,000 between the years 2001 and 2011, indicating an increase of 44.1 per cent in ten years. This large growth of the upper middle group of professionals and skilled labourers came to represent 26.1 per cent of employed people in 2005 and 34.6 per cent in 2012. However, not all members of the work-force holding higher education qualifications are working in occupations that require these qualifications. In this sense, it can be said that Madrid, which has been characterised over the past two or three decades as having a polarised struc-ture, has changed rapidly to re-enforce large middle categories which could be divided into two factions. The first of which can be referred to as the upper-middle category, made up of professionals and people with technical qualifications, both self-employed and salaried, and characterised by their higher education through university studies, and in jobs that correspond to their qualifications, working in both the public and private sectors. Madrid has the advantage of having the coun-try's public administration located within the city.

The other part of the middle categories is largely composed of mid-level work-ers, some with university studies, and others who have only reached the level of high school completion. Middle-level occupations range from administrative positions in private companies or public institutions to tradesmen, highly skilled labourers, etc. In contrast with the other group, it has not grown considerably over the last few years, but it has experienced a change in its composition and a self-rejuvenation. Furthermore, a distinction must be made between the old middle categories of professionals and technically qualified workers and the young mid-dle categories, highlighting the intergenerational social mobility process driven by the latter, which explains its dispersion over the city. Moreover, the increase in volume of these middle-high categories is followed by its social and economic devaluation, expressed in terms of a below-average growth in their wages.

There are two consequence of this devaluation. First, there is an increasing and significant distance between the group of young and senior professionals, particu-larly in their real capacity for consumption and in their access to housing. The second consequence is the increasing gap between professionals and directors and managers. As a result, the precarious living conditions of younger salaried profes-sionals (especially those working in public services) are becoming more similar to that of the lower middle categories. The importance of having a university degree decreases in comparison to other qualities such as work experience or lan-guage skills. Careers are no longer linear systems of promotions in one company; instead, they require greater diversification, labour mobility and specialisation, and thus the differences between managerial and technical positions are becoming more and more pronounced.

There are also some differences concerning the traditional living areas of the dif-ferent socio-economic groups that compose the category of professionals. Whereas traditional living areas of upper middle professionals follow some of the managerial trends, younger middle categories tend to be located in the same neighbourhoods that their family used to live in. As a result, professionals used to be settled through-out the whole Metropolitan Area. Familial dimension is a key factor in explaining socio-economic segregation in societies where family networks of mutual support are a common strategy in the context of a weak welfare state. For example, according to Eurostat, the age of nest-leaving is later in the case of Spain (28.9) than in the European Union (26.2). Although the Spanish indicator lessened during the bubble years (from 29.0 in 2004 to 28.2 in 2009), it is growing again since the crisis began. In this regard, in southern European cities this kind of process leads to socio-economic mixing in neighbourhoods which had previously enjoyed lower socio-economic status. Finally, in the last years of the considered period, between 2007 and 2012, the members of the highest groups have moved from accounting for one-third of the total of categories (33.1 per cent) before the crisis, to 43.6 per cent four years later. This growth demonstrates that these categories' resistances to the crisis were far greater than others, since their decrease in absolute numbers of workers is low in comparison to the decline that occured among manual workers (Table 9.1).

The decline of manual categories

In the light of this decline, there are two exceptions: freelancers (unsalaried workers) and the service and sales workers. First, the rise in self-employment is also a consequence of the crisis. A certain number of unemployed workers, who were previously salaried, have set up on their own to try to survive at very competitive rates. Among them, there are also workers who are hired by companies as self-employed, which

Table 9.1 Numbers of people employed by occupational group (using Economically Active Population Survey Double encoding matrices ISCO88-ISCO08) and year. Difference and percentage increase (2001–2011). Urban Region of Madrid

ISCO major group	2001	2011	2001–2011	
			Difference	% Increase
Unemployed	340,195	832,825	492,630	144.8
Armed forces occupations (0)	19,892	22,405	2,513	12.6
Managers (1)	162,082	176,635	14,553	9.0
Professionals (2)	433,872	573 770	139,898	32.2
Technicians and associate professionals (3)	298,396	385,620	87,224	29.2
Clerical support workers (4)	338,072	444,430	106,358	31.5
Service and sales workers (5)	441,174	499,615	58,441	13.2
Skilled agricultural, forestry and fishery workers (6)	16,975	18,990	2,015	11.9
Craft and related trades workers (7)	307,312	230,920	−76,392	−24.9
Plant and machine operators, and assemblers (8)	166,476	142,835	−23,641	−14.2
Elementary occupations (9)	261,448	274,770	13,322	5.1
Total	2,785,895	3,602,815	816,920	29.3

Source: Produced by the authors based on the Census of Population and Housing 2001 and 2011 (INE) Development.

exempt the companies from paying social security expenses. And, second, the category formed by the service and sales occupations is largely composed of workers in the personal service industry: domestic workers, caregivers, hairdressers, etc. Of these, a large portion are foreigners who often compensate in part for the shortage of public support services, as is the case with the elderly care providers.

However, the overall result is that in the period of crisis, from the second quarter of 2008 to that of 2012, a decline of 25.6 per cent took place in absolute terms in the employment of the traditional working categories, formed by manual workers and skilled and unskilled workers in the service sector, while the lower middle categories fell by 16.4 per cent and the higher categories saw an increase of 9.1 per cent over this period. Each company's strategy needs be taken into account with respect to this data, yet in general it can be said that first the less qualified workers are laid off, allocating their tasks to those who have a higher category. These changes in social structure have a huge spatial impact. The conclusion is that the geography of unemployment is spatially differentiated, just because the socio-economic categories are distributed unequally within the territory. Traditionally, manual categories have lived in the south (Alcorcón, Fuenlabrada, Getafe, Leganés, Móstoles, Parla, Pinto) and the east (Alcalá de Henares, Coslada, San Fernando de Henares, Torrejón de Ardoz) of the Metropolitan Area of Madrid. These groups have also lived in some of the southern and central districts that have become devalued (Carabanchel, Centro, Puente de Vallecas, San Blas, Tetuán, Usera, Villaverde).

As a consequence, all these areas with the highest proportion of manual workers will be much more affected than those with high proportions of upper and upper middle categories. Naturally this would, in turn, lead to other types of inequalities, whereby foreigners would be more affected with higher proportions of unemployment and more complex segregation processes because of overcrowding in homes. Nevertheless, the insignificant dimension of contemporary social housing explains the absence of highly segregated places where some of these socio-economic categories could be concentrated in a similar way to other European countries.

Generational fracture and grassroots response

The other important consequence of the effects caused by the crisis is its unequal impact on different age groups. First, the cohort of young adults will have more acutely experienced the consequences of unbalanced economic growth and the crisis that followed. In this regard, current mortgage requirements imply indebtedness in the long term and are very different from the prices and repayment times available to older generations. Second, obtaining a job is more difficult for those who are trying to emancipate themselves in times of crisis. Thousands of young people search fruitlessly for jobs in the public and private labour market without much luck. The result is that some of the young people with the best training and knowledge of languages are being obliged to search for work in other countries.

In this context, the citizen's response was delayed, but had a series of completely innovative forms of expression that manifested themselves in the 15 May 2011 movement. A large portion of the population (mainly young adults) occupied Madrid's city centre and settled in the city's central plaza, while a series of public open debates on the topic of the crisis and the measures necessary to overcome it were taking place. In the second stage of the movement, it tried to base itself on other types such as the neighbourhood movements (mainly, anti-eviction movements). Finally, the partial dismantling of the welfare state gave way to new demands whereby protests and street demonstrations would join up with protests against mass dismissals at important companies. The generalised descent of activity meant a considerable reduction in the public tax revenue, which led to a great imbalance. The adjustment of the public sector in turn led to a retraction in construction activities, a lowering of salaries and, as a result, a reduction of the capacity to consume: a downwards spiral, a way out of which is difficult to imagine in the short term.

Data and methods

In the case of Madrid there are three main different spatial boundaries: first, *the Urban Region* constituted by the administrative 'Community of Madrid' with a population of 6,489,680 inhabitants in 2011, and second *the Metropolitan Area* defined by the Atlas of Urban Areas elaborated by the Ministerio de Fomento (2004) with a population of 6,030,413 people. Finally, *the city of Madrid*, in the centre of the Metropolitan Area, with its 3,265,838 habitants. Most of the data we used refers to the Urban Region, as this is the only spatial division for which this kind of information is available. However, from this point on, the study of residential segregation patterns is focused on the Metropolitan Area since this is the actual area in which significant movements concerning residential segregation (mainly residential mobility and commuting) take place. In Appendix 1, two maps can be consulted for more information on the geography of the Metropolitan Area and the central city of Madrid, especially concerning areas and districts that will be mentioned in the next section.

The 2001 and 2011 Censuses of Population and Housing offer information about the socio-economic composition of spatial units smaller than the neighbourhood scale. In particular, the spatial units on which the calculation of different indicators of residential segregation are based are groupings of census tracts, as, unlike the 2001 Census, the sample in the Census of Population and Housing of 2011 is not representative at a more disaggregated territorial level. Then, the 2001 census tracts have been added to match the 2011 spatial units as closely as possible. The resulting groupings have an average of 12,252 residents in 2011 and 10,623 in 2001. To facilitate comparisons between the results obtained from these territorial units with those of other cities analysed in this book (see also the introduction of this book for more detail: Tammaru *et al.* 2016), in Appendix 2 the values of the dissimilarity index obtained in 2001 are contrasted, based on the territorial scope of the employee (using census tracts or aggregations of these). In all cases, the index of dissimilarity is less when aggregated census tracts are used; while in the case of isolation indices, it is equal or slightly lower.

Notwithstanding, the change in intensity of the residential segregation of different labour categories in the Madrid Metropolitan Area must be interpreted with caution. This is because of the important changes across ISCO 88 and ISCO 08 that have been highlighted in the introductory chapter. However, some categories do allow for a good approximation to the processes of socio-spatial change, which can explain the increase, or the maintenance, of segregation intensity. In particular, two occupational categories that allow for comparison are very important in the context of Madrid: the unemployed category remains unchanged; while the categories of professionals and manual workers (both skilled and unskilled) have not seen their composition altered in a remarkable manner. Finally, throughout the analysis, the categories of craft and related trades workers (ISCO-7) and plant and machine operators and assemblers (ISCO-8) have been grouped into a single category to solve the problems of statistical representation of the latter, because of the sample the Census of Population and Housing in 2011 is based on.

Residential segregation in the Madrid Metropolitan Area (2001–2011)

Residential segregation between different labour categories in Madrid has increased from 2001 to 2011. This process has, in short, been fomented by transformations in the structure of urban society during this period. Specifically, three groups can be understood to characterise this dynamic, seen in: the increase and diversification of the social conditions of professionals; the decline in traditional worker categories; and the socio-economic homogeneity of the unemployed from 2007 onwards. Thus, this ongoing process aids an understanding of the reasons for the spatial exception which characterised urban societies in the south of Europe in 2001, such as Madrid, where huge social inequality did not translate to an equivalent residential segregation (Arbaci 2008; Domínguez *et al.* 2012; Malheiros 2002; Martínez and Leal 2008).

The end of the southern exception: the reconciliation between social inequality and spatial distance

The relevant residential segregation of 2011 reveals the dynamics of socio-spatial inequality that were masked by the southern exception at the beginning of the century. Until the start of the economic crisis in 2007, this paradoxical increase in inequality combined with a reduction in segregation is seen as an intermediate step within the socio-economic model. It involves an increase in some service activities that lead to the growth of middle and upper categories at the same time as reinforcing personal service jobs, which create manual labourer categories with very different profiles than seen before. That is to say, it is a model, developed throughout Spain from 1994 to 2007, of a speculative, socially regressive character (Colectivo Ioé 2009). This growth cycle has primarily developed through the production of urban space, so that its impact on the segregating processes is crucial (López and Rodríguez 2010). However, some of the dynamics involved were temporally expressed at the start through the social mixing between different labour categories. The result of which was the concealment of the unequal relationships that defined them. In the first place, the years of Spanish (and Madrid) economic growth (up to 2007) permitted upward social mobility processes for a large part of the most disadvantaged households. Thus, in their neighbourhoods of residence, unemployment was replaced either by work in low qualified occupations, often related to the construction sector; or by technical jobs, as a result of the inclusion of their new generations into the Spanish education system, thereby facilitating intergenerational social mobility.

The contribution of this dynamic to the decrease in segregation is, in itself, paradoxical, given that the reduction in intensity is due, precisely, to the characteristics of an insufficient welfare state. To summarise, the *familist model* of southern European countries is based on family networks of mutual support, in the absence of far-reaching social policies (Esping Andersen 1997; Moreno 2001). This fact, linked to the preference for family closeness in residential decisions, explains how, in the first stages of intense growth, socio-economic segregation can diminish. As a consequence, the greater dependency on family solidarity in the case of young people with working-categories backgrounds explained their permanence on the outskirts of their urban zones of origin, in new developments that combine better housing with easy access to family support networks. In conjunction, these processes encouraged processes of social mixing (Leal 2004). However, ascending social mobility was supported, to a great extent, by a real estate bubble pregnant with the seeds of processes of profound social inequality. Thus, the bursting of the bubble (in 2007) has resulted in the dramatic return of unemployment to the most humble households and neighbourhoods. In this way, the social mixing promoted during the heyday of this model of economic growth has been replaced by the concentration of poverty and job insecurity in certain urban areas of the Madrid Metropolitan Area.

Second, the Spanish accumulation process has used house prices as the centrepiece of its development model. Thus, the construction of the city has been driven by the needs of the capital accumulation process to a greater extent than by social housing needs. In particular, the city has been progressively structured into areas that are relatively differentiated, according to their social value, which is clearly manifest in the territorial differences of their homes (Roch 2008). Throughout this stage, while the real estate bubble lasted, it promoted the financialisation of domestic economies and the creation of an ownership society in which the wealth effect was produced and linked to the inflation of home ownership (Lopez and Rodriguez 2010; Naredo 2010). This dynamic allotted a newfound prosperity to households from different socio-economic categories.

However, in the race towards the elite club in which said bubble consisted, the efforts of different social groups are not comparable: 'it has supposed a greater real effort, on the part of the worse off areas, to approach the (unattainable) values of true exclusive spaces, than that which had to be made in order to increase that distance' (Fernández and Roch 2012: 52). Lower-income households, whose collapse has been far greater than those socio-economic categories living in the areas that retain their centrality, are facing both a crisis of mortgage debt and of the value of their domestic assets. Therefore, the upper end has accumulated at the expense of the lower end, as a result of mechanisms of asymmetric force.

Another key aspect to consider is the conditions of housing built between 1950 and 1970 to accommodate the migrant population from rural environments, the rapid production of which resulted in neighbourhoods with negligible residential standards (Musterd and van Kempen 2007). Given that these settings are highly devalued in the market, these homes have been acquired by the social sectors (immigrants and low-income young people) that only pursue an affordable use value (for them) in these spaces, allowing some traditional working categories to get relatively richer and turn to new suburban developments (Nel-Lo 2004). The result is the formation of neighbourhoods that are home to people who all enjoy weak social positions but who come from very diverse age and ethnic backgrounds (from native old working class and unemployed young people to greatly impoverished immigrants who belong to different ethnic groups), making the establishment of community networks of mutual support difficult. Insofar as these spaces are seldom the receivers of regenerating public investment, these spaces are at the spearhead of precarious conditions of urban life.

Coming from the opposite end of the social spectrum, over the same period, the categories that have been most responsible for the processes of social and spatial change in the Madrid Metropolitan Area (managers and professionals) have consolidated their hold on the most valued spaces (areas where higher socio-economic groups are overrepresented could be found in the north-west of the Metropolitan Area as well as in the districts of Chamartín and Salamanca in Madrid). In the process, the social structuring of the Madrid area has secured the categories that direct these processes with the ability to accumulate (material and symbolic) benefits. As a result, a significant socio-spatial polarisation is revealed in the Madrid Metropolitan Area that gradually exposes the regressive nature of the socio-economic change. In sum, the true meaning of present differences in the residential patterns of different social and labour categories is being revealed, as social inequality begins to manifest itself in spatial terms (Table 9.2).

The diagonal line that runs from the south-west to the north-east of the territory of the Metropolitan Area of Madrid represents a border, that is less and less

Table 9.2 Segregation index (IS) by activity group (ISCO categories and unemployed) and year (%)

ISCO major group	2001		2011	
	D	%	D	%
Unemployed	0.08	0.12	0.14	0.23
Managers (1)	0.26	0.07	0.35	0.05
Professionals (2)	0.33	0.15	0.31	0.16
Technicians and associate professionals (3)	0.10	0.13	0.11	0.11
Clerical support workers (4)	0.08	0.11	0.10	0.12
Service and sales workers (5)	0.11	0.13	0.13	0.14
Craft workers, plan and machine operators (7 and 8)	0.27	0.17	0.23	0.10
Elementary occupations (9)	0.15	0.10	0.21	0.08

Source: Produced by the authors based on the Census of Population and Housing, 2001 and 2011 (INE) Development.

(a)

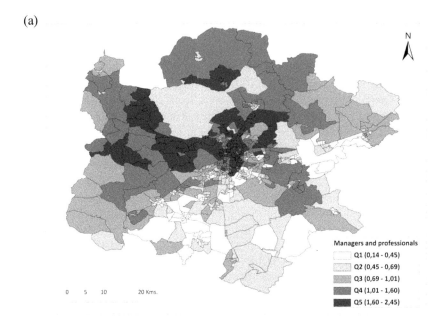

Managers and professionals

Q1 (0,14 - 0,45)
Q2 (0,45 - 0,69)
Q3 (0,69 - 1,01)
Q4 (1,01 - 1,60)
Q5 (1,60 - 2,45)

0   5   10   20 Kms.

(b)

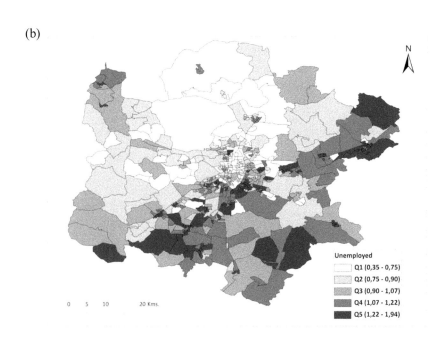

Unemployed

Q1 (0,35 - 0,75)
Q2 (0,75 - 0,90)
Q3 (0,90 - 1,07)
Q4 (1,07 - 1,22)
Q5 (1,22 - 1,94)

0   5   10   20 Kms.

(c)

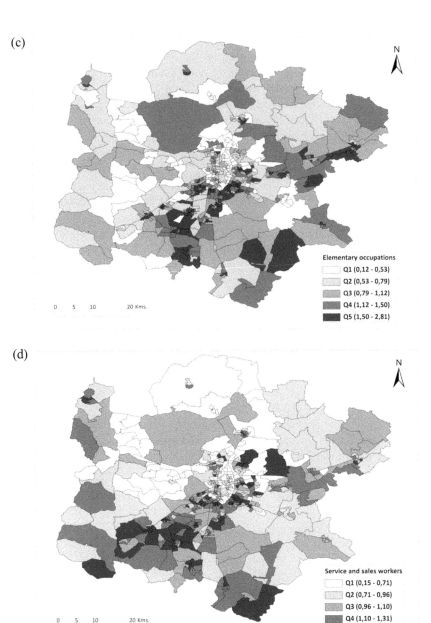

Elementary occupations
- ☐ Q1 (0,12 - 0,53)
- ☐ Q2 (0,53 - 0,79)
- ☐ Q3 (0,79 - 1,12)
- ☐ Q4 (1,12 - 1,50)
- ■ Q5 (1,50 - 2,81)

0   5   10   20 Kms.

N

(d)

N

Service and sales workers
- ☐ Q1 (0,15 - 0,71)
- ☐ Q2 (0,71 - 0,96)
- ☐ Q3 (0,96 - 1,10)
- ☐ Q4 (1,10 - 1,31)
- ■ Q5 (1,31 - 1,84)

0   5   10   20 Kms.

Figure 9.2a–d Distribution of the location quotients of (a) managers and professionals, (b) unemployed, (c) elementary occupations and (d) service and sales workers in the territory of the Madrid Metropolitan Area, according to quintiles, 2011.

Source: Produced by the authors based on the Population and Housing Census 2011 (INE) Development.

porous, between positions that are both socially and spatially different: on the one hand the job insecurity and unemployment of residents in the south and east Madrid Metropolitan Area; in contrast, on the other hand, are the job security and social distinction of the citizens of the north and west (see Figure 9.2). Three labour categories, professionals, the traditional working categories and the unemployed, stand out within the general processes of residential segregation in the Madrid Metropolitan Area between 2001 and 2011. This is due to both the change in their weight in the social structure and the residential behaviour of the groups.

Professionals' expansion: from social mix to colonisation

In the entire working population, professionals are the category whose weight has increased the most. However, as discussed earlier, this category is far from homogeneous. The more established professionals are characterised by their greater age and job security, while new fractions of younger professionals are emerging whose careers are shot through with uncertainty and insecurity. This division between professionals explains the slight decline in segregation reflected in Table 9.3. The reason is that the large increase in the number and proportion of professionals has motivated the exploration of new urban areas not previously dominated by this category. In this regard, it is crucial that the expansion has been produced by the younger, more precarious fractions.

In particular, the central districts of the city of Madrid stand out as the places with the most pronounced growth in the location quotient of professionals between 2001 and 2011. For example, the case of the neighbourhoods of the historic centre of Madrid is relevant in that they have been subject to significant urban regeneration interventions. These operations have contributed to increasing the attractiveness of these areas for the younger fractions of professionals, whose dispositions are favourable towards urban values (Ley 1996; Savage *et al.* 2005). As shown, the

Table 9.3 Dissimilarity index matrix between activity groups (ISCO categories and unemployed) with 2001 results being above the main diagonal and 2011 results below

ISCO major group	(U)	(1)	(2)	(3)	(4)	(5)	(7&8)	(9)
Unemployed (U)		0.30	0.33	0.15	0.10	0.07	0.19	0.09
Managers (1)	0.42		0.12	0.19	0.26	0.33	0.44	0.36
Professionals (2)	0.35	0.19		0.23	0.30	0.37	0.49	0.39
Technicians and associate professionals (3)	0.19	0.31	0.23		0.08	0.17	0.30	0.22
Clerical support workers (4)	0.16	0.34	0.25	0.10		0.11	0.24	0.16
Service and sales workers (5)	0.10	0.43	0.34	0.18	0.15		0.16	0.09
Craft workers, plan and machine operators (7 and 8)	0.15	0.51	0.45	0.27	0.24	0.17		0.17
Elementary occupations (9)	0.13	0.49	0.42	0.27	0.24	0.15	0.17	

Source: Produced by the authors based on the Census of Population and Housing, 2001 and 2011 (INE) Development.

location quotient of professionals and managers has grown in central neighbourhoods that were not dominated by those categories in 2001. At the same time the location quotient of the blue-collar workers, those employed in elementary occupations and the unemployed, has fallen more than average. This applies to Centro and Tetuán, certain emblematic central districts of Madrid.

In any case, as previously mentioned, the decrease in the index of segregation of professionals is skewed by the increase in their population size. The fact that size usually influences the value of this index must be borne in mind, in that the larger the size the smaller the index, except when this increase does not alter the distribution between territorial units of each of the contrasted groups, in which case it remains unchanged (Simpson 2004). However, this premise is rarely fulfilled, since the increase in population implies non-random residential settlement in new urban areas, altering the above distributions (Echazarra 2010). For professionals, the expansion caused by the saturation of traditional settlement areas entails, in the first stages, the development of areas with greater social mix.

In this regard, there are more dimensions, or features, that make the characterisation of residential segregation possible (Masseandy and Denton 1988). Among these, residential isolation stands out. Johnston *et al.* (2005) demonstrate that the maintenance of the segregation index, in a context where the proportional size of the minority group increases even when its distribution doesn't change between territorial units, leads to an increase in the isolation index. The reason is that the relative size of the minority group in the areas of residence increases, and with it, the probability of meeting between members of the same group. This is the case of professionals, whose expansion into new areas of the city by its most precarious fractions does not negate the maintenance of their isolation. Inversely, the increased appreciation of their traditional places of residence explains the maintenance of its high isolation, since the consolidation of these territories with the arrival of new professionals compensates for their dispersal into new spaces. In

Table 9.4 Isolation index (I), modified isolation index (MI), by occupation group (ISCO88 in 2001, ISCO-08 in 2011) and year, in relation to the rest of the working population

ISCO major group	I			MI		
	2001	2011	Δ (01–11)	2001	2011	Δ (01–11)
Managers (1)	0.11	0.11	−0.01	0.029	0.043	0.01
Professionals (2)	0.24	0.27	0.03	0.069	0.061	−0.01
Technicians and associate professionals (3)	0.15	0.15	−0.01	0.006	0.006	0.00
Clerical support workers (4)	0.13	0.17	0.04	0.004	0.007	0.00
Service and sales workers (5)	0.16	0.20	0.04	0.010	0.019	0.01
Craft workers, plan and machine operators (7 and 8)	0.26	0.17	−0.08	0.057	0.040	−0.02
Elementary occupations (9)	0.13	0.13	0.00	0.014	0.028	0.01

Source: Produced by authors based on the Census of Population and Housing, 2001 and 2011 (INE) Development.

urban areas where they are the majority, this concentration is reproduced by the continuous arrival of established professionals. Thus, professionals are the most isolated category of all occupations: that is to say, the probability that a professional has of meeting another in their place of residence is the highest, even when this rate is controlled against the population size of each category (see Table 9.4).

In conclusion, between 2001 and 2011 the professionals' dominion over areas where they previously resided has been maintained and hence its settlement patterns consist of a process closer to colonisation than to socio-spatial integration. Finally, it is important to note that, even more segregated than the professionals, the directors are the most segregated category in the Madrid Metropolitan Area. This position contrasts with that of 2001, when the directors shared the category with the heterogeneous group of entrepreneurs, within which very different social positions coexisted depending on the number of employees and type of business in question. Thus, in 2011 a clear pattern has emerged by which the segregation of the most privileged socio-economic positions in exclusive, and excluding, spaces is revealed to be very extreme. This phenomenon is related to the construction of low-density developments, of a closed nature with a high surveillance of users, in the north and north-west of the Metropolitan Area. These developments are shared with the more established professionals. Furthermore, they are located in residential contexts without environmental problems for those who have the material means to choose their place of residence, and are endowed with such attributes valued by these types of household, such as comfort or tranquillity (Pujadas *et al.* 2007).

In summary, both categories (professionals and managers) are the most segregated according to all of the indices considered. After them, the blue-collar workers are the next most segregated group, although the process of their uneven residential distribution is fundamentally altered because of the destruction of jobs and the corresponding reduction in their numbers.

The unemployed and traditional manual categories: restructuring social peripheries.

In contrast to the professional categories, the traditional working categories have registered the most important proportional reduction of the employed population. However, there are important differences between their qualified categories and those working in elementary occupations. Moreover, the increase in the inequality of the residential distribution of workers in elementary occupations is outstanding. This process, in a context where the impact of elementary occupations on the total employed population is stable, suggests their concentration in specific parts of the Metropolitan Area. These parts are mainly characterised by lower house prices, like some southern districts of Madrid (Carabanchel, Puente de Vallecas, Usera, Villaverde) or the Henares strip (Alcalá, Coslada, San Fernando), in the east of the Metropolitan Area (see Figure 9.2). Yet the skilled workers, whose residential distribution is linked to both their economic resources and the location of their employment centres, reflect a significant decline in segregation that is directly related to the transfer of many of its members to the category of unemployed, as detailed in the following section.

Finally, the other categories (service, administrative and technical workers) are the least segregated. However, those employed in the most precarious services are slightly more isolated than technical and administrative workers. The explanation for this difference lies in their internal composition, largely linked to the most precarious foreign population. As a result of this composition, those working in personal services and business are found in the central city of Madrid due to the availability of rental housing there, pre-existing networks of mutual support and transport facilities. In any case, within the city this category focuses on very specific districts in the south, such as Carabanchel, Puente de Vallecas and Usera. These neighbourhoods are favourable for their residential settlement, in contrast not only to the more expensive areas of the city but also to other areas that are impenetrable for them for various reasons, including the low residential mobility of working and aged native populations (for example some parts of Usera or San Blas) (see Figure 9.2). Indeed, these are prime neighbourhoods in terms of their degree of centrality that nevertheless have a reduced average house price because of stigmatisation, meaning that users of these neighbourhoods are trapped because leaving them would mean losing residential quality.

The unemployed are the category with the most pronounced growth within the active working population. However, the segregation index does not drop but increases very significantly, along with their isolation index. This joint variation is possible because this group is composed of a high proportion of manual workers who are concentrated in a number of specific territorial units. This socio-spatial process contrasts with that of the professionals, due to differences in the internal composition of the two categories: while professionals have become differentiated throughout the last decade with one fraction as established and the other as devalued; up until 2011 those unemployed as a result of the economic crisis remained very similar in their social composition.

The percentage and absolute increase in unemployed has been inflated exclusively by the job losses of the traditional working categories. Therefore, the unemployed categories have risen in urban areas where the workers who have lost their jobs reside. This concentration of its population growth does not translate, as expected, into a decline in inequality in its geographical distribution. By contrast, the index of segregation grows with the index of isolation. In this sense, the change in the correlation between the location quotient of the blue-collar workers and the unemployed over the decade is very telling: although in both of the compared censuses the coefficient is high and positive, the intensity of the Pearson correlation coefficient is much higher in 2011 (0.75) than in 2001 (0.51). Consequently, in 2011 the coexistence of the unemployed and the blue-collar workers is very likely, since these very categories are more related than in 2001 as a result of the economic crisis. Moreover, Table 9.3 shows that the dissimilarity index between both categories has dropped from 0.19 in 2001 to 0.15 in 2011.

Thus, the intimate relationship between unemployment and the most precarious employment categories is not only social but also spatial. The reason is the previous concentration of blue-collar workers in the Madrid Metropolitan Area: in 2001, the skilled blue-collar workers category was the most isolated and also the category with the second-most segregated territorial distribution. All in all, the loss of jobs in the Madrid Metropolitan Area is the result of the economic crisis linked to the bursting of the housing bubble. Consequently, most of the destruction is concentrated among the working categories which were spatially located in the south and east of Madrid in 2001. Thus, in 2011, unemployment is concentrated in these neighbourhoods, strengthening the spatial distance between the most devalued, on the one hand, and professionals and managers, on the other. In confirmation, the relationship between the first and the second is intensely negative and significant: the overrepresentation of professionals and managers (combined) precludes large presences of both blue-collar workers (Pearson correlation coefficient equal to minus 0.86) and the unemployed (minus 0.79); and vice versa.

In short, the characterisation of spaces as more or less segregated in metropolitan Madrid in 2001 has been disrupted by emerging processes of segregation over the following decade. On the one hand, trends are detected towards both the reproduction and extension of Metropolitan Areas where the most privileged socio-economic positions are concentrated; while at the same time the exclusive character of historic districts (Centro, Tetuán) and bourgeois extensions (Chamberí, Salamanca, Retro) is consolidated. On the other hand, the dispersal of the most devalued categories (often composed of foreign immigrants) in some of the peripheral segments, inhabited by the most precarious native categories, is critical, both in sociological and in residential terms. These territories have been, right from the start of the economic crisis, the places with the highest number of evicted households and therefore the scene of numerous protest actions by social movements. In a context of a severe economic crisis like the present, such spaces are places where the social malaise produced by the current regime of capitalist accumulation is deployed with greater intensity. 'the result is a clear concentration of the most vulnerable populations in the worst equipped areas; and this is exactly what makes them the territory par excellence of the new social peripheries' (López and Rodríguez 2010: 448).

Conclusions

The problematic at stake is that the different stages of a process of change can go through stages of transition in which the differences in the positioning of socio-economic categories are reduced to and, consequently, understood as stable situations. This appears clearly in some gentrification processes whereby an intermediate stage can be perceived to reveal an increase in the social mix. Conversely, these very processes often end up with the dominant settlement of a socio-economic category that previously had little presence in that urban space.

In the case of Spain and, to a greater extent, in the city of Madrid, economic changes over the past twenty years have led to the growth of medium-high categories formed by salaried and self-employed professionals. This growth has led to territorial expansion in different directions: in central areas of the city that they had scarcely occupied previously; in outlying areas, which before their settlement had been characterised by having a majority composition of blue-collar workers; and finally, in new urban areas of the extreme periphery, usually in low-density settlements.

This spatial distribution change contributes to the reduction in their previous segregation indices and can lead to misunderstandings, if the transformation of the greater part of this relation to other socio-economic categories is not taken into account. To explain this we must take into account households' tendencies in southern Europe towards locating themselves in the vicinity of their families. This is due to the necessity of solidarity for the provision of certain services that a weak welfare state does not provide (Musterd 2005). This fact, where there is a process of strong intergenerational social mobility, will promote the development of differentiated residential areas, with a majority settlement of these new middle classes next to places traditionally occupied by the blue-collar workers that are their families. That being said, both in the Spanish and the Italian cases professionals and managers remain as the most segregated categories (Petsimeris 1998; Rubiales *et al.* 2012).

Moreover, the reduction of traditional blue-collar categories linked to industrial production has brought two types of processes with it. On the one hand, the neighbourhoods traditionally stigmatised for being markedly working class have become closed off with respect to their socio-economic composition: their characteristics are maintained and the great expansion of immigrant workers has come up against a barrier there. In these working-class neighbourhoods, with improved living conditions, there is a certain freezing of conditions, meaning that even the children of workers who reside there cannot find housing, due to the low residential mobility that characterises these neighbourhoods in southern European countries (Musterd and van Kempen 2007).

On the other hand, the growth of blue-collar service workers, especially personal services, is reaffirmed. This category is made up of a high proportion of immigrant workers and their composition and residential settlement are more heterogeneous than other manual workers. This is because the majority of them rent housing, while there is a predominance towards property ownership in the other occupational groups, formed mostly of Spanish households. The result is a greater dispersion around the city and therefore a lower segregation index than the rest of the manual workers, although their working and residential conditions are not better. Therefore, in southern European cities like Madrid, the low levels of residential segregation of lower classes conceal the real problem of residential marginalisation (Arbaci 2008; Bayona 2007; Domínguez *et al.* 2012; Maloutas 2007; Martori and Hoberg 2004).

It is also important to consider what has happened to the unemployed. The tremendous increase of unemployment in Spanish cities, as an effect of the crisis, has brought with it a concentration in certain areas that expresses a very high correlation with the neighbourhoods where there is a high presence of blue-collar workers. In this sense, unemployment affects blue-collar workers more intensely and has had very segregated effects, at least in the initial stages of the economic crisis. Finally, the low production of social housing in Spain has meant that the vast majority of the population, including the households with the least resources, have turned to the free market. In short, not only is the housing policy weak, but it has also been focused on middle categories, keeping more precarious categories out. As a consequence, lower socio-economic categories are more spread out than expected. This has meant that at the smallest scale there is some heterogeneity in the composition of neighbours or even within buildings, just like other southern European cities like Athens (Maloutas and Karadimitriou 2001). This may slightly mitigate the perception and awareness of the intensive residential segregation according to socio-labour categories in the city.

In conclusion, the interactions between contemporary socio-economic changing trends and specific southern European urban societies have led to complex processes where social inequality is hidden behind paradoxical free-market dynamics. However, the increasing privileges of upper categories, together with austerity policies implemented in the southern European urban societies, are putting an end to this exception. In short, there is a re-composition of socio-economic categories that, as a whole, implies an increase in segregation, although some categories could exhibit temporal tendencies that are contrary to these. Therefore, spatial distance among socio-labour categories is progressively matching the extent of their social inequality.

Appendices

Appendix 1: Towns and districts composing the Metropolitan Area and the city of Madrid.

Figure 9.3 Towns composing the metropolitan area of Madrid.

Source: Authors' creation based on the Atlas of Urban Areas elaborated by the Ministerio de Fomento (2004).

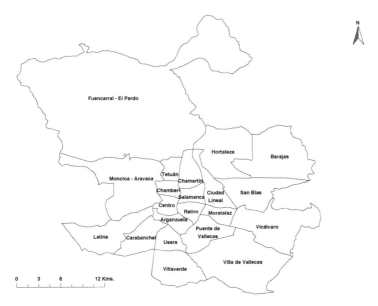

Figure 9.4 Districts composing the city of Madrid.

Source: Authors' creation based on the Comunidad de Madrid.

Appendix 2: Differences in segregation according to the population size of the considered territorial unit.

Table 9.5 Value of the indices of dissimilarity (D), isolation (I) and modified isolation (MI) in relation to the active labour force, according to the territorial unit used (census tract or aggregation), 2001

ISCO major group	D		I		MI	
	C.Tracts	Aggreg.	C.Tracts	Aggreg.	C.Tracts	Aggreg.
Unemployed	0.11	0.08	0.13	0.13	0.01	0.00
Managers (1)	0.29	0.26	0.11	0.10	0.04	0.03
Professionals (2)	0.35	0.33	0.22	0.21	0.08	0.06
Technicians and associate professionals (3)	0.13	0.10	0.14	0.14	0.01	0.01
Clerical support workers (4)	0.10	0.08	0.11	0.11	0.01	0.00
Service and sales workers (5)	0.13	0.11	0.14	0.14	0.01	0.01
Craft workers, plan and machine operators (7 and 8)	0.28	0.27	0.23	0.22	0.05	0.05
Elementary occupations (9)	0.19	0.15	0.12	0.11	0.02	0.01

Source: Authors' creation based on the Population and Housing Census, 2001 (INE).

References

Arbaci, S 2008, '(Re) viewing ethnic residential segregation in southern European cities: Housing and urban regimes as mechanisms of marginalisation' *Housing Studies* 23(4), 589–613.

Bayona, J 2007 'La segregación residencial de la población extranjera en Barcelona: ¿una segregación fragmentada?', [Residential segregation of the foreign population in Barcelona: a fragmented segregation?], *Scripta Nova. Revista Electrónica de Geografía y Ciencias Sociales*, 11(235). Available online: http://www.ub.edu/geocrit/sn/sn-235. htm. Accessed 14 May 2015

Colectivo Ioé 2009, '1994–2007: se cierra un ciclo de expansión especulativa y regresión social' [1994–2007: speculative expansion and social regression cycle closes] *Papeles de Relaciones Ecosociales y cambio social* 105, 141–152.

Domínguez, M, Leal, J and Martínez, E 2012, 'The limits of segregation as an expression of socioeconomic inequality: The Madrid case' in *Residential segregation around the world: Why context matters*, eds T Maloutas and K Fujita, Ashgate, London, pp. 217–236.

Echazarra, A 2010, 'Segregación residencial de los extranjeros en el área metropolitana de Madrid: Un análisis cuantitativo' [Residential segregation of foreigners in the metropolitan area of Madrid: A quantitative analysis], *Revista Internacional de Sociología* 68(1), 165–197.

Esping-Andersen, G 1997, *The three worlds of welfare capitalism*, Polity Press, Cambridge.

Fernández, C and Roch, F 2012, 'La quiebra de la ciudad global y sus efectos en la morfología urbana. Madrid, bajo la lógica inmobiliaria de la acumulación–desposesión' [The collapse of the global city and its impact on the urban morphology. Madrid, under the real-estate logic of accumulation–dispossession] *Urban NS03*, 45–63.

Johnston, R, Poulsen, M and Forrest, J 2005, 'On the measurement and meaning of residential segregation: A response to Simpson' *Urban Studies* 42(7), 1221–1227.

Leal, J 2004, 'Segregation and social change in Madrid metropolitan region' *The Greek Review of Social Research* 113, 81–104.

Ley, D 1996, *The new middle categories and the remaking of the central city*, Oxford University Press, Oxford.

López, I and Rodríguez, E 2010, *Fin de ciclo: financiarización, territorio y sociedad de propietarios en la onda larga del capitalismo hispano (1959–2010)* [End of cycle: financialisation, territory and ownership society in the long wave of Hispanic capitalism (1959–2010)], Traficantes de Sueños, Madrid.

Malheiros, J 2002, 'Ethni-cities: Residential patterns in the northern European and Mediterranean metropolises – implications for policy design' *International Journal of Population Geography* 8, 107–134.

Maloutas, T 2007, 'Segregation, social polarization and immigration in Athens during the 1990s: Theoretical expectations and contextual difference' *International Journal of Urban and Regional Research* 31(4), 733–758.

Maloutas, T and Karadimitriou, N 2001, 'Vertical social differentiation in Athens: Alternative or complement to urban segregation?' *International Journal of Urban and Regional Research* 25(4), 699–716.

Martínez, A y Leal, J 2008, 'La segregación residencial, un indicador espacial confuso en la representación de la problemática residencial de los inmigrantes económicos: El caso de la Comunidad de Madrid' [Residential segregation, a confusing spatial indicator representing the residential problems of economic migrants: The case of the Community of Madrid] *Architecture, City and Environment* 3, 53–64.

Martori, J C and Hoberg, K 2004, 'Indicadores cuantitativos de segregación residencial: El caso de la población inmigrante en Barcelona' [Quantitative indicators of residential segregation: The case of the immigrant population in Barcelona] *Geo Crítica / Scripta Nova. Revista Electrónica de Geografía y Ciencias Sociales* 8(169). Available online: http://www.ub.es/geocrit/sn/sn–169.htm. Accessed 23 April 2015.

Massey, D and Denton, N 1988, 'Suburbanization and segregation in U.S. metropolitan areas' *American Journal of Sociology* 94, 592–626.

Ministerio de Fomento 2004, *Atlas Estadístico de las Áreas Urbanas* [Statistical atlas of urban areas]. Madrid, Ministerio de Fomento.

Moreno, L 2001, 'La vía media española del modelo de bienestar mediterráneo' [The Spanish middle way of the Mediterranean welfare model] *Papers: revista de sociología* 63(64), 67–82.

Musterd, S 2005, 'Social and ethnic segregation in Europe: levels, causes, and effects. *Journal of Urban Affairs* 27(3), 331–348.

Musterd, S and van Kempen, R 2007, 'Trapped or on the springboard? Housing careers in large housing estates in European cities' *Journal of Urban Affairs* 29(3), 311–329.

Naredo, J M 2010 'El modelo inmobiliario español y sus consecuencias' [The Spanish real-estate model and its consequences] in eds Belil, M, Borja, J and Corti, M, *Ciudades, una ecuación imposible*. Madrid, Icaria, 65–98.

Nel-lo, O 2004, '¿Cambio de siglo, cambio de ciclo? Las grandes ciudades españolas en el umbral del siglo XXI' [Change of century, cycle change? The large Spanish cities in the twenty-first century threshold] *Ciudad y Territorio. Estudios Territoriales* 36(141/142), 523–542.

Petsimeris, P 1998, 'Urban decline and the new social and ethnic divisions in the core cities of the Italian industrial triangle' *Urban Studies* 35(3), 449–465.

Pujadas, I, Prats, P and Coll, M 2007, 'Elección residencial y nuevas formas urbanas' [Residential choice and new urban forms] in *Los procesos urbanos postfordistas, Actas del VIII Coloquio de Geografía Urbana*, eds A Bauza *et al.*, Universitat de les Illes Balears y AGE, Palma, 215–234.

Roch, F 2008, 'La deriva patológica del espacio social en el modelo inmobiliario neoliberal madrileño' [The pathological drift of the social space in the neoliberal real-estate model of Madrid] in *Diez años de cambios en el Mundo, en la Geografía y en las Ciencias Sociales, 1999–2008*. Actas del X Coloquio Internacional de Geocrítica, Universidad de Barcelona. Available online: http://www.ub.es/geocrit/–xcol/179.htm. Accessed 23 April 2015.

Rubiales, M, Bayona, J and Pujadas, I 2012, 'Patrones espaciales de la segregación residencial en la Región Metropolitana de Barcelona: Pautas de segregación de los grupos altos' [Spatial patterns of residential segregation in the metropolitan area of Barcelona: Voluntary segregation of the upper groups] *Scripta Nova. Revista Electrónica de Geografía y Ciencias Sociales.* 16(423). Available online: http://www.ub.es/geocrit/sn/sn–423.htm. Accessed 23 April 2015.

Savage, M, Bagnall, G and Longhurst, BJ 2005, *Globalization and belonging*, Sage, London.

Simpson, L 2004, 'Statistics of racial segregation: measures, evidence and policy' *Urban Studies* 41, 661–681.

Tammaru, T, Musterd, S, van Ham, M and Marcińczak, S, 2016, 'A multi-factor approach to understanding socio-economic segregation in European capital cities' in *Socio-economic segregation in European capital cities: East meets West*, eds T Tammaru, S Marcińczak, M van Ham and S Musterd, Routledge, London.

10 Urban restructuring and changing patterns of socio-economic segregation in Budapest

Zoltán Kovács and Balázs Szabó

Abstract

Since the systemic changes of 1989–90 the socio-spatial structure of Budapest has gone through gradual changes. These changes could be linked with a solid occupational stratification caused by deindustrialisation and the growing role of services. In this process the share of more educated and higher-income groups increased, whereas the weight of lower-status groups shrank. Economic restructuring generated not only occupational reconfiguration but also increasing wage differences. According to our findings growing income differences have only slowly translated to new patterns of social segregation in Budapest. One important aspect of the new segregation pattern is that lower socio-economic groups became more segregated while upper occupational categories, especially professionals, became more evenly dispersed in the city.

Introduction

The issue of social differentiation, residential mobility and socio-economic segregation in post-socialist cities is clearly among the most intensively studied fields in contemporary urban geography (Brade *et al.* 2009; Gentile *et al.* 2012; Kovács 2012; Leetmaa *et al.* 2015; Marcińczak *et al.* 2012; Marcińczak *et al.* 2013; Marcińczak *et al.* 2014; Marcińczak *et al.* 2016; Ruoppila and Kährik 2003). As Marcińczak *et al.* (2016) recently pointed out, Budapest is the most segregated post-socialist capital city north of the Balkans with regard to the spatial separation of different occupational groups. In this phenomenon historical factors (both socialist and pre-socialist), as well as recent socio-economic restructuring, equally play a role.

Socio-economic segregation has a complex history in Budapest. Before World War II the dimensions of segregation and the driving forces behind them were very similar to other Central European cities (for example Vienna, Berlin). Segregation was basically the outcome of class differences and a market-based housing system where the private rental sector prevailed (Szelényi 1983). However, central planning along with state ownership of land introduced by the state-socialist system in the late 1940s distorted the historically evolved pattern of segregation and resulted in new ('socialist') types of socio-spatial inequalities. Better-off people and members of the *nomenklatura* segregated themselves in the villa quarters of the Buda hills, where previously aristocrats and members of the bourgeoisie concentrated. From the late 1960s the construction of large housing estates with good quality housing provided the younger and better-off part of the society with a new niche for segregation. At the same time a large part of the densely built inner-city neighbourhoods became dilapidated, losing their earlier prestige due to neglect and a lack of maintenance, and some of them becoming enclaves of poverty by the early 1990s (Ladányi 1997; Kovács 1998).

After 1990, in line with the political and economic transformation of the country, the socio-economic pattern of Budapest went through gradual changes again. The principles of state-socialist redistribution of income and goods (for example housing) were replaced by the rules of the market. Due to the re-establishment of a market economy and the privatisation of housing, the liberalisation of the property market and the growing presence of global capital, large-scale socio-economic differentiation took place in the society. This resulted in new types of socio-spatial inequalities. New forms of segregation, including severely deprived neighbourhoods on the one hand, and the mushrooming of gated communities and new upmarket housing compounds on the other, became symbols of the neoliberal 'post-socialist' political and economic conditions, and underlining the weakness of the welfare state (Kovács 1998).

Analysing the socio-spatial differentiation and residential segregation in post-socialist cities, some authors came to the conclusion that growing income inequalities inevitably bring about more distinctive intra-urban spatial divisions and socio-economic disparities (Brade *et al.* 2009; Kovács 1998, 2012; Smith and Timár 2010; Weclawowicz 1998). Others, supported by census data, argue that the level of residential segregation in post-socialist cities did not increase after the systemic changes; on the contrary, despite all the consequences of capitalist transition it actually lowered (Sýkora 2009; Marcińczak and Sagan 2011; Marcińczak *et al.* 2013; Marcińczak *et al.* 2014). Their explanation about the 'paradox of post-socialist segregation' seems to be fairly plausible: 'post-socialist segregation processes operate in their initial phases against the socialist heritage, bringing some higher social status neighbourhoods (housing estates) as well as lower social status zones (suburbanisation of rural hinterland) closer to the city average'(Sýkora 2009: 394). This controversial debate is our point of departure here.

The aim of this chapter is to investigate the long-term pattern of socio-economic segregation in Budapest. First, we provide an account of socio-spatial differentiation in Budapest from a historical perspective. It will be then followed by the introduction of the local context (Maloutas and Fujita 2012), portraying the main factors that have influenced socio-economic stratification and spatial separation in the city after 1990. In the empirical part we analyse occupational data of the 1990, 2001 and 2011 censuses in order to shed light on the new, post-socialist patterns of segregation in the city. Since the chapter is aimed at providing a deeper insight into the current processes of socio-spatial differentiation and segregation, we would like to focus on the following research questions:

1   What are the impacts of post-socialist transformation on the socio-spatial structure of the city?
2   How has the socio-economic segregation of population in the city changed since 1990?
3   Have growing income differences been translated to higher levels of social segregation in Budapest since 1990; in other words, has the city become more segregated since the fall of communism?

Inequalities and socio-economic segregation in Budapest before 1990

Existing literature on the residential segregation of Budapest focuses basically on two aspects: socio-economic and ethnic segregation. From the first strand of investigations the pioneering study of Probáld (1974) should be mentioned, where the level of residential segregation in the city was first statistically examined. Deep in the middle of the communist era the author stated: 'Though some of the causes, which have given rise to the residential segregation, ceased to exist in the socialist societies, it is obvious, that the Hungarian and other East Central European cities are not at all free from that phenomenon' (Probáld 1974: 105). In order to justify his proposition, the author measured the segregation of white-collar workers. The

Figure 10.1 The ratio of white-collar workers at sub-district level in Budapest, 1960.

Source: Probáld (1974).

Note: 1 = 0–19.9%, 2 = 20.0–29.9%, 3 = 30.0–39.9%, 4 = 40.0–49.9%, 5 = 50.0–59.9%

territorial framework of his study was the 22 districts of Budapest for the 1949, 1960 and 1970 censuses, and the 59 subdistricts for 1960 and 1970. As a result of his study, Probáld came to the conclusion that the level of residential segregation in Budapest somewhat decreased between 1949 and 1960 but slightly increased again between 1960 and 1970. White-collar workers tended to congregate in the hilly Buda side of the city, west of the Danube but relatively close to the city centre (Figure 10.1).

The first more comprehensive analysis of socio-spatial differentiation was carried out in the mid-1980s by Csanádi and Ladányi (1985), who investigated the historical development of the urban structure and trends in residential segregation covering the period of 1930–80. To reveal long-term tendencies of residential segregation, the authors calculated segregation indices for different groups of the economically active owners and tenants of inhabited apartments for the pre-World War II period (i.e. using the 1930 and 1941 censuses). The territorial framework of analysis was provided by the 14 districts of the then Budapest. For the state-socialist period, dissimilarity and segregational indexes for groups of economically active earners were computed using data from the 1960, 1970 and 1980 censuses. District-based calculations were also extended with census tract analysis. As the authors commented, they had faced enormous difficulties because the methods of data collection and the social categories employed in statistics changed frequently, and spatial units with different levels of aggregation were used over the studied period of time (Csanádi and Ladányi 1985).

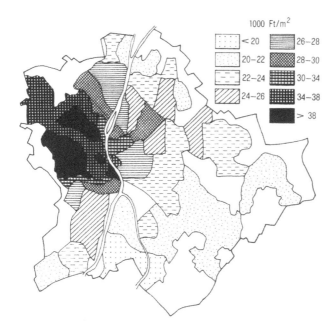

Figure 10.2 Apartment prices in Budapest, 1988.

Source: Kovács (1990).

Kovács (1990) used dwelling prices as a proxy for socio-spatial inequalities within Budapest shortly before the collapse of communism. On the basis of private advertisements, a map of the spatial distribution of dwelling prices was produced that reflected more or less accurately the then residential differentiation within the city. As the author found, the physical geographic features of the city were strikingly reflected by price patterns. On the one hand, the most expensive and highest-status areas of the city could be delimited in the second and twelfth districts of the Buda side, in the traditional upper-class areas of the city, where a high proportion of local residents belonged to the *nomenklatura*. On the other hand, the cheapest price zones could be found in the industrial outskirts (for example Csepel) and monotonous pre-fab housing estates, where most of the lower-class resided (Figure 10.2).

The second group of papers dealing with ethnic segregation in Budapest is much narrower. This is not least because of the ethnic homogeneity of the city compared to other (for example post-Soviet) cities in the region (Leetma *et al.* 2015). Also, these papers focused unequivocally on the segregational patterns of the Roma (gypsy) people, the largest minority group in the city. In 1971 István Kemény registered almost one-third of the Roma of Budapest living in 'traditional gypsy colonies' which were usually located in the peripheries and were inhabited nearly exclusively by Roma (Kemény 1975). Kemény's work turned the attention of the public to the topic. His work was followed by a more systematic analysis by Ladányi who collected data about Roma children attending the first four grades of the elementary schools and special schools for mentally handicapped in Budapest in the summer of 1987 (Ladányi 1993). Altogether data from 3,889 children were collected, and segregation indices of Roma pupils and those of the population under 14 were calculated and compared for the 490 urban units of Budapest. The author found exceptionally high segregation indices for this low-status ethnic group.

The importance of these early studies is not at all negligible both from methodological and scientific points of view. They were the first academic publications that drew the attention of researchers to the concept of segregation in Hungary and provided a broad picture about social differences in Budapest before and during state-socialism.

Pre-socialist legacies of segregation

The ecological structure of Budapest coincides very much with the physical geographic features of the city. The traditional high-status areas of the city are located close to the city centre on either side of the Danube, on the hilly Buda side in the west, and in the centre of Pest in the east (Figures 10.3 and 10.4). Prior to 1945 the pattern of social segregation was very similar to other Central European cities: moving from the city centre towards the urban periphery the social status of residents traditionally declined (Szelényi 1983). Although the enlargement of the territory of Budapest through the annexation of the suburbs in 1950 and mass housing construction of the 1960s and 1970s somewhat altered this general picture, the traditional centre–periphery dichotomy remained strong until today.

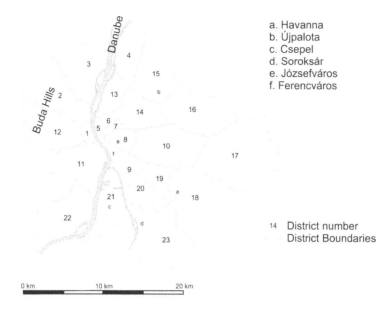

a. Havanna
b. Újpalota
c. Csepel
d. Soroksár
e. Józsefváros
f. Ferencváros

14   District number
     District Boundaries

Figure 10.3 Local districts in Budapest.

Source: Designed by the authors.

inner city
villa quarter
industrial zone
housing estates
family houses
other

Figure 10.4 Morphological zones in Budapest.

Source: Designed by the authors.

Before World War I, due to strict planning control the housing stock of the inner city was generally of high standard with a socially rather heterogeneous milieu. The typical form of housing was the 3–4 storey tenement building with an inner-courtyard containing dwellings of very varying size. High-status families normally occupied the street-facing larger apartments, whereas low-status families rented the smaller, back apartments facing the inner-courtyards. This architectural pattern allowed a relatively strong social mix on the level of buildings, streets and neighbourhoods. At the fringe of the compact city, overcrowded shanty towns were expanding with low-quality tenement blocks that were in sharp contrast with the inner part of the city both in terms of the quality of the housing stock and the social status of the residents (Enyedi and Szirmai 1992).

After World War I, the development of Budapest slowed. Housing rents were frozen during the war in order to protect the families of soldiers from eviction and these remained intact as late as 1926. New housing projects were rare and served predominantly the needs of better-off strata. In the interwar period social inequalities increased mainly due to the world economic crisis of 1929–1933 which brought about a massive decline in factory employment and the impoverishment of wide sections of the society. According to Ladányi (1989), the segregational index of manual and non-manual workers at the level of districts slightly increased in Budapest from 21.2 to 23.3 between 1930 and 1939. Changes in the housing market exacerbated the growing social inequalities. New housing projects in the 1930s, like Újlipótváros or Lágymányos, also contributed to growing segregational indices as high-status social groups started to move to these new fashionable neighbourhoods. Through these new housing projects, smaller or larger high-status 'islands' developed in different parts of the city in addition to the Buda hills and the city centre.

Socio-economic segregation during state-socialism

Due to the significant social changes that took place in the country, the level of segregation decreased in Budapest from the middle of the 1940s till the 1960s. According to Probáld (1974) the segregation index of the white-collar and blue-collar workers calculated for the 22 districts of Budapest decreased from 16.8 to 16.2 between 1949 and 1960. This trend was also confirmed by Csanádi and Ladányi (1985). The reasons were manifold. First of all, the wealthiest sections of the former landlord and capitalist strata (7.9 per cent of the population according to the 1941 census) left the country by the end of the 1940s. Several thousand families, mainly members of the former upper class were deported from Budapest in 1951–52, partly for political reasons. At the end of the 1940s a new communist constitution was implemented in Hungary, land and property were nationalised and nearly all commercial functions were prohibited or severely controlled (Enyedi and Szirmai 1992). Capitalist extremes of social inequality were attacked and to a large extent eliminated via different channels (for example narrowing wage differences, social housing provision, etc.). According to the statistics, before World War II wage differences between white- and blue-collar employees in Budapest stood at

2.5–3.0 to 1.0 in favour of white-collar professionals. Due to the new wage system this difference was virtually eliminated by the early 1960s (Kovács 1998). The capitalist system of housing production and distribution, blamed for the previous inequalities and segregation, was abolished and replaced by a communist-type housing system. Housing was proclaimed to be a universal right which meant that every family was entitled to its own dwelling at low cost. Thanks to a radical nationalisation policy the private rental sector, dominant in the inter-war period, was abolished and replaced by a growing public rental sector. By 1953 the share of public rental sector reached 77 per cent in Budapest. After nationalisation, rents were kept artificially low for political reasons. Mass state housing programmes from the beginning of the 1960s were also meant to decrease the level of segregation. The intense development of large-scale housing estates on peripheral urban locations, with standardised dwellings, was to assist in making the society more homogeneous (Compton 1979).

However, despite all the state interventions the decrease of residential segregation gradually turned into an increase from the early1960s. The segregation index of the white-collar and blue-collar workers increased from 16.2 to 17.2 between 1960 and 1970 (Probáld 1974; Ladányi 1989). The main reason was that after the 1956 revolution Hungary moved away from the Stalinist model of redistributive economy and egalitarianism, and started to liberalise its economy. The series of liberalisation policies culminated in the so-called 'New Economic Mechanism' of 1968, which recognised the multi-sector nature of the economy, where state, co-operative and private small-scale economic activities enjoyed equal rights. At the individual level it meant more opportunities for capital accumulation, and more freedom in cultural, private life, etc. This was basically the so-called 'goulash communism' – a mixture of economic policies and personal opportunities. This had also its impacts on the functioning of the housing market and the residential mobility of different strata. As Probáld (1974) noted, one of the possible causes of increasing segregation in this period was that most of the new condominium projects requiring higher personal financial contributions were realised on the Buda side. White-collar earners, 'with average salaries by about 20 per cent higher than the manual workers' could more easily afford the costs of such more expensive dwellings (Probáld 1974: 110).

The increase in residential segregation stopped after 1970 and gradually turned into a decrease. The index of segregation for the white-collar and blue-collar workers decreased from 17.2 to 15.9 between 1970 and 1980 (Ladányi 1989). The reasons were twofold. First of all, after 1970 Budapest entered the epoch of mass housing construction in the form of large pre-fabricated housing estates where different social groups could be systematically mixed via housing allocation policies. Second, this was the period when the post-World War II generation of women entered the labour market in great numbers, mostly in service jobs. Thus, the proportion of households where there were both manual and white-collar workers significantly increased.

After 1980 social inequalities and residential segregation started to grow again, but this time to a considerable extent (Ladányi 1997: 84). Housing policy played an important role in intensifying residential segregation. New measures introduced in 1983 were to abolish the previous heavily subsidised nature of the housing system. Mass housing production financed by the state was replaced by the mushrooming of private forms of housing provision. Consequently, the share of public housing shrank to 51 per cent of the housing market by the end of the 1980s. The expansion of private-sector housing generated growing inequalities in the housing market. The increasing share of co-operative and private housing construction allowed those with substantial resources, mostly earned in the second economy, both a way out of the state rental tenure and a method of capital accumulation (Szelényi 1987).

In addition, the green light for the second economy further enhanced social inequalities. The term 'second economy' was used in opposition to the first (i.e. state sector) economy during communism (Hann 1990). It included full-time entrepreneurs and artisans in the private sector, and many kinds of 'informal' work performed by persons who also had 'formal' employment in some branch of the state sector. Estimates of the extent of the second economy varied considerably. According to Lackó, in 1980 already 13 per cent of the Hungarian GDP was generated by the informal sector, which rose to 16 per cent by 1989 (Lackó 1995). As Szelényi (1987) noted, by the mid-1980s 70 per cent of the households in Hungary earned incomes from the second economy, and about a fifth of the income earners received a third or half of their incomes from such activities. With these figures – together with Poland – Hungary was clearly the front-runner among the communist countries. Economic difficulties in the second half of the 1980s further intensified segregational trends, which led to a relatively high level of segregation in Budapest, especially when compared with other cities of more orthodox East Central European communist countries (Kovács 1990).

Factors influencing socio-economic segregation in Budapest after 1990

It is generally acknowledged that the post-socialist transition consists of multiple transformation processes that include both the political application of normative concepts as well as spontaneously proceeding societal changes with the re-established market environment (Sýkora and Bouzarovski 2012). With regard to the socio-economic stratification of the population and the formation of new patterns of residential segregation, we consider the transformation of the economy and the housing market the two most relevant factors. Due to historical legacies the transformation policies, as well as the dynamics of economic and social changes in post-socialist cities, differed significantly (Stryjakiewicz *et al.* 2013).

Hungary belonged to the 'fast track' group of transforming countries, with a highly liberalised economy and housing system well before 1990 (Marcińczak *et al.* 2016). As part of the transformation, large state companies were privatised and/or disintegrated after 1990. The economic breakdown was accompanied by rapid deindustrialisation (for example the share of industrial workers fell from 36 to 14 per cent of the active population between 1990 and 2011) and skyrocketing unemployment rates (Dövényi 1994). The replacement of the state-socialist economy by a post-Fordist flexible economy intensified income differences, with a growing distinction between the lowest and the highest segments of the society. Income inequalities are well reflected by the Gini coefficient. According to Éltető and Havasi (2009), the value of the Gini coefficient of income was 0.362 for Budapest in 2004 (mean values for villages (0.312), whereas other cities (0.348) were significantly lower). Even though the Gini value for Budapest was below the international alert line (0.40), it increased significantly, from 0.252 to 0.362 between 1987 and 2004, which clearly reflects the process of growing income differences in the city. Typically, the income difference between managers and elementary occupations stood at 5.0 to 1.0 in Budapest in 2010.

As Ladányi and Szelényi (1998) pointed out, the major beneficiary of the transformation was the previous communist technocracy and the managerial elite. While the majority of the former communist *nomenklatura* lost their positions, a new economically privileged stratum emerged, composed of the technocratic-managerial elite, their opinion-forming intellectual allies and private entrepreneurs. Later this group was extended by the new wave of young, highly educated technocrats working in the wide array of financial and business services.

On the other hand, the widening group of urban poor was formed mainly by low-skilled industrial and service workers who became unemployed in large numbers after 1990 and other socially disadvantaged groups, for example Roma, the elderly and the disabled. They could be considered commonly as losers in the post-socialist transformation (Smith and Timár 2010).

In addition to economic transformation and labour-market segmentation, the liberalisation of the housing market also actively contributed to the development of new patterns of residential segregation. In the transformation of the housing market, privatisation of public dwellings played a very important role. Within a relatively short period of time the overwhelming majority of the public housing stock became privatised. The share of the public sector in the housing market of Budapest fell drastically from 51 to 14 per cent within six years after 1990, and it shrank further to 5 per cent by 2011. Privatisation of public housing in Budapest meant a pure 'give away' type of privatisation to sitting tenants, at a very low price. Most state dwellings were sold for between 15 and 40 per cent of their estimated market value depending on the physical conditions of the dwelling. A further 40 per cent discount was offered for cash transactions, which meant that the great majority of public dwellings were sold for 9 per cent of the market value.

Given these circumstances, it is easy to understand that the best quality (i.e. most valuable) segment of the public housing stock was first sold in the course of privatisation. The logic of privatisation favoured the better-off families, since tenants (now 'buyers') of the best quality dwellings with a desirable location gained the biggest amount of value gap. Tenants of spacious villa dwellings on the Buda side (mostly members of the communist *nomenklatura*) could realise an extra profit through privatisation compared to tenants of standardised blocks in pre-fab housing estates.

These changes in the housing market had far-reaching ecological implications. First of all, households had more opportunity to actualise relocation desires as they became owners; second, new conditions allowed a greater plurality of values and promotion of self-interest. Factors in housing preferences such as security or accessibility of green spaces and the residential mobility of households gained great importance, while rent regulations completely lost their relevance as the overwhelming majority of flats were converted to owner-occupation. The outcome was a rapid segmentation of the housing market. The public rental sector became residualised as the direct consequence of the give-away privatisation: only the 'leftovers of privatisation' remained in the public rental sector (Tosics 2012). While public housing became residualised and served as a shelter for the urban poor, new upmarket residential areas for the better off were developed. Perhaps the most eye-catching among them are the new gated residential compounds, signifying the new and more intense physical separation of the 'new rich' (Kovács and Hegedűs 2014). The establishment of new enclaves of affluent population, as well as segregated districts of socially excluded went hand in hand (Sýkora 2009).

Methodological framework

To detect changes in the pattern of social segregation in Budapest, we used occupational data from the three post-socialist censuses of 1990, 2001 and 2011. Occupation is generally considered to be the best single variable indicator of socio-economic status and of a person's position in the social hierarchy (Morgan 1980). A census occupational breakdown of the economically active population relies on the International Standard Classification of Occupations (ISCO). ISCO data seem to be appropriate for examining the labour market segmentation, occupational stratification, income inequalities and social disparities within cities (Marcińczak *et al.* 2012).

In order to simplify the analysis we disregarded two occupation groups out of the ten ISCO categories: the group of agricultural workers and armed forces. As the first group has no relevance in metropolises and the weight of the second group drastically decreased in Budapest between 1990 and 2011, the omission of these two occupation categories does not seem to distort our results.

For the sake of fine geographical resolution, Budapest was divided into discrete territorial units (ca. 1,600) on the basis of functional and morphological attributes. The spatial units chosen for segregation analysis are compact and small, and similar in population size (ca. 1,000 inhabitants) in the three censuses. Occupational data were available for these small-scale units for each census, making fine spatial resolution possible.

To detect the evolving patterns of segregation, two basic measures were used (see also the introduction of this book for more detail: Tammaru *et al.* 2016). The traditional indices of segregation (IS) and dissimilarity (ID) summarise well the overall intensity of residential separation, illuminating the degree to which socio-economic distance follows spatial distance. The index of dissimilarity (ID) is calculated as:

$$D = \frac{1}{2} \sum_{i=1}^{n} \left(x_i - y_i \right)$$

where x_i and y_i are the proportions of two different social groups residing in areal unit i, and n is the number of areal units in the city. The absolute proportional differences of all areal units are summed and half of that is the ID value. The index has a theoretical range from 0 to 1, where 0 reflects no segregation and 1 indicates a perfect segregation between the two groups. Essentially it measures the percentage of an occupational group (x) which would have to move to make its distribution identical with another occupational group (y).

If the value of ID is computed between one occupation group and all others combined, it gives the second measure, the index of segregation (IS). The index can be defined as:

$$S = \frac{D_s}{1 - \frac{\sum x_{ai}}{\sum x_{ni}}}$$

Main research findings

Occupational stratification and professionalisation after 1990

Census data reflects robust shifts among the main occupational categories in Budapest for the periods 1990 and 2011. In 1990 the largest occupational category was the 'industrial workers', with nearly one-fifth of the economically active population. By 2011 their proportion dropped significantly as an outcome of deindustrialisation, whereas already one quarter of employees belonged to the category of 'professionals'. In general, the weight of highly skilled occupations (i.e. those that require university education) substantially increased in the labour market, whereas the proportion of less-educated categories (i.e. industrial workers and machine operators) shrank considerably (Table 10.1).

Table 10.1 Labour market segmentation by ISCO occupation groups in Budapest, 1990–2011 (without the occupation groups of agricultural workers and armed forces)

	1990		2001		2011	
1 Managers	93310	10.6%	80181	11.0%	66387	8.6%
2 Professionals	135261	15.4%	152526	21.0%	196183	25.4%
3 Technicians	145707	16.6%	143311	19.7%	168254	21.8%
4 Clerks	110019	12.5%	70506	9.7%	79473	10.3%
5 Sellers	60433	6.9%	105932	14.6%	99433	12.9%
6 Industrial workers	175401	19.9%	99261	13.7%	65161	8.5%
7 Machine operators	84971	9.7%	37259	5.1%	38293	5.0%
8 Unskilled workers	73980	8.4%	37766	5.2%	57418	7.5%
Total	879082	100.0%	726742	100.0%	770602	100.0%

Source: National Census 1990, 2001, 2011, Hungarian Central Statistical Office.

If we aggregate the top three and bottom three occupational categories, the effects of deindustrialisation as well as the internationalisation of the economy and the professionalisation of the labour force becomes even clearer. The share of the top three occupational groups (managers, professionals and technicians) increased from 42 to 56 per cent between 1990 and 2011, whereas the share of the last three categories decreased substantially (from 38 per cent to 21 per cent). The reasons behind this massive occupational stratification were economic restructuring, on the one hand, and the robust improvement of the educational level of the population triggered by the democratisation of higher education, on the other. Typically, while in 1990 only 16 per cent of the population in the 15-years-plus age group had a university or high-school diploma in Budapest, by 2011 the percentage was already 31. With this process Budapest followed the global trends of professionalisation of the labour force which had already begun during communism but remained limited until the advent of the democratic system and a service-sector-based market economy.

Changing levels of socio-economic segregation

This part of the study is divided into two stages: first, we analyse the long-term changes of IS, then the separation among different occupational groups through their computed ID values is highlighted. Overall, the results of the IS reveal gradual shifts in the socio-economic segregation of the city, both in upwards and downwards directions (Figure 10.5). However, abrupt changes are not to be seen in any of the occupational groups and more smooth trends than fluctuations are prevalent.

Among the higher-status occupational groups, the level of segregation of managers seems to be very stable over time, whereas the segregation of professionals

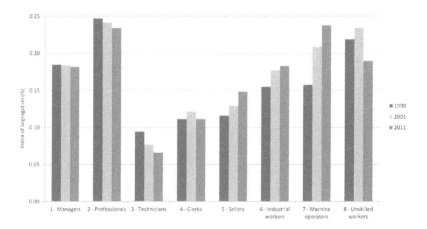

Figure 10.5 Indices of segregation (IS) of occupational groups in Budapest, 1990–2011.

Source: National Census 1990, 2001, 2011, Hungarian Central Statistical Office.

has slightly decreased since 1990. This trend is not at all unique, or post-socialist specific; lower segregation indices for higher occupational categories were found for example in Athens (Maloutas 2016), or Madrid (Leal and Sorando 2016). Perhaps the most plausible reason for the lowering segregation level of professionals is the substantial growth of their number and proportion, and their more even distribution in urban areas due to better relocation opportunities triggered by new housing projects.

The decrease of segregation indices was more pronounced for the group of technicians. Technicians and clerks, the two occupation groups in the middle, are the two least segregated groups in Budapest, which coincides with experiences of other European cities (Kährik *et al.* 2016; Leal and Sorando 2016; Maloutas 2016; Marcińczak *et al.* 2016). What is more remarkable, however, is the growing segregation of lower-status groups, for example sellers, industrial workers and machine operators. With an 0.238 IS, the group of machine operators was the most segregated in Budapest in 2011, followed by the professionals (0.234). The IS for unskilled workers first grew then decreased in the two decades after 1990.

The increase in segregation of lower-status groups is a completely new, 'post-socialist' phenomenon in Budapest. As Csanádi and Ladányi (1985), and later Ladányi (1997, 2002) pointed out, the segregational curve of Budapest between 1930 and 1980 was characteristically different from what was described in the literature for North American cities (Duncan and Duncan 1955), as the indices of segregation of the lower-status groups were significantly lower than those of the higher-status ones. Thus, the segregational curve did not follow the regular U-shape described by American sociologists, but it had a 'U' with a truncated right stem. Ladányi (1997: 85) also added that 'the irregular shape of the segregation curve seems to be fairly universal in the case of European cities'.[1] This irregular U-shape seems to be over now, as lower-status groups became at least as strongly segregated in Budapest as the higher-status groups by the early 2010s.

Our data also confirm that the lowering segregation thesis (Marcińczak *et al.* 2013; Marcińczak and Sagan 2011; Sýkora 2009) does not fit for the case of post-socialist Budapest. Even though professionals and technicians have become less segregated since 1990, for lower-status groups higher IS figures became clearly evident. However, the reasons behind this are quite different. On the one hand, professionals and technicians became by far the two most populous groups by 2011, comprising nearly half of the active earners. Their more even spatial distribution can therefore also be linked with a spatially more balanced distribution of diplomas and higher technical qualifications. This is less related to residential mobility and more to the improving opportunities for young people to obtain a diploma. On the other hand, the growing spatial separation of employees with low socio-economic status is much more related to residential entrapment. Neighbourhoods inhabited predominantly by lower-status people have become less diversified since 1990, due to the outmigration of better skilled higher-status people who have left lower-class neighbourhoods, partly as an outcome of suburbanisation (Kovács and Tosics 2014). In the next section we make an attempt to figure out the geographical concentrations of such neighbourhoods.

The index of dissimilarity (ID) can shed light on the correlation between socio-economic status and spatial distance. IDs were calculated between each pair of occupational categories for each census (Table 10.2). Stronger spatial separation (ID values over 0.25) is indicated by grey shading in the table. A closer look at Table 10.2 reveals generally growing ID figures over time, especially between the upper two (managers, professionals) and the bottom three (in 2011 already

Table 10.2 Index of dissimilarity by ISCO occupation groups in Budapest, 1990–2011 (1 – Managers, 2 – Professionals, 3 – Technicians, 4 – Clerks, 5 – Sellers, 6 – Industrial workers, 7 – Machine operators, 8 – Unskilled workers)

1990

	1	2	3	4	5	6	7	8
1	0.00	0.12	0.14	0.22	0.22	**0.27**	**0.29**	**0.34**
2		0.00	0.18	**0.28**	0.25	**0.32**	**0.34**	**0.36**
3			0.00	0.13	0.14	0.18	0.20	0.26
4				0.00	0.12	0.12	0.13	0.21
5					0.00	0.16	0.17	0.20
7						0.00	0.10	0.17
8							0.00	0.17
9								0.00

2001

	1	2	3	4	5	6	7	8
1	0.00	0.15	0.18	0.24	0.25	**0.32**	**0.35**	**0.30**
2		0.00	0.20	**0.27**	**0.28**	**0.37**	**0.37**	**0.32**
3			0.00	0.12	0.14	0.22	0.25	0.21
4				0.00	0.11	0.16	0.21	0.18
5					0.00	0.17	0.19	0.16
7						0.00	0.21	0.20
8							0.00	0.18
9								0.00

2011

	1	2	3	4	5	6	7	8
1	0.00	0.16	0.18	0.24	**0.27**	**0.41**	**0.28**	**0.34**
2		0.00	0.18	0.25	**0.29**	**0.44**	**0.33**	**0.39**
3			0.00	0.11	0.15	**0.39**	0.18	0.24
4				0.00	0.11	**0.39**	0.13	0.18
5					0.00	**0.39**	0.13	0.17
7						0.00	**0.37**	**0.39**
8							0.00	0.13
9								0.00

Source: National Census 1990, 2001, 2011, Hungarian Central Statistical Office.

bottom four) categories. Extreme ID values, ranging from the mid-20s to the mid-30s in 1990, grew to the mid-30s to mid-40s range by 2011. The highest values of dissimilarity are computed for industrial workers in 2011; these are by far the most segregated among the investigated occupational groups. It seems that the relationship between socio-economic distance and spatial distance in Budapest is sensitive to the level of socio-economic inequalities. Finally, the dissimilarity index clearly indicates that the middle occupational categories (groups 3, 4, 5) are not only the most evenly distributed, but they also tend to share residential tracts with lower rather than with higher socio-economic groups.

The changing geographical pattern of socio-economic segregation

Using the typology of Marcińczak *et al.* (2016), we delimited higher- and lower-socio-economic status neighbourhoods within Budapest. The common weight of the top two occupational categories (managers and professionals) was 34 per cent in 2001, whereas the proportion of the bottom three occupation groups (industrial workers, machine operators and unskilled workers) made up 21 per cent. Therefore, to alleviate possible distortions caused by the different size of the upper and lower strata, we applied a 50 per cent threshold for the delimitation of higher-status neighbourhoods, and 30 per cent for lower-status neighbourhoods. In order to get a comprehensive picture about the long-term trends of spatial segregation, we display the 1990, 2001 and 2011 occupational data with the same thresholds (Figure 10.6).

Budapest has a very distinct pattern of socio-economic segregation when compared with other CEE capital cities (Marcińczak *et al.* 2016). This distinctiveness

(a)

High status (MAN+PROF > 50%)
Low status (IND+MOP+UNSK > 30%)

(b)

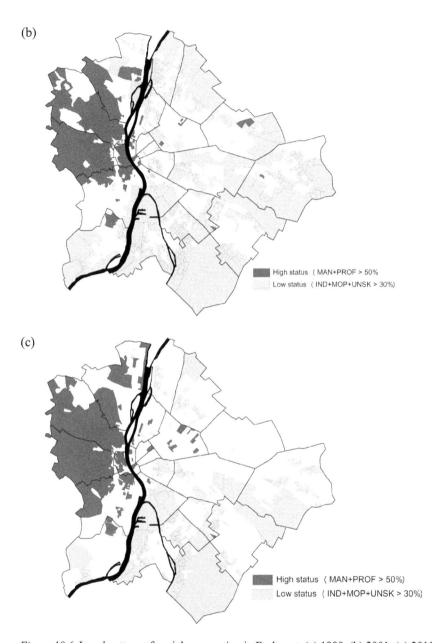

(c)

Figure 10.6 Local pattern of social segregation in Budapest, (a) 1990, (b) 2001, (c) 2011.

Source: National Census 1990, 2001, 2011, Hungarian Central Statistical Office.

is rooted partly in the physical geography of the city, which makes the physical separation of the better off easier, and historical legacies such as planning regulations and zoning back in the nineteenth century. In Figure 10.6 a clustering of higher socio-economic status neighbourhoods is clearly visible. They form a compact zone on the Buda hills, west of the Danube, which is the traditional high-status villa area of the city, developed earlier in the pre-World War II period but further expanded during state socialism. After 1990 this compact zone of affluence was massively extended both north and south along the river. In the 2000s, even some smaller pockets of high-status neighbourhoods appeared east of the Danube as well, in the inner city, as a result of both market-led renewal and public-led regeneration programmes (Egedy 2010; Földi 2006; Kovács 2009), and also outside the compact city due to the mushrooming of new upmarket residential compounds (for example rowhouses, gated and guarded neighbourhoods) (Hegedűs 2009; Kovács and Hegedűs 2014). Due to urban regeneration programmes, the majority of the original residents of these neighbourhoods have been replaced by younger, better-off families in a gentrification process (Kovács *et al.* 2013).

Low-status neighbourhoods are clearly shrinking on the map and in 2011 they are mostly located in the outer part of Pest. The shrinkage of low-status neighbourhoods goes hand in hand with the occupational stratification of society. While in 1990 these neighbourhoods dominated the scene, by 2011 their contiguous zone became heavily fragmented. Low-status neighbourhoods consist of three different types: decaying inner-city quarters, high-rise housing estates and low-rise mixed residential-industrial neighbourhoods.

In the inner city, next to upgrading areas decaying neighbourhoods are located where the outcome of post-socialist transformation was not revitalisation but further physical and social decline (Kovács 1998; Ladányi 2002). They are typically old, working-class quarters with multi-storey tenement buildings in the eastern periphery of the inner city, for example in Józsefváros and Ferencváros. The reasons for the physical decay of these neighbourhoods are complex. One of them is the lack of maintenance and infrastructural development during communism. The deficit of investment was not alleviated by the transformation and the subsequent transfer of ownership (i.e. privatisation), either. The deterioration process of the building stock has been accompanied by the erosion of the local society. Residential mobility played an important role in this process, as younger and more-educated people gradually left these neighbourhoods. Later they were followed by the blue-collar workers of an active age, and finally the mobile part of the elderly, for example those with second homes or with children/relatives in the countryside. As a result of this filtering-down process, the population of these old residential quarters has become more and more marginalised (Ladányi 2002).

High-rise housing estates of the state-socialist period, especially the more peripheral ones (for example Havanna, Újpalota, Centre of Csepel) are also strongholds of lower-class families. These pre-fab housing estates built in the 1970s and 1980s rapidly lost their popularity after 1990 due to their architectural monotony, lack of green spaces, decreasing security and relatively high costs of amenities (especially heating) (Egedy 2012). Even though radical downgrading or ghettoisation similar to that in Western cities is not seen (Kovács and Herfert 2012), the filtering-down process on some of these housing estates is clearly visible due to the selective out-migration of the younger and better-off strata. As demand for such housing estates becomes less and less (especially towards those with peripheral locations), they seem to be increasingly residualised – a phenomenon also described recently for other cities in Europe with a more solid welfare system (Andersson and Magnusson Turner 2014).

The third group of low-status neighbourhoods is comprised of low-rise residential areas, traditional villages (for example Soroksár) that were independent before 1950, and some of the mixed residential-industrial neighbourhoods of the periphery. They can be characterised by low-densities, poor accessibility and insufficient environment. Their inhabitants are mostly less skilled elderly people. Since land is cheap in these neighbourhoods, some of the new affluent gated compounds were located there, making the spatial separation of upper and lower social groups at the local (i.e. micro) level very contrasting (Kovács and Hegedűs 2014).

Discussion and conclusions

Post-socialist transformation in Budapest had multifaceted impacts on the socio-spatial structure of the city. On the one hand, the elegant Buda hills enclave became extended on its fringes due to new housing developments. On the other hand, new upmarket compounds appeared in former low-rise neighbourhoods with a village character and a lower-class profile, resulting in socio-economic upgrading. Some of the inner-city neighbourhoods have also gone through spectacular rejuvenation and upgrading due to large-scale regeneration programmes (Egedy 2010; Földi 2006; Kovács *et al.* 2013; Tosics 2006). However, there were also neighbourhoods where a lack of investment over the last two decades resulted in physical and social decline. Due to the complex intermix of investment-disinvestment and the concomitant residential mobility, the socio-spatial structure of the city changes. These changes are, however, rather smooth; no abrupt shifts have been experienced.

Our research findings showed that substantial occupational stratification took place in Budapest after 1990 in line with the advancement of a new, capitalist economy. In this process the share of more educated and higher-income groups increased, whereas the size of lower-status groups decreased. Economic restructuring in the form of deindustrialisation and the growing role of services triggered professionalisation of the labour force. With this process Budapest clearly followed global trends, together with other post-socialist capital cities (Marcińczak *et al.* 2016).

However, as our findings showed, growing income differences are only slowly translated to new patterns of social segregation in Budapest. This is because despite some sporadic new developments and regeneration programmes, the building stock and the physical pattern of the city remained rather stable over time. At least large-scale interventions with the magnitude of state-socialist housing projects have not taken place over the last two decades. Small-scale investments resulted in small but important changes in the socio-economic fabric of the city. Growing income differences and social distances were also not converted to radical social separation among different socio-economic groups due to the functioning of the local housing market. The local housing market in Budapest is absolutely dominated by owner-occupied housing (Tosics 2006).

As opposed to rental markets, the level of residential mobility is generally low, and many households are trapped in their current housing and unable to change. Greater mobility was also hampered by the dramatic ageing of the society after 1990, and the 2008 global economic crisis (Egedy 2012).

Regarding the intensity of segregation, it can be pointed out that lowering levels of socio-economic segregation referring to other post-socialist cities (Marcińczak *et al.* 2013; Marcińczak and Sagan 2011; Sýkora 2009) are not to be seen in Budapest. Among higher- and middle-status groups stagnation, and in some cases a slight decrease of segregation, could be observed. This is probably linked with the fact that higher social groups were more mobile and they could mix in previously lower-status neighbourhoods due to new housing projects or regeneration activities. At the same time lower social strata remained relatively immobile and stayed in certain pockets of the city. This is confirmed by our empirical findings reflecting steadily growing segregation indices for lower-status groups.

In terms of future developments regarding segregation, no dramatic changes in Budapest can be envisaged. First of all, since the outbreak of the global economic crisis in 2008 new housing construction has decreased dramatically, further decreasing the otherwise already very low residential mobility rates (Egedy 2012). Second, the long-wave of post-1990 suburbanisation also came to an end (Kovács and Tosics 2014). After 2009 Budapest started to have a modest migration surplus; thus, the mobility of higher-status groups will take place within the city boundaries. In the future this might result in a spread of smaller but more homogenised pockets of segregated neighbourhoods and hence the fabric of residential segregation in Budapest is probably getting much finer.

Note

1 Differences between the segregational curves of North American and European cities were brough about by the ethnic dimension of segregation which had been traditionally very strong in North Amercia. In US cities, social and ethnic differences were closely related to each other in the post-World War II period, when the vast majority of lower-status groups were from the black population. As the most unprivileged ethnic group, blacks were also afflicted by ethnic discrimination; they were as highly segregated as the members of the white upper-middle class (Ladányi 1997: 85).

References

Andersson, R and Magnusson Turner, L 2014, 'Segregation, gentrification and residualisation: From public housing to market-driven housing allocation in inner city Stockholm' *International Journal of Housing Policy* 14(1), 3–29.

Brade, I, Herfert, G and Wiest, K 2009, 'Recent trends and future prospects of socio-spatial differentiation in urban regions of Central and Eastern Europe: A lull before the storm?' *Cities* 26(5), 233–244.

Compton, P 1979, 'Planning and spatial change in Budapest' in *The socialist city*, eds R A French, and F E I Hamilton, John Whiley, New York, pp. 461–491.

Csanádi, G and Ladányi, J 1985, *Budapest – a városszerkezet történetének és akülönböző társadalmi csoportok városzerkezeti elhelyezkedésének vizsgálata* [Budapest – a study of the history of urban structure and the spatial distribution of social groups], University of Economics, Budapest.

Dövényi, Z 1994, 'Transition and unemployment – the case of Hungary' *GeoJournal* 32(4), 393–398.

Duncan, O D and Duncan, B 1955, 'Residential distribution and occupational stratification' *American Journal of Sociology* 60(5), 493–503.

Egedy, T 2000, 'The situation of high-rise housing estates in Hungary', in *Hungary towards the 21st century. The human geography of transition*, ed. Z Kovács, Studies in Geography in Hungary 31, Geographical Research Institute, Hungarian Academy of Sciences, Budapest, pp. 169–185.

Egedy, T 2010, 'Current strategies and socio-economic implications of urban regeneration in Hungary' *Open House International* 35(4), 29–38.

Egedy, T 2012, 'The effects of global economic crisis in Hungary' *Hungarian Geographical Bulletin* 61(2), 155–173.

Éltető, Ö and Havasi, É 2009, 'A hazai jövedelemegyenlőség főbb jellemzői az elmúlt fél évszázad jövedelmi felvételei alapján' [Main characteristics of income inequalities in Hungary on the basis of income records in the last half a century], *Területi Statisztika* 87(1), 5–40.

Enyedi, G. and Szirmai, V 1992, *Budapest – a Central European capital*, Belhaven Press, London.

Földi, Zs 2006, *Neighbourhood dynamics in inner-Budapest – a realist approach*, Netherlands Geographical Studies 350, Faculteit Rumtelijke Wetenschappen Universiteit Utrecht, Utrecht.

Gentile, M, Tammaru, T and Van Kempen, R 2012, 'Heteropolitanization: Social and spatial change in Central and Eastern European cities' *Cities* 29(5), 291–299.

Hann, C M 1990, 'Second economy and civil society', in *Market economy and civil society in Hungary*, ed. C M Hann, Frank Cass, London, pp. 21–44.

Hegedüs, G 2009, 'A review of gated communities in some Hungarian cities' *Geographica Pannonica* 13(3), 85–96.

Kährik, A, Tammaru, T, Leetmaa, K and Mägi, K 2016, 'Socio-economic segregation in the inherited dual ethnic context in Tallinn' in *Socio-economic segregation in European capital cities: East meets West*, eds T Tammaru, S Marcińczak, M van Ham and S Musterd, Routledge, London.

Kemény, I 1975, 'A budapesti cigányokról' [About the gypsies of Budapest] *Budapest* 13(5), 240–243.

Kovács, Z 1990, 'Rich and poor in the Budapest housing market' *The Journal of Communist Studies* 6(2), 110–124.

Kovács, Z 1998, 'Ghettoization or gentrification? Post-socialist scenarios for Budapest' *Netherlands Journal of Housing and the Built Environment* 13(1), 63–81.

Kovács, Z 2009, 'Social and economic transformation of historical neighbourhoods in Budapest' *Tijdschrift voor economische en sociale geografie* 100(4), 399–416.

Kovács, Z 2012, 'Residential segregation in Budapest before and after Transition' in *Residential Segregation in Comparative Perspective*, eds T Maloutas and K Fujita, Ashgate, Farnham, pp. 197–215.

Kovács, Z and Hegedüs, G 2014, 'Gated communities as new forms of segregation in post-socialist Budapest' *Cities* 36, 200–209.

Kovács, Z and Herfert, G 2012, 'Development pathways of large housing estates in post-socialist cities: An international comparison' *Housing Studies* 27(3), 324–342.

Kovács, Z and Tosics, I 2014, 'Urban sprawl on the Danube: The impacts of suburbanization in Budapest' in *Confronting suburbanization: Urban decentralization in postsocialist Central and Eastern Europe*, eds K Stanilov and L Sýkora, Wiley-Blackwell, Oxford, pp. 33–64.

Kovács, Z, Wießner, R and Zischner, R 2013, 'Urban renewal in the inner city of Budapest: Gentrification from a post-socialist perspective' *Urban Studies* 50(1), 22–38.

Lackó, M 1995, 'The underground economy in international comparison' *Közgazdasági Szemle* 42(5), 486–510.

Ladányi, J 1989, 'Changing patterns of residential segregation in Budapest' *International Journal of Urban and Regional Research* 13(4), 555–572.

Ladányi, J 1993, 'Patterns of residential segregation and the gypsy minority in Budapest' *International Journal of Urban and Regional Research* 17(4), 30–41.

Ladányi, J 1997, 'Social and ethnic residential segregation in Budapest' in *Prozesse und Perspektiven der Stadtentwicklung in Ostmitteleuropa*, eds Z Kovács and R Wießner, Münchener Geographische Hefte 76, Passau, pp. 83–95.

Ladányi, J 2002, 'Residential segregation among social and ethnic groups in Budapest during the post-communist transition' in *Of states and cities*, eds P Marcuse and R van Kempen, Oxford University Press, Oxford, pp. 170–182.

Ladányi, J and Szelényi, I 1998, 'Class, ethnicity and urban restructuring in post-communist Hungary' in *Social change and urban restructuring in Central Europe*, ed. G Enyedi, Akadémiai Kiadó, Budapest, pp. 67–86.

Leal, J and Sorando D 2016, 'Economic crisis, social change and segregation processes in Madrid' in *Socio-economic segregation in European capital cities: East meets West*, eds T Tammaru, S Marcińczak, M van Ham and S Musterd, Routledge, London.

Leetmaa, K, Tammaru, T and Hess, D B 2015, 'Preferences towards neighbour ethnicity and affluence: Evidence from an inherited dual ethnic context in post-Soviet Tartu, Estonia' *Annals of the Association of American Geographers* 105(1), 162–182.

Maloutas, T 2016, 'Socioeconomic segregation in Athens at the beginning of the 21st century' in *Socio-economic segregation in European capital cities: East meets West*, eds T Tammaru, S Marcińczak, M van Ham and S Musterd, Routledge, London.

Maloutas, T and Fujita, K (eds) 2012, *Residential segregation aound the world: Why context matters*, Ashgate, London.

Marcińczak, S, Gentile, M, Rufat, S and Chelcea, L 2014, 'Urban geographies of hesitant transition: Tracing socio-economic segregation in post-Ceausescu Bucharest' *International Journal of Urban and Regional Research* 38(4), 1399–1417.

Marcińczak, S, Gentile, M and Stępniak, M 2013, 'Paradoxes of (post) socialist segregation: Metropolitan sociospatial divisions under socialism and after in Poland' *Urban Geography* 34(3), 327–352.

Marcińczak, S, Musterd, S and Stępniak, M 2012, 'Where the grass is greener: Social segregation in three major Polish cities at the beginning of the 21st century' *European Urban and Regional Studies* 19(4), 383–403.

Marcińczak, S and Sagan, I 2011, 'The socio-spatial restructuring of Łódź, Poland' *Urban Studies* 48(9), 1789–1809.

Marcińczak, S, Tammaru, T, Novák, J, Gentile, M, Kovács, Z, Temelová, J, Valatka, V, Kährik, A and Szabó, B 2016, 'Patterns of socioeconomic segregation in the capital cities of fast-track reforming postsocialist countries' *Annals of the Association of American Geographers* 105(1), 183–202.

Morgan, B 1980, 'Occupational segregation in metropolitan areas in the United States, 1970' *Urban Studies* 17(1), 63–69.

Probáld, F 1974, 'A study of residential segregation in Budapest' *Annales Universitatis Scientiarium Budapestinensis de Rolando Eötvös Nominatae – Sectio Geographica 9*, 103–112.

Ruoppila, S and Kährik, A 2003, 'Socio-economic residential differentiation in post-socialist Tallinn' *Journal of Housing and the Built Environment* 18(1), 49–73.

Smith, A and Timár, J 2010, 'Uneven transformations: Space, economy and society 20 years after the collapse of state socialism' *European Urban and Regional Studies* 17(2), 115–125.

Stryjakiewicz, T, Gritsai, O, Dainov, E and Egedy, T 2013, 'Addressing the legacy of post-socialist cities in East Central Europe' in *Place-making and policies for competitive cities*, eds S Musterd and Z Kovács, Wiley-Blackwell, Chichester, pp. 77–94.

Sýkora, L 2009, 'Post-socialist cities' in *International Encyclpedia of Human Geography*, eds R Kitchin and N Thrift, Elsevier, Oxford, pp. 387–395.

Sýkora, L and Bouzarovski, S 2012, 'Multiple transformations: Conceptualising the post-communist urban transition' *Urban Studies* 49(1), 43–60.

Szelényi, I 1983, *Urban inequalities under state socialism*, Oxford University Press, Oxford.

Szelényi, I 1987, 'Housing inequalities and occupational segregation in state socialist cities' *International Journal of Urban and Regional Research* 11(1), 1–8.

Tammaru, T, Kährik, A, Mägi, K Novák, J and Leetmaa, K 2016, 'The "market experiment": Increasing socio-economic segregation in the inherited bi-ethnic context of Tallinn' in *Socio-economic segregation in European capital cities: East meets West*, eds T Tammaru, S Marcińczak, M van Ham and S Musterd, Routledge, London.

Tammaru, T, Musterd, S, van Ham, M and Marcińczak, S, 2016, 'A multi-factor approach to understanding socio-economic segregation in European capital cities' in *Socio-economic segregation in European capital cities: East meets West*, eds T Tammaru, S Marcińczak, M van Ham and S Musterd, Routledge, London.

Tosics, I 2006, 'Spatial restructuring in post-socialist Budapest' in *The urban mosaic of post-socialist Europe: Space, institutions and policy*, eds S Tsenkova and Z Nedovic-Budic, Physica-Verlag, Heidelberg, pp. 131–150.

Tosics, I 2012, 'Housing and the state in the Soviet Union and Eastern Europe' in *International encyclopedia of housing and home,* eds S J Smith, M Elsinga, L F O'Mahony, O S Eng, S Wachter and C Hamnett, Elsevier, Oxford, pp. 355–362.

Weclawowicz, G 1998, 'Social polarisation in postsocialist cities: Budapest, Prague and Warsaw' in *Social change and urban restructuring in Central Europe*, ed. G Enyedi, Akadémiai Kiadó, Budapest, pp. 55–64.

11 The velvet and mild

Socio-spatial differentiation in Prague after transition

Martin Ouředníček, Lucie Pospíšilová,
Petra Špačková, Zuzana Kopecká and
Jakub Novák

Abstract

This chapter deals with socio-spatial differentiation in Prague after transition. The empirical evidence shows decreasing segregation indices for the whole of the twentieth century, so this decrease cannot be ascribed solely to the period of post-socialist development. The process of professionalisation has flattening effects within the higher-status groups and has led to a decreasing share of lower-status groups in Prague's population during the last decennia. The decrease in socio-spatial differentiation is mainly a consequence of the location of new housing and in-migration of higher-strata groups into formerly poorer neighbourhoods. Moreover, the high price of housing has restricted the in-migration of the economically weak population. Thus we cannot find larger poor areas in contemporary Prague.

Introduction

The socio-spatial structure of contemporary Prague has been influenced by the long-term development of complex political, economic and cultural processes that formed the urban patterns in Europe over several decades. However, the consequences of these macro-processes differ depending on the state and city context (Kazepov 2005). The Czech settlement system was exposed to these processes at various levels of intensity and was highly dependent on the openness of the Czech border and the extent and nature of the contacts within the global and European economic and cultural system. During the interwar period the Czechoslovak state was among the top European economies and had a tight connection with Western countries (Musil 1997, 2005), but under socialism (1948–1989) Czechoslovakia was reoriented towards the Soviet Union and other countries on the eastern side of the Iron Curtain, which served also as a solid barrier against movements of various kinds including international migration, economic and cultural exchange, and the transfer of ideas (Musil 1997; Ruoppila 2004). The period after the Velvet Revolution (November 1989) is often depicted as a return to a capitalist or neo-liberal development of the economy, where political and economic transformations gradually produced winners and losers (Kornai 2006; Kovács 1999; Węcławowicz 1998). It is logical to assume that significant changes in social and economic systems would have been mirrored in the spatial organisation of the settlement structure and urban environment throughout the past 90 years of Prague's evolution (Musil 1993, 1997). However, the core question in urban studies on this point is: to what extent are social inequalities and transformations of the welfare state translated into the spatial patterns of the internal structure of the city? Thus the main aims of this chapter are twofold:

- To discuss evidence on the differences in socio-spatial differentiation in the capital city of Prague and provide details of the specific context and conditions that have produced these outcomes during the last 90 years of urban development, with special attention to the most recent stage of the post-transition period, specifically 2001–2011.
- To apply widely adopted analytical techniques to the available data to make an international comparison of the level of segregation in selected European capital cities.

We argue that one of the main attributes of Prague's recent history is its relatively stable progress and lack of sudden changes to the trajectories of urban development. Moreover, the spatial consequences of World War II, of 40 years of socialism and also of the post-socialist transformation are relatively mild compared to those experienced by some of the other cities discussed in this book. We illustrate that none of the historical urban layers was completely destroyed or overcome by succeeding development and that the physical structure, the functions of individual quarters and to a high degree also the symbolic values and social environment show considerable inertia and persist within the contemporary residential mosaic of the city (Matějů 1980; Musil 1987; Ouředníček and Temelová 2009).

In the first part of this chapter, we provide a description and explanation of the long-term context of the pre-socialist, socialist and transformation eras. Then, we turn our attention to the main focus of this study, namely the recent evolution of socio-spatial differentiation in Prague and especially the question of segregation. Our discussion is based mainly on the results of quantitative analyses of data on socio-professional structure for the period 2001–2011. In the last part of this chapter we focus on the differential development of six types of neighbourhood in Prague and on explaining the processes that have influenced changes to these types in the context of the contemporary processes of urban development.

Historical context of socio-spatial differentiation in Prague

The socio-spatial differentiation of Prague was one of the most discussed topics in this field during the interwar period in Czechoslovakia. The books and papers published during that time are mostly studies of the demographic and socio-spatial structure of interwar Prague based on population census data (Boháč 1923; Lehovec 1944; Moscheles 1937) or provide in-depth knowledge of the city's development

(Král 1945; Ulrich 1938). Most of these authors used the theoretical concepts and methods of social ecology and anthropogeography. Indeed, Boháč (1923) evaluated ethnic structures for census tracks and spatial development of demographic processes in five concentric zones two years before the now-famous concentric model of Chicago was presented by Burgess (1925). The ecological tradition in urban research strengthened after World War II, when the Western-inspired quantitative analysis approach was widely applied in Prague for the indices of residential segregation (Musil 1960, 1968), the methods of factorial ecology (Matějů 1980; Matějů et al. 1979), and the typology of urban areas (Linhart et al. 1977). After the Velvet Revolution, the processes of socio-spatial differentiation or segregation were discussed by just a few authors (Ouředníček and Temelová 2009; Sýkora 1999; 2009), which we draw on in our discussion below.

Prague has undergone several significant changes in its history. During the thirteenth (Ottokar II) and fourteenth (Charles IV) centuries and the turn of the sixteenth and seventeenth (Rudolph II) centuries, it belonged to the group of principal cities of Europe that were home to a concentration of social and cultural elites of Europe-wide importance. In contrast to those periods of rapid growth, during the industrialisation era Prague remained a rather provincial city while other large European cities were reinforcing their positions within the European settlement system (Musil 1997). The largest industrial cities and capitals of the colonial empires became the target of extensive domestic and international migration and grew into European metropolises, but Prague's catchment area covered only the central part of Bohemia, and the population of other parts of Bohemia and the whole of Moravia migrated mostly to Vienna (Horská 2002). Consequently, the social and economic elites tended to concentrate in Vienna, the capital of Cisleithania. Later, the residential differentiation of Prague – divided into an historical core and newly built quarters for clerks and workers in growing nineteenth-century suburbs – was enriched during the interwar period by 30 new villa estates and several temporary dwelling (slums) dating mainly from the economic crisis of the 1930s (Votrubec 1959). Even though the Prague of the 1930s has been described as differentiated in terms of housing type and also social status (Matějů 1977; Musil 1987), the level of segregation was rather low compared to other European cities (Musil 2005).

The relative homogeneity of Prague's population was further strengthened by the events of World War II, when the traditional diverse ethnic structure of the city was diminished (Musil 2005; compare Węcławowicz 1998). The expulsion of Germans (out of a total population of around 25,000 in Prague, approximately 80 per cent were expelled) and the genocide of the Jewish population brought about a flattening of the socio-economic stratification within the city as both the Germans and the Jews were often more wealthy than the Czechs. At first glance, the indices of dissimilarity for four social groups based on a comparison of data from the 1930 and 1950 population censuses (see Table 11.1) reveals that there was a relatively large decrease in socio-spatial differentiation. However, this decrease can be partly explained by the use of different statistical units for the measurement of dissimilarity; 46 cadastral units in 1930 and 16 city districts in 1950. The different

Table 11.1 Indices of dissimilarity in Greater Prague, 1930–1950

Social group	Social group					
	Clerks		Foremen, non-manual employees		Workers	
	1930	1950	1930	1950	1930	1950
Self-employed, tenants, employers	12.29	8.13	18.50	9.58	25.11	13.28
Clerks	–	–	19.36	10.88	27.45	14.63
Foremen, non-manual employees	–	–	–	–	13.03	5.51

Note: Indices were constructed for 46 cadastral units (1930) and 16 city districts (1950).

Source: Musil (1968: 254).

population size of the city districts seems to have resulted in lower numbers than the use of cadastral units would probably uncover (this effect is well documented for the contemporary situation; see later in Figure 11.5).

The industrial growth of Prague defined the functional structure of the city and divided the quarters of Prague according to social status and symbolic values, and these survived without fundamental change until the policy of Complex Housing Construction was applied in Czechoslovakia during the era of state socialism. Musil notes that the social structure of Prague at that time 'was already formed in the period prior to World War II and that very little of this general pattern has changed during the past 30 years' (1968: 251). However, the urban growth of Prague was considerably slower than that of the largest European cities. Moreover, the housing shortage of the 1930s and 1940s blocked the population growth of the city, whose working power was secured by the intensive commuting of industrial workers. Together with post-war ethnic and to some extent also socio-economic homogenisation, these developments led to lower socio-spatial differences than in the other cities presented in this book. This homogenisation was consequently strengthened by 40 years of socialism.

The development of Prague's ecological structure and socio-spatial differentiation under socialism has been the main topic of many publications since 1989 (Musil 1993; Ouředníček and Temelová 2009; Sýkora 1999) but is surprisingly also referred to in the sociological literature before the Velvet Revolution (Matějů *et al.* 1979; Matějů 1980; Musil 1968, 1987). Socialist developments were considerably influenced by the policies of the state, such as those on urban growth control in the form of the Central Settlement System and Complex Housing Construction policies. These policies were applied during the whole period of socialism and had different impacts on distinctive size categories of settlements that were set up by the communist government. Generally, in light of the differing impacts of these policies, we can distinguish three periods of development of the Czechoslovakian settlement system and Prague's socio-spatial structure under socialism.

First, the immediate post-war period of development, from circa 1945 to 1959, can be described as one that strangled urban growth. Investment in medium-sized cities and industrialised regions as well as the redistribution of the workforce through fixed job assignments (*umístěnky*) to depopulated areas of the Sudetenland were distinctive at the level of the organisation of the settlement system. The administrative area of Greater Prague established during the 1920s remained the same, but the size of the population was even lower than before World War II, and housing construction rather stagnated (see Figure 11.1) and residential mobility decreased (Matějů *et al.* 1979). Working power was provided by intensive commuting from relatively large catchment areas. Musil (1987) described this period as a phase of redistribution, which involved the implementation of specific housing and social policies. It was typical to divide large apartments and villas, formerly owned by the upper and middle classes, into two or three dwelling units and allocate them to households in need (Musil 2001). This mixing of households was accompanied by the removal of temporary dwellings (Votrubec 1959), which together smoothed the differences between the most obvious poles of the housing stock.

In the second period of development, during the 1960s and early to mid-1970s, the Complex Housing Construction and the Central Settlement System policies were introduced and affected mostly the outer parts of Czechoslovakian cities. While the Complex Housing Construction led to investment in specific zones on the outskirts of built-up areas, the latter had an impact on the hinterlands of Czech cities. The Central Settlements System originated in the so-called concept of urbanisation and used tools of regional planning derived from the theory of

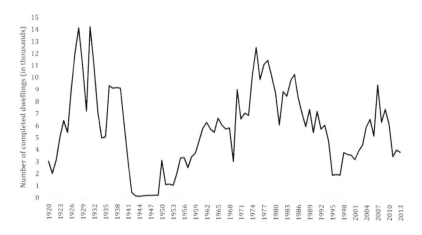

Figure 11.1 Number of completed dwellings, 1920–2013.

Source: Czech Statistical Office 2014.

central places. Socialist regional planning employed this theory for the creation of a network of central settlements with a specific hierarchy. This blocked the development of non-central settlements where investment in social, transport and technical infrastructure was restricted. Thus the creation of inner peripheries was one of the most pronounced impacts on the settlement system (Musil 2002). In the case of the metropolitan regions, investment in the outer parts of only some selected cities and towns meant a lack of resources for the rest of the region – mainly inner parts and hinterland. Thus the Central Settlement System policy influenced many small municipalities within the hinterland of Prague, where distinctive features of the inner periphery have survived to date (Ouředníček 2007).

The Complex Housing Construction policy aimed at the mass construction of apartments and thus the spatial structure of socialist cities began to be determined by the construction of housing estates (*sídliště*). This development resulted in the first significant enlargement of Prague's administrative territory in 1968 (24 municipalities; 100 sq. km) and led to a considerable increase in housing construction beyond the area of former Greater Prague (see Figure 11.1). The three different forms of ownership – state, cooperative and company – were mixed within the same areas of new construction and diversified the socio-economic structure of the population of housing estate neighbourhoods, distinguishing the social structure in Prague from that of other post-socialist cities, where this mix was not usual (Musil 2001). For example, cooperative apartments, which were characterised by the growing financial participation of households in housebuilding, were of better quality and led to the presence of new dimensions in the social differentiation of urban space (Musil and Ryšavý 1983). The allocation of apartments to younger families changed the inert socio-economic patterns of the capital that have continued to the present day and caused a smoothing of the socio-economic differences between the inner city and periphery of Prague during the 1960s (Musil 1987), but it also created quite differentiated patterns of family status within the city (Matějů *et al.* 1979). The substantial investment in housing estates led to the stagnation or regression of inner-city tenement houses. In contrast, Matějů (1980) describes the growing residential attractiveness of the villa quarters, Prague's West End, and also its historical centre based on data from a migration preferences survey conducted in Prague.

During the third development period, during the late 1970s and 1980s, the socialist state showed a strong preference for developing the capital, which was the main economic development area (Musil and Ryšavý 1983; similarly Enyedi 1998). Development of the capital city of Prague was designated a priority of the national economic plan in the main conclusions of the Fourteenth Congress of the Communist Party (1971). In practical terms, it meant the stimulation of the growth of the city and its agglomerative effects (Musil and Ryšavý 1983). A series of measures covered, among others, the enlargement of Prague's territory in 1974 (30 municipalities; 200 sq. km), and the establishment of a new subway (metro) system. This created the conditions for the evolution of mass pre-fab housing construction in the form of autonomous residential districts outside the built-up area of former urban quarters – for example South Town (for 100,000 people) and South Eastern Town (for 130,000 people).

The socio-spatial structure of Prague during socialism was more homogenous and the level of segregation was lower than in the interwar period (Musil 2005). While the index of segregation of manual workers in 1930 was 0.32 (Musil 1968), according to our calculations, it was considerably lower in 1970 (0.10). This decrease was achieved by increasing the share of manual workers in the total population (33 per cent in 1930 to 43 per cent in 1970) and their more equitable distribution within the city. From the population censuses held in 1970 and 1991 we can measure indices of segregation on the level of basic settlement units (BSUs). However, for 1970 we can measure only the category of manual workers (index of segregation (IS) = 0.14) because the other occupational groups were subsumed under the 'employees' and 'other' categories. After the end of the socialist era, in 1991 more detailed occupational categories were used in the census and the indices of segregation for lower status occupational groups were even lower (0.11 in the case of industrial workers, 0.12 for machine operators and 0.10 for unskilled workers). This confirms that a decrease in segregation is not an attribute of post-socialist development but rather has its roots in the post-war and socialist eras (compare Marcińczak *et al.* 2013 for Polish cities; Csanádi and Csizmady 2006 for Budapest).

The main features of the development of socio-spatial differentiation in Prague during the socialist era can be summarised as follows: first, the role of socio-economic status retreated in favour of the role of family status and was less applicable than in capitalist cities. Both the city centre and inner city of Prague were characterised by the continuity of their physical fabric (Musil 1987), but their attractiveness was considerably weakened by years of underinvestment in maintaining the physical state of the housing stock and infrastructure. Beyond the former area of Greater Prague, three generations of pre-fab housing estates were built and housed a demographically homogenous but socially differentiated population. The hinterland of Prague was significantly affected by the Central Settlement System policy because of underinvestment in non-central settlements that created an inner periphery characterised by physical and social decline close to the city. These conditions were the starting point for post-socialist transformation in Prague.

Developments after the Velvet Revolution

Prague's socio-economic structure has been affected by various local and global processes during the last 25 years (post-socialist transformation, economic globalisation, deindustrialisation, EU enlargement). In academic debates, these processes have been associated with the emergence of new or the growth of existing socio-economic inequalities (Musil 2005; Sýkora 1999). Mainly sociological studies have discussed the question of earnings disparities (Večerník 2001a) or new classes of differentiation or inequalities in accessing education (Matějů *et al.* 2008). However, their conclusions are rather ambiguous and highly dependent on the data and methods used for the analyses. We would argue that, despite the dynamic economic transformation in the Czech Republic, the country retained, rather uniquely, a high degree of equality inherited from its socialist past (Večerník 1996) and that the impacts of transformation have also had a rather smaller effect on the spatial pattern of cities, at least at the level that the statistical evidence allows us to evaluate.

Growing social inequalities have been mostly documented as a widening of the gap between rich and poor. The 1990s in the Czech Republic were characterised by a slight increase in wage inequalities as measured by the decile ratio[1] (2.5 in 1985, 2.7 in 1992 and 2.9 in 1999; Večerník 2001a), and a gradual and relatively stable increase can be observed since 2000 (2.9 in 2001, 3.0 in 2004 and 3.4 in 2012; MPSV 2013). If we take only the private sector into account, the variability is greater (decile ratio 3.7 compared to 2.6 in the case of state employees in 2013; MPSV 2013). Household income inequalities as measured by the Gini index (per capita) increased at the beginning of the post-socialist era (Večerník 2001b), but in recent years there has been a stagnation or slight decrease (25.3 in 2006, 25.1 in 2009 and 24.6 in 2013; Eurostat 2013). In the case of Prague alone, the development of wage inequalities is not that different from the rest of the Czech Republic but the gap between the rich and poor working in the private sector is wider and has been increasing more rapidly (from 4.2 in 2003 to 5.3 in 2013; MPSV 2013). However, if we compare the Czech Republic with other European countries utilising the Eurostat data,[2] the Czech Republic is among those with the lowest income inequalities (Eurostat 2013) together with the Scandinavian countries, which are known as highly developed welfare states. Also, when compared to other CEE countries, poverty has remained relatively low in the Czech Republic during the whole transition period (Musil 2005; Večerník 2004).

The spatial patterns of the city seem to reflect the post-revolutionary societal processes only to a limited extent, and overall a relatively high level of inertia has persisted. Socio-spatial differentiation is manifested mainly through the housing market, which has weakened rather than strengthened the spatial differences in recent times. The restitution of tenement houses within the inner city to former owners and the privatisation of housing stock in housing estates in favour of sitting tenants have created a new housing tenure structure that has significantly decreased the role of the public sector in housing provision. According to the 2011 census, out of 542,000 of apartments, 28.7 per cent are in the hands of dwelling owners associations, which were established especially in the privatised parts of housing estates, 24.8 per cent of apartments are owned by a private owner (family houses and restituted tenement houses), 17 per cent by housing cooperatives and 12 per cent by the local authority or the state. Thanks to generous social assistance[3] and the survival of rent regulation in large Czech cities (until 2012), lower-income residents have been pushed out from attractive neighbourhoods very slowly and have remained in the inner parts of the cities. The privatisation of former state housing stock and company-owned apartments has led to hundreds of thousands of people remaining in their flats. This, together with a relatively small amount of housing construction and low migration, has fixed the spatial patterns of the city. Former tenants have remained in their dwellings and now, as homeowners, they have started to invest in the modernisation of their high-rise blocks located in large pre-fab housing estates. Such behaviour will help to continue to maintain the social mix in different neighbourhoods and housing types for several decades at least (Ouředníček *et al.* forthcoming).

The existing research shows that the spatial concentration of urban problems has been very limited and that the seeds of poverty appear only at the micro level in particular houses or block of houses in the Czech Republic (Macešková *et al.* 2009). This has also been confirmed in the case of Prague, where social segregation is found to exist only here and there in a micro-local form, encompassing individual buildings or at most several blocks (Kostelecký *et al.* 2012). No signs of pauperisation or ghettoisation in Prague are evident, at least within the statistic data. Other aspects such as homelessness, ethnic differences (Roma people and guest workers) and unrecorded types of housing for example, shared apartments, dormitories) are not covered adequately by the data available. This makes it impossible to undertake extensive analysis on those aspects; however, this does not mean that more pronounced forms of segregation might be or not be revealed in the case of their inclusion.

Methodological framework

Our research reflects the discussion on the expected increase in residential segregation as a response to growing income inequalities in post-socialist countries (for example, Marcińczak *et al.* 2013; Sýkora 2009). In their work, Marcińczak *et al.* (2013) question this broadly accepted assumption and call for more empirical research to explore the development of segregation patterns in post-socialist countries. Our aim is to make a contribution to this discussion by exploring the development of socio-spatial differentiation in Prague during the period 2001–2011, which could be termed 'post-transition development'. Our methodology is based on the well-established procedures for the assessment of segregation in the European context and we further develop them by applying some new evaluations. The main analysis of changes in socio-economic segregation in Prague investigates the data on occupational structure from population censuses. The Czech Classification of Occupations (CZ-ISCO) employed by the Czech Statistical Office is built on the International Standard Classification of Occupations (ISCO-08), making international comparison possible (see also the introduction of this book for more detail: Tammaru *et al.* 2016). The classification is based on type of work (occupational task) and skill level. Nine out of 11 occupational groups are included in our analysis. Two groups were excluded: armed forces and agricultural workers. Thus, 87 per cent of the economically active population of Prague is considered in our evaluation (see Table 11.3).

Even though occupational data are widely used for the evaluation of socio-economic status and segregation (Duncan and Duncan 1955; Marcińczak *et al.* 2012), there are some limitations that need to be addressed. For instance, these data cover the economically active population only (this equates to 50.8 per cent of Prague's population in 2011),[4] but society is much more differentiated when pensioners, unemployed, children or homeless people are included. For this reason we use some additional socio-demographic data (unemployment rate, education, age) in further analyses. Another issue concerns the drawback of the assessment of segregation only on the basis of place of residence and excluding the temporal dimension (see Silm and Ahas 2014). However, the social environment of urban localities may be influenced significantly by encounters between daily users from different parts of the city or the wider region during the day (Pospíšilová 2012).[5]

The data analysis enabled us to examine the socio-spatial differentiation of various strata of the population based on their socio-professional characteristics. Two types of indices, the IS and the ID, were calculated to measure the overall level of segregation. To visualise the spatial pattern of socio-economic differentiation, we employed the locational quotient (LQ), which allows us to compare the variable in a given spatial unit to the values for Prague as a whole. The main dataset used in the analysis consists of occupational data from 2001 and 2011. Indices based on data from 1991 are presented only in the introductory part of this chapter because a different occupational classification (NACE) was used in that census so it is not fully compatible with the ISCO. However, the comparison of the data from the last two censuses is also complicated by an important methodological discrepancy. During the period between 1961 and 2001 the data were sorted and published according to registered permanent residency (not necessarily identical to the place where the person actually lived), whereas in the 2011 census (and also in the period between 1921 and 1950) usual residency was recorded. Because the latter type of residency should better correspond to where one actually lives (regardless of formal registration), the spatial differentiation of the population based on usual residency could be more accurate. It is necessary to bear these differences in criteria in mind when interpreting the overall development of spatial patterns.

To reveal the effect of socio-economic differentiation/segregation at different spatial scales, we compute segregation indices and display the spatial patterns for four types of spatial units: cadastral units (112 units in Prague; with an average population of around 10,000 people), BSUs (916; 1,000), discrete territorial units[6] (1,404; 400) and census tracts (5,663; 200). Finally, we compare socio-economic differentiation in various types of BSU. The typology is based on the prevailing character of housing, the construction period and distance from the city centre (for details, see Table 11.2 and Figure 11.2).

Research findings

First we provide an overview of the development of the occupational stratification of Prague's population between 2001 and 2011. Then we evaluate the general patterns and measures of segregation. In the last part of this section we focus on the analysis of residential differentiation in distinct types of neighbourhood in Prague.

Socio-occupational structure of Prague

The data from the two most recent population censuses conducted in 2001 and 2011 show that the process of professionalisation (rather than polarisation) significantly influences the change in the occupational stratification of Prague's population. The workforce in the bottom three occupational categories (industrial workers, machine operators and unskilled workers) decreased by one third, and the number

Table 11.2 Typology of residential areas

Type of residential area	Characteristics	Number of basic settlement units	Number of inhabitants in 2011 (share in %)
Historical core	Housing located in historical city centre	23	46,939 (3.7)
Tenement houses	Prevailing share of tenement houses located predominantly in inner city	141	331,855 (26.2)
Villas	Prevailing share of family houses, mainly bigger houses with own garden, located predominantly in inner city	52	99,281 (7.8)
Housing estates	Prevailing share of prefabricated apartment housing, which emerged after World War II	153	530,626 (41.9)
Working-class houses	Prevailing share of family houses, rather small, basic and working-class houses, located mainly in outer city, often original village centres	82	103,443 (8.2)
Inner-suburbs	Prevailing share of family houses, centres of original rural settlements or/and newly built suburbs	131	154,001 (12.2)
Newly built areas	(i) Prevailing share of newly built houses – 90% of flats built since 1991	(i) 14	(i) 11,901 (0.9)
	(ii) Significant share of newly built houses – 30% of flats built since 1991	(ii) 62	(ii) 11,1640 (8.8)

Note: This typology does not involve non-residential areas or indistinct units, which were not possible to assign to any category (all smaller than 50 inhabitants; total population of 2,651 people). The last category of newly built areas was delimited additionally for the evaluation of new construction impact on socio-spatial structure. BSUs and number of population of this type were distributed to particular types.

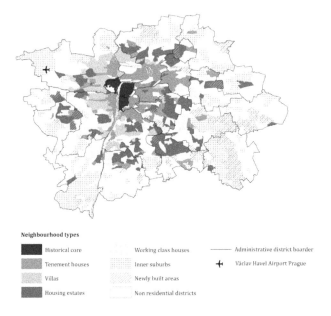

Neighbourhood types

■ Historical core	▦ Working class houses	—— Administrative district boarder
■ Tenement houses	⋮⋮ Inner suburbs	✈ Václav Havel Airport Prague
▦ Villas	▨ Newly built areas	
■ Housing estates	Non residential districts	

Figure 11.2 Residential areas in Prague.

Source: Own typology, see Table 11.2.

of unskilled workers halved over the course of the decade (see Table 11.3). On the other hand, the share of the top three occupational groups (managers, professionals and technicians) rose from 57 per cent to 62 per cent between 2001 and 2011. This is caused not only by the tertiarisation of economy (Musil 2005) but also by the changes in the social structure of the population (exemplified by the increase in the proportion of the university-educated population in Prague from 19 per cent in 2001 to 24 per cent in 2011).

This change is in accordance with the trends in the occupational stratification of the Czech population as a whole during the transformation period for which very similar changes can be observed. However, the exclusive position of the capital city as a national economic centre with a concentration of progressive sectors of the economy is reflected in the fact that the share of the top three groups in the workforce is considerably higher than the national average (62 per cent and 37 per cent respectively). Also, a high proportion (20 per cent) of Czech managers and professionals is concentrated in Prague (the share of Prague's economically active population is 13 per cent).

However, as mentioned above, the volume of any shift may be influenced to some extent by the methodological change in the registering of residents according to their permanent or usual residence in the censuses of 2001 and 2011, respectively. The number of inhabitants with permanent residence was 10 per cent lower than the number of inhabitants who reported that they have their usual residence in Prague.[7] This should be borne in mind when interpreting both the changing share of occupational groups and the measures of segregation.

Table 11.3 Labour market segmentation by ISCO occupational groups in Prague, 2001–2011

	2001		2011	
	Total number	In %	Total number	In %
Managers (1)	47,003	7.9	50,785	9.0
Professionals (2)	107,741	18.0	159,087	28.2
Technicians (3)	185,387	31.0	136,552	24.2
Clerks (4)	52,039	8.7	43,590	7.7
Sellers (5)	78,088	13.1	85,406	15.1
Industrial workers (7)	65,414	10.9	44,221	7.8
Machine operators (8)	32,742	5.5	30,106	5.3
Unskilled workers (9)	29,037	4.9	14,536	2.6
ISCO 1, 2, 3, 4, 5, 7, 8, 9	597,451	100.0	564,283	100.0
Armed forces and agricultural workers (ISCO 0, 6)	6,790		3,182	
No response	30,864		77,178	
Economically active – total	635,105		644,643	

Sources: Population Census 2001, 2011, Czech Statistical Office.

General patterns and measures of segregation

From our results, the degree of segregation, as measured by the traditional index of segregation (IS), followed a standard U-shape in both years (see Figure 11.3). The least segregated groups are traditionally middle-ranked groups of technicians,

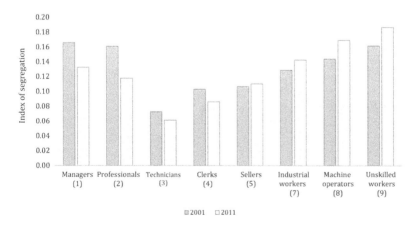

Figure 11.3 Development of segregation indices in Prague by ISCO occupational groups, 2001–2011 (on the level of discrete territorial units).

Sources: Population Census 2001, 2011, Czech Statistical Office.

Table 11.4 Development of dissimilarity index in Prague by ISCO occupational groups, 2001–2011 (on the level of discrete territorial units)

2011

	Managers (1)	Professionals (2)	Technicians (3)	Clerks (4)	Sellers (5)	Industrial workers (7)	Machine operators (8)	Unskilled workers (9)
Managers (1)	—	0.12	0.13	0.17	0.19	**0.21**	**0.24**	**0.26**
Professionals (2)	0.17	—	0.10	0.14	0.16	**0.20**	**0.23**	**0.23**
Technicians (3)	0.17	0.14	—	0.09	0.11	0.14	0.17	**0.20**
Clerks (4)	**0.20**	0.19	0.11	—	0.11	0.14	0.16	0.19
Sellers (5)	**0.21**	**0.20**	0.12	0.12	—	0.13	0.14	0.17
Industrial workers (7)	**0.22**	**0.22**	0.14	0.13	0.12	—	0.14	0.18
Machine operators (8)	**0.23**	**0.25**	0.16	0.15	0.13	0.12	—	0.18
Unskilled workers (9)	**0.25**	**0.25**	0.18	0.17	0.14	0.15	0.15	—

2001

Sources: Population Census 2001, 2011, Czech Statistical Office.

clerks and salespersons, whereas the high- and low-status groups show a greater level of segregation. Between 2001 and 2011, the level of segregation changed in two ways. First, it significantly decreased in the case of the top two occupational groups (managers and professionals). This is connected particularly with the localisation of new housing construction in the formerly lower-status neighbourhoods, the migration of high-income groups to both newly built and renovated apartments in such areas and the consequent processes of gentrification and suburbanisation (as discussed below). Second, the index of segregation of lower-status groups increased, especially in the case of industrial workers, machine operators and unskilled workers. The IS of these groups is even higher than in the case of managers and professionals. Although these workers decreased in number, it can be assumed that those who remained became trapped in the less attractive areas that the high- and middle-income residents were able to move away from. However, such localities are not numerous in the capital. Yet, it can be concluded that, in general, the rates of segregation are relatively low compared with other post-socialist metropolises such as Budapest (Kovács and Szabó 2016).

The index of dissimilarity (ID) indicates the degree to which social distance is accompanied by spatial distance. From Table 11.4 it is obvious that although the values of the ID are generally quite low, the relationship between the spatial and the social is evident. The highest level of separation can be observed between the groups of managers and professionals on the one side and the groups of industrial workers, machine operators and unskilled workers on the other side (ID ranging from 0.2 to 0.26). For those groups whose social distance is small, the ID takes a low value. Similar to the indices of segregation, the indices of dissimilarity show an upward trajectory in some cases but a downward trend in others. The increase can be observed in the case of the group of unskilled workers (in relation to the majority of all other groups apart from managers and professionals) and to a limited extent also in the case of machine operators. In contrast, the values of the dissimilarity index decreases in the case of managers and professionals whose spatial distance, especially from technicians, clerks and salespersons considerably diminishes.

Spatial patterns and types of residential areas

The second part of our empirical analysis is devoted to the detailed evaluation of the spatial patterns of occupational groups that lie behind the measured values of segregation indices. While the spatial structures of cities such as Budapest or Vilnius are relatively intelligible, with easily recognisable sectors of low- and high-social status, Prague's spatial arrangement is much grainier with the housing of rich and poor often located side by side (Marcińczak *et al.* 2016). This is clear from the spatial distribution of occupational groups (Figure 11.4) within Prague´s territory, which is quite difficult to explain without knowledge of the local conditions of individual neighbourhoods. The aim of the following paragraphs is to shed more light on the regularities of the spatial distribution of occupational categories by exploring the patterns on the level of BSUs, which

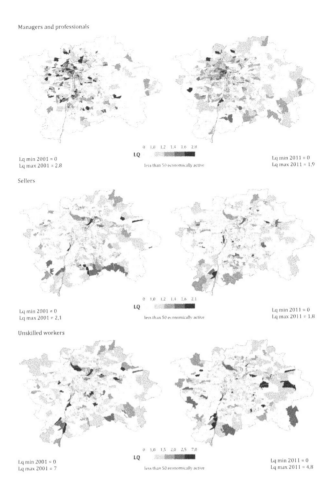

Managers and professionals

Lq min 2001 = 0
Lq max 2001 = 2.8

LQ   0 1,0 1,2 1,4 1,6 2,0
less than 50 economically active

Lq min 2011 = 0
Lq max 2011 = 1,9

Sellers

Lq min 2001 = 0
Lq max 2001 = 2,1

LQ   0 1,0 1,2 1,4 1,6 2,1
less than 50 economically active

Lq min 2011 = 0
Lq max 2011 = 1,8

Unskilled workers

Lq min 2001 = 0
Lq max 2001 = 7

LQ   0 1,0 1,5 2,0 2,5 7,0
less than 50 economically active

Lq min 2011 = 0
Lq max 2011 = 4,8

Figure 11.4 Location quotient of selected ISCO occupational groups 2001–2011 (on the level of discrete territorial units).

Sources: Population Census 2001, 2011, Czech Statistical Office.

are categorised according to prevailing housing type into six groups (historical core, tenement houses, villas, housing estates, working class houses and inner suburbs).

However, first it is necessary to show how the values of segregation measures change at various spatial levels in Prague (i.e., at the level of census tracts, discrete territorial units, BSUs and cadastral units). As reported in other empirical studies (Duncan and Duncan 1955; Musil 1968; Wong *et al.* 1999), we found that the higher the spatial level of analysis of Prague's units, the lower the values of the segregation indices (see Figure 11.5). This is in accordance with the findings of previous research on segregation in the Czech Republic that claims that manifestations

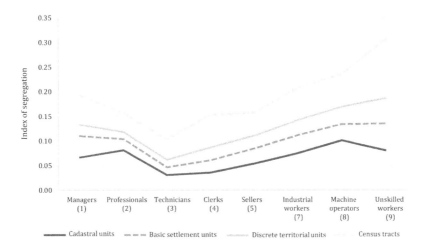

Figure 11.5 Segregation index in Prague by ISCO occupational groups in 2011 on various spatial levels.

Source: Population Census 2011, Czech Statistical Office.

of segregation are often registered in small spatial units, even at the level of one or more houses (Kostelecký *et al.* 2012).

Although the calculated indices for all occupational groups fit this rule, the differences between the values of IS at different spatial levels vary considerably among these groups. The characteristic U-shape is most apparent at the lowest spatial level of the census tracts. On the other hand, the variability of IS values at the level of cadastral units is relatively low. The gap is widening in the case of groups with the lowest social status (unskilled workers, machine operators and industrial workers) and the highest social status (managers). A significant part of differentiation in the distribution of these groups takes place especially at the lower spatial level. On the other hand, cadastral units are relatively more homogenous in terms of the distribution of professionals and technicians. For the purposes of further analysis, it is important to note that the differences between IS values at the levels of discrete territorial units (used in the previous analysis) and BSUs are quite small and that the variability in the differences between groups is quite low.

We also searched for regularities in the spatial pattern that might explain the segregation measures in Prague. As a part of our analysis, we assessed the heterogeneity of the six selected types of residential neighbourhoods by using the segregation indices for both years 2001 and 2011 (see Table 11.5). The historical core and the housing-estates types show the lowest level of segregation and can therefore be regarded as the most mixed types of neighbourhood, while the greatest differentiation is registered in the inner suburbs, working class houses and tenement houses (but only in the case of low-rank occupational groups in the case of the latter).

Table 11.5 Indices of segregation in types of residential areas in Prague, 2001–2011

	Managers (1)		Unskilled workers (9)	
	2001	2011	2001	2011
Historical core	0.08	0.07	0.06	0.11
Tenement houses	0.15	0.10	0.12	0.15
Villas	0.12	0.06	0.14	0.13
Housing estates	0.11	0.07	0.09	0.10
Working class houses	0.13	0.11	0.12	0.15
Inner suburbs	0.13	0.11	0.14	0.16

Source: Population Census 2011, Czech Statistical Office.

Undoubtedly, there is a considerable differentiation across neighbourhood types in terms of the socio-economic composition of residents. First, it is necessary to point out that new housing construction is one of the shaping factors in Prague's residential differentiation. As shown in Figure 11.6, residents with high-ranking occupations account for almost 50 per cent of the inhabitants in neighbourhoods with a high share of newly built housing (this category consists of 62 BSUs and covers 8.8 per cent of Prague's population). As discussed in the following paragraphs, new construction takes place predominantly in the types of neighbourhoods where lower or moderate social status residents are present, thus contributing to the more even socio-spatial development of Prague's neighbourhoods.

The historic core (23 BSUs with 3.7 per cent of the population) and villa neighbourhoods (52 BSUs; 7.8 per cent of the population) are traditionally areas of the highest social status and even 40 years of socialist policies were unable to change this. The share of high-ranking occupational groups (managers, professionals and technicians) is very high (45 per cent) in both of these types of residential area compared to the rest of the city (see Figure 11.6). At the same time, about half of the BSUs of these areas belong to the top 20 per cent of Prague units with the most progressive occupational structure. Although the historical core has been experiencing commercialisation (Ouředníček and Temelová 2009) connected with the displacement of some of the original residents, there have not been any drastic changes in terms of the transformation of the structure of the economically active population. However, although the high-status population continues to reside in the historical core and villa neighbourhoods, these areas are losing their exclusivity as part of this population gradually spreads to other areas of the city (to tenement houses, suburban areas). This is definitely one of the reasons for the decreasing of the segregation indices in the case of managers and professionals.[8]

In contrast, one of the types of residential area where significant changes have taken place is tenement houses, which are home to 330,000 people (141 BSUs; 26.2 per cent of the population). The average share of high-ranking occupational groups within the population in this type of residential area has increased considerably since 2001 (and is slightly above the city average) and, more interestingly,

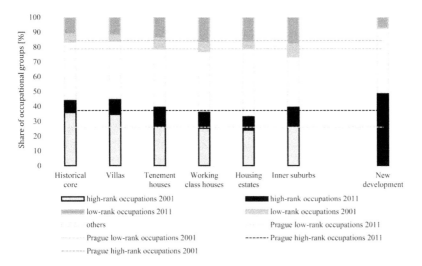

Figure 11.6 Share of residents with high-rank and low-rank occupations in types of residential areas in Prague in 2001 and 2011.

Source: Population Census 2001, 2011, Czech Statistical Office.

30 per cent of BSUs belong to the top 20 per cent of all Prague units with the highest share of managers and professionals. Conversely, the proportion of low-ranking occupational groups in this population diminished between 2001 and 2011. This shift in population structure is connected with processes of revitalisation, gentrification, and/or incumbent upgrading (Sýkora 1999; Temelová 2007). However, these processes have affected (at least for the time being) only a part of this housing stock. Our analysis of additional socio-economic characteristics reveals that neighbourhoods of tenement houses are extremely heterogeneous and that this heterogeneity has been growing over the past decade. This is evidenced by the fact that approximately one third of BSUs belong to the fifth of Prague's units with highest unemployment rate and worse educational structure, while also having the highest proportion of university educated (the latter proportion has even doubled since 2001). Moreover, a number of changes will not be recognisable at the level of the statistical units analysed in this study because they often take place at the level of streets and even houses.

The housing estates in Prague represent a type of residential area where any changes in the population's socio-economic structure are very carefully observed by both scientists and politicians, because they are home to over 530,000 people (153 BSUs; 41.9 per cent of the population). Indeed, they are also located in the parts of the city that are the worst off: the share of low-ranking occupational groups is slightly above the city average and the proportion of high-ranking occupational groups is the lowest compared with all other residential areas. However, because there have been quite intense regeneration efforts made in these areas, we assume that the fear of a steep decline taking place in these neighbourhoods appears so far to be groundless in the large majority of Prague's housing estates (compare Temelová *et al.* 2011). Concerning the spatial pattern, housing estates seem to be the least heterogeneous type of residential area in the city. Thus it can inferred that these areas contribute to lowering of the values of the segregation indices.

Similar to housing estates, the working-class-housing type of residential area (82 BSUs; 8.2 per cent of the population) has a slightly higher share of the economically active population that are in the lower part of the socio-professional hierarchy (and this was the case especially for 2001). These neighbourhoods were originally independent villages that were absorbed into the city's fabric during periods of industrial and socialist growth; they represent a relatively heterogeneous part of the urban landscape and consist of family houses of different quality, ranging from former working-class colonies to more spacious housing near the outer city limits.

The residential space that witnessed the second-most significant set of changes over the period of interest is the suburban neighbourhood (131 BSUs; 12.2 per cent of the population), where the share of the low-ranking occupational group declined considerably, while that of managers and professionals increased greatly. This recent change is certainly a consequence of the suburbanisation process (Ouředníček 2003, 2007). Formerly underdeveloped parts of the city on its administrative border that house rather low-status population groups have seen the arrival of new high-status in-migrants who can afford to buy recently built houses and apartments. This has led to a mixture of different status inhabitants living near each other (Špačková and Ouředníček 2012; compare Marcińczak 2013). Although the decline in the share of low-ranking occupational groups has been recorded in inner suburbia, it is still the highest among all six types of neighbourhood investigated in this study. On the other hand, a high proportion of suburban BSUs belong to the top 20 per cent of Prague units with the most progressive occupational structure. Thus, as the suburbanisation process creates clearly delimited areas of housing for 'the rich' and 'the poor', it leads generally to a growing heterogeneity in the inner suburban zone and to increasing values of segregation indices.

In general, there has been a gradual spreading of the higher-ranking social groups to areas of Prague that were hitherto thought of as rather worse than those of the historical core and villa neighbourhoods for instance. On the other hand, there still remain areas of lower social status population that are composed of a higher proportion of people of older productive age who generally have a lower level of education and a consequent lower occupational status. This process of spreading has changed the level of segregation the most in the outer city areas (inner suburbs, working-class houses) and to some extent also in areas of tenement houses where a deeper polarisation on the lower scale has taken place.

Discussion and conclusions

An examination of the long-term development of Prague shows that the largest disparities in socio-spatial differentiation were created during the economic and population booms of the 1930s, 1970s and 2000s and are connected to the growing stratification of urban society and diversification of the housing stock. The allocation of housing during the interwar period produced rather homogenous neighbourhoods built for similar social classes – villa quarters for the bourgeoisie, tenement houses for officers or workers and housing colonies for the working class, as well as temporary dwellings for the urban poor. This resulted in a relatively differentiated city structure consisting of particular neighbourhoods with distinctive characteristics that to a certain degree persisted in the form of the contemporary inner city. From this time, measures of the social differentiation and segregation started to decrease gradually. Generally speaking, Prague has always been a very stable city in terms of its spatial organisation. Under socialism there was a unified policy for the construction of prefabricated housing estates throughout the outer parts of the city for all social groups to live in the same place or even in the same apartment block. The empirical evidence, i.e., the segregation indices, illustrate that socio-spatial differentiation decreased gradually during the second half of the twentieth century and that this decrease cannot be ascribed to post-socialist development (for similar findings, see Marcińczak *et al.* (2013) for Polish cities based on an analysis of data for the period 1978–2002).

Our evaluation of post-socialist development, based on detailed measures for socio-professional groups and types of residential neighbourhoods, has confirmed that professionalisation rather than polarisation has had an effect on the social structure of Prague. This is illustrated by the increase in the proportion of higher occupational categories in the economically active population and the decrease in the number and share of those in the lower occupational categories. During the post-socialist development period, indices of segregation and dissimilarity have decreased in the case of higher occupational groups. This could be explained partially by the increase in the number and share of people in the higher socio-economic categories and a consequent increase in the variance within these groups. In a simplified way, we could say that non-manual professions can be taken up by a much bigger proportion of the population than before and that these categories contain more heterogeneous people in terms of social stratification (in terms of assets, incomes, lifestyles and so on). The opposite is happening to the categories of manual and unskilled workers, whose share in the city population is decreasing and who are essentially becoming relicts of dwindling neighbourhoods of worse housing stock in parts of the urban environment that are located especially within the outer city and periphery. However, in contemporary Prague, we cannot actually find larger truly poor areas or neighbourhoods characterised by considerable urban decay.

The decrease in socio-spatial differentiation is mainly a consequence of the location of new housing. It may seem surprising that new small-scale developments in the form of in-fills are often located in places representing the socially least developed parts of the metropolitan region at the end of the socialist era. Such new projects are located within or on the edge of former suburban villages, in working-class quarters (Karlín, Smíchov, Holešovice), and in specific inner-urban peripheries, alongside railways and industrial brownfield sites. Because new housing construction is focused almost solely on the middle- and higher-income strata of population, the incoming population is socially and economically stronger than the indigenous population of these quarters. It is not clear at this stage whether this inflow will strengthen the social structure of these quarters or will lead to social polarisation and segregation on the level of individual houses or blocks of houses that reflects the dichotomy between old and new housing stock.

Although migration to newly constructed housing is the most important factor in the changes to socio-spatial differentiation that have been occurring in Prague, the Czech population is characterised by low spatial mobility. This low mobility was even reinforced for a large part of Prague's population by several waves of privatisation of apartments during the transformation period, which still continues today, and this together with regulations on restituted property has fixed the inhabitants in their places of current residence. This 'velvet' housing policy has protected tenants from growing commercial rents[9] and together with low unemployment has actively blocked out-migration from the city. Additionally, due to the relatively high price of housing and rent, the capital city is almost 'restricted' in terms of preventing a significant inflow of the economically and socially weak population. These aspects of development can be considered as specific factors that have influenced the low level of segregation in Prague, when we compare the city with other parts of the Czech Republic, and also with other CEE capital cities (Kovács and Szabó 2016; Kährik et al. 2016; Marcińczak et al. 2016; Valatka et al. 2016).

Of course, all these conclusions are valid only in terms of the statistically registered economically active population permanently living in Prague, as recorded by the population census. The decrease in socio-spatial differentiation could be partially influenced by the fact that we excluded economically non-active people, mostly pensioners, who represent a growing proportion of Prague's population and who have declining purchasing power and rather specific spatial concentrations, especially in the oldest housing estates (Temelová et al. 2011). Second, foreigners, both from the West and the East, account for the most important part of the migration to Prague, but there is limited information recorded about them in the population census. Moreover, Prague's social environment is structured according to the perpetually changing social spaces of different social groups which, in addition to residents, covers roughly 600,000 non-residents, tourists, workers and clients of shops and services. This mix of social spaces is more complicated and more diversified than the socio-professional structure of Prague's residents. Although this comparative analysis of the socio-professional structure provides an important insight into the overall picture of the socio-spatial structure of this contemporary city, future investigations of socio-spatial differentiation could focus on these other groups of people who together create the social environment of the city.

Acknowledgements

This chapter was supported by the Czech Science Foundation (grant number GA14-00393S).

Notes

1 Namely, decile ratio of gross earnings (D9/D1). The decile ratio does not take into account the earnings of the lowest and highest 10 per cent of the population (Večerník 2001a).
2 Income inequalities are measured by the Gini coefficient of equalised disposable income and the S80/S20 income quintile share ratio.
3 In particular, the provision of housing allowance and housing supplement, which address cases where the income of the family is insufficient to cover housing costs. For families with no income, the housing supplement may actually cover total housing costs. Such arrangements make demand-side subsidisation of housing in the Czech Republic very generous – at least in comparison with other post-socialist states (Hegedüs *et al.* 2013; Ouředníček *et al.* forthcoming).
4 Furthermore, persons who did not supply their occupational group or complete the census form at all are not included in the analysis, i.e., 77,178 of Prague's inhabitants are not included in our analysis (CZSO 2014).
5 In the city centre of Prague, the daily population can be as much as five times higher than the night-time population (Pospíšilová 2012).
6 Discrete territorial units were defined especially for this comparative analysis by the authors to create spatial units of similar population size.
7 It is obvious from this fact that the labour market of the capital city is very attractive to broad groups of people who seek employment there.
8 We must bear in mind the deficiencies of the last census, which was, for instance, unable to cover part of the population (among them especially foreigners).
9 The average rents in the regulated part of Prague's housing stock are still about half the price of market rents.

References

Boháč, A 1923, *Hlavní město Praha: Studie o obyvatelstvu* [Prague: A population study], Bursík a Kohout, Praha.
Burgess, E W 1925, 'The growth of the city: An introduction to a research project' in *The city*, eds R E Park, E W Burgess and R D McKenzie, Chicago University Press, Chicago, pp. 47–62.
Csanádi, G and Csizmady, A 2006, 'Trends in residential segregation and local policy in post socialist cities' *First Bi-Annual European Urban Research Association (EURA) Conference*, 11–14. May 2006, Warszawa, Poland.
CZSO, 2014, Population and Housing Census 2011. Czech Statistical Office. Available at https://www.czso.cz/csu/czso/home. Accessed 15 May 2015.
Duncan, O D and Duncan, B 1955, 'Residential distribution and occupational stratification' *American Journal of Sociology* 60(5), 493–503.
Enyedi, G 1998, 'Transformation in Central European postsocialist cities' in *Social change and urban restructuring in Central Europe,* ed. G Enyedi, Akadémiai Kiadó, Budapest, pp. 9–34.
Eurostat, 2013, The European Union Statistics on Income and Living Conditions (EU-SILC). Eurostat. Available at http://ec.europa.eu/eurostat/web/income-and-living-conditions/overview. Accessed 15 May 2015.
Hegedüs, J, Lux, M and Teller, N eds 2013, *Social housing in transition countries*, Routledge, New York, London.
Horská, P 2002, 'Klasická urbanizace v českých zemích (1830–1930)' [Classical urbanisation in Czech Lands] in *Zrod velkoměsta: Urbanizace českých zemí a Evropa*, P Horská, E Maur and J Musil, Paseka, Praha, Litomyšl, pp. 121–236.

Kährik, A, Tammaru, T, Leetmaa, K and Mägi, K 2016, 'Socio-economic segregation in the inherited dual ethnic context in Tallinn' in *Socio-economic segregation in European capital cities: East meets West* eds T Tammaru, S Marcińczak, M van Ham and S Musterd, Routledge, London.

Kazepov, Y ed. 2005, *Cities of Europe: Changing contexts, local arrangement and the challenge to urban cohesion*, Wiley-Blackwell, Malden, MA.

Kornai, J 2006, 'The great transformation of central Eastern Europe' *Economics of Transition* 14(2), 207–244.

Kostelecký, T, Patočková, V and Illner, M 2012, 'Problémové rezidenční čtvrti a politiky k jejich regeneraci v postsocialistickém městě – studie Prahy' [Problem residential neighbourhoods and policies aimed at their regeneration in the post-socialist city: A case study of Prague] *Sociologický časopis/Czech Sociological Review* 48(1), 39–63.

Kovács, Z 1999, 'Cities from state-socialism to global capitalism: an introduction' *GeoJournal* 49(1), 1–6.

Kovács, Z and Szabó, B 2016, 'Urban restructuring and changing patterns of socio-economic segregation in Budapest' in *Socio-economic segregation in European capital cities: East meets West*, eds T Tammaru, S Marcińczak, M van Ham and S Musterd, Routledge, London.

Král, J 1945, *Zeměpisný průvodce Velkou Prahou a její kulturní oblastí* [Geographic guide to greater Prague and its cultural area], Melantrich, Praha.

Lehovec, O 1944, *Prag, Eine Stadtgeographie und Heimatkunde*, Volk und Reich, Praha.

Linhart, J, Rak, V and Voženílek, J 1977, 'Sociální aspekty ekologické zónace hlavního města Prahy' [Social aspects of the socio-ecological zonation of Prague] *Sociologický časopis/Czech Sociological Review* 13(1), 94–115.

Macešková, M, Ouředníček, M and Temelová, J 2009, 'Sociálně prostorová diferenciace v České republice: implikace pro veřejnou (regionální) politiku' [Socio-spatial differentiation in the Czech Republic: Implications for public (regional) policy] *Ekonomický časopis* 57(7), 700–715.

Marcińczak, S, Musterd, S and Stępniak, M 2012, 'Where the grass is greener: Social segregation in three major Polish cities at the beginning of the 21st century' *European Urban and Regional Studies* 19(4), 383–403.

Marcińczak, S, Gentile, M and Stępniak, M 2013, 'Paradoxes of (post) socialist segregation: Metropolitan sociospatial divisions under socialism and after in Poland' *Urban Geography* 34(3), 327–352.

Marcińczak, S, Tammaru, T, Gentile, M, Temelová, J, Novák, J, Kährik, A, Valatka, V, Kovács, Z and Szabó, B, forthcoming 'Patterns of socio-economic segregation in the capital cities of fast-track performing post-socialist countries' *Annals of Association of American Geographers*.

Matějů, P 1977, 'Sociologické aspekty vývoje bydlení v Praze' [Sociological aspects of housing development in Prague] *Sociologický časopis/Czech Sociological Review* 13(1), 39–58.

Matějů, P 1980, 'Vývoj sociálně prostorové struktury Prahy v letech 1930–1970 ve světle faktorové analýzy' [Development of socio-spatial structure of Prague 1930–1970 in the light of the factor analysis] *Sociologický časopis/Czech Sociological Review* 16(6), 572–592.

Matějů, P, Večerník, J and Jeřábek, H 1979, 'Social structure, spatial structure and problems of urban research: The example of Prague' *International Journal of Urban and Regional Research* 3(1–4), 181–202.

Matějů, P, Smith, M L and Basl, J 2008, 'Rozdílné mechanismy – stejné nerovnosti. Změny v determinaci vzdělanostních aspirací mezi roky 1989 a 2003' [Different mechanisms – the same inequalities. Changes in the determinants of educational aspirations between 1989 and 2003] *Sociologický časopis/Czech Sociological Review* 44(2), 371–399.

Moscheles, J 1937, 'The demographic, social, and economic regions of greater Prague: A contribution to urban geography' *Geographical Review* 27(3), 414–429.

MPSV, 2013, Regional statistics on the price of labor. Ministry of Labour and Social Affairs. Available online: http://portal.mpsv.cz/sz/stat/vydelky. Accessed 14 May 2015.

Musil, J 1960, 'Vývoj demografické struktury Prahy' [Development of Prague's demographic structure] *Demografie* 2(3), 234–249.

Musil, J 1968, 'The development of Prague's ecological structure' in *Readings in urban sociology*, ed. RE Pahl, Pergamon Press, Oxford, pp. 232–259.

Musil, J 1987, 'Housing policy and the sociospatial structure of cities in a socialist country: The example of Prague' *International Journal of Urban and Regional Research* 11(1), 27–36.

Musil, J 1993, 'Changing urban systems in post-communist societies in Central Europe: analysis and prediction' *Urban Studies* 30(6), 899–905.

Musil, J 1997, 'Potentials and limits of Prague's future in the context of long-term development' *Sociologický časopis/Czech Sociological Review* 5(1), 23–38.

Musil, J 2001, 'Vývoj a plánování měst ve střední Evropě v období komunistických režimů' [Urban development and planning in Central Europe under communist regimes. The perspective of historical sociology] *Sociologický časopis/Czech Sociological Review* 37(3), 275–296.

Musil, J 2002, 'Urbanizace českých zemí a socialismus' [Urbanisation of Czech lands and socialism] in *Zrod velkoměsta: Urbanizace českých zemí a Evropa*, eds P Horská, E Maur and J Musil, Paseka, Praha, Litomyšl, pp. 237–297.

Musil, J 2005, 'Prague returns to Europe' in *Transformation of cities in central and Eastern Europe: Towards globalization*, eds F E I Hamilton, K Dimitrovska Andrews and N Pichler-Milanović, United Nations University Press, Tokyo, pp. 281–317.

Musil, J and Ryšavý, Z 1983, 'Urban and regional processes under capitalism and socialism: A case study from Czechoslovakia' *International Journal of Urban and Regional Research* 7(4), 495–527.

Ouředníček, M 2003, 'Suburbanizace Prahy' [The Suburbanisation of Prague] *Sociologický časopis/Czech Sociological Review* 39(2), 235–253.

Ouředníček, M 2007, 'Differential suburban development in the Prague urban region' *Geografiska Annaler: Series B, Human Geography* 89(2), 111–126.

Ouředníček M, Lux M and Přidalová I forthcoming, 'Changes in urban social environment in times of crisis: A case study of the Máj housing estate, the Czech Republic'.

Ouředníček, M and Temelová, J 2009, 'Twenty years after socialism: The transformation of Prague's inner structure' *Studia Universitatis Babes-Bolyai, Sociologia* 54(1), 9–30.

Pospíšilová, L 2012, 'Denní rytmus lokalit pražského centra' [Daily rhythm of localities in Prague's centre] in *Sociální proměny pražských čtvrtí*, eds M Ouředníček and J Temelová, Academia, Praha, pp. 136–158.

Ruoppila, S 2004, 'Processes of residential differentiation in socialist cities: Literature review on the cases of Budapest, Prague, Tallinn and Warsaw' *European Journal of Spatial Development* 9, 1–24.

Silm, S and Ahas, R 2014, 'Ethnic differences in activity spaces: A study of out-of-home non-employment activities with mobile phone data' *Annals of Association of American Geographers* 104(5), 542–559.

Špačková, P and Ouředníček, M 2012, 'Spinning the web: New social contacts of Prague's suburbanites' *Cities* 29(5), 341–345.

Sýkora, L 1999, 'Processes of socio-spatial differentiation in post-communist Prague' *Housing Studies*, 14(5), 679–701.

Sýkora, L 2009, 'New socio-spatial formations: Places of residential segregation and separation in Czechia' *Tijdschrift voor Economische en Sociale Geografie*, 100(4), 417–435.

Tammaru, T, Kährik, A, Mägi, K Novák, J and Leetmaa, K 2016, 'The "market experiment": Increasing socio-economic segregation in the inherited bi-ethnic context of Tallinn' in *Socio-economic segregation in European capital cities: East meets West*, eds T Tammaru, S Marcińczak, M van Ham and S Musterd, Routledge, London.

Tammaru, T, Musterd, S, van Ham, M and Marcińczak, S, 2016, 'A multi-factor approach to understanding socio-economic segregation in European capital cities' in *Socio-economic segregation in European capital cities: East meets West*, eds T Tammaru, S Marcińczak, M van Ham and S Musterd, Routledge, London.

Temelová, J 2007, 'Flagship developments and the physical upgrading of the postsocialist inner city: The Golden Angel project in Prague' *Geografiska Annaler: Series B, Human Geography* 89(2), 169–181.

Temelová, J, Novák, J, Ouředníček, M and Puldová, P 2011, 'Housing estates in the Czech Republic after socialism: Various trajectories and inner differentiation' *Urban Studies* 48(9), 1811–1834.

Ulrich, Z 1938, *Soziologische studien zur verstädterung der Prager Umgebung.* Verlag der Revue Soziologie und Soziale Probleme, Prag.

Valatka, V, Burneika, D and Ubarevičienė R, 2016, 'Large social inequalities and low levels of socio-economic segregation in Vilnius' in *Socio-economic segregation in European capital cities: East meets West*, eds T Tammaru, S Marcińczak, M van Ham and S Musterd, Routledge, London.

Večerník, J 1996, 'Earnings disparities in the Czech Republic: the history of equalisation' *Sociologický časopis/Czech Sociological Review* 4(2), 211–222.

Večerník, J 2001a, *Mzdová a příjmová diferenciace v České republice v transformačním období* [Distribution of earnings and income in transitional Czech Republic], Sociologický ústav Akademie věd České republiky, Praha.

Večerník, J 2001b, 'From needs to the market. The changing inequality of household income in the Czech transition' *European Societies* 3(2), 191–212.

Večerník, J 2004, 'Who is poor in the Czech Republic? The changing structure and faces of poverty after 1989' *Sociologický časopis/Czech Sociological Review* 40(6), 807–833.

Votrubec, C 1959, 'Zanikání nouzových kolonií na území Prahy. Příspěvek k zeměpisu velkoměsta' [Clearing Prague slums] *Sborník Československé společnosti zeměpisné* 64(1), 6–12.

Węcławowicz, G 1998, 'Social polarisation in postsocialist cities: Budapest, Prague and Warsaw' in *Social change and urban restructuring in Central Europe*, ed. G Enyedi, Akadémiai Kiadó, Budapest, pp. 55–66.

Wong, D W S, Lasus, H and Falk, RF 1999, 'Exploring the variability of segregation index D with scale and zonal systems: an analysis of thirty US cities' *Environment and Planning A* 31(3), 507–522.

12 Occupation and ethnicity
Patterns of residential segregation in Riga two decades after socialism

Zaiga Krišjāne, Māris Bērziņš and
Kalju Kratovitš

Abstract

This chapter discusses the patterns of socio-economic and ethnic residential segregation between 2000 and 2011 censuses. In our study, we draw our empirical evidence from the capital city because it is widely acknowledged that the most notable social change and the fastest economic growth has tended to be concentrated and much more advanced in capital cities. Moreover, little is known about the ethnic dimension of socio-economic segregation, despite the existence of sizeable minority populations. The focus on ethnicity is important, since Riga is the only capital in the Baltic States where the ethnic majority in absolute numbers is less than the non-Latvian minority. In our research, most importantly, we need to clarify how growing socio-economic inequality in the light of systemic changes and economic restructuring relates to patterns of socio-economic and ethnic segregation. Our key findings show that despite growing income inequality, the levels of socio-economic segregation in Riga are rather low but slightly increasing over the observed decade. This chapter concludes that ethnic segregation dominates over socio-economic segregation in Riga and that the increase in ethnic segregation was found for higher occupational categories of Latvians.

Introduction

The fundamental political, economic and social transformations that have been unfolding since the collapse of state socialism in Central Eastern Europe (CEE) drew scholarly and public attention to increasing socio-economic inequalities and socio-spatial differentiation in post-socialist cities. The new urban reality and related processes of post-socialist transition has been driven through the neo-liberalisation of their economies, the withdrawal of the welfare state and the internationalisation of the financial services (Hegedus *et al.* 2005; Smith and Timar 2010; Sykora and Bouzarovski 2012). Some scholars generally endorsed that these systemic transformations contributed to the increase of social and ethnic residential segregation in CEE (Sykora 1999; Vendina 1997). However, the aforementioned large-scale transformations that in Eastern Europe started almost twenty-five years ago did not result in uniform effects across the region.

Historically developed, context-sensitive and path-dependant characteristics have to be taken into account in order to gain a better understanding of urban social inequalities (Burgers and Musterd 2002; Marcińczak and Sagan 2011; Marcińczak *et al.* 2012). Thus, the level of socio-economic inequalities is rooted in the city's historically developed functions of the pre-socialist and socialist periods and in recently adopted post-socialist development policies.

The socialist period particularly had a significant influence on urban development and urban living in the formerly centrally planned countries. Some researchers have argued that socialist cities were more homogenous, socially mixed, spatially compact and generally characterised by a lower level of residential segregation than their capitalist counterparts (French and Hamilton 1979; Szelényi 1996). However, despite the egalitarian aims of the socialist system, numerous studies have shown that residential differentiation does exist, but was lower, as expected, than in capitalist cities (Ruoppila 2004; Smith 1996; Sailer-Fliege 1999). Several studies reveal residential and housing segregation by education, occupation and ethnicity in cities under socialism (Ruble 1989; Rukavishnikov 1978).

The return to the democracy and a market economy initiated multiple simultaneous processes that strongly changed and continue changing the urban structures in the post-communist context. The emerging patterns of more contemporary urban residential segregation involve the socio-spatial results of deindustrialisation, suburbanisation, gentrification, demographic change, thus downgrading the social status of some neighbourhoods while others retained a relatively good image and social mix (Brade *et al.* 2009; Kabisch and Haase 2011; Kiss 2002; Kovacs and Herfert 2012; Kährik and Tammaru 2010; Steinfuhrer and Haase 2007; Temelova *et al.* 2011; Gentile *et al.* 2012). In this context, it is somewhat surprising that only very recently empirical studies exploring the levels and patterns of social segregation have started to appear (Marcińczak and Sagan 2011; Marcińczak *et al.* 2012; Marcińczak *et al.* 2013; Marcińczak *et al.* 2014). Besides, ethnic segregation still remains a modestly studied aspect of residential segregation in post-socialist cities (Gentile and Tammaru 2006; Ladányi and Szelényi 2001).

A distinct feature of Soviet cities, compared to those in Central Eastern Europe, is a considerable share of ethnic minorities. Moreover, during the Soviet period the formation of minority groups in Baltic countries, particularly in Estonia and Latvia, was shaped by the interrelated processes of immigration, industrialisation and urbanisation (Gentile and Sjöberg 2010). Immigration was part of a deliberate political and ideological agenda used to disperse a predominately Russian-speaking workforce through 'organized channels' of migration (Gentile and Tammaru 2006; Lindemann 2009). Approximately half of all the Soviet immigrants came from the present territory of the Russian Federation. During the 1970s and 1980s the share of Belarusian and Ukrainian immigrants increased (Monden and Smits 2005). The immigrants were mostly located in the largest industrial cities with their own ethnic infrastructure and were given priority to access the newest and better urban housing (Hess *et al.* 2012; Kährik and Tammaru 2010). As a result of large-scale immigration the share of ethnic minorities reached 42 per cent of the total population of Latvia and almost

64 per cent in Riga at the time of the last Soviet census in 1989. According to the 2011 census, Russians comprised 40 per cent of the total population in Riga and 75 per cent of the minority population. Other large ethnic groups are Belarusians (7 per cent) and Ukrainians (6 per cent) who mostly speak Russian. Therefore, even today Riga is the only capital in the Baltic States where the ethnic majority in absolute numbers is less than the predominantly Russian-speaking minority. The societal changes and economic reforms in the 1990s have placed minorities in a new situation that substantially alters inherited patterns of labour market and housing segmentation from the Soviet period. The studies have confirmed that the members of the Russian-speaking minority in Estonia and Latvia have adjusted worse to economic restructuring and suffered more from employment losses in different industrial sectors in which they were overrepresented (Aasland 2002; Aasland and Flotten 2001; Hazans 2011; Hess *et al.* 2012; Lindemann 2009). Therefore Latvia and Estonia with homogeneous minority communities, where the large-scale immigration stopped almost three decades ago, provide an interesting starting point for studies of social and ethnic segregation. Despite many common features, some studies found that the Russian-speaking minority in Estonia is less dispersed geographically and socially more separated than in Latvia (Lindemann 2013; Rozenvalds 2010). Moreover, socio-economic inequalities between ethnic groups increased in Estonia but decreased in Latvia (Muiznieks *et al.* 2013).

Nevertheless, until the present day no detailed studies on residential segregation in Riga exist. Therefore, the purpose of this contribution is to analyse the post-Soviet social inequalities in urban space, with a specific focus on ethnicity. In our study, most importantly, we need to clarify how growing socio-economic inequality in a light of systemic changes and economic restructuring relates to patterns of socio-economic and ethnic segregation. Therefore, this chapter seeks to answer the following questions:

- What were the levels and patterns of socio-economic and ethnic segregation and intermixing in the capital of Latvia?
- To what degree do ethnic divisions relate to the patterns of socio-economic segregation?

For the purpose of this study *segregation* is defined as the uneven distribution of socio-economic/ethnic groups across the city, while *concentration* we understand as the socio-economic and ethnic composition of neighbourhoods (Musterd 2005; Reardon 2006). The ethnic differences in segregation are measured by comparing ethnic Latvians with the largest minority group – Russians. Intra-urban differentiation at the neighbourhood level is an important aspect as this study for the first time examines socio-economic and ethnic residential segregation based on neighbourhood characteristics in Riga. In describing the internal spatial structure of a post-socialist city, with the classic wedge-like model and the concentric model were assessed (Ott 2001; Ruoppila 2004; Sailer-Fliege 1999). Thus, we distinguish between inner city, large-panel housing estates and the outer city. In our study, we draw our empirical evidence from the capital city because it is widely acknowledged that the most notable social changes and the fastest economic growth has tended to be concentrated and much more advanced in capital cities (Smith and Timar 2010; Stanilov 2007; Stenning 2004). The following section begins with the context-related urban development of Riga. Next, there is a description of the research materials and methods used in this study. Then we present global and local patterns of contemporary socio-economic and ethnic segregation in Riga, interpreting them within the spatial framework of neighbourhoods. Finally, we present our conclusions.

Setting the scene

According to the latest census of 2011, Riga, the capital and largest city of Latvia, houses 658,640 residents or around 32 per cent of Latvia's population of two million. Riga traditionally has been the main attracter of investment and employment and has held significant primacy in the country's urban system and in political, social and cultural functions. The capital houses almost half (47 per cent) of country's urban population. Similarly, Riga accounts for half of the country's GDP and still represents a highly centralised system of governance with the dominant role in the Latvian economy (Paalzow *et al.* 2010). Riga is one of the oldest European capitals, founded at the beginning of the thirteenth century. More rapid development started in the late nineteenth century when it experienced fast industrial growth, becoming one of the main port cities in the Russian Empire (Tsenkova 2005). Nevertheless, the most significant influence on Riga's urban development was the socialist period after World War II. Soviet policies of industrialisation and urbanisation were reinforced by the immigration of predominantly Russian-speaking people from other parts of the Soviet Union (Bleiere 2012; Tsenkova 2005). During the Soviet regime large industrial facilities were established in Riga, particularly in the 1960s and 1970s. The population significantly increased, reaching almost one million in 1989 (Table 12.1).

Table 12.1 Long-term migration trends and share of immigrants in Riga

	Immigration	Emigration	Net migration	Population at the end of period	
				Total (000s.)	Share (%) of immigrants
1946–1950	273,100	119,700	153,400	482,3 (1950)	n.d.
1951–1960	407,171	314,492	92,679	574,7 (1959)	55.5 (1959)
1961–1970	314,722	231,364	83,358	729,0 (1970)	59.1 (1970)
1971–1980	344,038	262,032	82,006	828,5 (1979)	61.7 (1979)
1981–1990	276,832	239,631	37,201	910,5 (1989)	63.5 (1989)
1991–2000	77,471	170,361	−92,890	764,3 (2000)	59.0 (2000)
2001–2011	224,230	297,852	−73,622	658,6 (2011)	55.3 (2011)

Source: Riga in figures 1993; Riga in figures 2005; Statistical database of the Central Statistical Bureau of Latvia.

Today, similarly to other large cities in CEE, Riga witnessed a process of steady population decline (Kabisch and Haase 2011; Turok and Mykhnenko 2007). Processes of both negative demographic growth rates and out-migration due to sub-urbanisation and international migration intensified sharply during the 2000s. Thus, the population of Riga has declined rather fast over the past decade (Table 12.2). In addition, post-socialist transition has given rise to a substantial change in the redistribution of population within the city. Intra-urban population dynamics in Riga reveals that inner-city neighbourhoods have lost their population most obviously over the last decade. Similarly, the Soviet-era housing estates are losing population but much more moderately. Nevertheless, the share of inhabitants in the zone of housing estates has slightly increased and only outer and peripheral areas of Riga have experienced population growth mostly due to suburban-type residential developments.

The proposed division of Riga into three distinctive urban zones is based on historical development and general patterns of built-up areas following the boundaries of neighbourhoods. However, it should be noted that the urban landscape of these zones has its own set of internal disparities and to a greater or lesser extent industrial areas can be found in all zones. The inner city, or historical neighbourhoods, constitutes a more or less compact area in the texture of the city, located on both sides of the river Daugava (Figure 12.1).

The Old Town lies in the very centre of this zone, representing a well-preserved medieval core and the cultural heritage of the old Hanseatic Town cityscape. The Old Town is surrounded by blocks of the art nouveau buildings and attractive parks on the right bank of the river. Neighbourhoods situated on the left bank and the external part of the inner city could be characterised as pre-socialist middle- and working-class apartment blocks with adjacent industrial estates offering good

Table 12.2 Indicators of the socio-demographic and economic conditions in Riga

	2000	*2011*
Population size	764,329	658,640
Net migration rate per 1,000 inhabitants	−8.7	−7.2
Share of population by urban zones		
Inner city	21.5	17.1
Soviet-era housing estates	73.7	75.9
Outer city	4.8	7.0
Share of main ethnic groups		
Latvians	41.0	46.3
Russians	43.9	40.2
Others	15.1	13.5
Share of owner-occupied housing	63.6	74.5
Gini index (Latvia)	33.2	35.7
Share in country's GDP	55.4	50.2

Source: Census 2000 and 2011; Statistical database of the Central Statistical Bureau of Latvia.

Note: Other large ethnic are Belarusians (7% of minorities in 2011), Ukrainians (6%) and Poles (4%). Russians comprise 75% of the ethnic minorities in Riga.

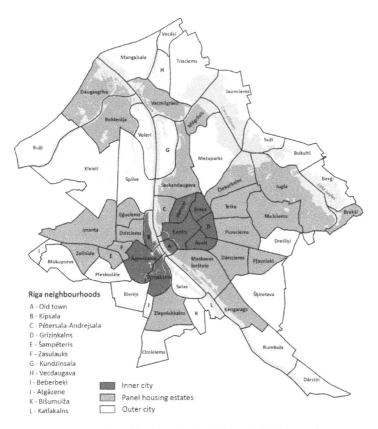

Figure 12.1 Map of neighbourhood units in Riga divided into urban zones.

Source: Riga City Council, authors' figure.

opportunities for work. Under the Soviet rule most of these buildings became communal apartments, but the best ones were reserved for the privileged classes (members of the *nomenklatura*).

The most distinctive type of housing in Riga is high-rise standardised and pre-fabricated panel housing estates found in many neighbourhoods. These residential districts were conceived during the Soviet era as social units complete with all necessary residential services, being the most significant spatial manifestations of the ideological goals of a collective social system (Grava 2007; Smith 1996). In Latvia, the large-scale construction of prefabricated housing estates started in the 1959. The height of the houses, size and quality of the apartments increased in the 1970s and the 1980s (Smith 1996; Treija 2009). In Riga, Soviet prefabri-cated panel housing estates represent all periods of construction and occupy vast areas on both banks of the river. A distinct feature of Soviet cities, compared to those in CEE, is the significant proportion of Russian-speaking immigrants in the panel housing districts (Gentile and Tammaru 2006; Hess *et al.* 2012; Kährik and

Tammaru 2010). Apartments in those panel housing estates were centrally allo-cated to the newly arrived labour force according to the 'need' of large industrial enterprises. Thus, the immigrant population had preferential access to new housing in Riga.

The outer city is the most diverse with respect to land use patterns and housing stock. This type generally covers neighbourhoods with single-family housing districts including pre-socialist villas and summer cottages, Soviet-era dacha set-tlements and extensive territories of allotment gardens. There are also large lakes, wetlands and marshes, as well as nature reservations along the sea coast. During the 1990s but especially in the 2000s the outer city experienced an increase in the construction of owner-occupied housing and commercial structures (office build-ings, shopping centres, warehouses, etc.).

The withdrawal of the state from the housing market during the 1990s was con-ducted with privatisation vouchers, which were given to all individuals who had permanently lived and worked in Latvia. Thus, large numbers of sitting tenants, mostly, in the Soviet-era prefabricated panel housing estates, became owners. As a result of large-scale privatisation, the structure of the housing stock in Riga is now dominated (almost 75 per cent) by the owner-occupier sector (Table 12.2). Whereas the people who had been living in the restituted houses could not buy their flats, but instead they became tenants of the people to whom ownership was returned. Rent regulation in restituted dwellings was abolished in 2007. In Riga approximately 60 per cent of the housing stock has been built after World War II, during the Soviet period (Tsenkova 2005; Bertraud 2006) and most people today still live in pre-transition housing stock.

With regard to the scale of socio-economic inequalities, we use the widely adopted Gini index to capture the scale of income disparities. The available data reveal that the socio-economic inequalities have grown and index values increased in the 2000s. Numerous studies (Aidukaite 2013; Aidukaite 2004; Bohle and Greskovits 2007; Fenger 2007; Rajevska 2009) have indicated that the Baltic States have been reformed into a neoliberal model of the welfare state, based on macro-economic indicators of low welfare state spending, high income inequality and a low minimum wage. With regard to ethnicity, it has been found that in Latvia socio-economic inequalities between persons belonging to different ethno-linguistic groups decreased in the 2000s and ethnic disparities in employ-ment rates had largely disappeared (Hazans 2011; Muiznieks *et al.* 2013; Pabriks 2002). However, some studies reveal a significant impact on segregation beccause of the divided school system inherited from Soviet era. This resulted not only in a two-community state but also in the very low knowledge of the Latvian language among adolescents from schools with Russian as the main language of instruction (Cara 2010; Lindemann 2013; Pisarenko 2006). Some earlier research notes that language skills are more important in the Latvian labour market (Hazans 2011) and thus can be seen as a factor in encouraging residential segregation. We can assume that Russian speakers who have poor Latvian language skills are clearly the most disadvantaged group in the labour market. It should be noted that under the Soviet regime the largest non-Russian minorities (Belarusians, Ukrainians and

Poles) were deprived of their cultural and educational infrastructure and many use Russian as their native language (Muiznieks *et al.* 2013).

Data and methods

Data and spatial division

The data used in this chapter are drawn from the Latvian censuses for 2000 and 2011, focusing on Riga city. We have used data on the socio-economic and ethnic structure of the population. The available dataset is the most reliable source of information on the occupational and ethnic composition of the population in Latvia. Unfortunately, the census reporting hierarchy of Latvian statistics does not support statistical units at the intra-urban scale (such as census tracts, wards or enumeration areas) that are widely used in segregation research across the world. Therefore, in order to achieve homogenous spatial units for proper statistical analysis, we produced a hexagon grid and converted census data to cells of this grid (cf. Brown and Chung 2006; Reardon and O'Sullivan 2004). We chose the specific scale of 16.5 ha for the hexagon grid. There are 996 of such areas in Riga, with an average population of 602 in 2011, allowing fine-grained analyses of the city's geography. Therefore, we used them as the primary units of global and local segregation analysis. With such data, it is possible to map in detail where members of particular social strata were concentrated within Riga, and the occupational and ethnic composition of the population of the neighbourhoods within those concentrations.

The analysis of the global and local patterns of socio-economic segregation relies on the division of the economically active population into eight major socio-professional groups based on the International Standard Classification of Occupations (ISCO-08). Similarly, this classification was employed in earlier studies on socio-economic segregation (Butler *et al.* 2008; Johnston *et al.* 2010b Musterd 2005) and reflects the main social and income divisions of post-socialist countries (Marcińczak *et al.* 2012; Marcinczak *et al.* 2013 Sýkora 1999). Although the Latvian census does not provide income data, the available occupational division is very useful for studying local income disparities. The total gross salaries have increased since the 1990s in Latvia. The ratio of average gross monthly salary between the top earning occupational group (managers) and the lowest earners (elementary occupations) was 2.2 in 2010. The inequality of income distribution, as measured by the Gini index, indicates a relatively high increase, from 33.2 in 2000 to 35.7 in 2011 (Table 12.2).

Methodologies and methods

Residential segregation is a spatial process, and a wide variety of ways has been developed over a long period for measuring spatial inequalities (Duncan and Duncan 1955; Johnston *et al.* 2005; Massey and Denton 1988; Peach 1996). A more traditional index-based approach has been most widely used to compare segregation across different social and ethnic groups (Peach 2009; Simpson 2007). Massey and Denton claimed that segregation is a multidimensional phenomenon that should be measured on many different indices, among which the indices of dissimilarity and segregation are still most common. In total, there are 40 indices belonging to one or another of the five spatial dimensions of segregation defined by Massey and Denton (Granis 2002; Martori and Apparicio 2011). The traditional index-based approach has been limited to global studies of segregation summarising general patterns and allowing comparisons with former studies (Peach 2009). The more recent approach investigates segregation as concentration and examines multivariate relationships temphasising local patterns of social and ethnic mixing rather than separation (Johnston *et al.* 2009; Johnston *et al.* 2010a).

For simplicity and easier comparison with other case studies in this book, we will refer to the global and local patterns of socio-economic and ethnic segregation, analysing them sequentially. Thus, our first results represent the contemporary situation in the socio-occupational and ethnic composition of the population in Riga. The dissimilarity index (ID),[1] the segregation index (IS)[2] and the isolation index (II)[3] were calculated for each of the eight socio-professional categories and both main ethnic groups. Additionally, in order to examine the patterns of concentration of the distinct social groups (classes) more closely, concentration profiles were produced for the opposite ends of the socio-economic hierarchy. The second part of our results characterises city-wide patterns and local geographies of socio-economic and ethnic segregation. The location quotient (LQ)[4] was used to illustrate spatial patterns of concentration (Brown and Chung 2006). LQs were independently calculated and scaled for higher and lower social strata and both main ethnic groups were distinguished.

Results

Occupational structure and neighbourhood socio-economic composition in Riga

The two decades of transition triggered obvious changes in the overall occupational structure of Riga. Based on original ISCO categories, we aggregate three general socio-economic groups. Thus the managers and professionals become the higher socio-economic group (HSG). The technicians, associate personnel and clerical support workers fall into the middle socio-economic group (MSG), whereas service and sales workers, craft and related workers, plant and machine operators and assemblers, and elementary occupations form the lower socio-economic group (LSG). This approach was used to analyse the local patterns of residential mix within the neighbourhoods. The most evident trend is represented by professionalisation of the labour force (Figure 12.2). The expansion of the professional category has been the most noticeable. However, professionalisation was much more evident for Latvians than for Russians. Moderate expansion took place at the bottom of the socio-economic hierarchy. By percentage, professionals, service and sales workers and unskilled workers all increased their relative share of the occupational composition. The smallest and least changed group is clerks in the middle category. The most substantial decrease over the past decade took place within industry, illustrated by the decline in the share of skilled industrial workers and machine operators. When aggregated, the lower socio-economic group (ISCO 5–9) plus the unemployed still comprises the largest share of all economically active people at the time of both censuses, but its relative share decreased from 56.6 per cent in 2000 to 53.5 per cent in 2011. At the same time the share of the middle socio-economic group slightly decreased by 0.5 per cent

We have added the ethnic dimension to analyse the patterns of occupational structure and residential segregation for Latvians and Russians. The occupational

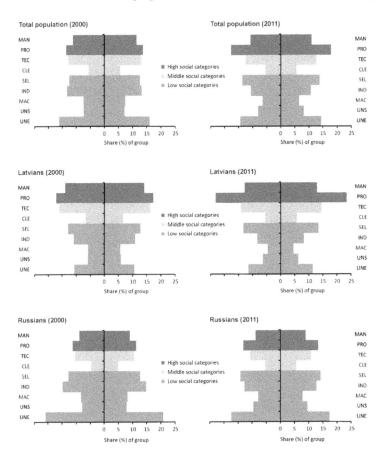

Figure 12.2 Occupational pyramids for ISCO occupational groups and unemployed in Riga.

Source: Census 2000, 2011, authors' calculations and figure.

Note: We present our data by centring 0 into the mid-point of each bar. MAN – managers, PRO – professionals, TEC – technicians and associate professionals, CLE – clerical support workers, SEL – service and sales workers, IND – craft and related workers, MAC – plant and machine operators, and assemblers, UNS – elementary occupations, UNE – unemployed.

pyramids shed light on the differences between the main ethnic groups. Both in 2000 and 2011 among Latvians the share of managers, professionals, technicians and associate professionals and clerks are higher than for Russians. Thus, ethnic Latvians more often belong to a higher and middle socio-economic group, while the Russian minority more frequently belong to lower socio-economic groups. Russians had a greater than average proportion working in industry. The restructuring of the economy in the 1990s had great effects on macro-economic changes and the employment situation, accompanied by rising unemployment. The unemployment rate of Russians in 2000 was two times higher than for Latvians. The differences in unemployment rates between Latvians and minorities were explained to some extent by the lack of language skills (Aasland 2006; Hazans 2007, 2011). Nevertheless, we see that differentiation in employment and occupational structure of Russians decreased between 2000 and 2011. Similar to Latvians, the share of the lower socio-economic group among Russians has decreased. The same trend towards professionalisation, however, has also been observed among Russians but to a lesser extent than for Latvians.

Another way of displaying occupational structure is to apply a neighbourhood sorting approach based on the socio-economic composition of residents. This approach has recently been used to investigate local geographies of socio-economic residential intermixing and the extent to which particular groups share residential neighbourhoods (Marcińczak *et al.* 2015; Musterd 2005; Reardon and Bischoff 2011). The same three general socio-economic groups (HSG, MSG and LSG) were used to capture the socio-economic status of the neighbourhood according to different threshold combinations of particular groups. In Riga, most of neighbourhoods fall into the polarised and low socio-economic status categories in both census years (Figure 12.3). Almost all the largest socialist panel housing estates fall into the polarised category. The low-status neighbourhoods are mainly concentrated along the river Daugava in the north and south of the city. These neighbourhoods in both directions contain remarkable

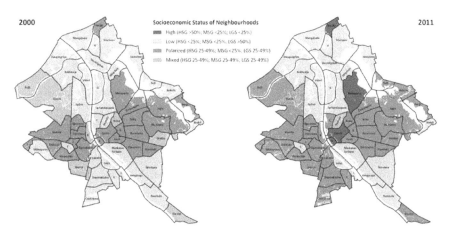

Figure 12.3 Riga's neighbourhoods by socio-economic composition.
Source: Census 2000, 2011, authors' figure.

concentrations of minorities (Daugavgrīva, Bolderāja, Vecmilgrāvis and Ķengarags), which might indicate an overlapping pattern between socio-economic and ethnic divisions. From 2000 to 2011, the socio-economic status has changed in several previously low- and mixed-status neighbourhoods on the urban periphery, where new housing developments were observed. The high-status neighbourhoods appear only in the last census and are located in the core of the inner city and in the villa quarters (Mežaparks and Vecāķi) from the pre-war period. Interestingly, only a few mixed neighbourhoods were observed where none of the three general groups clearly dominates. Such neighbourhoods in Riga are rare because the middle socio-economic categories did not form a substantial part of those economically active, not in 2000 and even less in 2011.

Socio-economic disparities and ethnicity divisions

The results of the analysis of the single-number indices summarise the spatial effects of the overall socio-economic and ethnic change. Overall, the results of the index of segregation (IS) reveal a generally low level of socio-economic segregation (Figure 12.4). The distribution of the index values takes an irregular 'U' shape pattern, with occupational categories in the centre of the classification the least segregated (service and sales workers the least segregated followed by the technicians and associate professionals). The most segregated categories are at the top (managers) and lower end (plant and machine operators and assemblers) of the classification.

There is remarkably little change between 2001 and 2011, with the values of 2011 matching those of 2001 or falling very close. The managers and unskilled

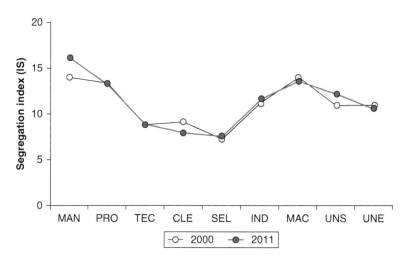

Figure 12.4 Segregation index (IS) for ISCO occupational categories and unemployed of total population in Riga.

Source: Census 2000, 2011, authors' figure.

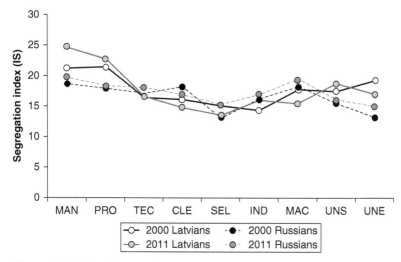

Figure 12.5 Index of segregation (IS) for ISCO occupational categories and unemployed of Latvians and Russians in Riga.

Source: Census 2000, 2011, authors' figure.

workers have become more segregated while the largest decline occurred for the clerical-support workers.

Figure 12.5 reports the outcomes of the index of segregation for the occupational categories of Latvians and Russians. The index values for occupational categories have been higher in both years (2000 and 2011) when measured separately for both main ethnic groups. The index values for ethnic groups are rather similar, with the highest values for Latvian managers and professionals an increasing trend over time. Furthermore, the index values for occupational categories of Russians have remained relatively stable over the particular time period.

The exposure dimension – of how much groups share common residential areas, as measured by the isolation index, reveals interesting notions about segregation in Riga. The values of the indices suggest a generally low level of isolation among socio-economic groups. This index also confirms the trend illustrated by the analysis of separation – higher and lower socio-economic groups were more isolated compared with middle socio-economic groups (Table 12.3). Contrary to the index of segregation, the 2011 outcome of the isolation index does not fall so close to the 2001 outcome. The increase in isolation occurs in the all groups but the most relevant changes in the values can be observed for higher and lower socio-economic categories.

As for the ethnic dimension of segregation, the values of the segregation index suggest a small difference in the overall spatial distance between ethnic groups (Table 12.3). Latvians are slightly more segregated compared to Russians and other minorities. The values of the segregation index increased for both ethnic groups during the 2000s. A different outcome was found for the

Table 12.3 Indices of residential segregation and isolation of major social and ethnic groups in Riga

Social categories	Segregation index			Isolation index		
	2000	2011	Change	2000	2011	Change
Higher socio-economic categories (ISCO 1+2)	13.8	15.2	+	13.4	21.0	+
Upper-middle socio-economic categories (ISCO 3+4)	7.7	7.1	–	9.4	12.3	+
Lower-middle socio-economic categories (ISCO 7+8)	11.9	12.1	+	11.1	12.5	+
Lower socio-economic categories (ISCO 5+6+9)	7.5	8.9	+	10.1	15.1	+
Unemployed and searching for job	11.0	10.7	–	8.5	10.3	+

Ethnic groups	Segregation index			Isolation index		
	2000	2011	Change	2000	2011	Change
Latvians	22.5	24.6	+	45.4	51.0	+
Russians	17.1	20.1	+	46.4	43.6	–
Others	11.4	13.0	+	16.1	14.6	–

Source: Census 2000 and 2011.

values of the isolation index; they were much higher. The increase in the isolation index reveals that Latvians are less likely to live in mixed residential areas, while for Russians and other minorities the isolation declines.

The separation of socio-economic groups was further illuminated by the indices of dissimilarity (ID). The matrixes of occupational categories with IDs indicate the degree to which the social distance is accompanied by spatial distance. Indices of dissimilarity among major occupational categories show that higher distances are observed between extreme categories, with the managers/professionals and the plant and machine operators/elementary occupations presenting the more dissimilar spatial distribution (Figure 12.6).

Over the past decade the indices between the professionals on one hand, and the plant and machine operators, and assemblers on the other have slightly grown from 21 in 2000 to 26 in 2011. By contrast, the managers and the professionals record index values of 14 for 2000 declining to 11 in 2011, depicting occupational categories that are closely integrated in the residential space. The higher and middle occupational categories present some similarity in spatial distribution and the same applies to lower categories. The dissimilarity index indicates that the middle occupational categories are the most evenly distributed and tend to share residential space with higher rather than lower socio-economic groups. The general trend between 2001 and 2011 shows that almost all dissimilarity indices are increasingly widening the gaps between the top and bottom socio-economic

2000 \ 2011	MAN	PRO	TEC	CLE	SEL	IND	MAC	UNS	UNE
MAN	--	11	15	19	20	24	25	25	22
PRO	14	--	15	19	20	24	26	24	22
TEC	14	11	--	14	15	19	21	20	18
CLE	18	15	13	--	14	18	19	18	17
SEL	19	16	13	12	--	15	16	14	14
IND	22	19	15	13	11	--	13	14	13
MAC	23	21	17	14	13	13	--	15	14
UNS	22	19	17	14	12	13	15	--	14
UNE	21	18	16	14	12	15	16	14	--

Figure 12.6 Index of dissimilarity (ID) for the occupational categories of total population in Riga.

Source: Census 2000, 2011, authors' figure.

Note: In shadowed cells dissimilarity index values is over 20.

		LATVIANS (2011)									RUSSIANS (2011)								
		MAN	PRO	TEC	CLE	SEL	IND	MAC	UNS	UNE	MAN	PRO	TEC	CLE	SEL	IND	MAC	UNS	UNE
LATVIANS (2000)	MAN	--	14	18	22	22	26	27	27	24	33	33	35	36	35	37	39	35	35
	PRO	17	--	18	22	22	26	28	27	24	34	34	35	36	35	37	39	35	35
	TEC	17	13	--	17	17	21	23	22	20	31	30	31	32	31	32	35	31	30
	CLE	21	18	17	--	17	21	22	21	20	30	30	31	31	29	30	33	29	29
	SEL	21	18	16	16	--	18	20	18	17	31	31	31	30	29	30	32	28	28
	IND	23	21	17	17	14	--	18	18	17	30	29	29	28	26	26	29	25	25
	MAC	25	24	20	19	17	19	--	20	19	31	30	30	28	27	27	29	26	26
	UNS	24	21	19	18	16	19	20	--	18	33	32	32	31	29	29	32	28	27
	UNE	23	20	19	20	16	19	21	18	--	35	35	35	33	32	32	35	29	29
RUSSIANS (2000)	MAN	32	30	28	28	28	31	29	32	31	--	14	16	20	21	25	24	25	23
	PRO	32	30	27	27	27	30	29	32	31	16	--	16	19	20	24	24	25	22
	TEC	34	32	28	27	27	29	27	31	30	16	12	--	16	16	20	20	21	19
	CLE	35	33	28	26	27	28	27	30	30	21	18	18	--	18	21	20	21	20
	SEL	33	30	26	23	22	24	23	25	25	21	17	17	15	--	16	17	16	15
	IND	35	32	28	25	24	25	23	27	27	24	20	19	16	13	--	14	15	15
	MAC	36	33	29	27	25	26	24	28	28	25	21	21	18	16	15	--	16	16
	UNS	34	31	27	24	23	24	23	26	26	25	22	22	18	16	16	17	--	16
	UNE	32	29	25	22	21	23	22	24	24	24	21	20	17	16	17	18	16	--

Figure 12.7 Index of dissimilarity (ID) for the occupational categories of Russians and Latvians in Riga.

Source: Census 2000, 2011, authors' figure.

Note: In shadowed cells dissimilarity index values is over 20.

groups. Stronger spatial separation (ID values over 30) is indicated with a dark-grey shading (Figure 12.7).

The values of the dissimilarity index are much more similar between occupational categories within the same ethnic group (Figure 12.7). Furthermore, over the past decade these indices have been relatively stable, with a slight increase between most pairs of occupational categories. The higher and middle occupational categories are the most segregated in relation to the lower categories and the unemployed for the both ethnic groups alike. However in both years (2000 and 2011), none of the occupational categories exceeded the value 30 with any other category. The dissimilarity index values between the ethnic groups are more pronounced, with the highest values being 36–39 in 2011. In the segregation literature such values are interpreted as moderate (Massey and Denton 1993). Overall, the Latvian higher and middle occupational categories exhibited slightly higher levels of separation than Russian higher and middle occupational categories in both years. The high values of the dissimilarity index were observed even for the same occupational groups of Latvians and Russians. For example, ID for Latvian and Russian managers and professionals is as 32/33 for 2000/2011 and 30/34 for 2000/2011, respectively. Thus, not only the occupational structure of Latvians and Russians is different but the same occupational groups do not share the same residential neighbourhoods.

The geography of socio-occupational segregation

The final descriptive measure in this section is the location quotient (LQ). This measure describes how concentrated an occupational category is compared with the city's average. The Figure 12.1 at the beginning of this chapter will help readers to recognise local neighbourhoods. As the main socio-economic division in the city consistently indicates the population with higher (managers and professionals) and lower (service, shop and market sales workers) occupation categories, these two groups are targeted for further inquiry. Thus, we focus on the opposite ends of the socio-economic hierarchy by selecting two highest and one lowest category. Figures 12.8 and 12.9 depict the location quotient, offering a number of insights into the local patterns of spatial concentrations of the selected socio-economic groups. The intra-urban geography of the highest socio-economic group has rather similar patterns in both years (2000 and 2011). There is a clear concentration of managers and professionals in the core of the inner city. This area already existed in 2000 and has become spatially extended eastwards. Thus, the city centre has remained as a preferred residential environment. Interestingly, the Old Town has lost its attractiveness among high-status socio-economic groups. Higher occupations have also been located in the north-east periphery of the city in the form of small pockets of wealth. The concentrated pattern could be found in the villa quarter of pre-war summer homes in the north (Vecāķi) and in the traditional high-status villa area from the pre-war period in the north-east (Mežaparks).

Another feature of location of the higher strata is associated with the new residential developments in the city's south-west (Zolitūde, Pleskodāle, Bieriņi,

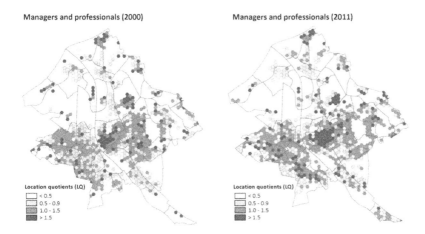

Figure 12.8 Location quotient (LQ) maps for managers and professionals (ISCO 1 + 2) in 2000 and 2011.

Source: Census 2000, 2011, authors' figure.

Figure 12.9 Location quotient (LQ) maps for service, shop and market sales workers (ISCO 5) in 2000 and 2011.

Source: Census 2000, 2011, authors' figure.

Atgāzene and Ziepniekkalns) and south-east (Dārziņi, Bukulti, Dreiliņi) periphery. The growing rate of new suburban-style construction in peripheral locations within the city limits is a result of the transformation of easily available and accessible former agricultural lands to residential areas. This shows that the higher socio-economic categories have largely moved towards investments in new housing (Marcińczak *et al.* 2012; Ouředniček *et al.* 2016). In contrast, the managers and professionals are underrepresented, compared to the Riga average, in the low socio-economic status neighbourhoods, especially in the northern periphery (Daugavgrīva, Bolderāja, Vecmilgrāvis).

The most evenly spatially distributed group within the city is sales and service workers (Figure 12.9). This group has increased its presence in some low socio-economic status neighbourhoods in the northern periphery (Bolderāja, Vecmilgrāvis, Trīsciems and Jaunciems) and within the polarised neighbourhoods in the southern periphery (Dārziņi and Mūkupurvs). Sales personnel tend to have the opposite location patterns as compared to managers and professionals. Compared to 2000, this particular group has slightly decreased in the inner city and in the high socio-economic status neighbourhoods.

Location maps for other socio-economic groups were also examined, but are not presented here. Overall, the geography of occupational structure in Riga reveals that socio-economic groups are widely dispersed across the city. The category of elementary occupations and the unemployed comprise a large per centage of the economically active population and have been relatively stable over the past decade. The areas in which the unskilled workers are concentrated largely overlap with the locations where the unemployed are overrepresented. Similarly to the unemployed, the share of elementary occupations has diminished in the inner city and in the high socio-economic status neighbourhoods. However, members of lower socio-economic group are also found concentrated in some centrally located neighbourhoods (Torņakalns) and neighbourhoods with decaying housing stock adjoining the inner city (Maskavas forštate). These residential areas could be characterised by a worsening of living conditions and a higher presence of wooden buildings compared with other neighbourhoods. Similarly, unskilled workers and the unemployed are overrepresented in the northern industry-based neighbourhoods (Daugavgrīva and Bolderāja) and some areas where the older socialist housing estates are located (Mīlgrāvis, Jugla, Brekši and Dzirciems). Another area of concentration for lower strata could be found in the south-east neighbourhoods in the outer city. Unemployed persons tend to form clusters in the neighbourhoods where the extensive territories of allotment gardens are located in the south (Dārziņi) and north (Spilve and Voleri). Some accumulation areas of low socio-economic groups in the outer city in 2000 have disappeared, being replaced by much lower levels of concentration or a more scattered distribution pattern in 2011. Interestingly, panel housing estates in general do not represent areas of increasing concentration of higher and lower socio-economic groups. The findings from Riga suggest that the housing estates have become differentiated during the transition towards a market economy. Some of these residential areas, especially older ones in peripheral locations, became downgraded, but the largest ones on both banks of the river have maintained a relatively good image and socio-economic mix.

Conclusions

The contemporary residential structure of Riga is inherited largely from the pre-war period and the Soviet urbanisation. As regards the influence of the post-socialist transitions on the level and patterns of social residential segregation, the conclusion seems to be that the two decades of post-socialist transformation in Riga have had an impact on the patterns of intra-urban socio-economic segregation, and on mixed rather than segregated neighbourhoods. However, the evolutionary nature of socio-spatial change takes time, with the socio-economic structure changing first and then followed by changes in the spatial structures (Sýkora 2009; Sýkora and Bouzarovski 2012). In this chapter we have provided evidence of how residential segregation patterns in Riga have evolved and transformed through the analysis of 2000 and 2011 census data. Besides emphasising the importance of socio-economic groups in understanding residential change, we have added the ethnic dimension of segregation and studied how these two dimensions are interrelated. For the first time in Latvia occupational and ethnic segregation has been studied at the intra-urban scale. The levels of socio-economic and ethnic residential segregation in Riga at the beginning of the twenty-first century are low, when compared with the levels in other capital cities of Central Eastern Europe (Marcińczak *et al.* 2015). The index values of socio-economic segregation follow an irregular 'U' shape pattern with occupational categories in the centre of the classification the least segregated. Socio-economic segregation during the post-socialist transition was driven by profound changes in the labour market, rapidly growing income inequalities, fast retrenchment of the socialist welfare state and extensive liberalisation of the economy. Over the past decade the employment structure of Riga followed a steady trend of professionalisation. Our findings suggest that socio-economic mobility and and increase in income differences between occupational categories, followed by an increase in residential mobility, have been responsible for transforming residential structures in the 2000s.

In Riga, based on detailed measures of the socio-economic groups, the changes in socio-economic structure have confirmed a mixed pattern of residential neighbourhoods. This is illustrated by the increase of economically active people in higher and lower occupational categories in sharing residential space. The increasing socio-economic polarisation of many neighbourhoods is probably related to two simultaneous processes – greater residential mobility among the higher occupational categories, and the relative immobility of the lower occupations and unemployed, as previously found in the case of Poland (Marcińczak *et al.* 2013). Although changes in the occupational structure were profound between the 2000 and 2011 censuses in Riga, the overall level of segregation remained stable, with a slight increase at the top (managers) and at the bottom (elementary occupations) of the occupational hierarchy. During the post-socialist development, indices of occupational segregation and dissimilarity have increased in the case of higher and middle socio-economic groups. This could be explained partially by the increase in number and share of people in these occupational categories. However, the segregation and separation are at a generally low level which in turn could be interpreted by the relatively high variety and heterogeneity of these groups (in terms of incomes, housing, lifestyles, etc.).

The empirical evidence of segregation indices has illustrated that ethnic segregation dominates over socio-economic segregation in Riga (cf. Musterd 2005).

The observed index values for occupational categories when measured separately for Latvians and Russians have been higher than for the total population. We found that ethnic differentiation is inherited from the Soviet period due to different employment structures for Latvians and Russians, and housing allocation mechanisms. The analysis of census data shows an increase in ethnic segregation at the opposite ends of the socio-economic hierarchy but especially for higher occupational categories. In other words, the number and share of Latvian managers and professionals has increased and they have become more segregated and isolated themselves from all Russian occupational groups in the 2000s. Moreover, the separation between Latvian managers and professionals is smaller in Latvian lower occupational categories than in Russian managers and professionals. Overall, the Latvian higher and middle occupational categories exhibited slightly higher levels of separation than Russian higher and middle occupational categories in both years. At the same time, the underlying parameters of stability in segregation levels for the occupational categories of Russians can be attributed to the relative stability of the occupational structure for this ethnic group. Nevertheless, our findings confirm previous studies revealing that segregation in the Latvian labour market between different ethnic groups is modest (Aasland 2006; Hazans 2011). Russians are only slightly disadvantaged compared to ethnic Latvians and much of this difference can be attributed to Latvian language proficiency.

Although the overall level of residential segregation was relatively low, with only a slightly increasing trend, there are, however, visible concentrations within the city landscape and these are indicated by the location quotients that demonstrate the differing residential patterns within Riga in the 2000s. The local patterns of concentration of the examined socio-economic groups not only highlight historically inherited socio-spatial differences but also illuminate the differences between more prosperous and less prosperous groups. In terms of geography, evidence clearly indicates that the observed socio-economic segregation has led to an increasing concentration of high socio-economic groups in the core of the inner city and in pre-war villa quarters. Thus, concentration areas of managers and professionals emerged as well as expanded around already prestigious neighbourhoods. The low socio-economic status neighbourhoods can be found alongside the river Daugava in the northern and southern periphery of the city. In addition, these neighbourhoods contain remarkable concentrations of ethnic minorities, which might indicate an overlapping pattern between socio-economic and ethnic divisions. The overall share of low socio-economic status neighbourhoods has decreased in Riga, indicating that polarisation is taking place in previously low-status areas, both as a result of the in-situ professionalisation of the workforce and in-migration from high socio-economic status groups.

To conclude, various global and local processes over the past 25 years of post-socialist transition have had an impact on the patterns of intra-urban socio-economic and ethnic segregation in Riga, and on mixed rather than segregated residential neighbourhoods. While society as a whole went through comprehensive changes, the socio-spatial patterns observed in Riga are firmly rooted in the city's past. The footprint of pre-war development and decades of Soviet rule left a lasting impact on the socio-spatial structures. Levels of socio-economic segregation slightly increased in the 2000s as managers, unskilled workers and Latvians were more inclined to separate. Moreover, despite the massive housing privatisation to sitting tenants, the residential mobility in Riga seems to be characterised as low and does not generate a significant increase in residential segregation. The analysis of local geographies of segregation indicates in most neighbourhoods a polarisation of socio-economic groups, particularly in almost all the largest Soviet panel housing estates and in the inner city.

Further studies should illuminate the population dynamics that drive the creation of polarised neighbourhoods in Riga. Similarly, attention should be paid to the circumstances in which substantial parts of the neighbourhoods retain a low socio-economic status. In addition, we expected that the ethnic dimension of segregation would be more pronounced. From this perspective, it would be particularly useful to examine more closely the housing segmentation of particular ethnic groups. Finally, it is important to note that the 2011 census captures the situation during the times of economic crisis. This should be borne in mind when interpreting both the changing share of occupational categories and the measures of segregation.

Acknowledgements

The authors are grateful to the book editors for their insightful comments and valuable suggestions. We would also like to acknowledge the Population Census section of the Central Statistical Bureau of Latvia and particularly Maranda Behmane, Uldis Ainārs, Uldis Ušackis and Pēteris Veģis. We also thank Ivars Bergmanis for cartographic help. This research was supported by the European Social Fund in Mobilitas postdoctoral research grant no. MJD334.

Notes

1 The dissimilarity index was calculated as: $ID = \left(0.5\sum \left|\left(x_i / X\right) - \left(y_i / Y\right)\right|\right) * 100$; where x_i is the number of people in first category in spatial unit i; X is the number of people in first category; y_i is the number of people in the second category in spatial unit i; and Y is the number of people in the second category. The index of dissimilarity indicates the degree of (un)evenness in the spatial distributions of social/ethnic groups. When multiplied by 100, the dissimilarity index is interpreted as the share of the population of a particular group that would have to move to resemble the dispersion of another group. Values below 30 are interpreted as low, whereas those greater than 60 are interpreted as high (Massey and Denton 1993).

2 The segregation index was calculated as: $IS = \left(0.5\sum \left|\left(x_i / X\right) - \left(t_i - x_i\right) / \left(T - X\right)\right|\right) * 100$; where x_i is the number of people in the first category in spatial unit i; X is the number of people in first category; t_i is the total number of people in spatial unit i and T is the total number of people in a city. The index of segregation compares the distribution of social/ethnic group with the remainder of the population. The values of the segregation index were interpreted in the same way as those of the index of dissimilarity.

3 The index of isolation was calculated as: $II = \left(\sum \left|\left(x_i / X\right) * \left(x_i / t_i\right)\right|\right) * 100$; where x_i is the number of people in the first category in spatial unit i; X is the total number of

people in first category; t_i is the total population of unit i. The index of isolation was interpreted as the probability that a person of category meets someone else of category in spatial unit X. The values i of the index of isolation were interpreted in the same way as those of the dissimilarity and segregation indices.

4 The Location Quotient was calculated as: $LQ = (x_i / t_i) / (X / T)$; where x_i is the number of people in the first category in spatial unit i; t_i is the total population of unit i; X is the total number of people in the first category and T is the total population of a city (Isard 1960).

References

Aasland, A 2006, 'Citizenship status and social exclusion in Estonia and Latvia' *Journal of Baltic Studies* 33(1), 57–77.

Aasland, A 2006, 'Russians and the economy' in *Latvian-Russian relations: Domestic and international dimensions*, ed. N Muižnieks, Riga, University of Latvia Press, pp. 53–63.

Aasland, A and Fløtten, T 2001, 'Ethnicity and social exclusion in Estonia and Latvia' *Europe-Asia Studies* 53, 1023–1049.

Aidukaite, J 2004, *The emergence of the post-socialist welfare state: The case of the Baltic States: Estonia, Latvia and Lithuania,* Södertörn Doctoral dissertation, Huddinge, Södertörns högskola.

Aidukaite, J 2013, 'Social policy changes in the three Baltic States over the last decade (2000–2012)' *Ekonomika/Economics* 92(3), 84–104.

Bertaud, A 2006 *The spatial structures of Central and Eastern European cities* (pp. 91–110). Physica-Verlag, Heidelberg.

Bleiere, D 2012, 'Eiropa ārpus Eiropa – Dzīve Latvijas PSR' [Life in the Latvian SSR] Riga, University of Latvia Press.

Bohle, D and Greskovits, B 2007, 'Neoliberalism, embedded neoliberalism and neocorporatism: Towards transnational capitalism in Central-Eastern Europe' *West European Politics* 30(3), 443–466.

Brade, I, Herfert, G and Wiest, K 2009, 'Recent trends and future prospects of socio-spatial differentiation in urban regions of Central and Eastern Europe: A lull before the storm?' *Cities* 26(5), 233–244.

Brown, L A and Chung, S Y 2006, 'Spatial segregation, segregation indices and the geographical perspective' *Population, Space and Place* 12(2), 125–143.

Burgers, J and Musterd, S 2002, 'Understanding urban inequality: A model based on existing theories and an empirical illustration' *International Journal of Urban and Regional Research* 26(2), 403–413.

Butler, T, Hamnett, C and Ramsden, M 2008, 'Inward and upward: Marking out social class change in London, 1981–2001' *Urban Studies* 45(1), 67–88.

Cara, O 2010, 'Lives on the border: Language and culture in the lives of ethnic Russian women in Baltinava, Latvia' *Nationalities Papers* 38(1), 123–142.

Duncan, O D and Duncan, B 1955, 'A methodological analysis of segregation indexes' *American Sociological Review*, 210–217.

Fenger, M 2007, 'Welfare regimes in Central and Eastern Europe: Incorporating post-communist countries in a welfare regime typology' *Contemporary Issues and Ideas in Social Sciences* 3(2), 1–30.

French, R A and Hamilton, F I eds 1979, *The socialist city: Spatial structure and urban policy*, Wiley & Sons, Chichester.

Gentile, M and Sjöberg, Ö 2010, 'Spaces of priority: The geography of Soviet housing construction in Daugavpils, Latvia' *Annals of the Association of American Geographers* 100(1), 112–136.

Gentile, M and Tammaru, T 2006, 'Housing and ethnicity in the post-soviet city: Ust'-Kamenogorsk, Kazakhstan' *Urban Studies* 43(10), 1757–1778.

Gentile, M, Tammaru, T and van Kempen, R 2012, 'Heteropolitanization: Social and spatial change in Central and East European Cities' *Cities* 29(5), 291–299.

Grannis, R 2002, 'Discussion: Segregation indices and their functional inputs' *Sociological Methodology* 32(1), 69–84.

Grava, S 2007, 'Urban transport in the Baltic republics' in *The post-socialist city: Urban form and space transformations in Central and Eastern Europe after socialism*, ed. K Stanilov, Springer, Dordrecht, pp. 313–343.

Hazans, M 2007, 'Coping with growth and emigration: Latvian labor market before and after EU accession' *Available at SSRN 971198*. Accessed 15 May 2015.

Hazans, M 2011, 'Labor market integration of ethnic minorities in Latvia' in *Ethnic diversity in European labor markets: Challenges and solutions*, eds M. Kahanec and K F Zimmerman, Cheltenham, Edward Elgar, pp. 163–197.

Hegedus, J, Tosics, I and Turner, B (eds) 2005, *Reform of housing in Eastern Europe and the Soviet Union,* Routledge, London.

Hess, D B, Tammaru, T and Leetmaa, K 2012, 'Ethnic differences in housing in post-Soviet Tartu, Estonia' *Cities* 29(5), 327–333.

Johnston, R, Poulsen, M and Forrest, J 2005, 'On the measurement and meaning of residential segregation: A response to Simpson' *Urban Studies* 42(7), 1221–1227.

Johnston, R, Poulsen, M and Forrest, J 2009, 'Research note – Measuring ethnic residential segregation: Putting some more geography in' *Urban Geography* 30(1), 91–109.

Johnston, R, Poulsen, M and Forrest, J 2010a, 'Moving on from indices, refocusing on mix: On measuring and understanding ethnic patterns of residential segregation' *Journal of Ethnic and Migration Studies* 36(4), 697–706.

Johnston, R, Sirkeci, I, Khattab, N and Modood, T 2010b, 'Ethno-religious categories and measuring occupational attainment in relation to education in England and Wales: A multilevel analysis' *Environment and Planning A* 42(3), 578.

Kabisch, N and Haase, D 2011, 'Diversifying European agglomerations: Evidence of urban population trends for the 21st century' *Population, Space and Place* 17(3), 236–253.

Kährik, A and Tammaru, T 2010, 'Soviet prefabricated panel housing estates: Areas of continued social mix or decline? The case of Tallinn' *Housing Studies* 25(2), 201–219.

Kiss, E 2002, 'Restructuring in the industrial areas of Budapest in the period of transition' *Urban Studies* 39(1), 69–84.

Kovács, Z and Herfert, G 2012, 'Development pathways of large housing estates in post-socialist cities: An international comparison' *Housing Studies* 27(3), 324–342.

Ladányi, J and Szelényi, I 2001, 'The social construction of Roma ethnicity in Bulgaria, Romania and Hungary during market transition' *Review of Sociology* 7(2), 79–89.

Lindemann, K 2009, 'Ethnic inequalities in labour market entry in Estonia: The changing influence of ethnicity and language proficiency on labour market success' Working Paper No. 125, Mannheimer Zentrum fur Europaische Sozialforschung.

Lindemann, K 2013, 'The school performance of the Russian-speaking minority in linguistically divided educational systems: A comparison of Estonia and Latvia' in

Integration and inequality in educational institutions, ed. Michael Windzio, Springer, Dordrecht, pp. 45–69.

Marcińczak, S, Gentile, M, Rufat, S and Chelcea, L 2013, 'Urban geographies of hesitant transition: Tracing socioeconomic segregation in post-Ceauşescu Bucharest' *International Journal of Urban and Regional Research,* 38(4), 1399–1417.

Marcińczak, S, Musterd, S and Stępniak, M 2012, 'Where the grass is greener: Social segregation in three major Polish cities at the beginning of the 21st century' *European Urban and Regional Studies* 19(4), 383–403.

Marcińczak, S and Sagan, I 2011, 'The socio-spatial restructuring of Łódź, Poland' *Urban Studies* 48(9), 1789–1809.

Marcińczak, S, Tammaru, T, Novák, J, Gentile, M, Kovács, Z, Temelová, J, Valatka, V, Kährik, A, and Szabó, B 2015, 'Patterns of socioeconomic segregation in the capital cities of fast-track reforming postsocialist countries' *Annals of the Association of American Geographers* 105(1), 183–202.

Martori, J C and Apparicio, P 2011, 'Changes in spatial patterns of the immigrant population of a southern European metropolis: The case of the Barcelona Metropolitan Area (2001–2008)' *Tijdschrift voor economische en sociale geografie* 102(5), 562–581.

Massey, D S and Denton, N A 1988, 'The dimensions of residential segregation' *Social Forces,* 67(2), 281–315.

Massey D S and Denton N A 1993, *American apartheid: Segregation and the making of the underclass,* Harvard University Press, Cambridge, MA.

Monden, C W and Smits, J 2005, 'Ethnic intermarriage in times of social change: The case of Latvia' *Demography* 42(2), 323–345.

Muiznieks, N, Rozenvalds, J and Birka, I 2013, 'Ethnicity and social cohesion in the post-Soviet Baltic states' *Patterns of Prejudice* 47(3), 288–308.

Musterd, S 2005, 'Social and ethnic segregation in Europe: Levels, causes, and effects' *Journal of Urban Affairs* 27(3), 331–348.

Ott, T 2001, 'From concentration to de-concentration – migration patterns in the post-socialist city' *Cities* 18(6), 403–412.

Ouředníček, M, Pospíšilová, L, Špačková, P, Kopecká, Z and Novák, J 2016, 'The velvet and mild: Socio-spatial differentiation in Prague after transition' in *Socio-economic segregation in European capital cities: East meets West,* eds T. Tammaru, S. Marcińczak, M. van Ham and S. Musterd, Routledge, London.

Paalzow, A, Sauka, A, Pauna, D, Kilis, R, and Dombrovsky, V 2010, *Policies and strategies in Riga: How to enhance the city's competitiveness* 10.9, AMIDSt, University of Amsterdam.

Pabriks, A 2002, *Occupational representation and ethnic discrimination in Latvia,* The Soros Foundation Latvia, Riga, Nordik Publishing House,

Peach, C 1996, 'The meaning of segregation' *Planning Practice and Research* 11(2), 137–150.

Peach, C 2009, 'Slippery segregation: Discovering or manufacturing ghettos?' *Journal of Ethnic and Migration Studies* 35(9), 1381–1395.

Pisarenko, O 2006, 'The acculturation modes of Russian speaking adolescents in Latvia: Perceived discrimination and knowledge of the Latvian language' *Europe-Asia Studies* 58(5), 751–773.

Rajevska, F 2009, 'The welfare system in Latvia after renewing independence' in *The handbook of European welfare systems,* eds K. Schubert, S. Hegelich and U. Bazant, London, Routledge, pp. 328–343.

Reardon, S F 2006, 'A conceptual framework for measuring segregation and its association with population outcomes' in *Methods in social epidemiology*, eds J M Oakes and J S Kaufman, Jossey-Bass, San Francisco, CA, pp. 169–192.

Reardon, S F and Bischoff, K 2011, 'Income inequality and income segregation' *American Journal of Sociology* 116(4), 1092–1153.

Reardon, S F and O'Sullivan, D 2004, 'Measures of spatial segregation' *Sociological Methodology* 34(1), 121–162.

Rozenvalds, J 2010, 'The Soviet heritage and integration policy development since the restoration of independence' in *How integrated is Latvian society? An audit of achievement, failures and challenges*, ed. N Muižnieks, University of Latvia Press, Riga, pp. 33–60.

Ruble, BA 1989, 'Ethnicity and Soviet cities' *Europe-Asia Studies* 41(3), 401–414.

Rukavishnikov, VO 1978, 'Ethnosocial aspects of population distribution in cities of Tataria' *Sociological Research* 17(2), 59–79.

Ruoppila, S 2004, 'Processes of residential differentiation in socialist cities: Literature review on the cases of Budapest, Prague, Tallinn and Warsaw' *European Journal of Spatial Development* 9, 1–24.

Sailer-Fliege, U 1999, 'Characteristics of post-socialist urban transformation in East Central Europe' *GeoJournal* 49(1), 7–16.

Simpson, L 2007, 'Ghettos of the mind: the empirical behaviour of indices of segregation and diversity' *Journal of the Royal Statistical Society: Series A (Statistics in Society)* 170(2), 405–424.

Smith, A and Timár, J 2010, 'Uneven transformations: Space, economy and society 20 years after the collapse of state socialism' *European Urban and Regional Studies* 17(2), 115–125.

Smith, M D 1996, 'The socialist city' in *Cities after socialism: Urban and regional change and conflict in post-socialist societies*, eds G. Andrusz, M. Harloe and I. Szelényi, Blackwell Publishers, Oxford, pp. 70–99.

Smith, A and Timár, J 2010, 'Uneven transformations: Space, economy and society 20 years after the collapse of state socialism' *European Urban and Regional Studies* 17(2), 115–125.

Stanilov, K ed. 2007, *The post-socialist city: Urban form and space transformations in Central and Eastern Europe after socialism*, Springer, Dordrecht.

Steinführer, A and Haase, A 2007, 'Demographic change as a future challenge for cities in East Central Europe' *Geografiska Annaler: Series B, Human Geography* 89(2), 183–195.

Stenning, A 2004, 'Urban change and the localities' in *East Central Europe and the former Soviet Union: The post-socialist states*, eds M. Bradshaw and A. Stenning, Pearson, Harlow, pp. 87–108.

Sýkora, L 1999, 'Processes of socio-spatial differentiation in post-communist Prague' *Housing Studies* 14(5), 679–701.

Sýkora, L and Bouzarovski, S 2012, 'Multiple transformations conceptualising the post-communist urban transition' *Urban Studies* 49(1), 43–60.

Szelényi I 1996, 'Cities under socialism – and after' in *Cities after socialism: urban and regional change and conflict in post-socialist societies*, eds G. Andrusz, M. Harloe and I. Szelényi, Blackwell Publishers, Oxford, pp. 286–317.

Treija S 2009, 'Housing and social cohesion in Latvia' in *Urban sustainability and governance: New challenges in Nordic-Baltic housing policies*, eds A. Holt-Jensen and E Pollock, Nova Science Publishers, New York, pp. 197–207.

Temelová, J, Novák, J, Ouředníček, M and Puldová, P 2011, 'Housing estates in the Czech Republic after socialism: Various trajectories and inner differentiation' *Urban Studies*, 48(9), 1811–1834.

Tsenkova S 2005, 'Latvia' in *Urban issues and urban policies in the new EU countries*, eds R van Kempen, M Vermeulen and A Baan, Ashgate, Aldershot.

Turok, I and Mykhnenko, V 2007, 'The trajectories of European cities, 1960–2005' *Cities* 24(3), 165–182.

Vendina, OI 1997, 'Transformation processes in Moscow and intra-urban stratification of population' *GeoJournal* 42(4), 349–363.

13 Large social inequalities and low levels of socio-economic segregation in Vilnius

Vytautas Valatka, Donatas Burneika and Rūta Ubarevičienė

Abstract

The city of Vilnius has experienced major shifts in occupational structure between 2001 and 2011 and at the same time there were major transitions in the housing market and suburbanisation. The main aim of this chapter is to get more insight in recent socio-economic segregation processes in Vilnius. We used occupational groups as a proxy for socio-economic status, and census tract level data to measure segregation in Vilnius and its three main housing zones during 2001 and 2011. Notwithstanding the major economic and social changes in post-communist society, we found low levels of segregation and modest change during the last decade. Local patterns of segregation were explored using location quotient maps. The analyses illustrated a deepening social divide in the city between the relatively rich north and the poorer south of the city, but the inner city changes are somehow ambiguous. In this chapter we argue that the main factors of socio-spatial change in Vilnius are related to an exceptionally high share of housing estates in the city and the polycentric urban system of the country. Together with 'fast-track' reforms after 1990 this urban system gave a unique character to the current processes and patterns of segregation.

Introduction

Vilnius, the capital of Lithuania (536.000 inhabitants in 2011), was greatly reshaped by processes of massive industrialisation and urbanisation during the communist period (Vanagas *et al.* 2002). The post-1990 period was also characterised by massive urban transitions triggered by reforms to a market-led neo-liberal economy (Aidukaitė 2014; Brade *et al.* 2009). These recent transitions resulted in an annihilation of public-housing policies and fast urban sprawl, stimulated by loosely regulated suburbanisation. At the same time fundamental changes took place in the Lithuanian society and economy, resulting in a changing occupational structure and an increase in social inequalities. It is likely that these inequalities also have a spatial dimension, but to date there has been no systematic research into the changing socio-spatial patterns of post-communist Vilnius.

The city of Vilnius, compared to other capital cities of Central and Eastern European (CEE) countries, has some unique characteristics that are shaped by its mutually dependant historical pathway and geographical situation. The capital city is located in the eastern part of Lithuania, just 30 km from the Belarus border. The deep valleys of the Neris and Vilnelė rivers, which penetrate the city, create a fragmented urban structure and land-use pattern. Due to the Holocaust and post-World War II repatriation of the Polish population of Vilnius, which previously constituted the majority of the residents in the city, Vilnius hardly has an inherited social structure from the pre-war period (Czerniakiewicz and Cerniakiewicz 2007; Eberhardt 2011; Mendelsohn 1983; Weeks 2008). Combined with the Soviet period of industrialisation and associated migration flows, this created a unique ethnic landscape of the Vilnius urban area: the city is dominated by migrants and their descendants from within Lithuania as well as from the other former republics of the Soviet Union (USSR), while the Polish population dominates in the poor region surrounding the city (Ubarevičienė *et al.* 2015). Another unique feature of Vilnius is its position in the settlement system of Lithuania. As a consequence of Soviet planning, the Lithuanian urban network was centralised to a much lesser degree than was the case in the other two Baltic countries of Estonia and Latvia. Since the 1990s this has resulted in the larger flows of inner migration directed towards the capital city and thus play an important role in the socio-spatial transformation of the country.

The main aim of this chapter is to get more insight into recent socio-economic segregation processes in the Vilnius city municipality (later, simply Vilnius or the city). Although we would have liked to focus on the surrounding region as well, data limitations forced us to concentrate on the city itself. Nevertheless, the processes that are taking place in the wider urban region will also be discussed because of their increasing importance. The chapter addresses the following three research questions:

1   How did the occupational structure of the population of Vilnius city change between 2001 and 2011 censuses? Is there evidence of polarisation or professionalisation of the workforce?
2   Do we find evidence of increasing or decreasing levels of occupational segregation in the 2000s following the growth of social inequalities since the 1990s?
3   How do the segregation processes vary between the city zones (inner city, large housing estates, outer city)?

In the next sections of this chapter we will present the wider historical and geographical context of Vilnius and the development of the labour and housing markets. The empirical investigation of changes in the social segregation of Vilnius is based on 2001 and 2011 censuses. We use ISCO occupational groups as proxy for socio-economic status. There is no data available on income at a low geographical level. We focus on comparing three major housing zones in the city: the inner city, large housing estates and the outer ring of the city. These three housing zones partly correspond with three major cycles of the urban growth. We hypothesise that large housing estates of the Soviet period, designed to facilitate communist society, play a noticeable role in preventing segregation processes in Vilnius.

Specific historical and geographical features

The history of Vilnius, and especially the frequent shifts of political borders in the twentieth century, has had a huge impact on the development of the urban structure of the city. Vilnius belonged to Russia, Germany, Lithuania, Poland, Lithuania, the Soviet Union, Germany, the Soviet Union and Lithuania during the last century. This means that the role of Vilnius in the hierarchy of the urban system was in constant flux. The inner city was built mainly before the beginning of the twentieth century when Vilnius was part of the Russian Empire, and this period corresponded with the first wave of industrialisation. The city centre, the first industrial districts, poor working-class neighbourhoods and rich nearby villa districts emerged and they form the backbone of the inner city of today's Vilnius. The construction of the railway from St Petersburg to Warsaw at the end of the nineteenth century also had an effect on the existing urban fabric. As a result, industrial areas and exclusively working-class neighbourhoods emerged mostly in the southern part, while more affluent residential neighbourhoods are located in the northern part of the city. This division is visible up to the present day.

During the interwar period, the growth of Vilnius was limited. The Vilnius region was subsumed under Polish governance and thus disconnected from the rest of Lithuania. The construction of owner-occupied single-family dwellings was minimal during this period unlike what happened in the other two Baltic capitals of Tallinn and Riga. The construction of single-family houses was also constrained in the Soviet period as large housing estates became the dominant form of housing. As a result, now only 15 per cent of the total living floor space in Vilnius is in buildings with one or two dwellings, and in 1990 in Vilnius the living space per capita was one of the smallest in the entire CEE (16 sq. m.).

Political shifts in the twentieth century also caused major and sudden changes in migration flows, the size of the urban population and its ethnic composition (Stanaitis and Česnavičius 2010). The population of Vilnius decreased from 270,000 in 1941, and down to as low as 110,000 in 1944 as the city shifted from German to the Soviet powers. In this period the number of Jews decreased from 57,000 to 2,000 because of the Holocaust (Mendelsohn 1983), and about 107,000 of the former Polish citizens who had constituted the majority of the city's population before World War II left Vilnius in 1945–1947 (Czerniakiewicz and Cerniakiewicz 2007; Eberhardt 2011).

The post-war mass industrialisation accelerated the growth of Vilnius city and led to a rapid increase of its population. The city received many in-migrants from other parts of Lithuania but also from the USSR, mainly from Russia. However, the proportion of in-migrants from the Soviet Union was much less compared to Riga and Tallinn. The region surrounding Vilnius has experienced many fewer social transformations, a unique ethnic landscape, characterised by a large ethnic segregation between the city and its surroundings, was created (Figure 13.1).

Lithuanians form the majority of the Vilnius population, while sizeable parts of the suburban ring are dominated by Poles. Ethnic segregation is marked in the city as well (Figure 13.1). Although this fragmentation is clearly visible at the

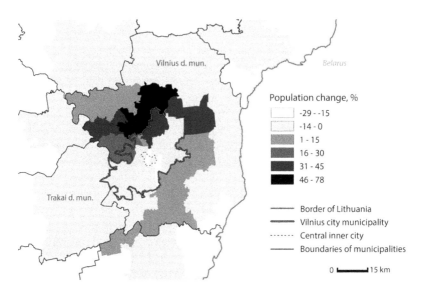

Figure 13.1 Ethnic fragmentation of the Vilnius urban region.

Source: Census 2011, Statistics Lithuania, authors' maps.

lowest spatial level (census tracts), it is less expressed on the higher level of LAU 2 regions (city districts). In 2011 there were no LAU 2 regions (out of a total of 21 in the city; see Figure 13.3) where Lithuanians accounted for less than 50 per cent of the population. It has to be mentioned that the northern part of the city has a larger portion of Lithuanians than the industrial southern part. While pre-empting the further outcomes of this research, we can state that the patterns of ethnic composition in Vilnius largely correspond with the distribution of the highest and lowest social status groups, indicating that there is an ethnic dimension in the socio-economic segregation in Vilnius.

Spatial planning and development in Lithuania during the Soviet period was dominated by policies directed at creating a 'unified settlement system', guided by the slogan 'erode the differences between city and country while building communism'. As a result of this policy, industry was spread throughout Lithuania during the Soviet period. The policy was based on the modified ideas of German geographer Christaller (Vanagas 2003) and the aim was to create a society with no spatial differences in terms of social and economic structure across the whole country. A polycentric urban network without a clear dominance of a single metropolitan region was created in Lithuania. Contemporary Vilnius has around 17 per cent of the country's population, while Riga and Tallinn have approximately a third of their national populations. Since 1990, when Lithuania regained independence from the Soviet Union, the country has experienced a period of metropolisation, resulting in the relative growth of the Vilnius population, and a shrinkage of rural areas and medium-sized cities as a result of internal migration processes. We stress that this is the relative growth as, overall, Vilnius lost 7.6 per cent of its population between 1996 and 2012, while other major cities lost more than 20 per cent because of natural decrease and emigration (the Lithuanian average was minus 16 per cent) (Statistics Lithuania 2014). The suburban areas surrounding the largest cities were the only areas in the country that gained population (Ubarevičienė *et al.* 2014). Although between 2001 and 2011 the total population in the Vilnius metropolitan area was growing due to the urban sprawl, the central city was shrinking (Figure 13.2).

The process of suburbanisation around Vilnius is largely unregulated and has an irregular pattern. Until 2011 the most intense suburbanisation had been taking place next to the city's administrative border, but new suburban settlements could be found as far as 40 km from the city centre (Ubarevičienė *et al.* 2011). Albeit the suburban zone contains a small fraction of the total urban population, socio-economically it is an important, integral part of the Vilnius housing market and, hence, of segregation processes. Therefore we will also discuss the processes that are taking place in the wider urban region.

The contemporary housing market in Vilnius

Residential mobility plays a dominant role in segregation processes and the housing market is an important factor influencing the location decisions of the population. More than 96 per cent of all dwellings in Vilnius are privately owned (Statistics Lithuania 2014). This is a consequence of voucher privatisation in the early 1990s and an absence of an active social housing policy. Only around 3 per cent

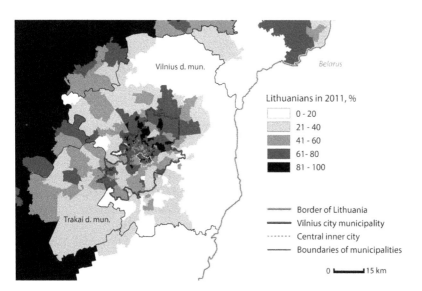

Figure 13.2 Population change in the Vilnius urban region, 2001–2011.

Source: Census 2001, 2011, Statistics Lithuania, authors' maps.

of non-privatised housing stock is social housing in Vilnius, and therefore it does not have much influence on the functioning of the regional housing market. Most of the social housing in Vilnius is located in the central part of the city and has low rents, housing the lowest-income households.

Limited land supply has also had an impact on the housing market in Vilnius. Forests, where changes of land use are largely prohibited, cover more than 40 per cent of the city's territory. New constructions are also strictly regulated in the Old Town, protected by the cultural heritage regulations. As a result, new residential construction is taking place in former industrial sites and empty areas in the inner city, and there is weakly controlled and dispersed sprawl of privately owned housing far beyond the city limits.

Banks play a significant role in the housing market as they control mortgages. As Harvey (2009) argued, an ability to obtain bank credit often makes a greater impact on housing decisions than savings or salaries. In Vilnius, it is easier to obtain a loan for a newly constructed dwelling as it is possible to take out a loan of up to 95 per cent of the dwelling's price if a property is no more than ten years old. To take out a loan for an older apartment, no more than 75 per cent can be borrowed. The loan policy and relatively high real estate prices encouraged middle-class and higher-income households to purchase apartments in new high-rise neighbourhoods developed in the former outer-city zone areas instead of older apartments at similar prices in the more central locations. This resulted in the vast construction of densely built-up multi-storey apartment neighbourhoods at the edge of the city. At the same time, favourable conditions for this housing boom were created by the rapidly growing number of higher-status groups in Vilnius, many of whom settled in the northern part of the city where the new developments were concentrated. It has to be noted that these processes are still relatively small since only 6.7 per cent of all households who owned their house had mortgages in 2011 (compared to 17 per cent in Estonia and 18 per cent in the Czech Republic) (Aidukaitė 2014).

A large inflow of internal migrants from other parts of Lithuania (more than 130,000 during 1994–2011) and a malfunctioning official housing rental market have been other major factors influencing the housing market in Vilnius. Data from the Lithuanian State Tax Inspectorate (2014) showed that 25–30 per cent of employees in Vilnius (70–80,000) are not registered as inhabitants of the city. The study of Tereškinas *et al.* (2013) found that almost a quarter of the population of the inner city live in rented housing, while only some 1,500 business certificates to rent housing are issued in Vilnius yearly. It is likely that some of these unregistered employees reside in the rented dwellings without a legal agreement and have a significant impact on the social segregation within the city.

Finally, heating cost compensation, an instrument of state social policy, has an impact on the functioning of the housing market and therefore segregation. According to the policy, households should not spend more than 20 per cent of their income on heating costs. Otherwise for poor households, in older apartments built in the Soviet period, heating costs would exceed their income in winter time. As a result of this compensation, lower-income groups (for example pensioners) can afford to live in expensive districts and large apartments. The compensations for heating preserve an existing residential structure by reducing market pressure on low-income residents to exchange their current dwellings for smaller and cheaper ones. Therefore, changing segregation patterns in Vilnius are mainly caused by the mobility of more affluent population groups.

Socio-economic segregation in Lithuania

The combined effects of major political, economic and social transitions have resulted in a large-scale socio-spatial transformation in the CEE countries since the early 1990s (Brade *et al.* 2009; Marcińczak 2012; Musil 1993; Sýkora 1999; Sýkora and Bouzarovski 2012; Ubarevičienė *et al.* 2011). Research that directly addresses issues of housing and socio-economic segregation in Lithuania has only been carried out recently (Krupickaitė 2014; Žilys 2013; Tereškinas *et al.* 2013). The survey-based study of Krupickaitė (2014) showed that most of the suburban residents have a higher socio-economic status (in terms of income and education). Results also demonstrate that the inner-city neighbourhoods are very dynamic: 50 per cent of the respondents living in the inner city have moved there in the last ten years, confirming the ongoing gentrification process. The least mobile population are those living in the typical high-rise multifamily apartments of the Soviet era (Krupickaitė 2014). Tereškinas *et al.* (2013) and Žilys (2013) found, also based on survey data, that levels of segregation are low in Vilnius.

The study that is most related to this chapter was made by Marcińczak *et al.* (2015). It employed 2001 census data and compared segregation in the CEE capital cities, including Vilnius. Some interesting differences between Vilnius and other capitals of CEE countries were found in this study: Vilnius had the lowest share of the middle-status and the highest share of low socio-economic status groups. It was also identified as having the highest share of 'bipolar neighbourhoods', where high- and low-status occupational groups live together. Our research could be regarded as a continuation of this study, based on recently released 2011 census data.

Data and methods

We base our quantitative analysis of socio-economic segregation processes in Vilnius on 2001 and 2011census data at the level of census tracts. Both of the censuses were carried out during the post-crisis periods and therefore represent periods of modest economic growth. The Asian–Russian crisis (1998–1999) mostly affected the peripheral parts of the country, while the global economic crisis (2008–2010) had a stronger influence on the development of the main cities, especially Vilnius. The labour market was stagnant and emigration was high during both census periods.

Our study focuses on the Vilnius city municipality within its administrative limits. Although data limitations do not allow us to analyse the wider urban region, the recent process of urban sprawl and some effects of suburbanisation on the socio-economic segregation are illustrated using data at the level of local administrative units (LAU 2) (Figure 13.1 and Figure 13.2). On the other hand, a significant part of the suburbanisation took place within the city limits, where the vast majority of the Vilnius region's population live.

We distinguished three major housing zones in Vilnius that differ in their housing stock, period of construction and location. Then we used census tract data to measure global indices of segregation in these three zones for both 2001 and 2011: indices of segregation, dissimilarity and isolation (see also the introduction of this book for more detail: Tammaru *et al.* 2016). We also created location quotient maps, illustrating differences in concentration of higher and lower occupational groups between the census tracts in Vilnius in 2001 and 2011. Our analysis is based on occupational data, where the main ISCO groups are used as a proxy for socio-economic status. Although occupation does not necessarily reflect income, the national labour force survey of 2010 (Statistics Lithuania 2014) showed that the differences in incomes between occupational groups are significant.

To make indices and spatial units comparable between the censuses we had to aggregate census organisational units (enumerator areas), which differed in 2001 and 2011. For this purpose we used AZTool software developed at the University of Southampton (Martin 2003; Cockings *et al.* 2011) based on Openshaw's work (1977) on automated zoning procedures. As a result we got 'census tracts' with an average size of 1,081 persons in 2001 and 1,143 in 2011. The limits of the census tracts in 2001 and 2011 do not correspond completely; therefore minor changes in location quotient maps of different years could be attributed to these border changes, and not to actual changes in the social structure. However, this does not affect the general picture of socio-economic segregation in Vilnius.

The housing zones of Vilnius

We categorised census tracts into three major housing zones according to the dominant housing type, density of population, period of construction and location (Figure 13.3). We distinguished the inner city, large housing estates and the outer ring of the city. The inner city could be divided into two parts. The central inner city covers the most prestigious locations of the historical city and former villa areas. The remaining part of the inner city consists of the oldest working-class neighbourhoods. The housing estate zone consists of high-rise multi-family buildings (5–12 storey) and houses around 70 per cent of the Vilnius population. The quality of housing increases with distance from the city centre, but the price levels are quite similar within this zone. The outer city is dominated by low-density single-family neighbourhoods and extends beyond the city limits. It includes newly suburbanised areas, old collective gardens (*datcha*), previous satellite towns, industrial areas and rural settlements that were recently incorporated into the city limits. There is a great division between the southern industrialised part, which includes former rural and suburban settlements with relatively low-quality housing, and the northern part, where new and more expensive single-family houses dominate.

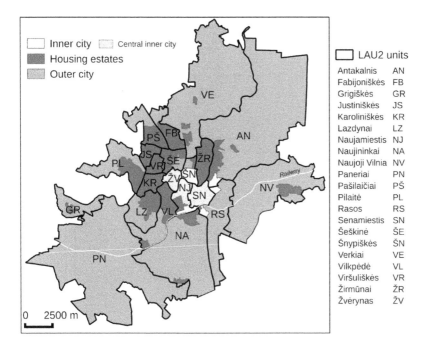

Figure 13.3 Main housing zones and LAU 2 regions of Vilnius.

Source: Census 2011, Statistics Lithuania, authors' map.

Different zones showed different trends in population change in the post-Soviet period. Since the early 1990s the sharpest population decline occurred in the inner city. It lost 40 per cent of its population between 1992 and 2011. This was mostly related to the process of commercialisation, when the housing function was taken over by offices, shops and catering establishments. An improvement in living conditions (increasing floor space) in the prestigious central locations was an important factor as well. The zone of large housing estates saw a population decline of around 15 per cent since 1992. At the same time, the population was constantly increasing in the outer city due to the process of suburbanisation: in some LAU 2 regions the population doubled between 2001 and 2011.

Labour market and occupational structure

After the 'full employment' in the Soviet-era, 40 per cent of jobs in Lithuania were lost between 1989 and 2001, mainly in industry (loss of 260,000), construction (130,000) and agriculture (120,000) (Statistics Lithuania 2014). In Vilnius, the number of workplaces decreased by 25 per cent during this period. It took several years for the economy to recover, until new economic sectors (business and other services first of all) started to develop and bring down the levels of unemployment. Employment and earnings grew rapidly and steadily in all economic sectors

Table 13.1 Changes in the occupational groups in Vilnius between 2001 and 2011

Abbr.	ISCO	Occupational group	2001	2011	2001–2011	2001–2011	2001	2011	2001–2011
			000s	000s	000s	%	%	%	pp
MAN	1	Managers	28,4	37,5	9,1	**32**	11.1	13.6	2.5
PRO	2	Professionals	55,0	80,3	25,3	**46**	21.4	29	7.6
APR	3	Associate professionals	27,0	27,5	0,5	2	10.5	10	-0.5
CLE	4	Clerks	11,7	11,0	-0,8	-7	4.6	4	-0.6
SER	5	Service workers	27,5	28,1	0,6	2	10.7	10.2	-0.5
CRA	7	Craft workers	30,6	23,3	-7,3	**-24**	11.9	8.4	-3.5
MAC	8	Machine operators	19,4	14,0	-5,4	**-28**	7.6	5.1	-2.5
UNS	9	Unskilled workers	15,5	15,6	0,1	1	6.1	5.7	-0.4
UNE	–	Unemployed	41,5	39,2	-2,3	-6	16.2	14.2	-2
		Total	256,6	276,4	19,8	8	100	100	
		Aggregated data							
	1–2	High	83,4	117,8	34,4	41	32.5	42.6	10.1
	3–4	Middle	38,7	38,5	-0,2	-1	15.1	14	-1.1
	5–9	Low (unemployed included)	134,5	120,1	-14,4	-11	52.5	43.6	-8.9
		Missing data							
		Occupation not indicated	26,1	14,5	-11,5	-44	12.1	6.2	-5.9
		Total employed	241,2	251,8	10,6	4.4			

Source: Census 2001, 2011, Statistics Lithuania, authors' table.

of Lithuania between 2001 and 2008. However, this growth had almost no effect on the income gap, which, according to the Gini index was constantly among the highest in the European Union (Eurostat 2014). For example, the gross salary of managers was 3.4 times higher than that of unskilled workers in 2010 (Statistics Lithuania 2014). That is more than in other Baltic States (2.6–2.9), but less than in most of the CEE countries (3.6–4.0).

Significant transformations of the occupational structure took place in Vilnius during the first decade of the twenty-first century (Table 13.1). First of all, there was a sharp increase of high occupational groups: a 32 per cent increase for managers and 46 per cent for professionals. In contrast, there was a decrease in low occupational status groups: minus 24 per cent for craft workers and minus 28 per cent for machine operators (an exception is a slight increase for service workers).The increase of high-status groups is illustrative for a concentration of capital and high-value-added economic sectors in the capital city; in Lithuania as a whole, the share of managers increased by 2 per cent and the share of professionals increased by 5 per cent. The decrease of the low-status group (it was the largest group previously) can be explained by shrinking construction and related industry sectors, as a result of the global economic crisis (this resulted in a peak of emigration in 2010) and deindustrialisation.

Occupational segregation in Vilnius according to the global indices

This section presents the main findings of occupational segregation in Vilnius and its main housing zones. We use an index of segregation (IS) and index of dissimilarity (ID) to study the evenness, and an index of isolation (II) to study the exposure dimension of occupational segregation. The values of all analysed global indices were low in Vilnius in 2001. This means that the representatives of different occupational groups were distributed quite evenly throughout the city and had a high chance to meet each other in each neighbourhood. A specific feature of Vilnius, compared to other CEE countries, was the high share of bipolar neighbourhoods: 34 per cent higher than in Tallinn and much more than in Budapest, Prague or Warsaw (Marcińczak *et al.* 2015). Hypothetically this could be explained by social differences within the occupational groups, which means that occupationally bipolar areas do not necessarily reflect income polarisation. It is likely that the housing estates are inhabited by middle- and low-income population from all professional groups (this could also be confirmed by an absence of higher-class cars in the courtyards of these neighbourhoods). Additionally, a high degree of homogeneity (in terms of balance between quality, price levels, prestige, accessibility, etc.) of the housing estates does not create substantially higher or lower demand for certain locations and therefore there is no strong sorting factor for different occupational groups. The lowest-income groups could afford living in the Soviet-era housing estates because of the previously mentioned heating compensation mechanism.

The analysis of IS for the city as a whole shows only minor changes in the evenness of distribution over the ten-year period (Figure 13.4, above). Segregation was still low in 2011 (below 20 for all occupational groups). There was only a modest increase among the middle- and lower- occupational groups and segregation remained constant for the highest-occupational groups. However, we find that the overall city-wide picture masks more detailed processes in the different housing zones; segregation is higher in the inner city and outer city compared to the housing estates. (Figure 13.4, bottom). Furthermore, we can observe an increased evenness of distribution of the higher-occupational groups in the inner city and outer city. There is a different situation in the case of the lower-occupational groups. Their IS increased slightly in the housing estates and inner city (service workers were an exception – for them IS increased by 6 per cent in the inner city) but substantially in the outer city. This shift together, with the decrease of IS for the higher-status groups, led to a situation where the lower-occupational groups were least evenly distributed in 2011, especially in the outer city. The changes did not have a clear structure for the middle groups; IS mainly decreased for associate professionals and increased for clerks.

New housing construction which took place during 2001–2011 often had an infill character. Higher-quality new housing stock is scattered around the whole city and is not concentrated in a specific area. The previously mentioned mechanism of compensation for heating costs reduces any incentives for lowe-income homeowners to move out from their 'luxury' (usually in terms of space) apartments. Additionally, the loan policy of banks is redistributing the higher-income groups (especially young families with small savings) to the new housing estates,

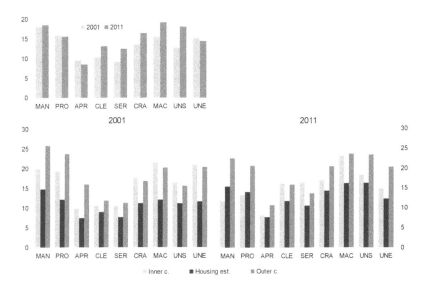

Figure 13.4 Indices of segregation.

Source: Census 2001, 2011, Statistics Lithuania, authors' graph.

mostly located in the periphery of the city. To sum up, socio-economic segregation in Vilnius is strongly conditioned by the housing estates, which have bipolar occupational structure reaching the higher levels in the outer city. IS would be higher if the study included the suburban neighbourhoods outside the city limits, where the higher social groups strongly dominate (Krupickaitė 2014). Global measurements of IS are not always sufficient when trying to evaluate ongoing processes under such circumstances, because growing uniformity in some areas may mask growing inequalities in others.

While the city-wide index of segregation is below 20 in Vilnius, which means even distribution of occupational groups, the index of dissimilarity (ID) tells a different story. Figure 13.5 shows the ID for different occupational group combinations in 2001 (ID values in the lower triangles) and 2011 (ID values in the higher triangles). The most evident trend (although not unexpected) is the increasing separation of the highest-occupational groups from the lowest- occupational groups. The growth between social and spatial distance is also visible in the housing estates' zone. Although the separation between managers and professionals was already low in 2001, it reduced even more in 2011. This implies that the higher-status groups moved closer to each other in all parts of the city. This might also explain why the IS did not increase for managers as much as, for example, in Tallinn (Tammaru *et al.* 2016).

Next we will analyse the exposure dimension of segregation. Figure 13.6 shows the distribution of occupational groups within the city in 2001 and 2011. The results show high and increasing levels of isolation for the higher-occupational groups. This trend is in line with previously established concentrations of the higher socio-economic groups in the most attractive locations of Vilnius (especially managers in the central

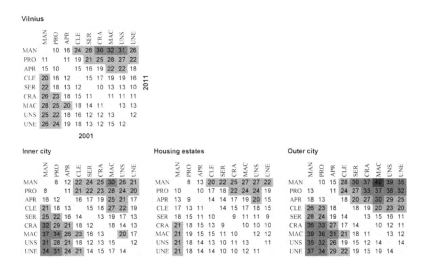

Figure 13.5 Indices of dissimilarity.

Source: Census 2001, 2011, Statistics Lithuania, authors' table.

inner city and suburbs). Apparently all occupational groups, except the higher ones, tend to live less isolated from each other. The lower the occupational status, the less isolated they are in all housing zones. The profiles in Figure 13.6 permit us to speculate that the higher-occupational groups are more residentially mobile than the lower-occupational groups. Though most of the groups are quite evenly distributed across the city, their isolation from each other is high within the neighbourhoods. Higher-occupational groups are large in Vilnius (Table 13.1), which mainly explains why they are strongly isolated from the rest of the workforce; i.e. they mainly potentially meet own-group members in the neighbourhoods they live in.

When analysing changes in the different housing zones, it can be seen that the higher-occupational groups experienced the fastest growth of spatial isolation in all of them. In 2011, managers' isolation in the outer city exceeded their previous isolation in the inner city, which could be seen as a sign of 'elite' suburbanisation. The middle-status groups are the most stable and the most evenly distributed in Vilnius. Two low-occupational groups (craft workers and machine operators) became less isolated in the inner and outer city in comparison to the housing estates. It could be an outcome of the overall decrease of their proportion in the occupational structure.

To sum up, our results show the growth of spatial isolation of higher-occupational groups, while isolation of the other groups is decreasing. Most likely this happened due to a growing share of managers and professionals in the workforce. The results also show a relatively low and stable isolation of the middle-status groups, with a moderate and increasing spatial separation of the higher-occupational groups.

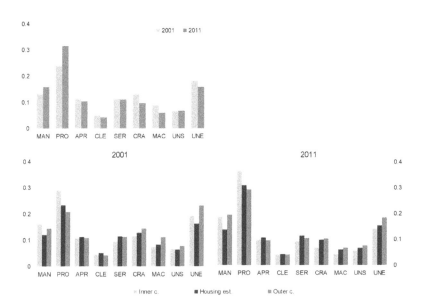

Figure 13.6 Indices of isolation.

Source: Census 2001, 2011, Statistics Lithuania, authors' figures.

Changing local patterns of segregation

Finally, we will analyse the geography of segregation by using location quotient (LQ) maps. This is a way of quantifying how concentrated a particular group is in a certain area compared to its concentration in the city as a whole. We have already established that a more uniform distribution of the higher-occupational groups was caused by their overall increase in the occupational structure of Vilnius. At the same time Figure 13.7 shows that they live in the most attractive locations in the inner and outer city. The concentration of the highest-status groups is the biggest (and growing) in the northern part of the outer city. We also observe their concentration in the peripheral parts of the southern outer city, but not in its more central industrial areas. Managers and professionals also spread into the formerly low-status areas within the inner city (former working-class neighbourhoods). This is why their distribution became more even there despite growing isolation from other groups in each neighbourhood. An increasing concentration of managers and professionals is visible in the tracts with the biggest post-Soviet housing estates. These are the new in-built neighbourhoods, mostly in the northern part of the city and formerly uninhabited areas next to the inner city. The concentration of higher groups is decreasing in the most typical Soviet-era neighbourhoods in the western part of the housing estate zone (Lazdynai, Karoliniškės; see Figure 13.3) and some northern areas (Fabijoniškės, Antakalnis). These are the only areas where the number of managers was dropping notwithstanding their general increase by 32 per cent in Vilnius.

The middle-occupational groups are the smallest and least segregated in Vilnius (map is not shown). The LQs for the unskilled workers (Figure 13.8) are higher than for most other groups and as high as in the case of managers. Unsurprisingly, the distribution of the unskilled is very different compared to the highest-occupational groups. The concentrations of unskilled workers in the southern and the least-attractive northern locations of the outer city (often old settlements with mixed

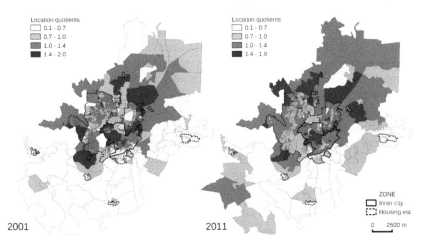

Figure 13.7 Location quotient maps for the managers and professionals.

Source: Census 2001, 2011, Statistics Lithuania, authors' maps.

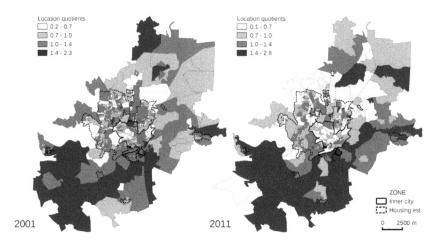

Figure 13.8 Location quotient maps for the unskilled workers.

Source: Census 2001, 2011, Statistics Lithuania, authors' maps.

ethnic composition) increased, and as a result a sharp gradient between the north and south of the city developed. Apparently because of the rising rental prices, lower-occupational groups are being pushed out of the city centre to more distant locations, especially to the south.

Finally, an important issue is the growing concentration of the low-status workers in the declining housing estates. We identified the main concentration areas of the low-status workers. The first and largest one covers almost the entire southern part of the city; the concentration of the low-status group was high and increasing there. Traditionally it has been a low-status area located to the south of the railway that is dominated by the sparsely populated industrial zones and involves only a few housing estate tracts. The concentration of the low-status workers is also increasing in the tracts of the quite central Soviet-era district Žirmūnai, built in the early 1970s, and it is most likely related to the former low-skilled workers' hostels, which are concentrated near the former industrial facilities. The increasing share of the low-status workers is also noticeable in the relatively new densely built-up Soviet-era neighbourhood Šeškinė (see Figure 13.3). Most of the 'darker' exclaves outside the core city are the former satellite settlements with their distinctive inherited social and ethnic structure and low-quality housing stock. One of the typical evidences of segregation processes could be illustrated by the deconcentration of the low-skilled groups from the northern part of the outer city close to the housing estate zone. These locations are attractive for the suburban developments and therefore the low-status population is being displaced (LQ below 0.7).

Conclusions and discussion

Like other East European capital cities, Vilnius experienced significant changes in its socio-spatial structure during the last decades. The processes of suburbanisation, gentrification and the professionalisation of the workforce made us expect increasing socio-economic segregation in Vilnius. Our main findings are as follows. The index of segregation, which indicates how evenly occupational groups are distributed across the city space, showed that segregation in Vilnius is low and quite stable, with a minor trend of growing inequality in the distribution of the middle- and lower-occupational groups and stability of higher-occupational groups. On the housing zone level we found an increasing concentration of wealthy households in the inner city and suburbs. The index of dissimilarity, which compares a distribution of two selected groups, showed the increase of spatial distance between lower- and higher-occupational groups. The exposure dimension brought this out even more clearly: the isolation for the higher-occupational groups increased significantly in the 2000s, while it decreased for other occupational groups. This is a result of residential mobility of more affluent households, which concentrate in the best inner and outer city locations.

We also used location quotient maps to explore the local patterns of occupational segregation. Like segregation indices, the maps showed the concentration of higher-occupational groups in the inner city and in the suburban zone in parallel with shrinkage of the middle- and lower-occupational groups there. The inner city is undergoing a wave of gentrification, since the share of professionals is increasing even in the formerly lowest-status areas. The middle-occupational groups have been dispersed throughout the rest of the city. The typical Soviet-era estates have lost more affluent groups. The lower-occupational groups tend to concentrate in less-attractive southern parts of the city and more distant areas, including the former satellite settlements, which is a sign of increasing deprivation in the worse locations. We find that lower- and higher-occupational groups are still living side by side in the large Soviet-era housing estates, but trends of change in the specific parts of the city are in line with the existing literature, stating that growing social inequalities will result in higher segregation. Finally, our results show that the historical divide between the relatively rich north and the poor south of the city is deepening. The corresponding pattern of the distribution of ethnic minorities permits us to speculate about the ethnic dimension of the socio-economic segregation as well.

In general, our results show that the socio-spatial structure in Vilnius is quite stable. This could be explained by an exceptionally high share of large housing estates, a concentration of workers in Vilnius from all over the country, the state social policy (heating subsidies) and the low supply of new higher-quality housing across the city. The absence of more rapid segregation could also be related to the low incomes of most of the occupational groups (low-middle, middle and even high-middle). The majority of households cannot afford anything other than an apartment in the Soviet-era or new economy-class housing estates. Such a situation keeps the demand for the ageing Soviet-era housing estates stable and prevents them from degradation.

To conclude, the legacy of the Soviet-era settlement system, without a strong dominance of a capital city, and an exceptionally large share of housing estates with their uniform character, have created special conditions for the socio-economic segregation of Vilnius. Our results show the main outcomes of socio-economic segregation under the conditions where market forces work in conjunction with a weak welfare state and a limited supply of high-quality housing. The Soviet-era housing estates, especially those in the more distant locations where the population is ageing, become stagnant and unattractive for younger or more affluent people. The contemporary state of such housing might be called the 'calm before the storm' because the demand for such housing could drop drastically as incomes of higher- and middle-occupational groups start to increase. This would result in large-scale deprivation and an intense growth of city-wide segregation in Vilnius.

Acknowledgments

This research was funded by a grant (agreement No. MIP 086/2014) from the Research Council of Lithuania. The authors are grateful to Maarten van Ham and Tiit Tammaru for their highly useful comments and suggestions about earlier drafts of this chapter. The authors also thank Statistics Lithuania for providing the census data. Some of Ruta's Ubarevičienė's time working on the research reported in this chapter has been funded by the Marie Curie programme under the European Union's Seventh Framework Programme (FP/2007-2013)/Career Integration Grant no. PCIG10-GA-2011-303728 (CIG Grant NBHCHOICE, Neighbourhood Choice, Neighbourhood Sorting, and Neighbourhood Effects).

References

Aidukaitė, J 2014, 'Housing policy regime in Lithuania: Towards liberalization and marketization' *GeoJournal* 79(4), 421–432.

Brade, I, Herfert, G and Wiest, K 2009, 'Recent trends and future prospects of socio-spatial differentiation in urban regions of Central and Eastern Europe: A lull before the storm?' *Cities* 26 (5), 233–244.

Cockings, S, Harfoot, D, Martin, D and Hornby, D 2011, 'Maintaining existing zoning systems using automated zone design techniques: Methods for creating the 2011 census output geographies for England and Wales' *Environment and Planning A* 43(10), 2399–2418.

Czerniakiewicz, J and Czerniekiewicz, M 2007, *Resettlements from the East 1944–1959*, Wydawnictwo Wyszej Szckoly Pedagogicznej TWP, Warsaw.

Eberhardt, P 2011, *Political migrations on Polish territories* (1939–1950), Polska akademia nauk, Warszaw.

Eurostat 2014, available online: http://epp.eurostat.ec.europa.eu/ Last accessed 27 April 2015.

Harvey, D 2009, *Social justice and the city.* Revised edition, University of Georgia Press, Athens.

Krupickaitė, D 2014, 'Vilnius – between persistence and socio spatial change' *Europa Regional* 3–4, 21–31.

Marcińczak, S 2012, 'The evolution of spatial patterns of residential segregation in Central European cities: The Łódź Functional Urban Region from mature socialism to mature post-socialism' *cities* 29(5), 300–309.

Marcińczak, S, Tammaru, T, Novák, J, Gentile, M, Kovács, Z, Temelová, J, Valatka, V, Kährik, A and Szabó, B 2015, 'Patterns of socioeconomic segregation in the capital cities of fast-track reforming postsocialist countries' *Annals of the Association of American Geographers* 105(1), 183–202.

Martin, D 2003, 'Extending the automated zoning procedure to reconcile incompatible zoning systems' *International Journal of Geographical Information Science* 17, 181–196.

Mendelsohn, E 1983, *The Jews of East Central Europe between the world wars*, Indiana University Press, Bloomington.

Musil, J 1993, 'Changing urban systems in post-communist societies in Central Europe analysis and prediction', *Urban Studies* 30(6), 899–905.

Openshaw, S 1977, 'A geographical solution to scale and aggregation problems in region-building, partitioning and spatial modelling' *Transactions of the Institute of British Geographers* 2, 459–472.

Stanaitis, S and Česnavičius, D 2010, 'Dynamics of national composition of Vilnius population in the 2nd half of the 20th Century' *Bulletin of Geography, Socio-economic series* 13, 31–44.

State Tax Inspectorate 2014, available online: http://www.vmi.lt/cms/en/ataskaitu-archyvas. Last access 27 April 2015.

Statistics Lithuania 2014, available online: http://osp.stat.gov.lt/en/web/guest/home. Last access 27 April 2015.

Sýkora, L 1999, 'Changes in the internal spatial structure of post-communist Prague' *GeoJournal* 49, 79–89.

Sýkora, L and Bouzarovski, S 2012, 'Multiple transformations conceptualising the post-communist urban transition' *Urban Studies* 49(1), 43–60.

Tammaru, T, Musterd, S, van Ham, M and Marcińczak, S 2016, 'A multi-factor approach to understanding socio-economic segregation in European capital cities' in *Socio-economic segregation in European capital cities: East meets West,* eds T Tammaru, S Marcińczak, M van Ham and S Musterd, Routledge, London.

Tereškinas, A, Žilys, A and Indriliūnaitė, R 2013, 'Emocijos ir socioerdvinė segregacija Lietuvos didmiesčiuose: ar aš galiu ką nors pakeisti?' [Emotions and socio-spatial segregation in Lithuanian cities: ampowerful enough to influence change?]. *Kultūra ir visuomenė* 4(2), 2029–4573.

Ubarevičienė, R, Burneika, D and Kriaučiūnas, E 2011, 'The sprawl of Vilnius city – establishment and analysis of growing urban region' *Annales Geographicae* 43–44, 96–107.

Ubarevičienė, R, Burneika, D and van Ham, M 2015, 'Ethno-political effects of suburbanization in the Vilnius urban region: An analysis of voting behaviour' *Journal of Baltic Studies*, forthcoming.

Ubarevičienė, R, van Ham, M and Burneika, D 2014, 'Shrinking regions in a shrinking country: The geography of population decline in Lithuania 2001–2011', IZA Discussion Paper No. 8026. Available online: www.iza.org. Last accessed 27 April 2015.

Vanagas, J, Krisjane, Z, Noorkõiv, R and Staniunas, E 2002, 'Planning urban systems in Soviet times and in the era of transition: The case of Estonia, Latvia and Lithuania' *Geographia Polonica* 75(2), 75–101.

Vanagas, J 2003, *Miesto teorija* [Urban theory], Technika, Vilnius.

Weeks RT 2008, 'Remembering and forgetting: Creating a soviet Lithuanian capital. Vilnius 1944–1949' *Journal of Baltic Studies* 39(4), 517–533.

Žilys, A 2013, 'Rezidencinė diferenciacija ir skirtumai Lietuvos moderniąjame mieste: (po)sovietinis ar Vakarų miestas?' [Residential differentiation in Lithuanian modern cities: Is it a (post-) Soviet or Western city'] in *Kultūra ir visuomenė*, Socialinių tyrimų žurnalas 4, 67–101.

14 The 'market experiment'

Increasing socio-economic segregation
in the inherited bi-ethnic context
of Tallinn

*Tiit Tammaru, Anneli Kährik, Kadi Mägi,
Jakub Novák and Kadri Leetmaa*

Abstract

This chapter examines the 'market experiment' unfolding in Tallinn, the capital city of Estonia, by focusing on how this experiment is beginning to reshape levels and patterns of socio-economic segregation as measured by occupation. The analysis contributes to discussion of the 'paradox of post-socialist segregation' i.e., the observed decrease in levels of segregation in tandem with an increase in social inequality as market forces are introduced into the Eastern European city. Together with the two other Baltic States of Latvia and Lithuania, the Estonian case is interesting for two reasons. First, the Baltic States are unique due to their radical institutional transition from a state-controlled socialist system to one of the most liberal market-oriented systems in Eastern Europe. This is the 'market experiment' unfolding in Tallinn. Second, a large Russian-speaking minority has a residential pattern determined largely by the new housing construction and central housing allocation regime in place during the Soviet period (1944–1991). Thus, unlike cities with ongoing high immigration elsewhere in Europe, Tallinn allows insights into what happens with long-established minorities when no significant new immigration is taking place and markets determine residential sorting. Our main finding is a considerable increase in occupational residential segregation as socio-economic inequalities become manifested in urban space, with increasing overlap between socio-economic and ethnic segregation.

Introduction

The urban fabric and population of Tallinn was greatly affected during the period in which Estonia was part of the Soviet Union between 1944 and 1991 (Bruns 1998; Kährik and Tammaru 2010; Leetmaa *et al.* 2009; Tammaru 2001a). During that era the city's population also increased significantly, from 165,000 to 475,000, and most of the housing stock, mainly in the form of estates of prefabricated apartment blocks, was constructed and centrally allocated to the residents. Tallinn, similarly to the other Baltic capitals of Riga and Vilnius, was an important destination for immigration. Migrants arrived through organised channels of migration but also, with time, on a voluntary basis as the Baltics were perceived as 'Western', not only due to their geographic location but also because of their more Western way of living (Kulu 2003). However, despite the strong Soviet footprint in the city in its patterns of both housing and population distribution, the age of the urban fabric of Tallinn is very diverse, with development having occurred since the thirteenth century. It is therefore possible to compare residential sorting in Tallinn with that in other European capital cities that underwent central planning, and have since undergone rapid social transformations: for example, the highly segregated Budapest and the moderately segregated Prague (Marcińczak *et al.* 2016).

As a result of Soviet-era immigration, the population of Tallinn linguistically divided into two major ethno-linguistic groups that are almost equal in size, i.e., the Estonian-speakers who form the national majority in Estonia, and Russian-speakers (consisting of mostly Russians but also Ukrainians and Byelorussians or Slavic groups). This adds an important dimension to analyses of the socio-spatial processes in Tallinn and the other Baltic capitals, in contrast to other cities in Eastern Europe but with some similarity to Western European cities. Although Soviet society aimed for social equality, ethnic segregation intensified for many reasons, also as a result of the sorting of residents by the central housing allocation system. Immigrants had to be housed somewhere on their very first day of arrival, and because new housing was built in spatially concentrated locations in order for construction to benefit from economies of scale, the Russian-speaking minority became strongly over-represented in the new high-rise housing estates in Tallinn (Kährik and Tammaru 2010; Tammaru and Kontuly 2011). The circumstances of migrants to Tallinn and the other Baltic capitals were rather different from those of many migrants to West European cities, however. As the main migrant group, Russians moved from Russia to the other republics of the Soviet Union, and Russian became the *lingua franca* among Soviet citizens. However, when the republics of the former Soviet Union (re)gained their independence in 1991, ethnic Russians became a minority group and lost their former privileged position in society. The integration of Russian-speakers has been an important challenge for many countries that were once part of the Soviet Union (Brubaker 1994).

Estonia belongs to the group of rapidly reforming Eastern European countries (Hamilton *et al.* 2005) that became members of the European Union in the first round of Eastward expansion in 2004. The re-establishment of the Estonian state and the desire to disconnect the country from Russia economically and to reconnect to the global capitalist world has resulted in far-reaching reforms. These reforms shifted Tallinn from a socialist paternal welfarism – in countries under central planning, the state nationalised the means of production and had thus a central role in the production and redistribution of goods with housing being one of the most valued of them (Verdery 1996) – to a situation where markets strongly shape the socio-spatial processes in the city. Especially in the context of segregation research, Tallinn represents a city almost completely subsumed under market forces; the public sector owns only 2 per cent of its housing stock. Hence, this study sheds light on the unfolding far reaching 'market experiment' taking place in the capital city of Estonia and how it shapes the patterns of residential segregation by occupation.

The over-arching goal of this chapter is to explore what happens to the socio-spatial structures of a city where there is a shift, almost overnight, from totalitarian state paternalism to almost exclusively market-driven liberalism. Previous literature from Central and Eastern Europe provides some insights as to what might happen with segregation patterns. As systemic changes start, higher social groups start to move into the formerly lower-status areas, for example, into the inner city as well as low-density areas in the outer city, thereby lowering levels of segregation, a phenomenon labelled a 'paradox of post-socialist segregation' (Marcińczak *et al.* 2014; Sýkora 2009). An important underlying reason for the lowering of segregation relates to the changes in the mental map of a city, including the relative prestige of different areas. Hybrid spaces emerge as different socio-economic groups start to mix together in the city in increasingly diverse ways as the socialist legacy and new capitalist forces interact in the city (cf. Golubchikov *et al.* 2014).

The egalitarian centrally planned city, homopolis, starts to transform into a heteropolis characterised by increasing socio-spatial diversity (Gentile *et al.* 2012). The most eye-catching changes of the heteropolitanisation process would be found in the inner city – in an area neglected by central planners but which became a very attractive residential location as the social transformation began to take place. Jana Temelová (2013) introduced the metaphor 'Cinderella' to characterise inner-city change in formerly socialist cities. However, it takes time for institutional changes and new forms of inequality to become manifest in urban space, i.e., new patterns of segregation emerge with a time lag (Marcińczak *et al.* 2014). It could be that local level mixing and diversification are a temporary phase that ultimately leads to new clear-cut patterns of segregation as the expanding higher social groups start to define the new geographies of the city (Sýkora 2009). Markets have only played a significant role in shaping segregation since 2000 because all the main institutions necessary for market-based transactions were by then established in the rapidly reforming Eastern European countries (Leetmaa *et al.* 2009). The defining power of higher-social status groups is a function of their purchasing power and their ability to manifest this in space, as evident from the 2010 round of censuses in European countries.

Following on from these core discussions on urban change in Eastern European cities, we seek answers to the following research questions:

1   Is there evidence of growing socio-economic segregation in the 2000s, following a clear rise of social inequalities in the 1990s and in the context of an ubiquitous market in the housing sector?
2   Or is there evidence of socio-economic mixing as higher-socio-economic groups move into areas over-represented by lower-socio-economic groups?
3   What happens to the inherited combination of high-level ethnic segregation and low-level socio-economic segregation under such conditions of social disruption and change in the minority status in the context of a far-reaching 'market experiment'?

The chapter starts by exploring the contemporary city of Tallinn. It is important to note at this point that detailed investigations of segregation were scarce in the former Soviet Union because population data were for administrative use only, and no data at low spatial resolutions were ever published. Next we introduce data and methods. We use data from the 2000 and 2011 censuses at a detailed neighbourhood level, with on average 300 economically active people in each unit, divided into occupational categories. Our results provide evidence of the changes in the levels and geographic patterns of socio-economic segregation in general, and by ethnic categories, across neighbourhoods. Finally, we discuss our findings in the light of core debates on urban change in Eastern European cities.

Setting the scene: social transformations, housing and residential segregation in Tallinn

There are several historical 'layers' that define the contemporary urban fabric of Tallinn. Its centre, the Old Town or medieval core, was mainly built in the thirteenth century when the city prospered from trade within the Hanseatic League. The population remained very small until the nineteenth century; only about 67,000 people lived in Tallinn in 1900 (Pullat 1972). However, being located at trade routes and ruled by several foreign powers, Tallinn was already multi-ethnic – Estonians formed about two-thirds of the city's population, while Germans and Russians were the two largest minorities (Tammaru 2001a). The industrialisation of Estonia took off in the second half of the nineteenth century when the country became part of the Russian Empire. The population of Tallinn started to increase largely due to the immigration of Russian industrial workers. Two-storey wooden houses were built for the migrants in the district of northern Tallinn (for the map of city districts, see Figure 14.1; then on the periphery and now part of the inner city of Tallinn), leading to considerable ethnic and socio-economic residential segregation (cf. Pullat 1972).

Estonia was independent between the two world wars, a period when its industrial importance diminished, and the growth of the urban population ceased. However, an important new layer was added to its urban fabric in the form of garden cities in Nõmme and Pirita (Tammaru 2001b) (Figure 14.1). Garden cities became an attractive living place for high-status officials, civil servants, businessmen and other professionals, turning them into prestigious residential neighbourhoods (Pullat 1968). Estonia was annexed by the Soviet Union during the course of World War II and this brought with it the rapid parallel processes of industrialisation and urbanisation. The population of Tallinn tripled, reaching 475,000 inhabitants by 1991. There was a strong ethnic dimension to these processes: large numbers of Russians and other mainly Russian-speaking migrants arrived in Estonia through 'organized migration channels' operated by state authorities and industrial enterprises (cf. Rybakovskiy 1987), leading to Russian-speakers being over-represented both in industrial as well as in public-sector jobs (Tammaru 2001a; Tammaru and Kulu 2003). The latter was a consequence of the privileged role of ethnic Russians and the Russian language in the former Soviet

Union (Brubaker 1994). The bi-ethnolinguistic population was thus formed during the Soviet years and remains the most important social characteristic of Tallinn. An important cornerstone of the Marxist ideological monopoly in the paternalist former Soviet state, as elsewhere in countries with central planning, was to create a collective and just society, and the spatial dimension of this ideology was the massive construction of housing estates of prefabricated apartment blocks (Kährik and Tammaru 2010; Leetmaa *et al.* 2014; Smith 1996). State housing (about 90 per cent of such housing in Tallinn, the rest was cooperative housing) in these estates was provided for free to people. The housing was equipped with all modern facilities unlike the pre-war houses, and rents were highly subsidised, which made them an attractive housing segment across Eastern Europe and the former Soviet Union (Bater 1980; Harris 1970; Morton and Stuart 1984; Sailer-Fliege 1999). Apartments were centrally allocated to households according to family need, with priority given to newly arrived workers. In Tallinn, the main areas of such Soviet high-rise housing estates are Mustamäe (built in the 1960s and 1970s), Õismäe in Haabersti district (1970s) and Lasnamäe (1980s) (Figure 14.1), but smaller developments of apartment blocks were also built elsewhere in the city and its hinterland (Kährik and Tammaru 2010). According to the 2000 census, about two-thirds of the population of Tallinn lived in this type of housing. The size of the apartments increased over time. The newest and largest housing estate Lasnamäe, with about 100,000 inhabitants, has the largest apartments, representing a true mass construction project.

As far as the composition of the population was concerned, migrants became over-represented in newly built housing estates, whereas Estonians remained over-represented in the decaying inner-city housing stock and in the low-density outer city (Ruoppila and Kährik 2003; Tammaru *et al.* 2013). High levels of ethnic housing segmentation and residential segregation thus characterised late-Soviet Tallinn. This reflects the combined effects of migration, mainly from Russia, and occupational differences between long-standing inhabitants and migrants. Immigrants often worked for employers who provided housing for workers, i.e., the large industrial enterprises that had divisions across the Soviet Union often controlled from Moscow. Thus, there was a strong corporatist dimension in the totalitarian Soviet society (cf. Sjöberg 1999). Russian-speakers became strongly attached to high-rise housing estates partly because of the specific own-language infrastructure that became established there (such as schools, child-care and leisure facilities, etc.). In most *mikrorayony*,[1] both Estonian-language and Russian-language educational institutions existed side-by-side. Despite some changes, this dual-language educational system has persisted, sustaining a continuous ethnic divide in social networks (Järv *et al.* 2014; Korts 2009; Silm and Ahas 2014).

The dominance of standardised apartment blocks implies that the city of Tallinn was spatially very compact until the end of the 1980s. As in other Eastern European cities (cf. Ladányi and Szelényi 1998), an important socio-spatial dividing line ran between the core city and the suburban ring outside the official city limits (Tammaru 2001b; Tammaru and Leetmaa 2007). In general, people working in lower-order industrial and agricultural sectors were over-represented

in the suburbs, while those – often more educated – working for priority industries and the public administration were over-represented in the cities (Gentile
and Sjöberg 2010; Kährik and Tammaru 2010; Tammaru and Leetmaa 2007).
This socialist suburban hinterland was diverse, consisting of smaller-scale satellite towns with mainly apartment buildings, as well as self-constructed detached
housing areas with houses of both high and low quality, and socialist-era seasonal
home settlements (Leetmaa *et al.* 2012; Leetmaa and Tammaru 2007; Tammaru
et al. 2013). Within the city, older quarters of the inner city decayed socially and
physically (Kährik *et al.* 2014). The low-density housing areas in the outer city
housed mainly ethnic Estonians with different social backgronds (Kulu 2003;
Ruoppila and Kährik 2003), and the more prestigious detached houses built
in the 1980s already reflected the nascent aspirations for a suburban lifestyle.
Soviet Tallinn remained spatially compact, however, with only a modest urban
sprawl (Tammaru 2001a).

Estonia was transformed from a highly state-controlled and state-paternal
system to one of the most liberal market-oriented systems in Europe during the
1990s. This transformation resulted in the large-scale privatisation of public
housing (such as apartments in Soviet-era blocks), making sitting tenants into
owners, while property confiscated by the Soviet regime, about 3 per cent of
the total housing stock in Tallinn (Kährik and Kõre 2013), was restituted to the
original pre-war owners or their heirs. Sitting tenants were given their apartments almost free of charge. Rent caps were established to avoid a potential
sharp increase in rent in homes returned to pre-war owners. Other measures were
also introduced, such as a guarantee system for down payments on mortgages for
special target groups such as young families, and a favourable tax treatment of
housing loans to stimulate home ownership (Hussar *et al.* 2014). Finally, Tallinn
has initiated municipal housing construction programmes (since the 2000s) to
accommodate tenants in housing restituted to previous owners and other socially
vulnerable groups (Kährik and Kõre 2013). However, all these policy measures
either support home ownership or pertain to a very marginal share of overall
housing stock in Tallinn.

Rent regulation was only a temporary measure introduced to cushion the immediate shock of restitution, and was abolished in 2004; rents have risen quickly
since then. Household income and borrowing capacity, as well as house prices,
dropped significantly during the economic crisis (2008–2010). In tandem, the private rental sector grew, as the large population cohorts born in the 1980s started
to enter the housing market at this time of crisis. The result was an increase in the
proportion of rented housing, mainly on account of the increased private rental
sector. According to the census, about 80 per cent of households lived in owner-
occupied dwellings in Tallinn in 2011, and 11 per cent lived in rental or other type
of housing. Only 2 per cent of the total housing stock was owned by the state or
local government, implying that the private renters dominate in the rental sector.
Renting is much more common among younger generations who did not gain
from the housing privatisation that took place in the 1990s, and is market based.
Estonian Finance Minister Maris Lauri explains it as follows:

I have nothing against having a bigger rental sector in Estonia, but this is mainly a task for the private sector. The role of the state is first all to set the rules of the game, but only in case that it is clear what are the exact problems on the rental market and what is the most efficient way to solve these very concrete problems. Here, the experience from other countries can be important, but we cannot adopt a blind copy-paste strategy. Such a strategy is even irresponsible since we lack a comprehensive understanding of the Estonia-specific problems on the rental market, and the Estonian context is certainly different compared to, say, the context of Finland or Sweden.

Maris Lauri blog, 10 November 2014 [authors' translation]

The Estonian labour market also went through a period of major change after 1991 (Eamets 2011; Marksoo *et al.* 2010). While housing was virtually given away by the state, the once mighty industrial enterprises were privatised, based on open international competitions. Those enterprises that survived reduced their workforce significantly. Ethnic minorities were over-represented in the industrial sector and were therefore especially hard hit by the economic reforms. Due to the generally limited Estonian-language proficiency of members of minority groups, they had greater difficulty adapting to the requirements of higher-status jobs in the emerging service economy; this led to higher levels of unemployment compared to the Estonians, and thus income inequalities between ethnic groups (Leping and Toomet 2008; Lindemann and Kogan 2013; Lindemann and Saar 2014; Marksoo *et al.* 2010). In other words, as an unintended consequence of the radical economic reforms that did not have explicit ethnic aims, ethnic Estonians became 'winners' in the social transformation (Titma *et al.* 1998).

While Estonia inherited an ethnically divided society from the Soviet period, the large socio-economic inequalities introduced by the economic reforms are a more recent phenomenon. Total gross salaries increased steadily from the mid-1990s in Estonia. The gap between the top-earning occupational group (managers) and the lowest earners (elementary occupations) peaked in 2000, with the ratio (gross hourly salary of managers/elementary occupations) being 3.3 (cf. in 1994 3.0 and 3.1 in 2010).[2] The inequality in income distribution, as measured by a Gini coefficient (of equivalised disposable income, source EU-SILC Survey), shows a moderate declining trend from 0.36 in 2000 to 0.32 in 2011. Therefore, social inequality peaked in the year 2000, after the first round of radical reforms had been completed, and has decreased ever since then. Estonia joined the EU in 2004 and it seems that both the accession negotiations as well as EU membership have mitigated income divides in Estonia, partly because institutional capacities for tackling social inequalities have strengthened after the system-change shock of the 1990s, and because of improved public and household finances overall. In other words, compared to many other countries in Europe, the welfare state grew somewhat in Estonia in the 2000s compared with the 1990s. However, the ethnic dimension in inequalities is still strong; for example, the salary of Estonian managers was 1.5 times higher than that of minority managers in 2010.

Despite the partial return migration of the Soviet-era immigrant population (which accounted for a large proportion of the vacant apartments on the market), housing privatisation (allowing the sale and purchase of residential property), and land privatisation (opening up suburban land for development), residential mobility levels remained modest throughout the 1990s (Leetmaa *et al.* 2009). Mobility was mainly restricted due to the low standard of living for most households as the hyper-inflation of the early 1990s and monetary reforms (switching from rouble to kroon) impoverished most households. The Soviet-era housing estates remained relatively attractive to all income groups through the end of the 1990s (Kährik and Tammaru 2010). Processes of both nation-wide population concentration towards the capital city and suburbanisation within its surrounding urban region, intensified sharply during the 2000s (Leetmaa *et al.* 2014; Tammaru *et al.* 2013). Estonians are more likely to leave housing estates and settle both in the inner city and the suburban ring than other ethnic groups (Leetmaa *et al.* 2014; Tammaru *et al.* 2013), thus potentially contributing to the increase in the proportion of Russian-speakers there.

Based on historical trajectories and current trends, four 'zones' with identifiable residential processes can be distinguished in the urban residential fabric of Tallinn today. First, the city centre (which is located in the northern part of central Tallinn; see Figure 14.1) and the inner city (merged to the category 'inner city' on Figure 14.1) are currently experiencing a period of selective gentrification (for example, Kährik *et al.* 2014) where lower socio-economic status

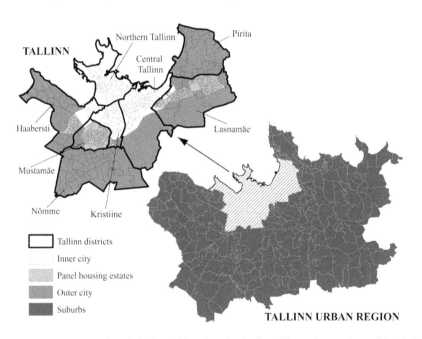

Figure 14.1 Map of statistical neighbourhood units in Tallinn urban region, with administrative city districts in Tallinn, and TUR's division into analytical urban zones.

Source: Census 2011, authors' figure.

residents increasingly reside side by side with higher socio-economic status incomers. Second, socialist-era housing estates are facing multiple trajectories of change – some are retaining their relatively high social status, while others suffer from selective out-migration (Kährik and Tammaru 2010). Third, the areas of detached houses within the city border and the outer city, with higher land prices and better connections with the city centre, now attract the higher-status groups, whereas the suburban ring (suburbs) around Tallinn with many greenfield sites for new low-density housing developments is more attractive to the emerging upper-middle class. People living in the suburbs, however, remain diverse; newcomers are mostly Estonians and have a higher social status and/or level of education compared to long-term residents (Kährik and Tammaru 2008). Understanding the transformations within these broad urban zones helps to interpret the changing segregation levels and patterns of the 2000s.

Data and methods

Our study area is the Tallinn urban region (Tallinn). Administratively this is defined as the city of Tallinn (including the inner city, Soviet-era housing estates and the outer city) and surrounding municipalities (suburban ring) (Figure 14.1). The total population of the Tallinn urban region was 470,000 in 2000 and 513,000 in 2011 (a 9 per cent increase). Despite migration from the rest of Estonia, the number of people living in the city of Tallinn decreased by 2 per cent between the 2000 and 2011 censuses, amounting to 393,000 people in 2011, whereas the suburban population increased from 70,000 to 120,000. Estonian-speakers make up 58.2 per cent of the population of the Tallinn urban region, Russian-speaking minorities 39.4 per cent and other linguistic groups 2.4 per cent, with very little proportional change between censuses.

Data for the study was obtained from the 2000 and 2011 censuses. The spatial units of our analysis are morphologically coherent neighbourhoods (following street and building structures, historical development and local identity patterns). We link these spatial units to census microdata in order to build the aggregated tables for our analysis of segregation. Our research population is the economically active population living in the Tallinn urban region. The average population size of neighbourhoods was 288 economically active inhabitants in 2000 and 347 inhabitants in 2011; this growth occurred due to the suburbanisation process – high-density areas (housing estates) lost population to other urban zones, especially to low-density areas in the outer city and suburban ring.

To measure socio-economic segregation we use the ISCO-88 (International Standard Classification of Occupations) occupational categories. We use the major groups of the ISCO classification,[3] excluding agricultural workers and military personnel, and including unemployed persons who according to the ILO (International Labour Organization) definition are part of the labour force. We calculate global indices of segregation to measure both the evenness (segregation index and index of dissimilarity) and exposure (modified isolation index) dimensions of segregation (see also the introduction of this book for more detail: Tammaru *et al.* 2016). We use a modified isolation index that is not sensitive to the relative size of groups since it allows for a better comparison of change over time. Local patterns of segregation are analysed by presenting location quotient maps. The ethnic differences in segregation are measured by comparing Estonians (Estonian first language) with Russian-speaking minority groups (Russian first language), omitting other ethnic categories (2.4 per cent in 2011) because the latter group is very heterogeneous when it comes to origins and time of migration. According to the 2011 census, 98 per cent of Estonians speak Estonian as their first language, and 99 per cent of Russians speak Russian as their first language.

Socio-economic segmentation: deepening ethnic divide in occupational structure

When studying occupational segregation, changes in the occupational composition over time should be taken into account. Figure 14.2a, occupational pyramids, reflects the ongoing 'professionalisation' process that has taken place in the Tallinn urban region. This is very different from, say, London, that was already highly professionalised in 2001 (Manley *et al*. 2016). Referring to the ISCO categories, the expansion of the 'professionals' category has been the most noticeable, but the share of 'technicians and associate professionals' has grown as well. When aggregated, the 'low-status' group (ISCO 5–9 plus unemployed) still comprised the largest share of all economically active people in 2011, but its relative share decreased from 53 per cent in 2000 to 48 per cent in 2011. At the same time the proportions of both 'middle-status' (ISCO 3–4) and 'high-status' (ISCO 1–2) groups increased. Professionalisation, however, seems to characterise

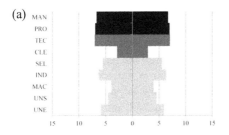
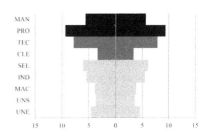
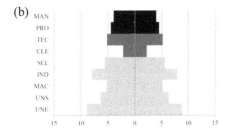
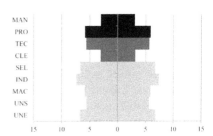

(c)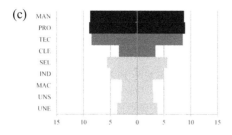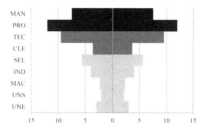

Figure 14.2a–c Occupational pyramids for ISCO occupational groups and unemployed in 2000–2011 in Tallinn urban region: (a) total population, (b) Russian speakers and (c) Estonian speakers.

Source: Census 2000, 2011; authors' calculations and figure.

Note: MAN – managers, PRO – professionals, TEC – technicians and associate professionals, CLE – clerical support workers, SEL – service and sales workers, IND – craft and related trades workers, MAC – plant and machine operators, and assemblers, UNS – elementary occupations, and UNE – unemployed.

only Estonians and not the ethnic minority group. The occupational pyramids by ethnic groups (Figures 14.2b and 14.2c) show the extent to which the occupational structure of the two major ethno-linguistic groups differ. Both in 2000 and 2011 Estonians are more often 'managers', 'professionals' and 'technicians and associate professionals', or otherwise belong to the top three categories, while Russian-speaking minorities more commonly work in lower-level occupations or are unemployed. We know that the major structural changes in the economy and also in the occupational structure occurred in the 1990s (for example Russians more often than Estonians lost their administrative positions and industrial jobs) (Tammaru and Kulu 2003); now we see that such differentiation further deepened between 2000 and 2011.

Socio-economic segregation: ethnic divide is increasingly projected spatially

Between 2000 and 2011 the segregation index (SI) and the index of dissimilarity (ID) reveal remarkable changes that by far exceed changes in the occupational composition. The values of SI for the total population (Figure 14.3) were below 20 for all socio-occupational categories in 2000, which is considered low and similar to what is found in many other Eastern European cities (Marcińczak *et al.* 2014). Because residential mobility was relatively modest in the 1990s, the 2000 census reflects mostly the low levels of segregation inherited from the Soviet era (cf. Raitviir 1987). The values of SI increased considerably for most of the groups during the 2000s, especially in the higher and lower ends of the occupational pyramid. The U-curve of occupational segregation (with the exception of the most diverse group of 'unemployed') steepened as well, implying that the increased levels of stratification in the labour market are reflected in increasing levels of residential segregation.

The matrix of occupational categories with IDs (Figure 14.4) presents the 'distance' of occupational groups from each other. The spatial distance is the highest between the two highest-status groups ('managers' and 'professionals') and the lowest-status occupational groups ('service and sales workers', 'craft and related trades workers' 'plant and machine operators', 'elementary occupations', and 'unemployed'; values >20 in most cases). The biggest ID value is between 'managers' on the one hand, and 'plant and machine operators', and 'unemployed' on the other. Over ten years these indices grew further, from below 30 in 2000 to close to

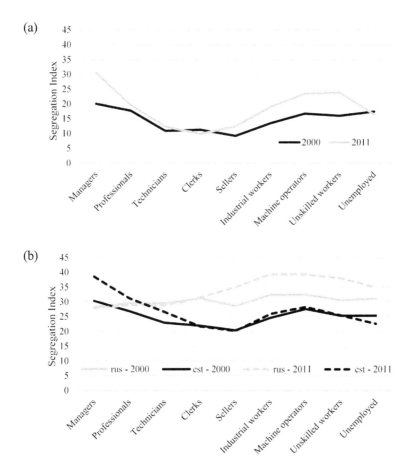

Figure 14.3a–b Index of segregation (IS) for ISCO occupational groups and unemployed: (a) total population and (b) Estonian and Russian speakers.

Source: Census 2000, 2011, authors' figures.

(a)

2000 \ 2011	MAN	PRO	TEC	CLE	SEL	IND	MAC	UNS	UNE
MAN	--	18	21	30	37	42	46	48	40
PRO	13	--	11	20	25	32	37	37	29
TEC	15	12	--	14	20	26	31	31	24
CLE	19	17	13	--	12	18	23	23	17
SEL	22	19	14	14	--	13	17	16	11
IND	27	25	19	17	13	--	11	13	12
MAC	30	29	22	19	16	12	--	13	15
UNS	29	27	22	19	15	12	14	--	14
UNE	30	28	23	21	16	14	16	15	--

(b)

2000 \ 2011		MAN	PRO	TEC	CLE	SEL	IND	MAC	UNS	UNE	MAN	PRO	TEC	CLE	SEL	IND	MAC	UNS	UNE
		ESTONIANS									RUSSIANS								
ESTONIANS	MAN	--	17	19	27	30	32	36	38	26	46	57	58	63	66	70	70	69	66
	PRO	14	--	12	20	21	26	31	30	19	44	50	51	55	59	63	63	62	59
	TEC	15	13	--	15	17	20	25	26	16	43	48	49	53	56	60	60	59	56
	CLE	20	19	15	--	14	17	22	21	15	42	44	45	48	50	55	55	53	51
	SEL	21	19	14	15	--	16	21	18	14	41	43	43	45	47	51	51	50	47
	IND	22	23	17	16	15	--	17	19	18	46	48	47	49	50	54	54	53	51
	MAC	28	28	23	22	20	17	--	21	22	47	49	49	50	51	54	54	53	51
	UNS	25	25	20	19	18	17	20	--	21	46	46	46	47	47	51	51	48	47
	UNE	25	25	20	20	18	18	23	21	--	43	46	46	49	51	55	55	54	51
RUSSIANS	MAN	47	50	52	54	53	56	56	54	54	--	23	25	30	33	37	38	38	33
	PRO	44	45	48	51	49	52	53	50	51	18	--	13	19	20	24	26	26	21
	TEC	44	44	46	48	46	50	50	48	48	19	17	--	16	17	20	22	23	17
	CLE	44	44	45	47	44	48	48	46	46	23	22	19	--	16	18	19	21	16
	SEL	43	43	45	46	43	46	47	45	45	21	20	16	19	--	14	15	15	11
	IND	47	48	49	50	47	49	50	48	48	24	24	19	21	15	--	11	13	12
	MAC	49	50	50	51	49	50	51	50	49	25	24	18	19	16	15	--	14	15
	UNS	47	47	49	49	47	49	50	48	48	24	24	20	20	15	13	15	--	14
	UNE	47	48	49	50	47	50	50	48	47	25	25	20	21	15	14	16	16	--

Figure 14.4a–b Index of dissimilarity (ID) for the occupational groups, 2000–2011: (a) total population and (b) Estonians and Russians.

Source: Census 2000, 2011, authors' figures.

Note: Shadowed cells = dissimilarity index value 20 and more.

40 or even 50 in 2011. Values above 40 could be considered to represent high levels of socio-economic segregation (Marcińczak *et al.* 2014). Furthermore, 'managers' have also become substantially segregated from some of the mid-level occupational groups (with an index of 30 in relation to 'clerical support workers').

SI values for occupational groups are higher in both years (2000 and 2011) when measured separately for Estonian-speakers and Russian-speakers – the most segregated group being Estonian 'managers' (showing an increasing trend over time). None of the groups stand out among Russian-speakers, however; the lowest status groups (ISCO 5–9) have become more segregated over time (Figure 14.3). The values of ID are much more similar between occupational groups within the same ethnic group (see Figure 14.4, for Estonians the upper-left cell, and for the Russian-speaking minority group the lower-right cell); in 2000 none of the socio-economic groups exceeded the ID value of 30 with any other occupational group. The distance between high- and low-occupational groups had increased within the same ethnic groups by 2011. The ID values between the ethnic groups (identical upper right or lower left cells) are striking, with the highest value being 56 in 2000, and increasing further to 70 by 2011. The most striking result is that even the ID values for the same occupational groups of Estonians and Russian-speakers differ considerably. For example, the ID for Estonian and minority 'managers' is as high as 47 and 46 for 2000 and 2011, respectively. Thus, not only is the occupational structure of Estonians and minorities different, but the same occupational groups do not share residential neighbourhoods either. We recall that this can partly reflect the fact that Estonian 'managers' earn about 1.5 times more than minority 'managers'. However, this cannot be the whole story since the spatial distance between Estonian 'managers' and 'elementary occupations' is smaller than between Estonian 'managers' and minority 'managers'.

The values of the modified isolation index (MII) for the total working population indicate that the separation of almost all ISCO occupational groups has increased during the period 2000–2011 (except for 'clerical support workers' and 'unemployed'; Figure 14.5a), and the isolation of 'managers' has increased the most. Estonian 'managers' are the most isolated group both in 2000 and 2011 (Figure 14.5b). Compared to Russian 'managers' they are three times more isolated from the rest of the workforce, and their isolation increases over time. The isolation of top occupations was lower for Russians and the levels did not change much between 2000 and 2011 either. Interesting changes took place in the lower end of the occupational pyramid: isolation decreased among Estonian-speaking

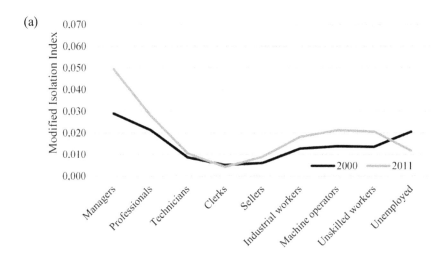

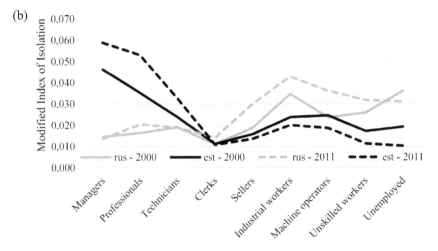

Figure 14.5a–b Modified index of isolation (MII) for ISCO occupational groups and unemployed: (a) total population and (b) Estonian and Russian speakers.

Source: Census 2000, 2011, authors' figures.

people working in lower-level occupations but increased among the same occupational groups in the case of Russian-speakers. Thus, the unfolding 'market experiment' has clear spatial consequences, with Estonian-speaking 'managers' and Russian-speaking 'elementary occupations' being the most segregated.

The geography of segregation

The increase in segregation between 2000 and 2011 is also reflected in local patterns of segregation. Figure 14.6 presents location quotients (LQs) for two selected occupational categories – 'managers and professionals' (ISCO 1 and 2 merged) or the high-status group, and 'elementary occupations' (ISCO 9) or the low-status group. The intra-urban geography of 'managers and professionals' has not changed dramatically; however, the concentration areas that already existed in 2000 have become spatially extended. The 'spill-over' effect of high-status groups has taken place in two directions. First, the historical (pre-World War II) high-status low-density outer-city districts Pirita and Nõmme[4] show an increase in their socio-economic status, together with areas of detached houses along the coastline in Haabersti. Second, the physical and social restructuring processes that have taken place in the inner city are clearly manifest in the local patterns of segregation. High-status groups are expanding their presence in many inner-city neighbourhoods in north Tallinn and in some neighbourhoods adjacent to the city centre in the south and east that were left to deteriorate during the Soviet period. The suburban ring still remains quite socially mixed, but the proportion of

348   *Tiit Tammaru* et al.

high-status residents increased from 2000 to 2011, especially in the most attractive coastal areas and, selectively, also inland south of Tallinn. Suburban development was restricted for security reasons in the coastal areas during the Soviet period because Estonia lay on the western border of the Soviet Union.

(a)

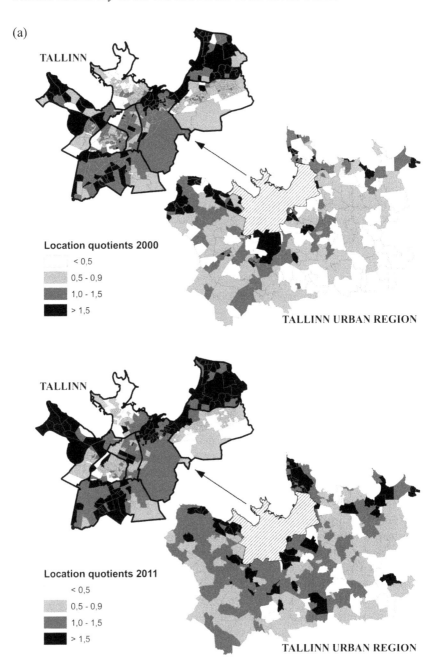

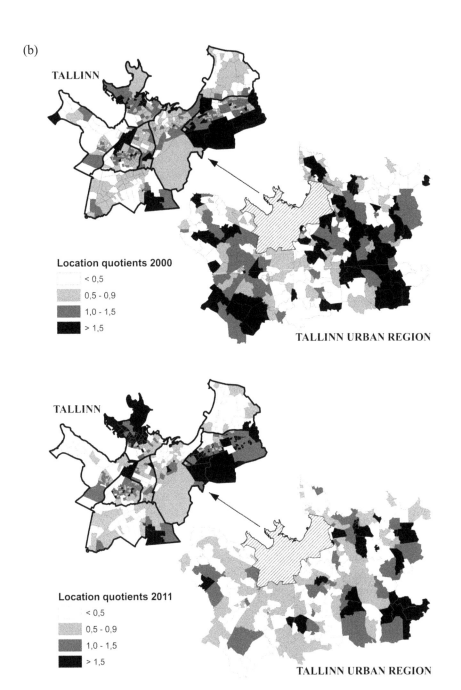

(b)

TALLINN

Location quotients 2000

- < 0,5
- 0,5 - 0,9
- 1,0 - 1,5
- > 1,5

TALLINN URBAN REGION

TALLINN

Location quotients 2011

- < 0,5
- 0,5 - 0,9
- 1,0 - 1,5
- > 1,5

TALLINN URBAN REGION

Figure 14.6a–b Location quotient (LQ) maps for selected ISCO occupational groups (a) managers (b) unskilled workers in 2000–2011.

Source: Census 2000, 2011, authors' figures.

Soviet-era housing estates have not gained from the redistribution of social status groups. Instead, the values for LQs of high-status groups have decreased in all large housing estates, especially in Lasnamäe where the share of 'managers' has declined compared to 2000, which is in striking contrast with the overall professionalisation of the Tallinn workforce. 'Managers and professionals' are also clearly under-represented in the more peripheral parts of northern Tallinn (untouched by the gentrification process).

The low-status group or 'elementary occupations' tends to have the opposite location patterns to 'managers and professionals'. Compared to 2000 when they were slightly over-represented in several inner-city neighbourhoods, their presence has dramatically declined in the city centre and also in the adjacent gentrifying neighbourhoods to the north, south and east of the city centre. This is because of replacement (natural decrease affects more low-status people who are over-represented in older age groups) and displaced (high-status groups often take over the houses that are undergoing major renovations), and because of the infills of new-built houses where high-status groups have settled (new-built gentrification), thus decreasing the relative presence of low-status groups, too. The latter have 'retreated' to estates of apartment blocks, particularly to Lasnamäe (the district where the share of Russian-speakers is also higher than in other housing estates), where a number of *mikrorayony* show LQ values over 1.5. The other large housing estates have retained a higher level of social mix. The peripheral parts of the district of north Tallinn, where pre-war housing is mixed with industry, with a decaying housing stock and high concentrations of Russian-speakers, is another area with an increasing concentration of low-skilled workers (LQ values over 1.5). However, this is a coastal area and subject to many new housing development projects. Low-status groups were widely present in most parts of the suburban ring in 2000, with LQ values over 1.5 in about one-third of the territory. Areas with a high concentration of this group can still be found in many parts of the suburban ring, mostly east of Tallinn, but they have increasingly been replaced by high-status areas.

Overall, the analysis of the changing geography of segregation indicates that the neighbourhood social mix inherited from the Soviet period can still be found in the Tallinn urban region, but increasingly clear-cut high-status and low-status areas are forming. Within Tallinn, the unfolding 'market experiment' pushes low-status groups out from the most attractive parts of the inner city, either to housing estates or to the less attractive and peripheral parts of the inner city. Within the suburban ring, high-status groups tend to settle in greenfield sites along the coast and near the city limits.

Discussion and conclusions

Tallinn had modest socio-economic residential segregation but was highly ethnically segregated during the Soviet period. In 1991, almost overnight, the socialist paternalistic welfare was lifted from the country, and it was subjected to market forces, almost universally. State budgets collapsed as the Estonian kroon replaced the Russian rouble, and underwent with very radical reforms to liberalise the economy and promote home ownership. It brought along a rapid rise in socio-economic inequalities in the 1990s, followed by a decline in this respect in the 2000s. In 2000, levels of socio-economic segregation were still low and comparable to those in many other Eastern European capital cities (cf. Marcińczak *et al.* 2015), and lower than those in West European capital cities (cf. Marcińczak *et al.* 2016). Sýkora and Bouzarovski (2012) explain this by the evolutionary nature of socio-spatial change in East European cities: institutional and socio-economic structures change first, only then followed by changes in spatial structures. More specifically, spatial mobility in Tallinn was modest until the 2000s for various reasons: for example, the housing market reforms (including mass privatisation, property restitution, changes in mortgage lending) were still ongoing and disposable household incomes (and thus opportunities to improve living conditions) were relatively low. In other words, it is difficult to move before the relevant institutions are in place and functioning, and before people have sufficient resources to do this. Hence, socio-economic segregation is delayed compared to other socio-economic inequalities. What this study shows, however, is that once the preconditions are in place and universal market forces take over the city as happened in the 2000s in Tallinn, levels of residential segregation start to rise quickly as well.

The segregation levels in 2000 were relatively low and the city was characterised by many neighbourhoods of mixed socio-economic composition. The 'paradox of post-socialist segregation' states that as the social transformations start in Eastern European cities, this brings about an increase in social inequalities but lowers levels of socio-economic segregation, because high-status groups start to move into areas previously over-represented by low-status groups such as the inner city (Sýkora 2009). However, this phenomenon should not be related to transforming Eastern European cities alone. Similar large-scale transformations have taken place in many cities in Europe, and different underlying processes, including *in situ* social mobility (people changing occupation but not residence) or *in situ* intergenerational social mobility (adult children get a higher occupation compared to parents but continue to live nearby) can mix people with different socio-economic backgrounds in the urban neighbourhoods (Leal and Sorando 2016; Maloutas 2016; Musterd and van Gent 2016).

The proportion of neighbourhoods with predominantly lower socio-economic-status residents decreased in Tallinn between 2000 and 2011, indicating both the ongoing professionalisation and socio-economic mixing that has taken place in previously low-status areas. Hence, we find some continued evidence of local level mixing. However, we also find that distinct spatial patterns of segregation are emerging once the markets are in place, with new clear-cut and internally homogenous neighbourhoods emerging in many parts of the city. Most importantly, 'managers' and 'professionals' are defining the new socio-economic residential geographies of the city by settling in increasing numbers in the areas neglected under socialism, the inner city and the suburbs (coastal areas and areas just beyond the city limits of Tallinn). The coastal areas were closed off during the Soviet period since Estonia was the western border of the Soviet Union, and what has happened is that there is an ongoing residentialisation of these areas, with mainly high-status groups as the Soviet-era compact city becomes more and more sprawled. Low-status groups, in contrast, get increasingly over-represented in the Soviet-era estates of apartment blocks.

Furthermore, there is a very strong ethnic dimension in this process. Tallinn was already ethnically segregated under socialism. This ethnic segregation has increased further as the 'market experiment' evolves in Tallinn, with Estonian 'managers' and Russians employed in 'elementary occupations' being the most segregated groups in the city. When compared to other 'fast-track' reforming cities or cities represented in this book (Marcińczak *et al.* 2015), we clearly see that together with Madrid, Tallinn is highly segregated despite its lower importance in the global city hierarchy (Tammaru *et al.* 2016). Today, levels of segregation in Tallinn are even higher than in Budapest, which used to be the most segregated fast-track reforming country in Eastern Europe before the large-scale societal transformations started in the 1990s (Kovacs and Szabó 2016). An income-based housing market and the absence of elaborate housing allow inequalities to be quickly translated into high levels of socio-economic segregation (Brown and Chung 2008; Marcińczak *et al.* 2015). Furthermore, the clear-cut occupational divisions between Estonians and mainly Russian-speaking minority groups are increasingly projected into urban space too, making Tallinn similar to clear-cut ethnic/racial divisions found in the the cities of the USA (van Kempen and Murie 2009).

The ethnic dimension probably also explains why the increase in segregation in Tallinn was bigger compared to the other Baltic capitals of Vilnius (Valatka *et al.* 2016) and Riga (Krišjāne *et al.* 2016). In Vilnius, the share of minorities is small and diverse. In Riga, the reverse is true: the Russian-speaking ethnic minority forms a clear majority in the city. Several more factors can be mentioned (Tsenkova 2006; Gentile 2015; pers. comm.): (a) Estonia is wealthier but with a less-regulated housing sector compared to Latvia and Lihtuania; (b) the prestige of Soviet-era large housing estates is higher in Latvia and well-regarded by both Latvians and Russian-speakers and, hence they have lower levels of inherited ethnic segregation; (c) the inner city in Riga is bigger and much more diverse compared to Tallinn, (d) deeper crises 2008–2010 in Latvia that froze settlement patterns because of the credit crunch. A more detailed comparative work on the Baltic capitals would help to better understand how residential sorting is related to such factors, making a difference regarding the way market forces operate along socio-economic and ethnic and dimensions between otherwise very similar cities when it comes to factors such as the city's role in the global network, level of social inequalities, type of welfare and housing regime (cf. Tammaru 2016).

To conclude, subjected to the far-reaching 'market experiment', levels of socio-economic segregation increased significantly in Tallinn between 2000 and 2011. High-status and low-status groups live increasingly apart from each other, with Estonian 'managers' and ethnic minority group members engaging in 'elementary occupations' being the two most segregated groups in the city. The spatial distance between Estonian 'managers' and 'elementary occupations' is less than it is between Estonian 'managers' and minority 'managers'. Segregation increased during times of lowering socio-economic inequality between the 2000 and 2011 censuses; despite a free market in the housing sector, the welfare state grew in

Estonia in the 2000s compared to the 1990s. It remains to be seen whether a decrease in socio-economic inequalities will bring down levels of socio-economic segregation, given that desegregation might also be delayed as the increase of segregation was delayed. In any case, while Tallinn was ethnically highly segregated and socio-economically modestly segregated under socialism, the 'market experiment' is leading towards a city that is characterised by an increasing overlap between ethnic and socio-economic segregation.

Acknowledgements

We are grateful to Dr Michael Gentile and Prof. Maarten van Ham for their helpful comments on our chapter. This research was supported by Grant No. 332265 by the Marie Curie Intra European Fellowship within the 7th European Community Framework Programme; Grant No IUT2-17, by the Ministry of Education and Science Estonia; and Grant No 9247 by the Estonian Science Foundation; European Union's Seventh Framework Programme (FP/2007–2013) / ERC Grant Agreement No 615159 (ERC Consolidator Grant DEPRIVEDHOODS, Socio-spatial inequality, deprived neighbourhoods, and neighbourhood effects).

In memoriam

This chapter is dedicated to the memory of our co-author Jakub Novák who recently passed away in a tragic car accident. We lost our good colleague and wonderful friend, and Czech urban geography lost one of its brightest scholars.

Notes

1 The main spatial buildings blocks across the former Soviet Union and Eastern Europe were *mikrorayony* ('micro-districts') or self-contained neighbourhoods, housing between 5,000 and 15,000 inhabitants, carefully planned according to the per-capita norms for social infrastructure (Kovács and Herfert 2012; Smith 1996). The aim was to build an environment that helps to approach equality in living standards (Smith 1996).
2 The within-group differentiation was the greatest among managers, with the ratio of the highest-income decile to the lowest being 8.0, whereas for other groups the average ratio was 3.
3 1 – managers, 2 – professionals, 3 – technicians and associate professionals, 4 – clerical support workers, 5 – service and sales workers, 7 – craft and related trades workers, 8 – plant and machine operators, and assemblers, 9 – elementary occupations, and 10 – unemployed.
4 These prestigous inter-war districts were somewhat downgraded socio-economically during the Soviet period.

References

Bater, J 1980, *The Soviet City*, Arnold, London.
Brown, L and Chung, S 2008, 'Market-led pluralism: Rethinking our understanding of racial/ethnic spatial patterning in US cities', *Annals of the Association of American Geographers* 98(1), 180–212.

Brubaker, R 1994, 'Nationhood and the national question in the Soviet Union and post-Soviet Eurasia: An institutionalist account' *Theory and Society* 23(1), 47–78.

Bruns, D 1998, *Tallinn: Linnaehitus Eesti Vabariigi aastail 1918–1940*, Tallinn, Valgus.

Eamets, R 2011, 'Labour market, labour market flexibility and the economic crisis in the Baltic states' *Estonian Human Development Report*, ed. M Lauristin, Tallinn, Eesti Koostöö Kogu, pp. 74–82.

Gentile, M and Sjöberg, Ö 2010, 'Spaces of priority: the geography of Soviet housing construction in Daugavpils, Latvia' *Annals of the Association of American Geographers* 100(1), 112–136.

Gentile, M, Tammaru, T and van Kempen, R 2012, 'Heteropolitanization: Social and spatial change in Central and Eastern European cities' *Cities* 29(5), 291–299.

Golubchikov, O, Badyina, A and Makhrova, A 2014, 'The hybrid spatialities of transition: Capitalism, legacy and uneven urban economic restructuring' *Urban Studies* 51(4), 617–633.

Hamilton, F, Andrews, K and Pichler-Milanovic, N (eds) 2005, *Transformation of Cities in Central and Eastern Europe: Towards Globalization*, Tokyo, United Nations University Press.

Harris, C 1970, *Cities of the Soviet Union: Studies in their Function, Size, Density and Growth*, Chicago, Rand McNally.

Hegedüs, J 2013, 'Housing privatisation and restitution' in *Social Housing in Transition Countries*, eds J Hegedüs, N Teller and M Lux, New York, Routledge, pp. 33–49.

Hussar, A, Kull, I and Kährik, A 2014, *National Report for Estonia*, EU TENLAW project.

Järv, O, Müürisepp, K, Ahas, R, Derudder, B, and Witlox, F 2014, 'Ethnic differences in activity spaces as a characteristic of segregation: A study based on mobile phone usage in Tallinn, Estonia' *Urban Studies*. Published online 22 September 2014, DOI 10.1177/0042098014550459.

Kährik, A and Kõre, J 2013, 'Social housing in Estonia after transition: In between the residual of privatization and the new developments' in *Social Housing in Transition Countries: Trends, Impacts and Policies*, eds J Hegedüs; M Lux and N Teller, London, Routledge.

Kährik, A, Novák, J, Temelová, J, Kadarik, K and Tammaru, T 2014, 'Patterns and drivers of inner city social differentiation in Prague and Tallinn', *Geografie*, forthcoming.

Kährik, A and Tammaru, T 2008, 'Population composition in new suburban settlements of the Tallinn metropolitan area' *Urban Studies* 45(5), 1055–1078.

Kährik, A and Tammaru, T 2010, 'Soviet prefabricated panel housing estates: areas of continued social mix or decline? The case of Tallinn, *Housing Studies* 25(2), 201–219.

Korts, K 2009, 'Inter-ethnic attitudes and contacts between ethnic groups in Estonia' *Journal of Baltic Studies* 40(1), 121–137.

Kovács, Z and Herfert, G 2012, 'Development pathways of large housing estates in post-socialist cities: An international comparison' *Housing Studies* 27(3), 324–342.

Kovács, Z and Szabó, B 2016, 'Urban restructuring and changing patterns of socio-economic segregation in Budapest' in *Socio-economic Segregation in European Capital Cities: East Meets West*, eds T Tammaru, S Marcińczak, M van Ham and S Musterd, London, Routledge.

Krišjāne, Z, Bērziņš, M and Kratovitš, K 2016, 'Occupation and ethnicity: Patterns of residential segregation in Riga two decades after socialism' in *Socio-economic Segregation in European Capital Cities: East meets West*, eds T Tammaru, S Marcińczak, M van Ham and S Musterd, London, Routledge.

Kulu, H 2003, 'Housing differences in the late Soviet city: The case of Tartu, Estonia' *International Journal of Urban and Regional Research* 27, 897–911.

Ladányi, J and Szelényi, I 1998, 'Class, ethnicity and urban restructuring in postcommunist Hungary' in *Social Change and Urban Restructuring in Central Europe*, ed. G Enyedi, Budapest, Akadémiai Kiadó.

Lauri, M 2014, Maris Lauri blog 10 November 2014. Riik ja üüriturg [State and the rental market]. Available online: https://mlauri.wordpress.com/2014/11/10/riik-ja-uuriturg/. Last accessed 27 April 2015

Leal, J and Sorando, D, 2016, 'Economic crisis, social change and segregation processes in Madrid' in *Socio-Economic Segregation in European Capital Cities: East Meets West*, eds T Tammaru, S Marcińczak, M van Ham and S Musterd, London, Routledge.

Leetmaa, K, Brade, I, Anniste, K and Nuga, M 2012, 'Socialist summer home settlements in post-socialist suburbanisation' *Urban Studies* 49(1), 3–21.

Leetmaa, K, Mägi, K, Kamenik, K, Org, A, Kratovitš, K and Tammaru, T 2014, *Internal Migration in Estonia in the Period 2000–2011: Input for National and Regional Population Prognoses 2013–2040 for Estonia*, Department of Geography, University of Tartu, Estonian Statistical Office.

Leetmaa, K and Tammaru, T 2007, 'Destinations of suburbanisers in the Tallinn metropolitan area' *Geografiska Annaler. Series B: Human Geography* 89, 127–146.

Leetmaa, K, Tammaru, T and Anniste, K 2009, 'From priorities to market-led suburbanisation in a post-communist metropolis' *Tijdschrift voor Economische en Sociale Geografie*, 100(4), 436–453.

Leetmaa, K, Tammaru, T, Hess, D B 2015, 'Preferences toward neighbor ethnicity and affluence: Evidence from an inherited dual ethnic context in post-Soviet Tartu, Estonia' *Annals of the Association of American Geographers,* Published Online, DOI: 10.1080/00045608.2014. Last accessed 27 April 2015.

Leping, K and Toomet, O 2008, 'Emerging ethnic wage gap: Estonia during political and economic transition' *Journal of Comparative Economics* 36(4), 599–619.

Lindemann, K and Kogan, I 2013, 'The role of language resources in labour market entry: Comparing Estonia and Ukraine' *Journal of Ethnic and Migration Studies* 39(1), 105–23.

Lindemann, K and Saar, E 2014, 'Contextual effects on subjective social position: evidence from European countries' *International Journal of Comparative Sociology* 55(1), 3–23.

Maloutas, T, 2016, 'Socio-economic segregation in Athens at the beginning of the twenty-first century' in *Socio-Economic Segregation in European Capital Cities: East Meets West*, eds T Tammaru, S Marcińczak, M van Ham and S Musterd, London, Routledge.

Manley, D, Johnston, R, Jones, K and Owen, D, 2016, 'Occupational segregation in London: A multilevel framework for modelling segregation' in *Socio-Economic Segregation in European Capital Cities: East Meets West*, eds T Tammaru, S Marcińczak, M van Ham and S Musterd, London, Routledge.

Marcińczak, S, Gentile, M, Rufat, S and Chelcea, L 2014, 'Urban geographies of hesitant transition: Tracing socioeconomic segregation in post-Ceauşescu Bucharest' *International Journal of Urban and Regional Research* 38(4), 1399–1417.

Marcińczak, S, Musterd, S, van Ham, M and Tammaru, T, 2016, 'Inequality and rising levels of socio-economic segregation: Lessons from a pan-European comparative study' in *Socio-Economic Segregation in European Capital Cities: East Meets West*, eds T Tammaru, S Marcińczak, M van Ham and S Musterd, London, Routledge.

Marcińczak, S, Tammaru, T, Novák, A, Gentile, M, Kovács, Z, Valatka, V, Temelová, J, Kährik, A and Balázs, S 2015, 'Patterns of socioeconomic segregation and mix in the capital cities of fast-track reforming post-socialist countries' *Annals of the Association of American Geographers* 105(1).

Marksoo, Ü, Białasiewicz, L and Best, U 2010, 'The global economic crisis and regional divides in the European Union: Spatial patterns of unemployment in Estonia and Poland' *Eurasian Geography and Economics* 51(1), 52–79.

Morton, H and Stuart, R (eds) 1984, *The Contemporary Soviet City,* London, Macmillan.

Musterd, S and van Gent, WPC, 2016, 'Changing welfare context and income segregation in Amsterdam and its metropolitan area' in *Socio-economic Segregation in European Capital Cities: East Meets West*, eds T Tammaru, S Marcińczak, M van Ham and S Musterd, London, Routledge.

Pullat, R 1968, 'Eesti linnarahvastiku dünaamika aastail 1917–1949' [Dynamics of urban population in Estonia 1917–1949] *ENSV Teaduste Akadeemia Toimetised* 17(4), 360–373.

Pullat, R 1972, *Eesti linnad ja linlased XVIII sajandi lõpust 1917. aastani.* [Estonian cities and city dwellers since the end of the eigthteenth centrury until 1917] Tallinn, Eesti raamat.

Raitviir, T 1987, *Tallinna faktorökoloogiline struktuur* [The factor-ecological structure of Tallinn] Tallinn, Eesti teadus- ja tehnikainformatsiooni ning majandusuuringute instituut).

Ruoppila, S and Kährik, A 2003, 'Socio-economic residential differentiation in post-socialist Tallinn' *Journal of Housing and the Built Environment* 18(1), 49–73.

Rybakovskiy, L 1987 *Migratsija naselenija: Prognosõ, faktorõ, politika* [Human migration: Forecasts, determinants and policies] Moskva, Nauka.

Sailer-Fliege, U 1999, 'Characteristics of post-socialist urban transformation in East Central Europe' *GeoJournal* 49, 7–16.

Silm, S and Ahas, R 2014, 'Ethnic differences in activity spaces: A study of out-of-home nonemployment activities with mobile phone data' *Annals of the Association of American Geographers* 104(3), 542–559.

Sjöberg, Ö 1999, 'Shortage, priority and urban growth: Towards the theory of urbanisation under central planning' *Urban Studies* 36, 2217–2235.

Smith, D 1996, 'The socialist city' in *Cities After Socialism: Urban and Regional Change and Conflict in Post-Socialist Societies*, eds G Andrusz, M Harloe and I. Szelényi, Oxford, Blackwell Publishers, pp. 70–99.

Sýkora, L 2009, 'Post-socialist cities' in *International Encyclopedia of Human Geography,* vol. 8, eds R Kitchin and N Thrift, Oxford, Elsevier, pp. 387–395.

Sýkora, L and Bouzarovski, S 2012, 'Multiple transformations: Conceptualising the post-communist urban transition' *Urban Studies* 49(1), 43–60.

Tammaru, T 2001a, 'Suburban growth and suburbanisation under central planning: The case of Soviet Estonia' *Urban Studies* 38(8), 1341–1357.

Tammaru, T. 2001b, 'The Soviet Union as a deviant case? Underurbanization in Soviet Estonia' *Urban Geography* 22(6), 584–603.

Tammaru, T and Kontuly, T 2011, 'Selectivity and destinations of ethnic minorities leaving the main gateway cities of Estonia' *Population, Space and Place*, 17(5), 674–688.

Tammaru, T and Kulu, H 2003, 'The ethnic minorities of Estonia: Changing size, location, and composition' *Eurasian Geography and Economics* 44(2), 105–120.

Tammaru, T and Leetmaa, K 2007, 'Suburbanisation in relation to education in the Tallinn metropolitan area' *Population, Space and Place* 13(4), 279–292.

Tammaru, T, Musterd, S, van Ham, M and Marcińczak, S, 2016, 'A multi-factor approach to understanding socio-economic segregation in European capital cities' in *Socio-economic Segregation in European Capital Cities: East Meets West*, eds T Tammaru, S Marcińczak, M van Ham and S Musterd, London, Routledge.

Tammaru, T, van Ham, M, Leetmaa, K, Kährik, A and Kamenik, K 2013, 'Ethnic dimensions of suburbanisation in Estonia' *Journal of Ethnic and Migration Studies* 39(5), 845–862.

Temelová, J 2007, 'Flagship developments and the physical upgrading of the postsocialist city: The Golden Angel project in Prague' *Geografiska Annaler: Series B* 89(2), 169–181.

Temelová, J 2013, 'Princess Cinderella? Multiple transformations in the CEE inner city' Presentation at 5th International Urban Geographies of Post-Communist States Conference, Tbilisi, Georgia, 11–13 September 2013.

Titma, M, Tuma, N B and Silver, B 1998, 'Winners and losers in the postcommunist transition: New evidence from Estonia' *Post-Soviet Affairs* 14 (2), 114–136.

Tsenkova, S 2006, 'Beyond transitions: Understanding urban change in post-socialist cities' in *The Urban Mosaic of Post-Socialist Cities*, eds. S Tsenkova and Z Nedović-Budić, New York, Physica-Verlag Heidelberg, pp. 21–50.

Valatka, V, Burneika, D and Ubarevičienė, R 2016, 'Large social inequalities and low levels of socio-economic segregation in Vilnius' in *Socio-economic Segregation in European Capital Cities: East Meets West*, eds T Tammaru, S Marcińczak, M van Ham and S Musterd, London, Routledge.

van Kempen, and Murie, A 2009, 'The divided city: Changing patterns in European cities' *Tijdschrift voor Economische en Sociale Geografie*, 100 (4), 377–398.

Verdery, K 1996, *What Was Socialism and What Comes Next?* Cambridge, Cambridge University Press.

15 Inequality and rising levels of socio-economic segregation

Lessons from a pan-European comparative study

Szymon Marcińczak, Sako Musterd, Maarten van Ham and Tiit Tammaru

Abstract

The *Socio-Economic Segregation in European Capital Cities: East Meets West* project investigates changing levels of socio-economic segregation in 13 major European cities: Amsterdam, Budapest, Vienna, Stockholm, Oslo, London, Vilnius, Tallinn, Prague, Madrid, Milan, Athens and Riga. The two main conclusions of this major study are that the levels of socio-economic segregation in European cities are still relatively modest compared to some other parts of the world but that the spatial gap between poor and rich is widening in all capital cities across Europe. Segregation levels in the East of Europe started at a lower level compared to the West of Europe, but the East is quickly catching up, although there are large differences between cities. Four central factors were found to play a major role in the changing urban landscape in Europe: welfare and housing regimes, globalisation and economic restructuring, rising economic inequality and historical development paths. Where state intervention in Europe has long countered segregation, (neo) liberal transformations in welfare states, under the influence of globalisation, have caused an increase in inequality. As a result, the levels of socio-economic segregation are moving upwards. If this trend were to continue, Europe would be at risk of slipping into the epoch of growing inequalities and segregation where the rich and the poor will live separate lives in separate parts of their cities, which could seriously harm the social stability of our future cities.

Introduction

The spatial sorting of residents according to socio-economic status is as old as the history of urbanisation (Nightingale 2012). Processes and patterns of segregation are far from uniform in historical and regional contexts (York *et al.* 2012). The intensity and geography of socio-spatial divisions in cities are related to the constant interplay between institutions that set the rules of the game and households that make residential location decisions. Most important, unlike other forms of segregation, such as those based on race, ethnicity or religion, socio-economic segregation is usually seen as a direct effect of economic inequality. Common sense may suggest that greater inequality in a city also entails higher levels of socio-economic segregation (Reardon and Bischoff 2011). Nonetheless, more often than not, the relation between the two is far from 'positive' and 'linear'. The seemingly obvious and logical regularity of this relation is mediated by a country/region-specific institutional setting and a city's trajectory of economic and population development (Burgers and Musterd 2002; Maloutas and Fujita 2012; Musterd and Ostendorf 1998). Moreover, socio-economic segregation will also be mediated by other forms of segregation, such as race-based and ethnic segregation (van Ham and Manley 2009; Manley and van Ham 2011). When a household 'selects' a certain place to live on demographic or cultural grounds, there will also be an impact on segregation in socio-economic terms. Viewed in this light, the studies on class-based spatial divisions in a selection of European cities brought together in this volume illuminate the complex relations between economic inequality, social disparities, and urban space. These relations unfold in the divergent historical, demographic, cultural and institutional contexts of the northern, southern, western and eastern parts of Europe at times of profound political and economic changes. Sweeping across the continent in the last two decades, these changes include the fall of the Berlin Wall (1989) and demise of the Soviet Union (1991), the enlargement of the European Union to include the new member states from East Europe[1] in 2004 and 2007, a concomitant massive East–West migration and, more recently, a deep economic crisis and its aftermath.

After an era of decreasing social inequality, which effectively started after World War II, from the early 1970s onwards, income inequality has been continuously increasing across the globe. In Europe, wealth inequalities are currently almost as high as they used to be in the heydays of laissez-faire capitalism in the late nineteenth century (Piketty 2013). Interestingly, one and a half centuries ago, similar levels of inequality were related to the formation of dreadful slums (Booth 1887, 1888; Engels 1892) and to clear-cut spatial divisions between the rich and the poor in the great industrial cities of that epoch (Park *et al.* 1925; Zorbaugh 1929). In the early 1990s, when globalisation was thriving and a new global division of labour evolved, some scholars predicted similar scenarios for urban areas at the turn of the twenty-first century. In brief, the end of the second and the beginning of the third millennium were heralded to be the advent of the era of mounting inequality, increasing class segregation and concentrated affluence and poverty (Massey 1996).

While there are several European studies of ethnic/racial segregation (Arbaci 2007; Huttman *et al.* 1991; Malheiros 2002; Musterd *et al.* 1998), European comparative research on class- or income-based socio-spatial divisions has received much less scholarly attention in the last 30 years. Although there are studies comparing European cities in the spheres of social inequality (for example Musterd 2005; Musterd and van Kempen 2007), these are rather crude, or limited to certain segments of a city, such as post-war neighbourhoods. Diligent up-to-date research on socio-economic (income or class) segregation in more than one city is hard to find. There are exceptions though, and some studies are dealing with socio-economic segregation in North America (Fischer *et al.* 2004; Reardon and Bischoff 2011;

Watson 2009), in West Europe and other western countries (Maloutas and Fuijta 2012; Musterd and Ostendorf 1998) or, recently, also in East Europe (Marcińczak *et al.* 2015). The contributions from 13 major European cities collected in this volume – Amsterdam, Budapest, Vienna, Stockholm, Oslo, London, Vilnius, Tallinn, Prague, Madrid, Milan, Athens and Riga – reveal that the levels of socio-economic segregation are moving upwards, and that the spatial gap between the more extreme socio-economic categories is widening in all capital cities across Europe.

The lack of studies that compare and contrast processes and patterns of socioeconomic segregation is in fact surprising as the field of urban studies is currently witnessing a revival and a reorientation of comparative research (McFarlane and Robinson 2012; Robinson 2011; Ward 2010). Essentially, this reinvigorated strand of urban studies aims at the systematic study of similarity and difference among cities or urban processes both through description and explanation (Nijman 2007). Even if the chances for a methodologically rigorous case selection are fairly slim (Kantor and Savitch 2005; McFarlane 2010; Pickvance 1986), comparative urbanism emphasises the merit of a cyclical movement between theorising and doing empirical research. This offers a unique opportunity to review established theories and to avoid further development of decontextualised universalist ideas and models of urban development (Robinson 2011).

In this final chapter an attempt is made to draw some general conclusions from comparing the findings from all the studies that were presented in this volume. Before doing that, however, we have to point out two caveats related to the crosscase comparisons we present. First, the very idea of 'a city' is not the same in every European country. The proposed definition of the city was a continuous built-up area (Tammaru *et al.* 2016b). Some contributors collected and analysed data for urban regions (metropolitan areas), while others had to limit their analysis to areas within administrative boundaries of the city, and still others did both. These choices partly reflect data availability and partly also the urban processes themselves, for example the extent of urban sprawl. This inconsistency, which is also present in previous comparative studies on segregation in Europe, may potentially bias direct comparisons, as tighter delimitations, arguably, conceal the effects of intraregional population dynamics that shape patterns of segregation, for example. suburbanisation. The second caveat relates to the fact that availability of data reflecting (socio) economic disparities varies from country to country, even when looking at relatively similar European countries, and impacts not only on the definition of the city but also the choice of socio-economic indicators. Because of this, contributors relied on the division of population into income groups, or classifications of socio-professional status or highest education completed. The latter two are imperfect proxies for income disparities, while a distinction on the basis of income falls short in covering the whole spectrum of social inequality as well. Finally, we decided to exclude Milan from direct comparisons with the other cities. The reason we did this is that the results from Milan pertain to the last decade of the twentieth century, while the focus of this chapter is on the evolving patterns of socio-economic segregation in the new millennium. However, we take on board the upshot of the Italian study.

The rest of this chapter is divided into three main sections. The first section summarises the changing patterns of socio-economic segregation in political and/ or economic capital cities of Europe in the first decade of the new millennium. In the introductory chapter of the book (Tammaru *et al*. 2016b) we presented a multi-factor approach to understanding segregation that resulted in the following theoretical ranking of cities with regard to their expected level of socio-economic segregation: London; Riga; Madrid and Vilnius; Milan and Tallinn; Amsterdam and Athens; Budapest, Oslo and Stockholm; and finally Prague and Vienna. The case studies presented in this book revealed a somewhat different ranking based on real data: Madrid and Milan; Tallinn; London; Stockholm; Vienna; Athens; Amsterdam; Budapest; Riga; Vilnius; Prague; and Oslo. In this concluding chapter we will elaborate on the differences between the theoretical and actual rankings of cities, mainly by scrutinising the similarities and differences in the levels and geographies of class-based spatial-disparities in our case cities. In the following section we elucidate how globalisation, economic inequality, different housing regimes and forms of welfare state relate to patterns of socio-spatial divisions in our selection of European cities. In the third and concluding section, we summarise the most important findings in the perspective of the multi-factor approach we developed in the introductory chapter of this volume.

Class and space in the European city

More than 50 years ago, Chicago scholars found that spatial distance grows with social distance and that a truncated U-shape characterises segregation profiles. Both high and low social categories appeared to be highly segregated, but higher social categories were consistently more segregated than lower social groups in the American city (Duncan and Duncan 1955). This was later confirmed in Europe by studies from England and Wales (Morgan 1975, 1980). The skewed U-shape of segregation profiles toward higher socio-economic groups also applied to the European cities that were developing under totalitarian socialist regimes (Dangschat 1987; Ladányi 1989; Szelényi 1987). Interestingly, it seems that the trend found and confirmed in different Fordist societies did not vanish with the end of Fordism; the profile still holds in the United States in the 2000s (Fischer *et al*. 2004; Reardon and Bischoff 2011). Yet, how persistent is the truncated pattern of socio-spatial divisions in Europe? Segregation outcomes from 12 European cities presented in this volume cast some doubt on the seemingly universal shape of relations between class and space. We used the index of segregation (IS) as a measure that summarises residential separation of one group from the remainder of the population. The IS illustrates the degree to which class-based disparities correlate with spatial distance. The indices of segregation for top and bottom social categories refer to the two ends of the segregation U-curve (Figure 15.1); the cities were ordered by the decreasing degree of residential separation of the highest socio-economic category in the early 2000s. The results presented in Figure 15.1, but also in other figures in this chapter, should be interpreted with care. The different variables used to distinguish the top (high) and bottom (low) social categories, as well as different spatial units, may influence the values of segregation measures. Notwithstanding the limitations of available data, it is clear that the rule that higher classes are more segregated than the lower classes is not ubiquitous. Even if in two-thirds of 12 European capital cities, the higher class is the most segregated social category (in Amsterdam, Stockholm, Oslo, Vienna, Madrid, Tallinn, Riga and Vilnius), the remaining cases show other outcomes. In Athens[2] and London, a counterintuitive segregation profile has been present for the last two decades. The 'anomaly' has been fading out in Budapest, but it has become a clear pattern in Prague. We must take into account that these differences between cases may be an effect of scale: the use of either cities or the whole metropolitan area. Essentially, metropolitan areas represent a spatial scale that allows more variation within its boundaries than a city does, for example concentrations of the affluent in inner London and more dispersed concentrations elsewhere in greater London can exist simultaneously. The stronger segregation of lower social groups could also result from inherited morphological structure and housing inequalities. But maybe also suburbanisation draws higher social echelons out of previously socially mixed neighbourhoods, as seems to be the case in Budapest and Prague. In other words, irrespective of the apparently unifying effect of neo-liberalisation and globalisation, the institutional, economic and demographic contexts still play a key role in determining which end of the social hierarchy is more segregated. The general conclusion about the shape of the distribution of segregation by social category is that profiles reported in 12 cities are skewed and that in most but not all cases, the highest social strata appear to be the most segregated.

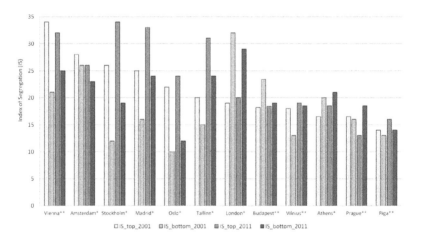

Figure 15.1 Index of segregation scores for top and bottom social categories.

Notes: * Metropolitan region, **city
Madrid, Tallinn, London, Budapest, Vilnius, Athens, Prague, Riga – managers and elementary occupations.
Amsterdam, Oslo, Stockholm – highest and lowest income quintile.
Vienna – university degree and compulsory education.

Figure 15.1 shows index of segregation scores for top and bottom social categories for 12 cities for both 2001 and 2011. There is a substantial difference between the levels of socio-economic segregation in our European case cities. In general, whereas in the early 2000s it was still possible to argue that West European cities were more segregated than those in the East, a decade later this is no longer so obvious. Most importantly, the intensity of socio-spatial divisions and its changes have not followed any clear regional pattern (Figure 15.1). The levels of segregation of the top and of the bottom categories decreased in Amsterdam (but see below). In Vienna and Prague (limited) desegregation was confined to the top social categories only, but we should take into account that the segregation level of the top social class in Vienna was already very high in 2001. In London and Budapest only the lower social groups became more evenly distributed; here we notice that segregation levels of the lowest class in London were already very high in 2001. Socio-economic spatial divisions of the social 'top' (relative to the rest) and 'bottom' (relative to the rest) became more pronounced in the other seven cities (Stockholm, Oslo, Madrid, Athens, Tallinn, Vilnius and Riga). The rise of segregation was especially high in Stockholm, Tallinn and Madrid. Interestingly, the recent crisis seems to contribute to both increasing segregation (Madrid) and desegregation (Amsterdam). In the latter case, the crisis implied a dynamic that was against the processes that were going on before and that created more segregation. Due to the crisis, people did not dare to make big (residential) decisions anymore; this resulted in (likely temporary) reduced segregation levels. In addition, there were swift changes in the formerly nineteenth-century neighbourhoods in Amsterdam that created – temporarily – more mix. Therefore, in a more structural sense segregation also seems to be increasing in Amsterdam. However, segregation also increased in Madrid also during the crisis. Here it seems that the crisis strengthened the segregation processes that were already ongoing: the poor became poorer in the neighbourhoods where they already lived; and the rich were able to retain their wealth, largely because the higher managerial and professional ranks managed to cope with the effects of the crisis. Moreover, Madrid only recently started to weaken the impact of family solidarity networks, networks requiring spatial proximity between different social classes and generations (Allen *et al.* 2004), implying that segregation could increase due to that process too. Also, gentrification started late in Madrid, and therefore the initial desegregating effects, which usually can be seen in the early phases of gentrification (cf. Freeman 2009; Galster and Booza 2007), are still negligible. Overall, for 9 of the 12 cities we had information on, we find increasing levels of segregation of the top social categories; and also for 9 of the 12 cities we found increasing segregation of the lowest social categories. Amsterdam may perhaps be added to these latter 9.

All in all, the main empirical finding of this comparative research is that socio-economic segregation levels increased in European capital cities between the 2001 and 2011. In those cases where desegregation occurred, this seems to be due to a lack of opportunities, economic uncertainty due to crises (Amsterdam) or simply because of the spatial distribution of affordable housing (Athens in the 1990s). In

Milan scholars point at demographic processes that are driving declining segregation: (1) gentrification leading to the substitution of working-class households in working-class neighbourhoods by white-collar workers; (2) under right-to-buy schemes working-class households purchased properties which they subsequently sold to white-collar households; (3) upgrading through inheritance, where a white-collar children inherit a house from their working-class parents; (4) the tendency for self-employed households on modest incomes to settle in the working-class periphery of the city where housing is affordable and where public and state-subsidised housing is mainly located. In other words, it seems that there are two general factors that appear to reduce levels of segregation, possibly both only temporarily. One is a limited or reduced level of residential mobility that leads to *in situ* social mobility: sitting residents become richer or poorer in their neighbourhoods. That creates more mix *in situ* and thus lower levels of segregation (cf. Galster and Booza 2007). When residential mobility increases again, we should see rising levels of segregation. The second factor is gentrification. Especially when gentrification is new in an area, this is typically a process where formerly homogeneous low-income households become accompanied by socially upward neighbours. This will initially reduce the level of segregation. More mature gentrification may again result in increasing segregation.

It would be misleading to attribute all changing levels of segregation to the effects of the crises and/or demographic processes only; these forces will be responsible for temporal deviations of the more general and structural changes in some cities, but not in all. The mounting socio-economic spatial disparities in Tallinn, a city that has also been in the grip of the recent economic crisis, may well have other roots. It is likely that the significantly higher levels of socio-spatial divisions in Tallinn in 2010 stem from the realised potential of the rapidly growing income inequality and employment change in the 1990s. Segregation has been on the rise in most of the other East European cities too. Essentially, while economic disparity skyrocketed throughout the region, the patterns of segregation did not change much in East Europe in the first decade after the collapse of socialism (Marcińczak *et al.* 2013, 2014; Sýkora 2009). However, from the second decade onwards, inequalities started materialising in space. Finally, institutional arrangements, housing regimes and the extent of the welfare state have had a tremendous impact on socio-economic segregation. In countries that virtually did not suffer from economic turmoil, levels of segregation either decreased somewhat (higher social strata in Vienna), or, as the case of Stockholm clearly exemplifies, increasing segregation could be observed before and after the crises. We will discuss the nexus between institutional arrangements, economic inequality and socio-economic segregation in the next section.

Figure 15.2 shows indices of dissimilarity between opposite social groups that gives a more coherent picture of changing levels of socio-economic segregation in Europe. Essentially, despite visible signs of desegregation of the top and/or the bottom social groups, residential separation of the rich from the poor has been consistently growing over the last decade in all cases included in our study, except for Amsterdam (Figure 15.2). However, if we leave out the effect of the

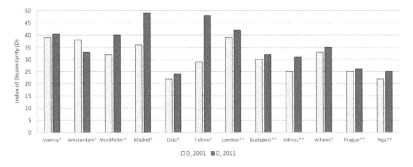

Figure 15.2 Index of dissimilarity.

Notes: * Metropolitan region, **city
Madrid, Tallinn, London, Budapest, Vilnius, Athens, Prague, Riga – managers and elementary occupations.
Amsterdam, Oslo, Stockholm – highest and lowest income quintile.
Vienna – university degree and compulsory education.

economic and housing crisis, which hit Amsterdam particularly hard, the separation between the rich and the poor also increased in Amsterdam, as shown in this volume. The reduced levels of segregation of the 'top' relative to the rest, or the 'bottom' relative to the rest (reported above for some cities), does not prevent increasing separation of the 'top' from the 'bottom'. This indicates that although socio-economic residential mixing may occur, this is limited to groups with a status that is not too far apart from each other. This corroborates the findings by Musterd *et al.* (2014), who showed that the tendency to move increases with the social distance between an individual and the social level of the neighbourhood (s)he is living in; larger social distances imply a larger propensity to move and subsequently a larger chance to end up in a socially more similar neighbourhood. However, the spatial gap between the more extreme categories, those that 'have' and those that 'have not' is pretty much widening all over Europe. However, so far, the socio-economic segregation is clearly lower than in the USA (Florida 2014) or in Brazil (Villaca 2011).

The ethnic and socio-economic dimensions of segregation are often linked. Even if the two dimensions do not overlap completely, immigrants in the West European countries, especially those newly arrived, are frequently overrepresented among the urban poor (Arbaci 2007). Yet, there is also class differentiation within categories of native and non-native residents. Some cities (Amsterdam, Stockholm) show that such class differentiation is even bigger for some non-native categories than for the native categories. Strong social divisions underpinned by ethnic disparities do not necessarily have to be a consequence of recent immigration. The Baltic States, principally Estonia, demonstrate the effect of deeply rooted ethnic divisions amplified by the downfall of socialism and the formation of independent statehood in the early 1990s. In Tallinn, the divisions between higher-class natives and lower-class minority groups are higher than in any other European city where ethnic divisions are present; such

Table 15.1 Major areas of concentration for top and bottom social groups in selected European cities, 2001–2011

City/region	Comments
Amsterdam	High SES is over-represented in some older neighbourhoods in the inner city and in specific suburban areas. Low SES is over-represented in post-war social housing neighbourhoods and in some of the older parts of the core city where social housing is prevalent.
Athens	Traditional social division between Low SES west and High SES East shapes Athens since the nineteenth century. Over the last decades, High SES is opting massively for residence in the north-eastern and south-eastern suburbs, creating strong city–suburb SES divide.
Budapest	Clear social division between High SES west sector stretching from the city centre to the suburbs, and the rest of the city. Three Low SES areas stick out: some decaying inner-city quarters, socialist high-rise housing estates and low-rise suburban residential–industrial neighbourhoods.
London	The High SES west and Low SES east is the most important macro-level social division already existing for centuries. A sector of High SES extends from west-central London towards the suburbs. Low SES location pattern is more mosaic compared to High SES, and concentrations can mainly be found in the distant suburbs.
Madrid	High SES is expanding from the core city towards the suburbs, especially to the north and north-west, creating clear divisions between the core city and suburbs. Those High SES who inherited, or who succeeded the prior inhabitants, stay in the core city. Low SES has long been over-represented in the core city and in the suburbs in the south and east.
Oslo	A key social division runs between the High SES west and the Low SES east. There are many locations in the city, however, where concentrations of both social groups are juxtaposed with each other.
Prague	Many locations in the city show concentrations of High SES and Low SES that are often juxtaposed all-over the city. A typical socio-spatial mosaic.
Stockholm	High SES is over-represented in inner-city neighbourhoods and in specific suburban areas. Low SES is over-represented in more peripheral post-war social housing neighbourhoods.
Tallinn	High SES predominates in the historical city centre and attractive inner-city neighbourhoods from the 1930s. Low SES is overrepresented in the socialist-era housing estates and in seedy, pre-World War II neighbourhoods in the inner city. In the periphery, High SES and Low SES concentrate in non-conterminous sectors and clusters.
Vienna	High SES residential patterns is sectoral, stretching from the western inner-city districts to the western outskirts of the city. Low SES are over-represented in the eastern parts of the city and strongly confined to public housing neighbourhoods.
Vilnius	Historical north–south division of the city is deepening. High SES is over-represented in the inner city and low-density villa areas in the outer city. Low SES is strongly over-represented in the south, especially in older socialist housing estates, as well as in the most peripheral parts in the north.
Riga	High SES concentrates in the city centre (historical core) and in small clusters sprinkled over the peripheral areas. Low SES are overrepresented in the lower quality housing in the inner-city and in the periphery. Both social categories mix in the socialist-era

a scale of disparities, arguably, evokes the picture of clear-cut ethnic/racial divisions epitomised by urban regions in the USA (Farley *et al.* 1978; van Kempen and Murie 2009).

Table 15.1 gives an insight into the major areas of concentration for top and bottom social groups in 12 cities. The descriptions in the table and the figures show that the geography of socio-economic segregation in European cities does not follow a uniform model. The only general characteristic shared by all 13 cities was a mosaic socio-spatial structure of the urban fabric. In the last 10 years this inherent feature of socio-economic spatial divisions in the European city (French and Hamilton 1979; Marcińczak *et al.* 2015; Musterd 2005) has somewhat changed. In the first decade of the twenty-first century we can now see emerging a more regular, often sectorial, pattern of socio-economic segregation in many cities. In short, the seemingly mosaic pattern of social disparities conceals divergent, context-sensitive, local patterns of class segregation (Table 15.1). In cities like Stockholm, London and Amsterdam, urban-oriented fractions of the middle class and certain professions increasingly concentrate in the central parts of the metropolitan area and the poorer households are consistently more dependent on housing in more peripheral residential areas. Social mix and anti-segregation policies may have reduced this process but failed to stop the overall trend. Interestingly, London is an excellent example of how persistent the legacy of historically developed segregation patterns might be: the social status of some neighbourhoods has not changed much for more than a century (Manley and Johnston 2015). The geographies of class divisions in Budapest and Vienna also point towards an important role for an 'inherited' urban fabric. Even though the two cities developed in radically different economic and political milieus in the second half of the twentieth century, higher social categories still occupy bourgeois tenements and villas, and lower classes are overrepresented in poor-quality buildings that housed the working class in the last days of the Habsburg Empire.

In Athens, more affluent sections of the population occupied specific suburban territory. This is a somewhat reverse image compared with West Europe. In Athens this was due to a stable professional structure, stable housing markets, limited residential mobility, reduced immigration and vertical segregation. A similar reversed pattern with elite in the suburbs and poorer households in the central districts can be found in Madrid, although independent professionals slowly seem to be 'taking over' the central parts of town as well. The effects of suburbanisation, a major trend in regional population dynamics after socialism (Stanilov and Sýkora 2014), on patterns of segregation are also clearly visible in East Europe. Top social groups have been incrementally moving to the peripheral and suburban estates where new housing was available. On the other hand, in five post-socialist cities, top social echelons are overrepresented in the inner-city too. Assuming that gentrification gained momentum in the 2000s (Kovács *et al.* 2013), and that large socialist-era residential estates, often the dominant form of housing, have been consistently losing the better-off residents, more clear-cut spatial divisions might actually materialise in East Europe in the future. However, new geographies of segregation might not necessarily be similar to elsewhere in Europe.

Economic disparities, globalisation, institutions and segregation

The starting point for this study was the multi-factor approach which we presented in the introduction of this volume (Tammaru *et al.* 2016b). This approach resulted in a theoretical ranking of our case study cities by the level of socio-economic segregation. Referring to theories explaining patterns of socio-economic segregation, the multi-factor approach lists a number of 'universal' and 'relative' characteristics determining levels and geographies of social divisions. The 'universal' factors are believed to cause ubiquitous effects that are not sensitive to spatio-temporal parameters, whereas the 'relative' factors are highly specific to particular social systems (Pickvance 1986). As a more parsimonious approach might still be beneficial for meaningful comparative analysis (Kantor and Savitch 2005), we selected four key variables for further examination. Essentially, we chose two universal factors (income inequality and level of globalisation) and two contextual factors (housing regimes and forms of the welfare state) to elucidate the complex relations between important structural economic and institutional changes and evolving patterns of residential segregation we encounter in European cities. We present a series of bivariate analyses of the relations between spatial separation of opposing social groups and the key contributory factors.

In general, it is taken for granted that socio-economic segregation is a product of socio-economic inequality, and that growing inequality results in increasing segregation (Massey 1996; van Kempen 2007; Watson 2009). However, the apparently universal and strong correlation between social and spatial divisions is not always existing (Fuijta 2012). In brief, the catalysing effect of income inequality on residential segregation hinges on context-specific institutional arrangements: for instance, a close and lasting link between segregation and inequality requires the presence of an income-based housing market and housing policies that relate income to residential location (Brown and Chung 2008; Reardon and Bischoff 2011). The results from the analysis of our 13 European cities shed some new light on these relations.

As in many other developed and developing countries across the globe (Stiglitz 2013), income inequality has been on the rise in most of Europe. In the last decade, societies became more equal income-wise in Estonia, and to a lesser extent in Norway and the Netherlands. Bearing in mind that generally the levels of socio-economic segregation also went up, it is tempting to suggest that the two phenomena are tightly linked. Figure 15.3 shows the relationship between income inequality (Gini index) and the level of residential segregation between top and bottom social categories measured by the index of dissimilarity. Indeed, in 11 out of 12 European cities the changing intensity of segregation reflects changes in income inequality; growing inequality involves increasing segregation, and, as the case of Amsterdam clearly illustrates, reduced levels of segregation follow income disparities (Figure 15.3). Nonetheless, it seems that segregation may surge irrespective of reducing economic inequality; in Tallinn, but also in Oslo, such a paradoxical situation is unambiguous. In both countries income inequality

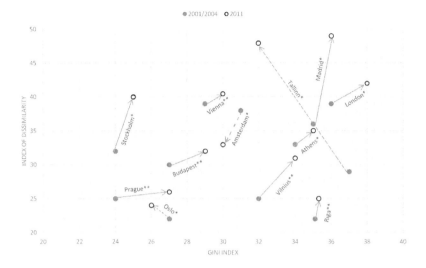

Figure 15.3 Income inequality and residential segregation between top and bottom social categories in selected European cities, 2001/2004–2011.

Notes: * Metropolitan region, **city.
Madrid, Tallinn, London, Budapest, Vilnius, Athens, Prague, Riga – managers and elementary occupations.
Amsterdam, Oslo, Stockholm – highest and lowest income quintile.
Vienna – university degree and compulsory education.

was consistently growing in the 1990s that may actually point to the lagged effect of income disparities on residential segregation; it simply takes time before spatial patterns catch up with socio-economic changes. Interestingly, a temporarily reversed relationship between economic inequality and segregation is also possible; in East Europe, rapidly growing income disparities after the collapse of socialism entailed short-term desegregation in the 1990s (Marcińczak *et al.* 2013: 2014; Sýkora 2009). A fairly similar trend could also be found outside former socialist Europe (Oslo in the last decade of the previous century). In fact, such a long-term perspective on the relation between social inequality and the level of socio-spatial segregation also proves to be more relevant for almost all of the cities included in this study. In that respect it is also important to filter out the temporary or conjunctural effects. With a view on social inequality over a longer period of time, we can show, for example, that Amsterdam (and the Netherlands) experienced substantially growing inequality over the past three decades, which also resulted in increasing socio-spatial segregation until 2008 when the crisis started. In 2011, compared to the start of the millennium, social inequality dropped a little, but compared to the late 1980s social inequality rose significantly. The more recent drop coincided with lower levels of segregation, which were also to be ascribed to the crisis. If crisis effects are left out, economic inequality has been on the rise for the last two or three decades.

Even if the widening spatial gap between the top social class and the bottom social class generally correlates with a growing economic inequality, as can be shown for 9 out of 12 cities, it does not necessarily mean that the most unequal cities are also the most segregated. Stockholm, the capital of one of the most equal countries in the world, is – at the moment – relatively high in the hierarchy of socio-economic segregation in Europe. Most important, the relationship between segregation and inequality is rarely linear. In other words, a relatively small increase in income inequality may relate to significantly growing residential segregation (Madrid, Stockholm). On the other hand, a more substantial growth of socio-economic disparities may well coincide with a negligible increase in residential segregation (Budapest, Prague). Thus, social inequality is not sufficient as the sole explanatory factor of the evolving patterns of residential segregation in Europe.

The globalisation of the economy and society and a series of massive and parallel changes that the processes involve, have been argued to stimulate the growth of socio-economic disparities and segregation in the contemporary city (Fainstein *et al.* 1992, Marcuse and van Kempen 2002; Massey 1996; Smith 2002). The evolution of the employment structure in major hubs and nodes in the global spaces of flows of money and people, amplified by a post-Fordist restructuring of the economy, may indeed lead to social and occupational polarisation (Sassen 1991). Essentially, the dwindling labour-intensive manufacturing industry in much of Europe and North America, in the aftermath of the new global division of labour (Massey 1995), has led to new economic activities that demand new types of labour, many of them with higher levels of education. Some cities will manage (or already have managed) to deliver the required new types of employees more easily than others. As Burgers and Musterd (2002) have set out, cities with a very strong history as a manufacturing industry centre, which were dependent on low-skilled or unskilled employees, may not immediately succeed in professionalising their population – transforming their professional structures to the newly required standards. In those cases a certain mismatch may develop between the demand for labour and the supply of it. This will result in rising unemployment levels in those cities, especially for the lower-skilled people. In contrast, cities that already had a profile in which service-sector jobs were more important and which were well-connected to important city networks, may have created a better position to fit the new economic requirements. These will be characterised by an easier expansion of activities in (international) services and knowledge-intensive industry sectors and are able to provide the correct skilled labour, and thus experience fewer mismatches and less unemployment. Some of the cities may, due to their connectedness and professional structure, become well positioned to connect with other major cities in the world and become essential nodes, or even centres of control in new economic networks. In truly global cities with such node or control functions, the rapid development of the service sector will involve the development of a large number of well-paid jobs in high-end producer services but also strong growth of low-paid, often dead-end, jobs associated with serving the better-off. The city type that will develop in such circumstances will typically be the polarised city Sassen (1991) was referring to.

In short, the future of cities is partly conditioned by the historically created economic profile of the city and the level of integration in the global economy. This may or may not lead to increasing social disparities, mismatches, social polarisation or duality (Castells 1989). Yet, even cities that manage to get a strong position in global networks will not automatically become the most segregated cities (Butler and Hamnett 2012); logically, actual social and spatial divisions are highly complex (Marcuse 1989; Hamnett 2012). Nevertheless, for some cities, globalisation brought about growing socio-economic inequalities (van Kempen 2007) and, at least in the USA, also more intensive spatial segregation (Fischer *et al.* 2004; Reardon and Bischoff 2011). In other cities existing economic structures did not suit the globalisation processes. This may have resulted in mismatches between demand and supply of labour, but may also have triggered active professionalisation policies, increasing professional skills throughout the social distribution, therewith reducing the share of lower strata while increasing the middle and upper strata. According to many, professionalisation, not polarisation, has in fact been the main trend in the transformations of employment profiles in European cities. The pattern that was clear in Europe already in the 1980s (Hamnett 1994), and that seems to have become even more prominent in the 1990s (Butler *et al.* 2008; Maloutas and Fujita 2012; Marcińczak *et al.* 2014, 2015; Préteceille 2000), may not have changed too much in the first decade of the new millennium, although there is difference between cities. In short, we expect a relationship between the 'global' character of a city and the level of social polarisation that will also be reflected in spatial segregation between top and bottom, but that relationship can be mitigated by a range of other forces.

It is hard to quantify such a multidimensional phenomenon as globalisation. We refer to a well-known typology of cities that reflects a city's connection with the global economy (Beaverstock *et al.* 2014) to differentiate between European cities that are more embedded in the space of flows and those that are less. There are three groups and several subcategories of world cities: *Alpha* cities link major economic regions and states to the world economy; *Beta* cities link their region or state to the world economy; and *Gamma* cities connect smaller regions or states to the world economy (Beaverstock *et al.* 2015) Figure 15.4 shows the relationship between world-city status and residential segregation between top and bottom social groups.

The European cities examined in this study virtually represent all categories distinguished by the world-cities taxonomy; major European urban areas range from the iconic *Alpha++* global cities like London to the much-less integrated capital cities of the Baltic States. Then, what do we see when we relate the classification based on this indicator of globalisation with the level of segregation of the cities studied in this volume? And how does that relation change over time?

It can be shown that in 2011 the paradigmatic global city, London, is not the most segregated in Europe anymore; in fact, it is clearly less divided than Madrid (*Alpha*), but also less than Tallinn, a *Gamma* city. This is in concordance with what we see in the United States where the most globalised cities (New York, Los Angeles or Chicago) are not among the top ten most segregated metropolitan areas (Florida 2014). However, we also see that Tallinn is, in fact, an outlier when it comes to the relation between globalisation and segregation. It used to be moderately socio-economically segregated like other East European cities but became highly ethno-linguistically segregated under socialism (Marcińczak *et al.* 2015; Tammaru and Kontuly 20101). What has happened in Estonia over the past two decades is a growing overlap between ethnic and socio-economic segregation, driven by marked occupational differences between the members of the minority and majority population in very market-driven social and housing contexts that may easily translate income differences into spatial differences (Tammaru *et al.* 2016a). Apart from Tallinn, there appears to be a firm relation between the 'global' position and the level of segregation between the 'top' and the 'bottom' of the social distribution (Figure 15.4). Lower levels of segregation go along with a more moderate position in global networks, while higher levels of segregation go together with a stronger position in global networks. The relation almost remains the same in terms of the strength (in fact it becomes slightly stronger) but was systematically at a higher level in 2011 compared to 2001. In short, there (still) is a firm relationship between globalisation and segregation.

Next to the dimensions we referred to so far – social inequality and globalisation – there are two context-sensitive dimensions that relate to the extent of welfare provision, indicating a type of welfare state, and the characteristics of

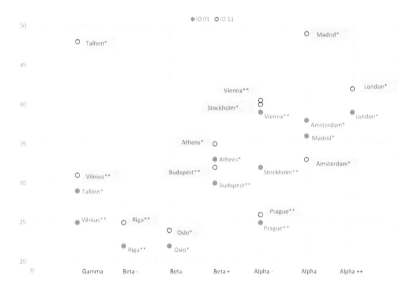

Figure 15.4 World city status and residential segregation between top and bottom social groups in selected European cities.

Notes: * Metropolitan region, **city.
Madrid, Tallinn, London, Budapest, Vilnius, Athens, Prague, Riga – managers and elementary occupations.
Amsterdam, Oslo, Stockholm – highest and lowest income quintile.
Vienna – university degree and compulsory education.

housing regimes. The forms of housing provision and the degree of housing com-modification are tightly linked to the type of welfare state, and both phenomena play a part in shaping levels of socio-economic and ethnic segregation (Arbaci 2007; Musterd and Ostendorf 1998). To further expose the contingent roots of the changing patterns of socio-economic segregation in Europe, we have adopted the well-known typology of welfare states proposed by Esping-Andersen (1990) along with its extensions to south Europe (Allen *et al.* 2004) and to the former socialist countries (Fenger 2007). Consequently, we distinguish between six types of European welfare regimes: democratic, corporatist, corporatist south European, corporatist post-socialist, liberal and liberal post-socialist. The former studies on ethnic divisions in Europe revealed that the liberal welfare-state correlates with evidently higher levels of segregation, while the corporatist and democratic welfare models are related to the lower scale of spatial disparities (Musterd and Ostendorf 1998).

With regard to housing regimes, an important element of the welfare state, we refer to Kemeny's (2002) general division between unitary and dual housing regimes that reflects the degree of government's direct (unitary) and indirect (dual) involvement in housing provision, regulations and subsidies. As this classification is somewhat crude, we are sensitive to regional variations of the two ideal types. Consequently, we also distinguish between the south European (Mediterranean) housing system (Allen *et al.* 2004) and the post-socialist variants of unitary and dual models. The Mediterranean and unitary housing regimes, especially when accompanied by different subtypes of the corporatist welfare-model, have been argued to result in lower levels of segregation than more market-oriented dual housing regimes (Arbaci 2007). It also seems that lower-income households in unitary regimes live in relatively better neighbourhoods compared with their counterparts in different forms of the dual regimes (Norris and Winston 2012). The results from the 13 European cities we included in this volume show that globalisation and post-Fordist economic restructuring contribute to the legible retrenchment of the welfare state in the new millennium (Figure 15.5).

Neo-liberalising states have tremendous impacts on urban housing markets. Urban economic restructuring, reduced welfare state interventions in several domains of life and high international in-migration (in many cities) have firmly affected structural changes over the past decades. Still, there is an enormous dif-ference between state provisions within Europe; this holds for the distinction between north and West European contexts compared to East and south European contexts, but after a closer look we also see important differences within these blocks. In north-west Europe, for example, the Dutch, the UK and Swedish wel-fare states all have their own character, albeit that the UK is standing out in terms of their liberal regime. In terms of housing and urban intervention, this makes a big difference. The Norwegian institutional milieu is also particularly interesting as a strong democratic welfare model coincides with a market-oriented dual hous-ing regime. Even in rather similar states, such as Sweden and the Netherlands, the types of interventions are different. In Sweden, for example, urban renewal is much less realised through demolition and replacement by building new dwellings than in the Netherlands. Institutional arrangements also differ between the countries mentioned because of different economic structures and differences in terms of how projects have been financed, how mortgage systems have been developed and the like. This has had evident impacts as we see that a city like Stockholm has hardly been hit by the recent crisis, whereas Amsterdam and the Baltic States clearly have experienced rather strong effects. Also within southern Europe there are differences. What we see is that family solidarity networks (requiring spatial proximity) are still very important drivers for changing levels of segregation in Athens and Milan but gradually less so in Madrid. In East Europe, with the exception of the Czech Republic that largely preserved the corporatist welfare regime and a significant public role in housing provision, the systemic transformation that started in the early 1990s brought about a massive privatisation of housing and a deep liberalisation and vanishing of social safety nets that, in turn, boosted the rising economic inequality.

In Figure 15.5 the index of dissimilarity of the 12 cities is plotted against seven welfare-state and housing regimes. Overall, it seems that the different types of welfare-state and housing regimes are only modestly related to the levels of socio-economic spatial divisions of the top and bottom social strata in European cities, and that the relationship has weakened (Figure 15.5). However, there is more structure in the data than initially expected. In the early 2000s, former socialist cities, even those in the most liberal contexts, were still the least segregated.

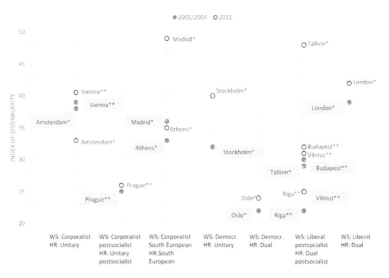

Figure 15.5 Welfare states, housing regimes and residential segregation between top and bottom social groups in selected European cities.

Notes: * Metropolitan region, **city.
Madrid, Tallinn, London, Budapest, Vilnius, Athens, Prague, Riga – managers and elementary occupations.
Amsterdam, Oslo, Stockholm – highest and lowest income quintile.
Vienna – university degree and compulsory education.

This may be ascribed to the forced egalitarianism that existed under the totalitarian socialist regimes some decades ago. That impact changed from 1989/1991 onwards but only with a time lag. The differences between north-west and south Europe are also evident, with the dual housing regime and liberal welfare state being the most segregated and the social-democratic welfare regime characterised by noticeably lower levels of segregation. One relation is particularly intriguing, however. There are several welfare states that are rather similar, such as the democratic welfare states in Norway and Sweden but perhaps also the Netherlands. Nevertheless, levels of segregation between the top and bottom of the social division are clearly different between the capital cities of these states (Oslo versus Amsterdam and Stockholm) or they develop in a different direction (Amsterdam versus Stockholm).

Levels of socio-economic segregation vary a lot within similar housing systems. In some countries with strong public involvement in the housing sector (unitary housing system), we find both low levels of segregation (Prague) and high levels of segregation (Stockholm and Vienna). True, we do not know what would be the levels of socio-economic segregation in the latter two cities if no elaborate housing policies existed. In countries with dual housing systems, we find significant variation too. Tallinn and London represent high levels of segregation, while Oslo represents low levels of segregation. The latter implies that market-based housing systems should not necessarily lead to high levels of segregation, at least in the context of an otherwise generous welfare system.

Finally, various developments interfere with each other. Amsterdam, with its stronger position in terms of globalisation (which drives segregation up) also experienced more than a decade of more liberal housing market intervention (also driving segregation up), while after 2008 the crisis had its effects as well (freezing segregation patterns). In Sweden neo-liberalisation also has had its effect and created more social spatial inequality, with higher levels of separation between top and bottom social categories than before. In fact, both cities have moved into a direction which is comparable to what we see elsewhere in more easily recognised liberal contexts, such as London, but also in more recent liberal environments, such as Madrid and the capital cities of the Baltic States. In all cases we may observe a positive correlation between the liberal welfare and housing regimes and socio-economic segregation, but the relationship between welfare regimes and housing systems with residential segregation is very complex and requires more in-depth analysis.

Conclusions and new perspectives

The comparative study of socio-economic residential segregation in European cities is almost new territory. So far, few studies have dealt with socio-economic segregation in a comparative research framework. This volume has the ambition to provide new insights related to socio-economic segregation and especially the factors which help to explain the levels and dynamics of segregation. In the theoretical framework we presented in Chapter 1, we elaborated on the potential changes in European capital cities and on the impact of globalisation, economic restructuring, welfare regime shifts and changing social inequality in general. We also referred to the previously developed historical development paths and to potential intervening factors, such as segregation in other domains, including ethnic/cultural and demographic domains. The introduction suggested that understanding social-spatial segregation in cities and/or their metropolitan areas is quite a challenge. Most importantly, the theory-grounded hypothesised ranking of European capital cities as introduced in Chapter 1 was not entirely confirmed by the actual patterns of socio-economic segregation. In this final section of the final chapter we will highlight some of the most salient findings from this volume and illuminate the mismatch between theory and reality.

We can draw two main conclusions from the analysis presented in this volume. The first is that the levels of socio-economic segregation in European capital cities are still rather modest. Segregation levels in cities in the Americas, Africa and parts of East Asia (Florida 2014; Maloutas and Fuijta 2012) are (much) higher than in Europe, and the negative side effects of high levels of segregation are only making their way into urban and political debates in Europe. However, the second main finding from this volume is that in the last decade Europe has been slipping, albeit slowly, into the epoch of growing inequalities and segregation. Under the influence of (neo-)liberal transformations in welfare states, and under the influence of the fact that several European cities also managed to become embedded in strong global networks and flows of people, the levels of socio-economic segregation are moving upwards. So far, this did not yet produce extreme levels of segregation in European cities, but Europe is clearly heading in the direction of higher levels of socio-economic divisions and especially in terms of the spatial separation of the top and bottom of social distributions. Three-quarters of the cities we included in this volume showed increasing levels of segregation of the top social categories, and a similar share showed increasing segregation of the lowest social categories. However, the spatial gap between the more extreme categories, those that have and those that have not, is widening in *all* capital cities across Europe.

We found that the shape of the 'segregation distribution' (low versus the rest; middle versus the rest and high versus the rest) is generally U-shaped, with more segregation of the higher-social strata than of the lower-social strata also in former totalitarian socialist environments. However, due to the complexity of the matter, we cannot speak of a universal shape of the relationship between class and space. In two-thirds of the European capital cities we investigated, higher social classes still form the most segregated social category; however, the remaining cases show other outcomes. All in all, it is clear that segregation between the two groups in European cities tend to be increasing. Nevertheless, we have also shown that there still is quite some variation in levels of segregation. Some of that seems to be caused by time lags between the development of socio-economic inequality and segregation. This was evident in the former socialist countries in the East of Europe but also elsewhere. Social inequalities that have developed three or four decades ago still have an enormous impact on current social spatial disparities. Other contributions to the variation in outcomes come from temporal factors, such as relatively short-term economic, financial or housing crises. These examples illustrate that for a fuller understanding of trends in socio-economic segregation, we would need an extended time frame on top of the ten years we used in this volume to fully grasp the complex relation between inequality and segregation. Finally, several contributions in this volume have discussed the relationship between socio-economic and ethnic segregation. In some places, neighbourhoods and cities, that relationship is strong, but it has also been shown that this is not a one-to-one relationship. In some cases social distances between social classes within the category non-natives were even bigger than social distances within the category natives. Caution is required here and researchers and policy makers should not automatically assume that 'non-western' migrants are all lower class.

Institutional arrangements – welfare-state regimes or housing regimes – may be developed in such a way that these can effectively temper social inequalities. However, welfare and housing regimes may also be designed in such a way that social inequalities are increased. We currently seem to have entered an era in which the latter type of regime has taken centre stage, with increasing segregation as a result. Currently, even a country like Sweden, which has long been the example par excellence for redistributing affluence and therewith was the prototype of a country that managed to avoid high levels of social spatial segregation, is showing rapidly increasing levels of segregation. Although there is no simple one-to-one relationship between the riots in Stockholm in the summer of 2013 and increasing socio-spatial segregation, the riots have caused much debate on the direction Sweden is taking and the causes of social unrest in the most deprived neighbourhoods (Malmberg *et al.* 2013). The actual European reality is that most welfare regimes have become more market oriented to stimulate the economy in a liberal way, with increasing social inequality as a side effect.

The relationship between increasing socio-economic segregation in Europe and situations that are seriously threatening urban social life (such as riots) is an issue that does not yet seem to be fully understood. Extreme forms of segregation include gated communities for the top end of the socio-economic distribution, and inaccessible ghettos or favelas for the bottom ends of the socio-economic distribution. The potential estrangement that may be the result of such contrasts – people increasingly will be unaware of the lives of contrasting classes – might be dynamite under the social stability of our future cities. The increasing number of no-go areas in our cities implies that ultimately major parts of cities are regarded to be no part of urban life anymore, which implies a serious limitation of freedom in such cities, and are having a major impact on the lives of those living in these no-go areas. Social apartheid, a process involving social discrimination and manifested in very high inequalities and spatial separation of the rich and the poor (Löwy 2003), could be the ultimate outcome of these urban social processes.

The explanatory framework for urban socio-economic segregation is highly complicated because of the many different dimensions simultaneously playing a role and over a longer period of time. One explanatory factor is not enough to illuminate the changing levels of segregation in Europe. In general, a liberal (market-oriented) institutional environment and higher levels of social inequality result in more separated spatial divisions. But less market does not necessarily entail lower levels of segregation (see Oslo versus Stockholm). Globalisation seems to be a relatively strong indicator of segregation, as long as we are satisfied with the general conclusion that *Alpha* cities (cities which link major economic regions and states to the world economy) are more segregated than other types of cities. Yet other factors may enhance or mitigate such a relation. A further explanatory factor of socio-economic segregation to consider is 'space' and inherited urban physical fabric. Some areas retain their attraction for certain niche groups over a long period of time, although a new valuation of spaces also may occur. Inner-city neighbourhoods that were regarded as not being attractive in the 1970s and 1980s have been gentrified by middle-class households that settled in originally blue-collar neighbourhoods. On the other hand, some neighbourhoods, large estates of mass-produced blocks of flats in particular, have been steadily losing middle-class residents. Put differently, the social and physical upgrading of neighbourhoods, as well as the reverse trend of social and spatial decay of neighbourhoods, plays an important role in shaping new social geographies of segregation.

To conclude, we have found that levels of socio-spatial segregation in Europe are still relatively modest compared to the rest of the world, but that they are increasing. We found that four central indicators of the multi-factor approach – welfare and housing regime, globalisation and economic restructuring, rising social inequality and historical development paths – all play a big role in changing the social urban landscape in Europe. It is also clear that understanding local institutional, social and physical contexts are crucial for a better understanding of changing social segregation patterns. These factors are, however, not stable over time, since contexts are changing continuously, through the enlargement of the European Union, neo-liberalization of states, immigration, economic crises and urban transformations. The ultimate lesson of this book is that a combination of both structural factors and a context-sensitive approach is needed to fully understand the socio-economic segregation processes to allow policy-makers to counter the negative effects that endanger the stability of European cities.

Acknowledgements

We thank Michael Gentile, Wouter van Gent and Thomas Maloutas for their helpful comments on this chapter. The research leading to these results has received funding from the Estonian Research Council (Institutional Research Grant IUT no. 2–17 on Spatial Population Mobility and Geographical Changes in Urban Regions); the European Research Council under the European Union's Seventh Framework Programme (FP/2007-2013) / ERC Grant Agreement no. 615159 (ERC Consolidator Grant DEPRIVEDHOODS, Socio-spatial Inequality, Deprived Neighbourhoods, and Neighbourhood Effects); and from the Marie Curie programme under the European Union's Seventh Framework Programme (FP/2007–2013) / Career Integration Grant no. PCIG10-GA-2011-303728 (CIG Grant NBHCHOICE, Neighbourhood Choice, Neighbourhood Sorting, and Neighbourhood Effects).

Notes

1 We use the term East Europe for countries that used to be part of the state-socialist centrally planned countries for the five decades after World War II (Czech Republic, Estonia, Hungary, Latvia and Lithuania in this book), and West Europe to the rest of Europe (Austria, Greece, Italy, Netherlands, Norway, Spain, Sweden, United Kingdom in this book).

2 The shape of segregation curves in Athens might also be the result of the heterogeneous composition of occupations included in the group of 'managers and higher representatives'. The group in Athens also includes middle and even low middle income categories.

References

Allen, J, Barlow, J, Leal, J, Maloutas,T and Padovani, L 2004, *Housing and welfare in Southern Europe,* Oxford, Blackwell Science.

Arbaci, S 2007, 'Ethnic segregation, housing systems and welfare regimes in Europe' *International Journal of Housing Policy* 7(4), 401–433.

Beaverstock, J, Smith, R and Taylor, P 2015, 'Global city network'. Available online: http://www.lboro.ac.uk/gawc. Accessed 10 May 2015.

Booth, C 1887, 'The inhabitants of Tower Hamlets (School Board Division), their condition and occupations', *Journal of the Royal Statistical Society* 50(2), 326–401.

Booth, C 1888, 'Conditions and occupations of the people in East London and Hackney' *Journal of the Royal Statistical Society* 51(2), 276–331.

Butler, T, Hamnett, C and Ramsed M 2008, 'Inward and upward: Marking out social class change in London, 1981–2001' *Urban Studies* 45(1), 67–88.

Brown, L A and Chung, C Y 2008, 'Market-led pluralism: Rethinking our understanding of racial/ethnic spatial patterning in U.S. cities' *Annals of the Association of American Geographers* 98(1), 180–212.

Burgers, J and Musterd, S 2002, 'Understanding urban inequality: A model based on existing theories and an empirical illustration' *International Journal of Urban and Regional Research* 26(2), 403–413.

Castells, M 1989, *The informational city*, Oxford, Blackwell.

Dangschat, J 1987 'Sociospatial disparities in a "socialist" city: the case of Warsaw at the end of the 1970s' *International Journal of Urban and Regional Research* 11(1), 37–60.

Duncan, O D and Duncan, B 1955, 'Residential distribution and occupational stratification' *American Journal of Sociology* 60(4), 493–503.

Engels, F 1892, *The condition of the working class in England in 1844* London, David Price.

Esping-Andersen, G 1990, *The three worlds of welfare capitalism*, Cambridge, Polity.

Fainstein, S S, Gordon, I and Harloe, M 1992, *Divided cities: New York and London in the contemporary world,* Oxford, Blackwell.

Farley, R, Schuman, H, Bianchi, S, Colasanto, D and Hatchet, S. 1978, 'Chocolate city, vanilla suburbs: Will the trend toward racially separate communities continue?' *Social Science Research* 7(3), 319–344.

Fenger, H 2007, Welfare regimes in Central and Eastern Europe: Incorporating post-communist countries in a welfare regime typology. Available online: http://journal.ciiss.net/index.php/ciiss/article/viewPDFInterstitial/45/37. Accessed 10 May 2015.

Fischer, C S, Stockmayer, G, Stiles, J and Hout, M 2004, 'Distinguishing the geographical levels and social dimensions of U.S. metropolitan segregation 1960–2000' *Demography* 43(1), 37–59.

Florida, R 2014, 'The U.S. cities with the highest levels of income segregation'. Available online: http://www.citylab.com/work/2014/03/us-cities-highest-levels-income-segregation/8632/. Accessed 28 April 2015.

Freeman, L 2009, 'Neighborhood diversity, metropolitan segregation and gentrification: What are the links in the US?' *Urban Studies* 26(10), 2079–2101.

French, R A and Hamilton F E I (eds) 1979, *The Socialist city: Spatial structure and urban policy*, New York, John Wiley & Sons.

Fujita, K 2012, 'Conclusions: Residential segregation and urban theory' in *Residential segregation around the world: Why context matters*, eds. T Maloutas and K Fujita, London, Ashgate, pp. 285–315.

Galster, G and Booza J 2007, 'The rise of bipolar neighborhood' *Journal of the American Planning Association* 73(4), 421–435.

Hamnett, C 1994, 'Social polarisation in global cities: Theory and evidence' *Urban Studies* 31(3), 401–424.

Hamnett, C 2012, 'Urban social polarization' in *International handbook of globalization and world cities*, eds B Derudder, M Hoyler, P J Taylor and F Witlox, Cheltenham, UK, Edward Elgar, pp. 361–368.

Huttman, E, Blauw, W and Saltman, J (eds) 1991, *Urban housing: Segregation of minorities in Western Europe and the United States*, Durham, NC, Duke University Press.

Kantor, P and Savitch, H V 2005, 'How to study comparative urban development politics: A research note' *International Journal of Urban and Regional Research* 29(1), 135–151.

Kemeny, J 2002, *From public to the social market: Rental policy strategies in comparative perspective*, London, Routledge.

Kovács, Z, Wiessner, R and Zischner, R 2013, 'Urban renewal in the inner city of Budapest: Gentrification from a post-socialist perspective' *Urban Studies* 50(1), 22–38.

Ladányi, J 1989, 'Changing patterns of residential segregation in Budapest' *International Journal of Urban & Regional Research* 13(4), 555–572.

Lowy, M 2003, 'The long march of Brazil's labor party. Brazil: A country marked by social apartheid' *Logos* 2(2). Available online: http://www.logosjournal.com/lowy.htm. Accessed 28 April 2015.

Malheiros, J 2002, 'Ethni-cities: Residential patterns in the northern European and Mediterranean metropolises – implications for policy design' *International Journal of Population Geography* 8(1), 107–134.

Malmberg, B Andresson, E and Östh J 2013, 'Segregation and urban unrest in Sweden *Urban Geography*, 34(7), 1031–1046.

Maloutas, T 2007, 'Segregation, social polarization and immigration in Athens during the 1990s: Theoretical expectations and contextual difference' *International Journal of Urban and Regional Studies* 31(4), 733–758.

Maloutas, T and Fujita, K (eds) 2012, *Residential segregation in comparative perspective. Making sense of contextual diversity.* City and society series, Farnham, UK, Ashgate.

Manley, D and Johnston, R 2015, 'London: A dividing city, 2001–11?' *City* 18(6), 633–643.

Manley, D and van Ham, M 2011, 'Choice-based letting, ethnicity and segregation in England' *Urban Studies* 48(14), 3125–3143.

Marcińczak, S, Gentile, M, Rufat, S and Chelcea, L 2014, 'Urban geographies of hesitant transition: Tracing socio-economic segregation in post-Ceausescu Bucharest' *International Journal of Urban and Regional Research* 38(4), 1399–1417.

Marcińczak, S, Gentile, M and Stępniak, M 2013, 'Paradoxes of (post)socialist segregation: Metropolitan sociospatial divisions under socialism and after in Poland' *Urban Geography* 34(3), 327–352.

Marcińczak, S,Tammaru, T, Novak, J, Gentile, M, Kovács, Z, Temelova, J,Valatka, V, Kährik, A and Szabo, B 2015, 'Patterns of socioeconomic segregation in the capital cities of fast-track reforming postsocialist countries *Annals of the American Association of Geographers* 105(1), 183–202.

Marcuse, P. 1989, '"Dual city": A muddy metaphor for a quartered city' *International Journal of Urban and Regional Research* 13(4), 697–708.

Marcuse, P and van Kempen, R (eds) 2002, *Of states and cities: The partitioning of urban space,* Oxford, Oxford University Press.

Massey, D S 1996, 'The age of extremes: Concentrated affluence and poverty in the twenty-first century' *Demography* 33(4), 395–412.

McFarlane, C and Robinson, J 2012, Introduction – experiments in comparative urbanism *Urban Geography* 33(6), 765–773.

Morgan, B 1975, 'The segregation of socio-economic groups in urban areas: A comparative analysis' *Urban Studies* 12(1), 47–60.

Morgan, B 1980, 'Occupational segregation in metropolitan areas in the United States, 1970' *Urban Studies* 17(1), 63–69.

Musterd, S 2005, 'Social and ethnic segregation in Europe; Levels, causes and effects' *Journal of Urban Affairs* 27(3), 331–348.

Musterd, S and Ostendorf, W (eds) 1998, *'Urban segregation and the welfare state: Inequality and exclusion in Western Cities*, London, Routledge.

Musterd, S, van Gent, W, Das, M and Latten, J 2014, 'Adaptive behaviour in urban space; Residential mobility in response to social distance' *Urban Studies* DOI: 10.1177/0042098014562344. Accessed 28 April 2015.

Musterd, S and van Kempen, R 2007, 'Trapped or on the springboard? Housing careers in large housing estates in European cities' *Journal of Urban Affairs* 29(3), 311–329.

Nightingale, CH 2012, *Segregation: A global history of divided city*, Chicago, University of Chicago Press.

Nijman, J 2007, 'Introduction – comparative urbanism' *Urban Geography* 28(1), 1–6.

Norris, M and Winston, N 2012, 'Home-ownership, housing regimes and income inequalities in Western Europe' *International Journal of Social Welfare* 21(2), 127–138.

Park, E P, Burgess, E W and McKenzie, R D 1925. *The city: Suggestions for investigation of human behavior in the urban environment*, Chicago, University of Chicago Press.

Pickvance, C1986, 'Comparative urban analysis and assumptions in comparative research' *International Journal of Urban and Regional Research* 10(2), 162–184.

Piketty, T 2013, *Capital in the 21st century*, Cambridge, MA, Harvard University Press.

Préteceille, E 2000, 'Segregation, class and politics in large cities' in *Cities in contemporary Europe*, eds A Bagnasco and P Le Gales, Cambridge, Cambridge University Press, pp. 74–97.

Reardon, S F and Bischoff, K 2011, 'Income inequality and income segregation' *American Journal of Sociology* 116(4), 1092–1153.

Robinson, J 2011, Cities in a world of cities: The comparative gesture' *International Journal of Urban and Regional Research* 35(1), 1–23.

Sassen, S. 1991, *The global city: New York, London, Tokyo*, Princeton, NJ, Princeton University Press.

Smith, N 2002, 'New globalism, new urbanism: Gentrification as global urban strategy' *Antipode* 34(3), 427–450.

Stanilov, K and Sýkora, L (eds) 2014, *Confronting suburbanization: Urban decentralization in postsocialist Central and Eastern Europe*, Oxford, Wiley Blackwell.

Stiglitz, J 2012, *The price of inequality: How today's divided society endangers our future*, New York, W.W. Norton.

Sýkora, L 2009, 'New socio-spatial formations: Places of residential segregation and separation in Czechia' *Tijdschrift voor Economische en Sociale Geografie* 100(4), 417–435.

Szelényi, I 1987, 'Housing inequalities and occupational segregation in state socialist cities. Commentary to the special issue of IJURR on east European cities' *International Journal of Urban and Regional Research* 11(1), 1–8.

Tammaru, T and Kontuly, T 2011, 'Selectivity and destinations of ethnic minorities leaving the main gateway cities of Estonia' *Population, Space and Place* 17(5), 674–688.

Tammaru, T, Kährik, A, Mägi, K Novák, J and Leetmaa, K 2016a, 'The "market experiment": Increasing socio-economic segregation in the inherited bi-ethnic context of Tallinn' in *Socio-economic segregation in European capital cities: East meets West*, eds T Tammaru, S Marcińczak, M van Ham and S Musterd, London, Routledge.

Tammaru, T, Musterd, S, van Ham, M and Marcińczak, S, 2016b, 'A multi-factor approach to understanding socio-economic segregation in European capital cities' in *Socio-economic segregation in European capital cities: East meets West*, eds T Tammaru, S Marcińczak, M van Ham and S Musterd, London, Routledge.

van Ham, M and Manley, D 2009, 'Social housing allocation, choice and neighbourhood ethnic mix in England' *Journal of Housing and the Built Environment* 24, 407–422.

van Kempen, R 2007, 'Divided cities in the 21st century: Challenging the importance of globalization' *Journal of Housing and Built Environment* 22(1), 13–31.

van Kempen R and Murie, A 2009, 'The new divided city: Changing patterns in European cities' *Tijdschrift voor Economische en Sociale Geografie* 100(4), 377–398.

Villaca, F 2011, 'São Paulo: urban segregation and inequality' *Estudos Avançadosvol* 25(71), 37–58

Ward, K 2010, 'Towards a relational comparative approach to the study of cities' *Progress in Human Geography* 34(4), 471–487.

Watson, T 2009, 'Inequality and the measurement of residential segregation by income in American neighborhoods' *The Review of Income and Wealth* 55(3), 820–844.

York, A M, Smith, M E Stanley, B W, Stark, B L, Novic, J, Harlan, S L, Cowgill, G L and Boon, CG 2012, 'Ethnic and class clustering through the ages: A transdiciplinary approach to urban neighbourhood social patterns' *Urban Studies* 48(11), 2399–2415.

Zorbaugh, HW 1929, *The gold coast and the slum: A sociological study of Chicago's near north side,* Chicago, University of Chicago.

Index

eBooks
from Taylor & Francis
Helping you to choose the right eBooks for your Library

Add to your library's digital collection today with Taylor & Francis eBooks. We have over 50,000 eBooks in the Humanities, Social Sciences, Behavioural Sciences, Built Environment and Law, from leading imprints, including Routledge, Focal Press and Psychology Press.

Free Trials Available
We offer free trials to qualifying academic, corporate and government customers.

Choose from a range of subject packages or create your own!

Benefits for you
- Free MARC records
- COUNTER-compliant usage statistics
- Flexible purchase and pricing options
- All titles DRM-free.

Benefits for your user
- Off-site, anytime access via Athens or referring URL
- Print or copy pages or chapters
- Full content search
- Bookmark, highlight and annotate text
- Access to thousands of pages of quality research at the click of a button.

eCollections
Choose from over 30 subject eCollections, including:

Archaeology	Language Learning
Architecture	Law
Asian Studies	Literature
Business & Management	Media & Communication
Classical Studies	Middle East Studies
Construction	Music
Creative & Media Arts	Philosophy
Criminology & Criminal Justice	Planning
Economics	Politics
Education	Psychology & Mental Health
Energy	Religion
Engineering	Security
English Language & Linguistics	Social Work
Environment & Sustainability	Sociology
Geography	Sport
Health Studies	Theatre & Performance
History	Tourism, Hospitality & Events

For more information, pricing enquiries or to order a free trial, please contact your local sales team:
www.tandfebooks.com/page/sales

www.tandfebooks.com

For Product Safety Concerns and Information please contact our EU
representative GPSR@taylorandfrancis.com
Taylor & Francis Verlag GmbH, Kaufingerstraße 24, 80331 München, Germany

www.ingramcontent.com/pod-product-compliance
Ingram Content Group UK Ltd.
Pitfield, Milton Keynes, MK11 3LW, UK
UKHW021022180425

457613UK00020B/1029